THE POPULATION CONTROVERSY

THE POPULATION CONTROVERSY

A collective reprint of material concerning the 18th century controversy on the trend of population in England and Wales

with an introduction

by

Professor D. V. Glass

1973

GREGG INTERNATIONAL PUBLISHERS LIMITED

© Editorial matter Gregg International
Publishers Limited, 1973

All rights reserved. No part of this publication
may be reproduced, stored in a retrieval system,
or transmitted in any form or by any means,
electronic, mechanical, photocopying, recording
or otherwise, without the prior permission of
Gregg International Publishers Limited

The Population Controversy and its companion
volume *The Development of Population Statistics* are
published in conjunction with *Numbering the People*
by D. V. Glass (D. C. Heath Limited, England).

ISBN 0 576 53502 8
Republished in 1973 by Gregg International Publishers Limited
Westmead, Farnborough, Hants., England

Printed in offset by Franz Wolf, Heppenheim/Bergstrasse
Western Germany

Table of Contents

THE FIRST CONTROVERSY

* W. Brakenridge	*Philosophical Transactions of the Royal Society*, Vol. 48, II 1755
* W. Brakenridge	*Philosophical Transactions of the Royal Society*, Vol. 49, I 1756
* W. Brakenridge	*Philosophical Transactions of the Royal Society*, Vol. 49, II 1756
* R. Forster	*Philosophical Transactions of the Royal Society*, Vol. 50, I 1757
* R. Forster	*Philosophical Transactions of the Royal Society*, Vol. 50, I 1757
* W. Brakenridge	*Philosophical Transactions of the Royal Society*, Vol. 50, I 1757
* G. Burrington	*An Answer to Dr. William Brakenridge's Letter*, London 1757

THE MAIN DISPUTE

* R. Price	'Observations on the expectations of lives . . .' *Philosophical Transactions of the Royal Society*, Vol. 59, 1769
* A. Young	Letter to *St. James's Chronicle* March 28, 1772, from *Political Arithmetic* London 1774
* W. Eden	*Letter to the Earl of Carlisle* 3rd edn London 1780
R. Price	*An Essay on the Population of England* 2nd edn London 1780
W. Wales	*An Inquiry into the Present State of Population in England and Wales* London 1781
[Anon]	*Uncertainty of the Present Population of this Kingdom*, London 1781
* R. Price	*Observations on Reversionary Payments* 5th edn London 1792 Vol. II
* John Howlett	Letter to J. Middleton in *View of the Agriculture of Middlesex* London 1798
* F. M. Eden	*An Estimate of the Number of Inhabitants in Great Britain and Ireland* London 1800

*Reproduced by kind permission of the Trustees of the British Museum

Preface

With one exception, this volume contains reprints of all the main contributions to the 18th century controversy on the trend of population in England and Wales (the exception is the contribution of John Howlett, *An Examination of Dr. Price's Essay*, Maidstone, 1781?, reprinted by Kelley, New York, 1970).

The controversy was in two stages. The first began with the papers of the Reverend William Brakenridge, published in the *Philosophical Transactions* of the Royal Society, and was largely carried on in that journal. Burrington's criticism of Brakenridge appeared in separate pamphlet form, perhaps partly because the author hoped thereby to reach a wider public. Not all of Forster's criticism was published. His unpublished reply to Brakenridge, to be found in the Birch Collection of manuscripts in the British Museum, has been printed in full in the companion volume to this book, *Numbering the People*, by D. V. Glass (D. C. Heath Limited, 1973) Appendix 1, Chapter 2.

The second stage of the controversy was initiated by the Reverend Richard Price and attracted much more attention. Price's contributions began in 1769 but took on full form in his *Essay on the Population of England*, originally published as an Appendix to William Morgan's *The Doctrine of Annuities and Assurances on Lives and Survivorships* (London 1779) but issued separately in a revised version in 1780. It is that revised version which is reprinted here.

The debate on the trend of population continued until shortly before the taking, in 1801, of the first of the periodic censuses of Great Britain, and found echoes in many of the political and economic writings of the period. The topic was also discussed in the contemporary reviews, while the 'depopulation of the countryside' was lamented by Oliver Goldsmith in 'The Deserted Village', first published in 1769.

D. V. Glass
1972

Biographical Notes on the Authors of the Works Reprinted in the present collection

Unless otherwise stated, the notes are based upon the information given in the *Dictionary of National Biography*.

Brakenridge [or Braikenridge], the Reverend William (B. ? D. ?)
He came from Glasgow and first studied at Aberdeen. He was subsequently a student at Queen's College, Oxford and later obtained the B.D. and D.D. degrees. In 1745 he became librarian to Sion College and was afterwards elected President of that College. (Source: *Alumni Oxonienses* and Guildhall Library).

Forster, the Reverend Richard (B. 1704? D. 1766)
He came from Lancashire and attended All Souls, Oxford. He became a Fellow of Brasenose and subsequently Vice-Principal and Senior Bursar of that college. In 1747 he was appointed Rector of West Shefford, Berkshire. (Source: Brasenose College, Oxford).

Burrington, George (B. c.1680 D. 1759)
Member of a Devon family. He was a captain in the army and in 1724 went to North America as Governor of North Carolina. He served initially for about eighteen months, being removed from office after attempting to assault Chief Justice Christopher Hale. He was again appointed Governor in 1731, promoted road and bridge building, financed out of his own fortune, and went on many expeditions in North Carolina. He resigned in 1734. He was murdered in London in 1759. (Source: *Dictionary of American Biography*).

Price, the Reverend Richard (B. 1723 D. 1791)
Born in the county of Glamorgan, the son of a Calvinist minister, Price was educated at various dissenting academies and completed his education at the Fund Academy in London. He became minister to various dissenting congregations, most of his life being associated with the congregation at Newington Green. He wrote widely on morals, was a champion of the American colonists, and supported the French Revolution in its early stages. He was a close friend of the distinguished nonconformists of his day, and especially of Dr. Priestly, who delivered the sermon at Price's funeral. Today Price is probably best known for his writings on mortality, annuities and population growth. (Sources: *D.N.B.* and R. Thomas, *Richard Price: Philosopher and Apostle of Liberty*, London, 1934).

Young, Arthur (B. 1741 D. 1820)
Born in London, he was apprenticed to merchants in Lynn, but his apprenticeship came to an end with the death of his father, heavily in debt. After an unsuccessful attempt to establish a monthly magazine, he took up farming, at which he was repeatedly unsuccessful. But from 1767 onwards, he began to collect, analyse and publish writings on agriculture, on economics and politics, and these writings were widely appreciated. In 1784 he began to publish *Annals of Agriculture*, of which 46 volumes had appeared by 1809 and some further parts in 1812 and 1815. Many distinguished writers contributed to the *Annals*, and not only on agriculture. Jeremy Bentham, for example, contributed an article which appeared to recommend contraception (the use of the sponge) as a means of reducing the cost of poor relief. In 1793 Pitt established a Board of Agriculture and Young was appointed Secretary to it—Sir John Sinclair, of whom he complained, being President. Young is best known for his writings on agriculture, but he was also a sharp general observer, as is evident in his books on his travels in Ireland and in France. (Sources: in addition to the *D.N.B.* and to Young's autobiography, edited by M. Betham-Edwards, London 1898, see G. D. Amery, 'The writings of Arthur Young', *Journal of the Royal Agricultural Society of England*, Vol. 85, 1924).

Eden, William (First Lord Auckland) (B. 1744 D. 1814)
Attended Christ Church College, Oxford, and was later called to the bar at the Middle Temple. After a promising legal career—which included the publication of *Principles of Penal Law* (1772), he gave up law for politics and became M.P. for Woodstock in 1774. He was involved in various governmental inquiries and negotiations and established the National Bank of Ireland. He was a close friend of Pitt.

Wales, William (B. 1734 ? D. 1798)
He was best known for his astronomical observations and accompanied Captain Cook in the Resolution on his second voyage round the world in 1772, and on his last voyage in 1776. After his return in 1780 he was appointed mathematical master at Christ's Hospital, where he remained until his death.

Eden, Sir Frederick Morton (B. 1766 D. 1809)
Eldest son of Sir Robert Eden, Governor of Maryland and nephew of William Eden (Lord Auckland). Attended Christ Church College, Oxford. He was a founder, and later chairman, of the Globe Insurance Company. The high prices of 1794 and 1795 led him to investigate the condition of the working classes and to produce his three-volume study, *The State of the Poor* (1797) by which he is best known. He also wrote on commerce, insurance and on Friendly Societies.

THE FIRST CONTROVERSY

PHILOSOPHICAL TRANSACTIONS,

GIVING SOME

ACCOUNT

OF THE

Present Undertakings, Studies, *and* Labours,

OF THE

INGENIOUS,

IN MANY

Confiderable Parts of the WORLD.

LONDON.
Printed for C. DAVIS, Printer to the ROYAL SOCIETY, over-againſt *Gray's-Inn Gate*, in *Holbourn.*

Republished in 1973 by Gregg International Publishers Limited
Westmead, Farnborough, Hants., England

XCV. *A Letter from the Reverend* William Brakenridge, *D.D. and F.R.S. to* George Lewis Scot, *Esq; F. R. S. concerning the Number of Inhabitants within the* London *Bills of Mortality.*

Dear Sir,

Read Nov. 21, 1754.

AS I have lately had the curiosity to consider, the number of inhabitants in London and Westminster, whether they increase or decrease; I presume to send you the observations I have made. For as no one understands numbers better than yourself, your approbation will much confirm me in my opinion, and perhaps have weight with many others, when you can easily find out any paralogism or mistake, that I may have made. And if you can spare any time from your great employment, to think upon the subject, and to rectify any thing that may be amiss in my method of computeing; it will be very obliging.

I have consulted the yearly bills of mortality for the last fifty years, which I imagine will be sufficient for my purpose; and from them I have extracted all the numbers of the baptisms and burials, both within the walls of London, and at large within the bills: for I thought that within the city walls, where the number of houses is nearly known, the baptisms and burials might be very useful to reason upon, concerning the whole inhabitants both within and without. And because it may be surer, to compute from a number of years taken at an average, than from the numbers in any one year as they stand in the bills; I have taken the sums of the numbers, for each five years of the fifty, and then the fifth part of each of these sums; which will at a medium be the number for any particular year. And in like manner, I have taken the sums of the numbers for each ten years, and the tenth part of each of the sums will be the number for any year, at an average. And the numbers so found will appear thus:

Years.	Baptisms.	Burials.	Baptisms.	Burials.
1704— 8	1870	2553	15867	22103
1709—13	1805	2551	15288	21701
1714—18	1890	2706	17586	24641
1719—23	1871	2719	18360	26978
1724—28	1829	2727	18442	27670
1729—33	1578	2532	17452	26267
1734—38	1406	2242	16762	26165
1739—43	1221	2397	15034	28219
1744—48	1062	1989	14402	23884
1749—53	1087	1790	14850	22006
1704—13	1837	2552	15577	21602
1714—23	1880	2712	18073	25809
1724—33	1703	2647	17920	27168
1734—43	1313	2320	15898	27192
1744—53	1074	1890	14626	22945

Where

Where the numbers are ranged in five columns. The firſt denotes the years, the ſecond and third the baptiſms and burials within the city walls, and the third and fourth ſhew the baptiſms, and burials at large within the bills. Thus, for inſtance, 22945 is the number of burials, at a medium, for any of the ten years within the bills from 1744 to 1753 incluſive. And in like manner, 1221 is the number of baptiſms for any year, at an average for five years, from 1739 to 1743 incluſive, and ſo of others. The numbers above the line are computed for five years, and thoſe below are for ten.

In the burials it is always to be conſidered, that there are perhaps 2000 more, than what the bills repreſent them. For there are burying-grounds belonging to the Proteſtant Diſſenters, the Quakers, and the Jews; of which there is no account taken, and that are very conſiderable. In the firſt of which in Bunyan-Fields, I have been informed there are about 400 burials in the year, and in the others, together, there may be about 400 more; which ſum of 800 we may ſuppoſe comes from all parts within the bills. But I think the one-half, *viz.* 400, muſt at leaſt come from within the city; where there are moſt Proteſtant Diſſenters and Jews. So that 400 may always be added to the burials, within the city. It is likewiſe to be remembered, that both from within and without the city, a great many burials go out into the country, of which there is no notice taken. But from what I have obſerved, if we were to ſuppoſe, that there are 1200 in the whole, carried out into the country, over and above the 800 mentioned above, in the burying-grounds; I ſhould imagine that to be the

out-

outmoſt. And therefore in our calculations we ſhall ſuppoſe 2000 burials yearly, more than in the bills at large. And which, whether we are exact enough or not in the ſuppoſition, will by no means hinder us to diſcover the increaſe, or decreaſe of the people.

It is next to be obſerved, that in the bills the baptiſms are always about two-fifth parts at leaſt, leſs than the burials, with the numbers added to them above-mentioned; and that this difference within the city ſeems continually to increaſe, ſo that it is much greater now than it was ſome years ago; which appears plainly to ariſe from two cauſes; the number of Diſſenters of various denominations, and the multitude of people that live unmarried. But I think it is rather owing to the laſt: for in London and Weſtminſter the one-half of the people at leaſt live ſingle, that are above twenty-one years of age; which muſt prevent almoſt as many more births, that might be reaſonably expected. And this is not mere conjecture; for I have had ſome proof from a particular detail given me of one pariſh within the city; where the greater part of thoſe that are above that age are ſingle. In the natural ſtate of mankind it ſeems plain, that the number of births ſhould be greater than the burials, and I believe that in many pariſhes in the country they are near double. I found it ſo in the Iſle of Wight, where I lived ſome time, and had an opportunity to ſee their regiſters; for there the births were generally near double. And even in London, before the great fire in 1666, it appears, from ſome pariſh regiſters, that the baptiſms were near about equal to the burials, and never afterwards: the reaſon of which I do not underſtand, unleſs it

be

be that more people were then married, and that from that time there was a greater confluence of ftrangers: for there certainly were more Diffenters at that time than ever after.

It is farther to be obferved, that in the bills from the year 1704 to the year 1728, without the city, both the number of chriftenings and burials continually increafed; and that from that time to 1743, they continued nearly the fame; but that after 1743 they gradually decreafed till this time; which plainly fhews, that the inhabitants were increafing till about the year 1728; and that from thence to 1743, they remained in the fame ftate nearly; but that afterwards, during the laft ten years, till 1753, they were conftantly diminifhing. For it is evident, that the number of inhabitants muft always be in proportion, to the number of births, and burials confidered together. And hence it appears, that the cities of London and Weftminfter, were in the moft flourifhing ftate, with regard to numbers, from 1728 to 1743, and that they are now paft their height, and in the fame ftate they were in the year 1708; and the firft decreafe feems to have been at the beginning of the laft French war, which was in 1744. Within the city walls the number of the inhabitants do not feem to fluctuate, in the fame periods of time, as without; for the moft numerous ftate of the city, appears to have been from the year 1718, to the year 1728, and then after that they have been continually decreafing: fo that when they were moft numerous within the walls, they were not then arrived at the height without; and when they were in the higheft ftate without, they were diminifhing in the city.

city. Perhaps the vaſt number of new buildings, within the liberties of Weſtminſter, may have in part cauſed this diminution. And as from the year 1718, within the city, the chriſtenings have been ſo remarkably decreaſing, that they are now but three-fifths of what they were at that time, and the burials are likewiſe diminiſhed above one-fourth in the laſt five years; this ſeems to ſhew that the inhabitants within the city walls muſt be near one-fourth fewer, than they were in the year 1718.

Now, in order to calculate the number of inhabitants, it will be neceſſary to obſerve, that in a year in London there generally dies one perſon in thirty. This Sir William Petty has long ago obſerved; and I have found it to be near the truth, upon conſulting my pariſh regiſter. For in the pariſh of Baſſiſhaw, London, there are not above 800 people, as appears from an account that I had lately given me: And the burials for the laſt ten years in the whole amount to 262; which at a medium gives 26 for one year, which is the thirtieth part of 800 nearly. In ſome pariſhes in London there die more than in this proportion, as in St. Giles's Cripplegate; and in others in the out-parts of the town there die fewer; but I believe, in general it will hold true, in and about the city. In the town of Breſlaw in Germany, from which Dr. Halley formed his famous table for the probabilities of life, there die about two in ſixty-nine, that is leſs than one in thirty-four; as is plain from an eaſy computation. But there certainly die more than in that proportion, within the London bills; for it appears, that one-third at leaſt of the children die under two years of age; whereas at Breſlaw there die under that age, only one-fifth; and therefore the difference being two-fifteenths, or four-thirtieths, there die four in thirty more at London than at Breslaw, under two years of age.

In the country the case is very different; for there does not die above one in fifty, in healthy places. Sir William Petty has likewise observed this, and I have found it true. For in the parish of Newchurch in the Isle of Wight, where I resided some time, there are about 900 people, and there does not die, at a medium, above eighteen yearly; which is one in fifty exactly. And I believe this will be found to be nearly the same, in most of the counties in Britain, where the people do not live in great towns; which shews the great difference between the effects of the air, in London and the country.

If then it be allowed, that in London and Westminster there dies one in thirty, it will be very easy to make a calculation of the whole number of the people nearly, that are within the bills. For if we take the number of burials at an average for some years, and multiply that by 30, the product must be the number of the people. Thus if we take the number of the burials, at large within the bills, for any one of the last ten years, at a medium, from 1744 to 1753 inclusive, to be 22945, and add to this 2000, for those burials omitted in the bills, as is supposed above, the total will be 24945, all the burials within the limits of the bills, for one year at 1753; and then multiply this by 30, the product 748350 will be the whole number of the people nearly, at present. But if we take 27192, the number of the burials, at a medium, for any one of the

ten

ten years preceeding 1743 inclusive, and add to this 2000, as above; the whole of the burials at that time within the bills will be 29192, which being multiplied by 30 gives 875760, for the number of the people at the year 1743. And therefore the inhabitants are fewer now than they were in 1743, by 127000. I have taken the numbers, at a medium, for ten years, to avoid any uncertainty, that might arise about a computation for a single year.

If we were to try the same calculation, by taking the burials, at a medium, only for five years to 1753, and also for five years to 1743 inclusive, the difference will be greater. For the numbers at these two times will be 720180, and 906570, of which the difference is 186390; so that the people would appear fewer at 1753 than they were in 1743, by 186000. But this is not so much to be depended upon as the numbers above; because there were two extraordinary bills at 1740 and 1741. Or if we should imagine that there might not more die at London than at Breslaw, that is one in thirty-four, still the difference would be greater than we found at first. For taking the burials at an average for ten years, at 1753 and 1743, as above, the numbers would at these two times be 848130 and 992528, of which the difference is 144398; so that it seems plain, if the bills are to be depended upon, that there is a decrease of the people since 1743 of above an hundred thousand, and that at present the number is about 740000. And this decrease has been annually continued: for if we try the thing farther, at the distance of five years, and take at a medium for five years, the burials for 1753 and 1748, the numbers will come out 720180 and 776520; of which the difference is 56340, the number decreased for the last five years.

There is another way of computing from the number of houses; but I think this not so certain as the other. For here are two difficulties, to ascertain the number of houses, and to fix on the number of persons for each house. As to the last, Sir William Petty thought we might allow eight persons to a house; which I have found to be a mistake. I have made an experiment of it, and got an exact account of the numbers in each house in a certain parish in London; and I find that they exactly come to six in a house, empty and full together, for there is seldom above one in twenty empty. And as in that parish the people are in a middle condition, and some of them have a number of servants; it may be presumed they are in a middle state with regard to numbers, between the very great families and those in the lowest rank. This is also confirmed, if we allow, as above, one in thirty to die yearly in London. For within the city walls there were 11857 houses in the 97 parishes, as appears from Mr. Smart's account, which was supposed to be very accurate at that time: But since he published that in 1741, there are not so many houses within the city walls; for in many parishes there are houses greatly enlarged, some rebuilt in place of two or three, and warehouses made of others. I know some parishes in which there is one in twenty fewer than in his time. In others perhaps there is no alteration. But I think they must, at an average, be diminished three in an hundred at least; and consequently

sequently there are about 354 fewer, and the number of houses within the city walls is about 11503; which being multiplied by 6, gives 69018, for the number of inhabitants; which is nearly equal to the burials 2290 multiplied by 30, or 68700; taking the burials at a medium for ten years, and adding 400 as above.

The number of houses within the bills may then be nearly come at, from the number of burials. For if we take the number of burials, for the last ten years, at an average, within the city to be 1890, and add 400, which makes 2290, we may say, if 2290 comes from 11503 houses, then the whole number 24945 of burials within the bills, having allowed 2000 as above, must come from 125302 houses. And there cannot be fewer; for there are more burials within the city, in proportion to the baptisms, than in the out-parishes; and therefore more burials in proportion to the number of houses; which shews that the number of houses cannot be less than 125302; which being multiplied by 6, will give 751812, for the number of people for this present time; and it is nearly equal to the number 748350 found above. So that the numbers produced from these two methods being almost equal, this is some farther proof that our supposition of six persons to a house, empty and full, is near to the truth. But if we suppose, that the number of houses within the walls is now the same, as in Mr. Smart's time, 11857; then all the houses within the bills will be 129158, and the number of people 774948 greater than 748350, found above, by 26598; which is not much in such calculations.

Sir

Sir William Petty likewife fays, that he was informed there were 84000 houfes tenanted within the bills, in the year 1682, in which he wrote; and if fo, the number of houfes feem to be increafed, near one-third fince that time. And, according to our way of computing, to fuppofe fix to a houfe, empty and full, there could not be more than 504000 people at that time; which is lefs than the number we found above for the prefent time, 748350, by 244350. But now, inftead of increafing, we are decreafing; for fince the year 1743 the inhabitants have been annually diminifhed; by which it appears that this great city is paft its height, and is rather upon the decline with regard to numbers. And hence we fee how far Sir William was miftaken, who imagined that it might increafe continually till the year 1800; when the number of people would be five millions, that is near feven times as much as they are at prefent.

Now, to account for this decreafe there may be various conjectures: I think three caufes may be affigned, that may all operate jointly. One may be the vicious cuftom that has prevailed of late years, among the lower people, of drinking fpirituous liquors; another the fafhionable humour of living fingle, that daily increafes; and a third may be the great increafe of trade in the northern parts of Britain, that keeps the people there employed at home, that they have no occafion, as formerly, to come hither for bufinefs; and it were to be wifhed that this caufe was the moft prevailing. But whatever be the caufe, it feems plain to me, that it could not be the late French war, as fome imagine. For by what was

was shewn above, there has been a decrease of 56000 since the year 1749, after the peace; but if the war had been the cause, there ought rather to have been an increase after it. And as in the whole, we could not have lost more than 150000, in the war by land and sea, of which there was not one-fifth, or 30000, taken from about the city; this can never account for 64000, the decrease before the year 1748. In the former war, between 1702 and 1711, the city never decreased, but continually increased: from which one would imagine that the last war could not diminish its numbers.

Nor can this decrease in the bills be accounted for, from a greater number than formerly leaving the town in summer; because it does not appear that there is a greater number of such, than was ten years ago. And if it could be allowed that the number was greater, it can never be thought that it can amount to 120000 more than in year 1743.

It is true, this decrease may appear suprising to some, when they see the number of new buildings in Westminster, continually increasing; but then, on the other hand, it is likewise to be considered, that there are a great number of houses enlarged, or rebuilt, in place of two or three others, as mentioned above; and others falling in, and empty, about the eastern parts of the city: so that for the last twenty years the inhabitants seem only to be moving, from the eastern to the western parts of the town, and not increasing.

And now, Sir, I am afraid I have tired you with this long letter, in which I have endeavoured to represent the present circumstances of this great city, with regard to numbers, and, if I have committed any miftake, I hope your ufual goodnefs will excufe,

Dear Sir,

Sion-College,
Novem. 20,
1754.

Your moft obedient fervant,

W^m. Brakenridge.

XLV. *A Letter to* George Lewis Scot, *Efq; F. R. S. concerning the Number of People in* England; *from the Reverend* William Brakenridge, *D. D. Rector of* St. Michael Baffifhaw, London, *and F. R. S.*

Dear Sir,

Read Nov. 20, 1755.

Having lately wrote to you my obfervations, concerning the number of inhabitants in London and Weftminfter, this has led me alfo to confider, whether there may not be fome way to compute nearly, the number of people throughout England; and if it can be done, there are many political ufes that may be made of it, and many conclufions that may be drawn, which may prevent miftakes in Government, and that will tend to promote the ftrength and riches of the Nation. The fubject is indeed intricate, and there cannot be

that

[269]

that accuracy in such calculations as might be desired; but I imagine we may come so near the truth, as is sufficient for any purpose to reason upon, or to be a foundation for any speculations in Policy. As you are a good judge of such computations, I presume to send you what I have done; and if I have your approbation, I shall be more satisfied that I am in the right; but, if I be mistaken in any particulars you will, I hope, make great allowance for the failure, when you consider the difficulties that occur.

There seems to me to be only two ways of discovering the number of people in England, where at present there are no Capitation Taxes, either by the number of *Houses*, or the quantity of *Bread* consumed. I shall consider both these methods of computing, so far as things are known to me; and the result from each of them being compared together, they will correct one another, from which at least the limits of the number may be nearly found. As to the first it is evident, that if the number of houses could be determined, it would then be very easy to compute nearly the number of people. For it might be easily known by trial, what number, at an average, could be allowed to each house, and from thence the whole number of people deduced. In my letter last year I have assigned six to a house in Town, which I found to be the nearest number, in some Parishes, by an account taken; but I think it is still more plain in the Country, that six is the number to be fixed on, where people do not go so much into single life, and where there are not so many Lodgers. For if we consider, that for every marriage there are

four

four births, at an average, as Dr. Derham, Major Graunt, and others have shewn, and which I have found to be true from the Regifters both in the Town and Country; then confequently, allowing for deaths, there cannot be three children that furvive, from every marriage to mature age, and indeed not much above two, as appears from Dr. Halley's Table of the probability of life. And therefore every family, where there are children, one with another, cannot confift of more than between four and five perfons, befides fervants or inmates; which fhews plainly that families, where there are children, cannot be eftimated at more than fix to a houfe, and where there are no children, they cannot be reckoned more at an average.

The number then being fix to be affumed, let us next confider what number of houfes is to be fuppofed. That I might come at fome certainty in this I lately applied to one of the Public Offices, where I thought they could very likely give me an account of them; and I there found, that before the year 1710, and near about that time, an account had been taken of all the houfes throughout England and Wales, in order for fome Affeffment upon them; and the number then did amount to 729048. In which it may be fuppofed, that a number of Cottages were omitted, that might be improper for that Affeffment; but I think there could not poffibly be above one-fourth part of that number more: For furely the Surveyors, if they had any care of the Public Revenue, would never omit above one in Five. Let us therefore fuppofe, that there might be one-fourth part of that number more; and then thofe omitted will be about 182262, and the whole number of houfes could not exceed 911310.

If

If now we take 911310 for the number, it is evident, if we allow six persons to a house at an average, according to what has been mentioned, the number of persons through England and Wales, before the year 1710, could not be above 5467860. And since that time, 45 years ago, by a method of computing which I shall presently shew, the increase could not be above 789558; and so the whole number of people now must be about 6257418; or six Millions, all ages included; for it must be remembered, that in our wars since 1710, there could not be fewer lost than 200000, which is to be deducted from that number.

As to the other way of determining this, by considering the quantity of *Bread* that is consumed, it may perhaps at first view appear more uncertain; but it will, I think, from some things that may be observed, at least help to ascertain the above number. For it is plain, if the quantity of *Wheat* that is produced in England could be known, it would then be very easy to make the computation, as it might be nearly discovered, by a little observation, what each person at an average might consume. But the great difficulty is to find out nearly the quantity of *Wheat*; and there seems to be no way at present of knowing it, but by considering what proportion it may have to the *Barley*; for the quantity of that is nearly known from the Malt-tax.

Now, if we compare the quantity of the Barley with that of the Wheat in England, it is evident, that there is at least as much ground sowed with the one as with the other. For there are vast tracts of land that will not bear good wheat, but are frequently sowed with

with barley; and even thofe lands that will produce good wheat, they are often alternately fowed with it: The land that is rich and well manured, after one crop of wheat, it is ufual to fow it with barley. And if this be admitted, that the quantity of land fowed with the one is equal to that fowed with the other, there muft then be a much greater quantity of barley; becaufe the fame number of acres will produce much more of it, and generally in a greater proportion than Three to Two. Thefe facts are fo well known that I believe every reafonable Farmer, when he confiders them together, will allow, that the barley cannot be in a lefs proportion to the wheat than Three to Two.

If then we allow, to make a calculation, that they are in this proportion, though I think, from what I have obferved in the Country, the difference is greater, we fhall then nearly find the quantity of wheat from the Malt-tax; becaufe the general confumption of barley is in malt. To ftate this as exactly as we can, it muft be remembered, that there are about 500000 quarters of wheat almoft annually exported, as appears from the Bounty-money paid by the Government; and fome of it is made ufe of in mechanical purpofes at home, befides food. And on the other hand there is fome barley exported, though nothing near to the quantity of wheat, and a great deal of it given to fatten Hogs; fo that the barley exported, and what is given for the purpofe of fattening, may be thought to be equal, or more than the wheat exported, together with what is ufed for mechanical purpofes. Let us imagine that they are equal, for the error will not be great in this grofs

manner

manner of computing, and then the remaining quantity ufed in malt muft be in a greater proportion to the remainder of the wheat ufed in food than Three to Two.

If then we affume this, that the barley ufed in malt is to the wheat ufed in food at home, as Three to Two, though I believe the malt is in a greater proportion to the wheat, we fhall then be able to compute the quantity of each of them in this manner: The Malt-tax from the year 1747 to the year 1753 inclufive, amounted to the fum of 4,254813 *l.* of which the feventh part, the Tax for one year, is 607830 *l.* and as the Tax is four fhillings upon every quarter of barley, it follows, that there are 3039150 quarters of barley confumed yearly in malt; and therefore, by what has been faid above, that this quantity cannot be in a lefs proportion to the wheat than Three to Two, there muft be 2026100 quarters of wheat confumed at home. Now, as it is known, and I have obferved it in the country, that labouring healthy people, at an average, confume about one quarter of wheat in the year, which is about 512 pounds of flower, or one pound and fix ounces in a day, we may allow that healthy and unhealthy, grown people and children, do not confume the half of that quantity, one with another. And therefore, that we may make the confumption of each perfon at an average, as fmall as can reafonably be imagined, we will fuppofe that three people, children included, do not confume more than one hearty labouring perfon, that is one quarter in the year, or each perfon about feven ounces in a day; and by this fuppofition, the above number of quarters of wheat 2026100, confumed at home, will be sufficient for 6078300, or six millions of people. And this quantity of a quarter to three persons, though it appears too little, may be admitted, as in some of the northern counties they use some Oat-bread and Rye-bread; and every healthy person may, one with another, be allowed to consume this quantity at least.

From this calculation it seems to me to be evident, that there cannot be above six millions of people in England: For the barley is certainly not in a less proportion to the wheat than Three to Two. And the quantity of wheat exported, and used in mechanical purposes at home, is not much less than the barley used in fattening, together with what is exported. And therefore the quantity of wheat used in food at home cannot exceed 2026100 quarters, which, computed at any reasonable rate, will not be sufficient for more than six millions of people; because it must always be supposed that labouring persons, or those in lower life, who have no great variety of food, consume much more bread, or food of wheat, than others in a more wealthy condition; and seven ounces a day, at an average, is rather too little allowance. And as from the other method of computing from houses, we found the number to be about 6,257400, from which at least 200,000 is to be taken for those lost in our wars since 1710, or near that time; it appears that both these calculations confirm one another, and that the number of people may be considered at about six millions, or rather less. In which, according to Dr. Halley's rule, there will be about fifteen hundred thousand men able to carry arms.

The

The worthy Dr. Derham, from the computations of Mr. King, which I never saw, suppoſes there is about five millions and an half of people in England; to which, if we add the increaſe that may be ſince that time, the number will be near about what we have made them. But Sir William Petty has endeavoured to make them, in his time, no leſs than 7369000, by ſuppoſing them to be in proportion to the Aſſeſſment, then eleven times greater than that in the city of London. In which, with regard to the city, he was certainly miſtaken, as I have ſhewn laſt year; for the number at that time, in 1682, was not much above 504000, and therefore eleven times that, *viz.* 5544000 muſt, according to his own hypotheſis, be the number of people in England. And if we allow 1355000 to be the increaſe in about 73 years ſince that time, by the method I ſhall preſently ſhew, the number could not be now, according to that aſſeſſment, above 6899000. From which we ought at leaſt to ſubtract 400000, which may be juſtly allowed for loſs in our wars ſince 1690; and the remainder 6,499000 is not half a million more than we have made them. But to compute the number of people from any pecuniary aſſeſſment that muſt ariſe from trade, circumſtances, and valuation of land, ſeems to me to be a much more uncertain method than either of theſe I have uſed.

The people then being computed at ſix millions, or rather leſs, it appears that England is but thinly peopled. For not only the exportation of at leaſt 400,000 quarters of wheat annually ſhews plainly, that we want people to conſume it at home, and that we maintain in bread about a million of foreigners abroad:

but if we examine more particularly we shall find, that the Country is capable of supporting one-half more inhabitants, or nine millions. According to Mr. Templeman's survey, England contains 49450 square miles, that is 31,648,000 acres, becaufe a fquare mile is equal to 640 acres. And if we suppose one-fifth of it waste ground, heaths, &c. there will remain about 25,300,000 acres of land proper to be cultivated. And as it can easily be made appear, that three acres, well manured, is sufficient for the maintenance of one person, I mean if a great number of acres are taken together, to produce the various necessaries of life in victuals and cloathing, then there will be maintenance in England for 8,430,000 people, children included; which, with the advantage of fishing, that the situation of the country gives, we may well allow that there is sufficient provision for nine millions of people, that is three millions more than we have at present. And this is only from the natural produce, without any of the advantages from trade, and the help of our Colonies in America, by which double the number might be maintained. The above allowance of three acres to each person, I think is too much; but some consideration must be had of the inclosures and pleasure-grounds, which those in higher life will always have.

But in Ireland the case is still worse: For if there is but a million of people, as is commonly supposed, and according to Mr. Templeman 27400 square miles, which is 17,536,000 acres, and one-fourth or more be supposed waste; then there will be at least 12,000,000 good acres. And consequently if four acres in that country be allowed sufficient, at an average,

average, for the maintenance of one perfon, Ireland, if duly cultivated, could maintain two millions more people than it has now, or three times its prefent number of inhabitants.

And in Scotland, if there be, as is faid, but a million and an half of people, for at prefent I know no way to compute them, and 27700 fquare miles, or 17,728,000 acres, and one-third be fuppofed wafte, which is not too much in that Country, then there will be 11,000,000 good acres; of which, if we fuppofe that five acres of that foil is not more than fufficient for each perfon, then there may be provifion for 2,200,000 people, or more, with the advantages of fifhing, that is 700000 more than there are at prefent. From all which it is plain, that if the land in both the Britifh ifles was duly cultivated, they might fuftain about fix millions more people than they do now; that is as many more people as England now contains. And this proportion of the number of people, to the quantity of provifions that may be raifed for them, from the natural produce of the country, I think is of great importance to confider, as it has many ufeful confequences, fome of which might be mentioned, if this was a proper place for political reflections.

And here, by the way, it may be obferved, if we extend our thoughts to the whole Globe of the Earth, and compare the quantity of land with the number of people, we fhall find, that it will maintain above twenty-fix times the prefent number of mankind. As this has hitherto not been taken notice of, I fhall briefly fhew it. The circumference of the Earth, fuppofing it to be a fphere, is, according to the measures of Messieurs Picard and Cassini, 123,249,600 Paris feet, or 131,630,572 English feet, which is 24930 English miles; and the diameter is 7935 English miles. And then the whole surface of the globe, by Prop. 38. lib. 1. *Archim. de Sphæra & Cylindro*, is 24930 × 7935 = 197,819,550 square miles. And as the whole surface is to the quantity of land, near about 8 to 3, the land will then be 74,182,331 square miles; of which, if we allow one-third to be waste ground, or unfit to produce the necessaries of life, we shall have 49,454,887 square miles, or 49,454,887 × 640 = 31,651,127,680 good acres. Now the number of mankind over the whole globe is computed by Sir W. Petty, and others, to be under 350,000,000; but we will suppose them 400,000,000, which is surely more than their number, that we may avoid any uncertainty in computation; and then there will be 79 good acres to each person. From which it is evident, if the soil in England be considered as a medium between the poor lands in the northern Climates, and the very fertile in the southern, and three acres be here sufficient for one person, that the earth can maintain more than twenty-six times its present number of inhabitants. And if we imagine the land to be in a greater proportion to the surface than 3 to 8, and the number of mankind less than we have supposed, the produce of the earth will then be in a greater proportion to them. And hence it plainly appears, that the earth is in a very imperfect state with regard to the number of people. And that if births and burials are supposed nearly in the same proportion, all over the Globe as in England, it will be above 1000 years before the earth can be fully peopled.

peopled. From which it seems probable, that the origin of mankind is not more antient than is commonly believed.

But now, to return to our purpose, let us in the next place see what may be the annual increase of the people in England, that we may be able to judge of the future improvement of the Country. Dr. Derham, in his *Physico-Theology*, has shewn, from some observations communicated to him, that the number of births are annually to the burials through England in general as 1,12 to 1, though I should imagine the births, if there was an exact account taken, would be in a little greater proportion. From which, if we could know the number of the burials, the increase would be easily found. And in my Letter last year I have there made it appear, that within the bills of mortality there die about one in thirty, and in some very healthy places in the country about one in fifty, which seem to me to be the two extreme degrees of health in England; so that in many Towns, and in fenny or marshy lands, the degrees of health must be between these two. Let us now take the mean between them, which is one in forty, and this will be nearly, at an average, the degree of health through England, or perhaps Britain in general, as Sir William Petty has observed, and which will very well serve to make a calculation of the increase of the people. For then, if we suppose the whole number to be 6000000, the fortieth part of it, *viz.* 150000 will be the number of the dead yearly. And the births, from the proportion of 1 to 1,12, will be 168000; from which, if we take the number of dead, the remainder 18000 must be the annual increase;

crease; which indeed is very small, and I believe much diminished, by the emigration of great numbers to our colonies in America, and settlements elsewhere, or by our wars, and losses at sea. So that if it was not for the accession of Foreigners, and those who come from Scotland and Ireland, the increase would be very inconsiderable, if any at all; which by the way shews the reasonableness and good policy of encouraging Foreigners to settle among us. However, let us suppose the annual increase to be 18000, and it will be easy from thence to find in what time the number of the people may be double, or in any given proportion; not by dividing 6,000,000 by 18000, considering the annual increase as a constant quantity, which is the method Sir William Petty uses by mistake, or perhaps not knowing how to do it otherwise; but by making this annual increase continually to increase as the whole number does. Let us propose the question first in general, the number of people being unknown, which is this:

The proportion being given of the living to the dead in one year, and also the proportion of the births to the dead, the number of the people being unknown; to find in what time the people shall be in any given proportion, to what they are at present.

Suppose n to be the unknown number of the people at present; and let the living be to the dead, in one year, as l to 1, and the dead to the births as 1 to b, the proportion given to what their number is at present as p to 1, and the number of years required to be y.

It

It is plain then, that the dead at the end of the first year will be $\frac{n}{l}$, and the births $\frac{bn}{l}$, and the whole number of people must be $n + \frac{bn}{l} - \frac{n}{l}$. In like manner, at the end of the second year, the dead will be $\frac{ln + bn - n}{l^2}$, and the births $\frac{lbn + bbn - nb}{l^2}$, and the whole number of people must be
$$n + \frac{bn}{l} - \frac{n}{l} + \frac{lbn + bbn - nb}{l^2} + \frac{n - ln - bn}{l^2} = n \times \frac{\overline{l+b-1} \times \overline{l+b-1}}{l^2}.$$
And so at the end of the third year the number of people will be $n \times \frac{\overline{l+b-1}|^3}{l^3}$. From which at length it is evident by induction, that the number of people at the end of the required number of years will be $\frac{n \times \overline{l+b-1}|^y}{l^y}$. But as the proportion is then to be as p to 1, we shall have $\frac{n \times \overline{l+b-1}|^y}{l^y} = pn$, and from thence $\overline{l+b-1}|^y = pl^y$, And because the logarithms of equal quantities must be equal, we shall have $y \times \log. \overline{l+b-1} = \log. p + y \times \log. l$, and also $y = \frac{\log. p}{\log. \overline{l+b-1} - \log. l}.$
And therefore the number of years y is determined by the logarithms of known quantities when the people shall be in the given proportion of p to 1.

It may be observed that the quantity $\frac{n \times \overline{l+b-1}|^y}{l^y}$ may be considered as the ordinate of the logarithmic curve, whose abscisse is the index y, and that the ordinate paſſing through the beginning of the abſciſſe, where $y = 0$, muſt be equal to n.

If now it be required to know when the people ſhall be doubled; let us ſubſtitute in the above formula, in place of b, l, p, the reſpective numbers 1, 12, 40, 2, and it will be $y =$
$$\frac{\log. 2}{\overline{\log. 40. + 1, 12} - 1 - \log. 40}; $$
and then the logarithms being taken we ſhall have $y = \frac{0,3010300}{0,0013009} = 231$; which ſhews, that, according to the preſent ſtate of births and burials, the people could not be doubled in leſs than 231 years.

And by the ſame method it appears, changing the ſigns of $b - 1$, that 230 years ago, in the time of Henry the VIIIth, the number could not be above one-half of what it is now, that is about 3,000,000.

And ſo if we were to find, when the number of people in England would be increaſed to nine millions, which, by what has been ſaid above, is near about the outmoſt that can be maintained, from the natural produce of the country; we ſhould then have $p = \frac{3}{2} = 1, 5$, becauſe nine millions is to the preſent number, as 3 to 2, and alſo $y =$
$$\frac{\log. 1, 5}{\overline{\log. 40 + 1, 12} - 1 - \log. 40} = \frac{0,1760913}{0,0013009} = 135;$$
which ſhews, that at the preſent rate of births and burials, it muſt be 135 years before England can be fully peopled.

If we ſuppoſe, as Sir William Petty does, that the burials are to the births as 9 to 10, that is 1 to 1, 111, which is ſomething leſs than that of Dr. Derham's proportion, and that one dies in 40 in a year; if we substitute these numbers in the formula, we shall then find the time of doubling to be 250 years. For then it will be $y = \dfrac{\log. 2}{\overline{\log. 40 + 1,111} - 1 - \log. 40} = \dfrac{0,3010300}{0,0012035} = 250$; which shews how far Sir William was mistaken, in his method of calculation, when he made the time to be 360 years.

After the same manner, the number of years being given, it will be easy to find the proportional increase. Suppose after 45 years. For then we should have $45 \times \log. \overline{l + b - 1} - 45 \times \log. l = \log. p$ which will give $45 \times 0,0013009 = \log. p$. and therefore $p = 1,1443$, from which if n be equal to 5,467,860, we have $pn = 6,256,872$. So that it appears if there was 5,467,860 of people in England at the year 1710, when the above-mentioned survey was made, there is now 6250000; if there was none to be deducted upon the account of our wars, and emigrations to our Colonies since that time.

From what has been found above, that $\overline{l + b - 1}|^y = p\, l^y$, it is evident, that the ratio of the increase in any number of years may be determined, without the number of people being known, or their proportion to the annual increase; and also that any one of the quantities l, b, y, p, may be found, the others being known. But if the ratio of the number of people to the annual increase be known; and consequently the proportion, of the number in any one year, to the number next year known, we shall then have a very simple equation. For if we suppose the number of people in any one year, to be to that number with the increase added in the next year, as 1 to r, we shall then have $n r^y = n p$, or $r^y = p$. And in like manner if the proportion of the number of people to their increase, in a given cycle of years, had only been known, and that cycle be c, we should then have $n r^{\frac{y}{c}} = n p$, or $r^{\frac{y}{c}} = p$.

From which formula it would be easy to calculate the numbers of mankind, in all ages through the world, if we suppose them to arise from a given number, and the rate of increase known, in any period of years. And this may sometimes be of use to discover the number in any age, that might be possible to reason upon, and to find out the truth of any hypothesis. But I shall not enter upon it farther, as such calculations are liable to great uncertainty, from the frequent and various devastations of mankind.

And thus I have endeavoured to discover the number of the people in England, and the rate of their increase, from the few things I had known, which I think are of such a nature, that I cannot be far mistaken. I have indeed made them fewer than they are commonly believed, but, if I am right, it will be so much the better, to be undeceived in a matter of such consequence. You will easily discern from your extensive knowlege where I have failed, which, as the subject is so difficult, I hope you will more readily excuse. And pray let me have your remarks, in the freest manner, on the whole, which will greatly oblige, Dear Sir,

Sion-College,
Nov. 19, 1755.

Your most faithful servant,

W^m. Brakenridge.

P. S.

P. S. I find some gentlemen have objected to my account last year, of the number of the people within the London bills of mortality, that the diminution of the burials may only be owing to an extraordinary degree of health, that may have been for the last ten years, and not to any decrease of the number of the living. But these gentlemen have not attended to what is there shewn in the Table, that the births are also greatly diminished, and that from the decrease of both together, it is concluded, that the people are fewer. For if greater health was the cause of the decrease of the burials, the births for that reason ought rather to be more. The truth is, the decrease of the people diminishes the practice of physic, which makes some of that profession imagine, that the times are more healthy.

CXIII. *A Letter to* George Lewis Scot, *Esquire, concerning the present Increase of the People in* Britain *and* Ireland: *From* William Brakenridge, *D. D. Rector of* St. Michael Bassishaw, London, *and F. R. S.*

Dear Sir,

Read Dec. 9. 1756.

YOUR favourable acceptance of my two former letters, concerning the number of people in this city, and throughout England, has encouraged me to add this as a supplement to them; in which if the observations are not so agreeable as could be wished, they may perhaps be useful in our reasoning upon matters of Government, and help us to discover some things that may be wrong, or inconsistent with the public utility.

From the proportion of births and burials in England, and the number of people found, you have already seen what the annual increase might be; which appeared so small, that I was in some doubt whether there was any increase at all, after the deduction of our losses by our ordinary commerce at Sea, our wars, and emigrations to our Colonies. However, supposing, that there was an annual increase, I shewed the method of computing it, after any number of years; which sometimes may be of use in considering the increase of mankind in general. But now, having considered this subject farther, I think it may be proved, that there is no increase at all from both our British Isles, after the deduction of our losses; and that in England, taken by itself, the natives would be in a decreasing state, if it were not for the supplies from Scotland and Ireland. As this seems to be of some importance to discover, because of its consequence with regard to Policy, and the influence it may sometimes have, I shall endeavour to shew it as plainly, as the present circumstances of things will allow.

Dr. Halley has shewn, from his Table of the Probabilities of life at Breslau, that the number of men able to carry arms in any country, between 18 and 56 years of age, or, as they are called, the fencible men, may be estimated as a fourth part of the whole people, children included. From which it demonstrably follows, that the fourth part of the annual increase will likewise be the increase of the fencible men; and that their increase or decrease will always be in that proportion. And therefore, if in England the annual increase of the people does not exceed 18000, as I have before proved from the proportion of births and burials, and the whole number being six millions, the annual increase of the fencible men will not be above 4500.

But in Scotland and Ireland this increase may be reasonably supposed to be more, in proportion as there are more marriages than in England. And therefore, to avoid any uncertainty in calculation, we will suppose the annual increase in those countries, to be double in proportion. That is, as we have from observation, assumed the births to be to the burials as 112 to 100 at an average through England, we will now allow them in Scotland and Ireland

Ireland to be as 124 to 100; where the difference, which is the increase, is double to the other, and by which the whole people would be doubled in about 114 years; which is surely as much as can be supposed. And then, by the method that has been shewn in my last letter, if the people in both countries do not exceed 2,500,000, the annual increase will be found to 15,000, and the fencible men will be 3750.

From the account given in the Philosophical Transactions, N°. 261, the number of people in Ireland, in the year 1696, did not appear to be more than 1,034,000; since which time there has been little increase, as I shall presently shew; and in Scotland they are supposed to be less than 1,500,000; and so both together they cannot be reckoned at more than 2,500,000: and therefore the annual increase of the fencible men cannot possibly be more than 3750, in both countries; which with those in England will be 8250, for the annual increase in Britain and Ireland, or a little above 8000 men. And no reasonable computation can make them more.

It is true it may be said, that besides this increase, there is a considerable number of Foreigners, who come from all parts of Europe to settle among us, especially at London; but it may be justly supposed, that they are nearly ballanced by the number that go from hence, to reside in other kingdoms, for the purposes of trade and other considerations. And there cannot be so great an accession of Foreigners, as is commonly imagined; for they almost all come to this City, and yet it is not in an increasing state, as has been shewn in my first letter, notwithstanding all

all its supplies from them, and from Scotland and Ireland.

The number then 8250 may be considered, at the utmost, as the yearly increase of the fencible men; from which all our public losses in our ordinary commerce at Sea, and in our wars by Land and Sea, and by our Colonies, are to be deducted. And it is plain, if in all these ways our losses are annually equal to about 8000 men, there can be no increase at all of our fencible men; and consequently no increase of our people, which must always be in proportion to them; but if our losses are more, we must be in a decreasing state.

To make a just and moderate estimate of our losses it will be proper, that we take fifty or sixty years at an average to avoid any uncertainty. And if we begin at the year 1690, which is 66 years ago, we shall find, that during that time, in our commerce at Sea, and in our wars by Land and Sea, we cannot have lost less than 450,000 men.

To shew this it may be observed, that in all bodies or armies of fencible men, which consist generally of those between 18 and 56 years of age, there dies annually about one in 54, by the natural decrease of life, as appears from Dr. Halley's Table. And therefore, if there are 80000 seamen or more, as is said in Britain and Ireland, the natural decrease, which is not here to be considered, will be about 1480 or 1500 annually. But the number must be much greater that is lost, by the various contingencies of the Sea, by wreck, scurvy, and the inclemency of different climates, &c; for fewer cannot be supposed to be destroyed by such incidents, than the

double

double of those that may be by natural mortality. I think there must be more; for if a ship goes a voyage for a year with an hundred men on board, and returns only with the loss of half a dozen, she is reckoned to have made a healthy voyage, though the loss is above three times what might be expected from natural decrease; that is, though the loss by the Sea only may be considered as double the other. And it often happens, that by sickness there will be much more than this, besides all the other hazards of the Sea. Our ships of war in long cruising have generally a greater consumption of their people: So that our losses by Sea are rather undervalued, when they are estimated to be the double, of what is from the natural decrements of life. And, if this be allowed, the loss by the various contingencies of the Sea will be more than 3000 annually, over and above the number that might die by natural casualties if they were at home; and in 66 years it must be 198,000.

And as to our losses by war at Land and Sea, of our own people, they are commonly reckoned to be 300,000, in all the three French wars, since 1690: But if we abate 50,000 from that number, that we may reason with more certainty, they cannot possibly be less than 250,000; for in all those wars, that taken together were about twenty years, there must be more than 10,000 lost yearly by Land and Sea. And therefore, both by our commerce and wars, from that time mentioned, we have at least lost about 448,000, or 6800 annually. In which are included those who died by fatigue, and other hardships, as well as those in actual Engagements.

And

And if we add to this, the number that is constantly and secretly drawn from Ireland, for foreign military service and on the account of religion; and likewise those taken from Scotland, for our Regiments in the Dutch service; all which cannot be less than 500 yearly, though some have thought it to be double this, we shall then appear to have lost 7300 annually, since the year 1690. To which if we put the loss of those who go from hence to our Colonies, and other settlements, particularly to Jamaica and the East Indies; and, last of all, the number we have lost by the use of spirituous liquors; it will be plain, that our whole loss cannot be less but more than 8250 annually; which is at most the yearly increase of our fencible men: And therefore that there has been no increase at all of our people these last 66 years; but rather perhaps a decrease, though it cannot be ascertained with any precision. And there is no avoiding this conclusion, unless it can be shewn, that the annual increment of our fencible men is much greater than 8250; which seems impossible, without proving the number of our people to be more than six millions, and the proportion of births to burials greater than any observations through England have lately made them.

And here it is to be observed, that if there has been no increase during that period of years, the people of England cannot be more than 5,500,000. Because, when they are computed from the number of houses at the year 1710, they do not exceed 5,467,000; and when in my last letter, I supposed there might be some increase, and gave a calculation of it to the present time, that, being added to the above,

above, made only about six millions. And therefore the annual increase of fencible men in England is not above 4130, and in both Islands it does not exceed 7900; which being less than what we have allowed above, seems to corroborate what has been said.

Now if this can be proved, as I imagine it has, that there is no increase of our people in Britain and Ireland, because of our losses, we may make this unpleasant reflection, that our country can never be fully peopled, while our losses continue so great as they have been these last sixty years. For it has been shewn in my last letter, that we want one third more people, to be fully inhabited, and which we could conveniently maintain from our own natural produce, if our land was duly cultivated. And it may be farther observed, that as the greatest part of those losses above-mentioned belong to England, because of its much greater trade, and the greater number of its people, it may be considered as in a decreasing state with regard to its natives; and, if it were not supplied from Scotland and Ireland, the decrease would be plainly discovered. For, as the people in England are double to those in both the two other countries, its losses must be in that proportion at least, or about 5300 annually, two-thirds of the whole; which is more than the increase of its fencible men.

In London and Westminster the decrease has been observable from the Bills of Mortality within these last twelve years, as I have shewn in my first letter; but the greatest part of that may, I believe, be attributed to other causes, rather than national losses.

From

From the above calculation we may likewise see, how small the annual increase of fencible men may be in Britain, or perhaps in any other country in Europe. For as that increase in both our Islands does not appear to be more than 8250, but rather less, or about 7900, and the number of our whole people in them is not found to exceed 8,000,000, the annual increase in each million must be less than 1000, or about 987; that is, less than one in a thousand; though we have allowed the increase in Scotland and Ireland to be double in proportion to what it is in England. And from this we may form a good rule, by which we may judge of the increase, or decrease of other nations. For though they may be supposed to increase perhaps faster than we do, by more frequent marriages, the annual increase of their fencible men will not generally much exceed 1000, for every million of people. And therefore, according as their losses by war, or other devastations are fewer, or exceed 1000 fencible men annually, for every million of their people, they are either in an increasing or decreasing state; and for every 1000 men that are lost, there is the increase of a million for one year destroyed; which it were to be wished, that Princes would attend to, in their ambitious schemes, by which they make such havock of mankind.

And hence by the way we may observe, that France cannot be in an increasing state, unless their late encouragement for marriage has had some considerable effect; because if the number of her people, as Sir William Petty and others have reckoned, does not exceed 14,000,000, the annual increase of her fencible

fencible men will not be much more than 14,000: Which number feems to be exhaufted during thefe laft 66 years, in her frequent wars, her ordinary commerce at Sea, and emigrations to her Colonies. For all the annual increments put together, in that time, will not make above a million, and the loffes cannot be computed at much lefs. And this is fome comfort to us in Britain, that our neighbours, who are rivals to us in trade and power, are not better œconomifts of their people than we are; and that their fcheme of Government and fuperftition will never fuffer them to increafe, fo much as they might reafonably do.

We may in general likewife obferve, that in all Europe the annual increafe of people muft be much lefs than it was in fome former ages. For the advancement of trade in the maritime countries, muft greatly augment the lofs of their fencible men. In Britain there is one-third of the increafe of them deftroyed by our concerns at Sea, and in Holland perhaps the whole of it; and this added to the fuperftitious celibacy of other nations, muft diminifh much the increafe of people.

The above method of fhewing our want of increafe, from the loffes of our fencible men; which are always in proportion to the whole body of the people, feems to me to be clear and demonftrative: But the fame thing may likewife be conjectured, from the exportation of our corn. For there is as much now fent abroad as was forty years ago, or perhaps more; befides a great deal of it diftilled, which was not formerly done. And if there is the fame quantity exported, there muft be nearly the fame con-

fumption

sumption at home, and consequently about the same number of people, unless there is a much greater quantity of land improved. But it seems evident, that if we were in an increasing state, our late improvements of land could not cause such a surplus, over our home-consumption. For there is near about a fifth part, of our whole crop of wheat exported annually. A quantity that shews we want people to consume our natural produce, and that our country is but thinly peopled.

Now, to account for the cause of the want of increase in our British Isles, it seems to be chiefly owing to three things, that operate together. The fashionable humour that greatly prevails, by which above one-third of our people in England above twenty-one years of age are single, occasioned by a variety of circumstances; and to our wars and commerce at Sea, which are rather beyond our natural strength, by destroying more of our people than can well be spared, and which, if preserved, might improve our country, and augment our power; and lastly, to the use of spirituous liquors, by which numbers have been and are daily lost. But there may be easy remedies for two of those evils, by a little attention of the Legislature; which would greatly conduce to the public happiness.

And thus, Sir, I have wrote this third Letter to you, upon a very uncommon subject: but I hope the importance of it will plead my excuse. And if I have discovered any thing that has not been known, and that may be useful in our speculations upon Government, I shall think my time and pains have not been misapplied; but if I have been mistaken, your usual goodness will, I trust, forgive

Your most affectionate
and faithful servant,

Sion College,
Nov. 25, 1756.

Wm. Brakenridge.

P. S. Since the above was written, I have been certainly informed, that from the survey lately made of the window lights, after the year 1750, there are about 690,000 houses charged to that Tax in England and Wales, besides cottages that pay nothing. And though the number of cottages is not accurately known, it appears from the accounts given in, that they cannot amount to above 200,000. And therefore there are not in England and Wales more than 890,000 houses, or 5,340,000 people, allowing six to a house; which well agrees with what I have said in this and my former letter, and corroborates the whole of my reasoning. For if the survey made before the year 1710 was near the truth, from which it appeared, that there was not above 729,048 houses, besides cottages, or 929,048 houses in the whole; which will make about 5,570,000 people; then there must have been no increment since that time, but rather a decrease, notwithstanding the continual supplies from Scotland and Ireland, and from Foreigners.

I beg leave likewise to mention, that I find some people have objected to the Bills of Mortality,

tality, from which I computed our numbers in London and Westminster, in my first Letter; That they are too uncertain to found any calculations upon; that sometimes in the weekly Bills there are omissions of some of the largest Parishes, and perhaps in the yearly Bills. To which it is answered. If there are omissions sometimes in the weekly Bills, these are afterwards supplied in the subsequent weeks, and at the end of the year the whole account to each parish is made up, as accurately as the circumstances will allow; so that upon the whole it is presumed, the yearly Bills are done in such manner, that they may be depended upon; for otherwise they would be a vile imposition upon the Publick. And if they are properly taken care of, they may be considered as the index of the health and numbers of the people, as they are in other cities in Europe; in which view they have always had some credit, for a century past, and been attended to as of some importance; and many ingenious men have deduced useful speculations from them. But if it should be allowed, that there are inaccuracies in them, it cannot reasonably be supposed, that there are more now than ever have been; for there is as much care taken of them lately as ever.

The argument then from which I inferred, that there is a decrease of the inhabitants within the Bills is this; That, before the year 1743, for twenty years, the burials in them were at an average above 27,000, and the baptisms between 15,000 and 17,000; but since that time they are both gradually decreased; so that now the
burials

burials are about 22,000, and the baptisms between 14,000 and 15,000, taken at an average for ten years: And therefore these different numbers, continued so long, cannot come from the same number of people; but that as the burials and baptisms are both decreased, the whole people must be also diminished. This seems be fair reasoning, if the Bills are true. The times were as healthy before the year 1743, as ever since; there were as many burials carried out into the country before that time as afterwards; and there were as many Diffenters to lessen the number of burials and baptisms before that time as ever after. What then is to be concluded, the circumstances being the same, but that there must be a diminution of the people? And this may be imperceptibly made; either by the increase of celibacy, or by fewer coming annually to reside in Town than formerly, and more retiring from it; which last case I consider rather as an advantage to the kingdom, as it may tend to the improvement of the country.

It is true, we do not see so great an increase of empty houses, that may answer to the decrease in the Bills; but it may be easily imagined, that some hundreds of families may be diminished, and not one house left empty. The one half of our people consist of Lodgers, Inmates, and Children; and therefore there may be a great decrease of these, and yet not many more houses empty: Though it is also to be considered, that there are much fewer houses now within the Liberties of the city, than were before 1743; many being built in place of two or three, or more, and warehouses

houses made of others. I know some Parishes, in which they have lost one tenth of their number, by this means, since that time; so that within the walls I find there is above double the number lost, that I mentioned in my Letter. To live in large houses is now a part of our luxury. But if there be an increase of houses in Padington, Mary le bone, &c. without the Bills of Mortality, this does not affect my argument; which was only to shew, that there was a decrease of the people within them; and surely such a small increment is not to be compared to the probable decrease on the whole.

In that first Letter I reasoned, and made my calculation, upon the same principles with Sir William Petty, Mr. Graunt, and other approved Authors. From a continued increase in the Bills they inferred, that there must be a proportional increase of inhabitants; and I from the continued decrease in them, in the same circumstances, have endeavoured to prove a similar decrease of people. If their reasoning is just, mine cannot be false; and if the Bills never again appear so high, as formerly for a continuance, in healthy times, it will be a demonstration.

XLIII. *An Extract of the Register of the Parish of* Great Shefford, *near* Lamborne, *in* Berkshire, *for Ten Years: With Observations on the same: In a Letter to* Tho. Birch, *D. D. Secret. R. S. from the Rev. Mr.* Richard Forster, *Rector of* Great Shefford.

Rev. Sir,   Great Shefford, near Lamborne, Berks, July 8. 1757.

Read Nov. 17, 1757.

WHEN I settled in the country, abundant leisure enabled me to keep an exact parish-register. I have now finished ten years, I trust, with sufficient care, having examined every thing accurately myself. The sight of three letters, lately published in the Transactions, upon the subject of political arithmetic, put me upon

over-

overlooking and methodizing my own account; which I here send you, to make what use you think proper of it.

From Lady-day 1747. to D°. 1757.

Baptized - { Males — 73 / Females — 75 } — — — 148

Buried -- { Males — 44 / Females — 39 } — — — 83

Increase — 65

Buried {
Under 2 years of age — 25
Between 2 & 5 ——— 4
5 — 10 ——— 3
10 — 20 ——— 4
20 — 30 ——— 5
30 — 40 ——— 9
40 — 50 ——— 4
50 — 60 ——— 4
60 — 70 ——— 9
70 — 80 ——— 11
80 — 87 ——— 5
}

83

And but one alive above 87, who is 91.

The Number of People 425.
The Number of Houses 90.
The Number of Acres 2245. whereof $\frac{1}{6}$ is waste.

I do not offer such trifling numbers as these, as a fit subject to build a canon of life upon; but only as they may furnish us with a few particulars, which may throw some small light upon a subject hitherto very little cultivated: and as what has been advanced this way has been always taken from great cities, a little from the country perhaps may not be disagreeable.

The first observable in my numbers is, that the two infancies of human life are exactly equal; i. e. as many die above 60 as under 2 years of age; and that these two periods of life are by much the most sickly, five eighths of the whole, nearly, dying in these two stages, which renders the intermediate numbers very small.

This will give us some reason to suspect, that capital cities are very improper to estimate the probabilities of life from. The continual flux of people from the circumjacent country, to seek for employment, makes the decrements of life seem much larger than they really are. London is very remarkable upon this account; and Breslaw must receive pretty large accessions, as a very considerable manufacture is carried on there.

The second thing I would observe from my table is, that it confirms what Dr. Brackenridge observes of the Isle of Wight; *viz.* that the births are to the burials as 2 to 1 almost; ours being as 15 to 8 nearly. Now if this is the case of all the country places in England, it will give us a strong presumption, that the increase of mankind is much quicker than Dr. Derham's proportion of 1 to 12; especially if we consider,

Thirdly, That of the living not 1 in 50 dies yearly; and this in a village not very healthy. We are situated upon the celebrated Lamborne stream, which dries up generally in August, and leaves a stagnated water, and stinking mud, at a critical season of the year, which bring on a putrid fever, and make our place sometimes very sickly. In the year 1751 we buried 17. and in 1756. 11: and therefore we may presume, that in the healthiest parts of the nation, the proportion is still greater, perhaps not one in 60. In order to clear up this, it were to be wished, that the actual number of the people was known, where-ever the bills of mortality are exhibited. All reasoning without this preliminary is really not much better than groping in the dark.

A fourth thing observable from my numbers is, that the quantity of people allotted to a house is too big in all former calculations: for if we divide 425, the number of people, by 90, the number of houses, it gives but 4.72, which is not quite 4 ¾ to a house; and therefore 5 to a house, I believe, is as much as ought to be allowed, taking the nation all together. Now if the number of houses, taken in Queen Anne's time, be any thing near the right, with one fourth more allowed for cottages, according to Dr. Brackenridge's computation, we shall make the people in England, allowing 5 to a house, to be only 4,556,550. which appears, at first sight, to be too small a number. However, of Shefford I would beg leave to observe, (and it is far from being the poorest of villages) that more than two thirds of all the houses are downright cottages, and must be excluded, one as much as another, from any proposed assessment. Upon this foundation we must grant, that at least half the houses in England, take towns and all together, must be cottages, and plead an exemption from taxation

all

all alike. And thus the number of houses will be 1,458,096. which, multiplied by 5, will give us the number of people, 7,290,480. If to this we add the proposed increase, 789,558. we shall have 8,080,038 for the number of people now alive in England.

The fifth and last thing I would observe from my numbers is, that we may hence guess at the number of people in the whole kingdom: for if 1871, the good acres in Shefford, demand 425 persons for their cultivation, then will 25,300,000 good acres in England require 5,704,168 for the cultivation of the land only. Now supposing one third part of the people only to live in towns, above what is necessary for the cultivation of the land belonging to such towns, then we must add 2,852,084 to the above sum, which gives us 8,556,252 for the number of people in England. It may probably here be said, that this is but little better than reckoning at random. Indeed I allow it is so. But then I must beg leave to observe, that it has full as good a foundation to stand upon, as any calculation, that I have seen hitherto advanced. It has one *datum*, viz. a certain number of persons to a certain number of acres. It ought to be noted at the same time, that we are an inland place, have no sort of manufacture carried on, and consequently no accession of strangers.

If we examine the calculation arising from the consumption of wheat, we shall see some reason to suspect, that the number of inhabitants in England is not short of eight millions. I am persuaded I do not exaggerate, when I affirm, that three fourths of the people north of Trent, and in Wales, do not

eat

eat wheat: and as this is near a third part of England, it will follow, that one fourth of the whole is left out of the calculation, and that we muſt add near two millions to it to make it complete.

Again, I compute, that in my pariſh there are killed annually 160 fat hogs, *viz.* above one to three perſons; and that this humour of pig-killing prevails over half of England at leaſt, and is in ſome meaſure indulged in all parts. Now we will ſuppoſe, that there are but ſix millions of people in the nation, and that what is killed in the northern half makes up for what is deficient by reaſon of towns in the ſouthern half; we muſt from hence conclude, that a million of fat hogs are killed in England every year. Now one hog with another takes two quarters of corn, ſometimes barley, ſometimes peaſe: if we put half barley, we ſhall be under the truth. And here we ſhall have a million quarters of barley, not only to balance the exportation of wheat, but alſo to be equivalent to, as much bread-corn as will maintain a full million of people.

Farther, it is well known, that the greateſt part of the corn-trade is, of late years, got into the hands of millers: and it has been whiſpered about for a conſiderable time, and, I think, now the millers do not deny it, that *ſome* whiting is carried to all the great mills. The excuſe alleged for it is, that it makes the flour *wet*, and conſequently *bake*, the better. I am rather inclined to be of opinion, that it is to give a colour to ſomething that wants colour. And indeed, whoever taſtes the common bakers bread againſt a piece of genuine wheat-bread, will have ſome reaſon to ſuſpect, that all is not gold, that glitters. Every body knows,

knows, that the millers buy large quantities of barley and peafe, they fay, to fat hogs: but then they have pollard, middlings, &c. to fat them with; and fo may poffibly mix the barley and peafe with wheat to grind. But as this is all furmife, I would have no more weight laid upon it than it deferves.

The next article is of the fame nature; I mean, fomething of a myftery in trade; and therefore to be touched very gently. What I would hint is, that it is the opinion of many very intelligent perfons, that a good deal of malt is made, which does not pay the excife. I do not pretend to afcertain the quantity: perhaps one eighth may not be an extravagant fuppofition. And if this be the cafe, we fhall find as much barley, as will weigh againft bread for half a million of people.

But here, in all probability, you will object, that if all thefe articles be admitted, we fhall make the number of people near eleven millions; which is undoubtedly too much. I am ready to grant it. And here, if I might take the liberty to fpeak my mind, I think, that the allowance of one quarter of wheat to three perfons is too fcanty, and muft quite ftarve the poor, whofe chief provifion is bread: and therefore, two perfons to a quarter may be pretty near the truth. And then the numbers will ftand thus:

Such as eat wheat, by fuppofition - 4,500,000
In the North, and in Wales - - 1,500,000
Againft the fatting article - - - 1,000,000
Againft the two laft articles - - 1,000,000
             8,000,000

I cannot conclude this long scroll without recommending it strongly to the members of the Royal Society, who have many of them seats in parliament, and most of them interest in those that have, to get an Act passed for perfecting registers. The trouble is trifling; the expence nothing. It would be of great service likewise to number the people: and this might be done with great ease. I was not three hours in finishing mine on foot; tho' it is, perhaps, as extensive, for the number of people, as most in England, being near five miles in length. I am,

Reverend Sir,

Your affectionate Brother,

and very humble Servant,

Richard Forster, *Rector.*

[457]

LVII. *A Letter to the Rev.* Thomas Birch, *D. D. Secr. R. S. concerning the Number of the People of* England; *by the Rev. Mr.* Richard Forster, *Rector of* Great Shefford *in* Berkshire.

Revd Sir,   Shefford, Nov. 9. 1757.

Read Dec. 22. 1757.

SINCE I did myself the honour of writing to you in July †, my bookseller has sent me part ii. of vol. xlix. of the Transactions; in which * I find another medium advanced to determine the amount of the people in England: and this is the number of houses, which pay the window-tax, and which " amount to about 690,000, " besides cottages, that pay nothing." To this is added, that " tho' the number of cottages be not ac" curately known, it appears from the accounts given " in, that they cannot amount to above 200,000."

Here I cannot but express my concern, that this very ingenious gentleman has not been a little more explicit, by informing us, what these accounts are, upon which he builds so positive a conclusion. The law requires no such accounts to be delivered in; and parish-officers cannot be accused of works of supererogation: besides (which is more to the purpose) I am very certain no such accounts have been given in from this part of the world. On the other hand, in all parts of England, which I have seen (and that is, I think, almost the whole) the number of cottages greatly exceeds that of all other houses, except in the middle of towns, and some villages about Lon-

† See above, p. 356.   * Page 887.

don.

don. This is agreeable to the general interpretation of that sentence passed upon our original parent, that *he should eat bread by the sweat of his brows*; which is, that the majority of his descendents should be poor labouring people. This I do not mention with design to defend the interpretation, but only to shew the general sense of mankind.

As my notion of the matter differs so widely from that of this worthy gentleman, I did every thing in my power to check any mistake, which might arise from a fondness of one's own opinion; and which, I hope, will vindicate me in the eye of every candid inquirer. In a word, I set myself to count all the houses in several contiguous parishes; and then examined how many of them paid the window-tax, or duty upon houses. And here I must observe, that if there be any small mistake, it can hardly be supposed to be in favour of my own scheme; because I had the whole number of houses, by counting as I rode along; and some might possibly be missed, tho' of this I took the utmost care: whereas the number of those, that pay the window-tax, I had from the collectors rolls.

The following table is the fruit of my labours:

Great Shefford	90	17
Little Shefford	12	3
Welford	162	62
Chaddleworth	62	20
Bright-Walton	72	21
Catmore	10	1
Farmborough	34	5
Fawley	47	7
East Garston	99	41
	588	177

Here

Here we fee, that out of 588 houses only 177 pay the window-tax. Now if we say with the philopher *ex pede Herculem,* and suppose, that 200,000 taxable houses stand in the country, we shall have the following proportion, 177 : 588 : : 200,000 : 664406, for the whole number of houses that stand in the country, commonly so called.

Again, Lamborn parish, in which is a market-town, contains 445 houses, of which 229 pay the window-tax. Now if we suppose, in like manner, 200,000 taxable houses to stand in country towns (I mean of the middling and inferior classes), we must then say 229 : 445 : : 200,000 : 388646, the whole number of houses, that stand in country towns.

The remaining 290,000 houses must be placed in cities and flourishing towns; and must have Dr. Brakenridge's proportion assigned them; for without all doubt he had some reason for pitching upon such numbers; and as they could not be taken from country towns or villages, must be assumed from the present state of some flourishing place. Upon this supposition, we must say 690,000 : 200,000 : : 290,000 : 84,058. for the number of cottages in great towns; which, if added to the houses that pay, makes the whole number in large towns to be 374,058. These three sums added together make the total amount of houses in the nation to be

$$\begin{array}{r} 664,406 \\ 388,646 \\ 374,058 \\ \hline 1,427,110 \end{array}$$

The two former of thefe numbers fhould be multiplied by 5, and the latter by 6. The reafon of this difference is the great quantity of fervants kept in large towns.

$$1,053,052 \times 5 = 5,265,260$$
$$374,058 \times 6 = 2,244,348$$
$$\overline{7,509,608}$$

By this way of proceeding it appears, that the whole number of people now alive in England is fomewhat more than feven millions and an half. I would not be underftood, as if I meant to recommend this as exact; tho' I am in hopes, that, upon trial, it will be found nearer the truth, than any thing hitherto advanced. Neither will I lay any ftrefs upon its approaching fo near to the numbers advanced in my former letter; being fenfible, that all the methods I have hitherto tried are liable to very great objections. Where certainty may be arrived at by a little induftry, all hypothefis fhould be defpifed and rejected.

The militia act levies 32,000 men upon the whole kingdom; and in the weft riding of Yorkfhire 1 in 45, if my intelligence is right, completed their quota. Now if this proportion be applied to the whole nation, 32,000 × 45 will give 1,440,000 for the number of ballotters; and this multiplied by 5 (which, confidering the number of perfons excepted, muft be under the truth) will amount to 7,200,000 for the total of our people. But I dare not build any thing upon this computation, as many parts of the nation may have heavier quota's laid upon them than the weft riding.

Whether the kingdom is really in a declining or increasing state, is, in like manner, a problem not to be solved, I think, by mere calculation. If there happens but a small mistake in the principles, what is built thereupon will be extremely wide of the truth. If one might take the liberty to guess by appearances, I should think we are greatly increased within these forty years, or since the accession of the present Royal Family. This conjecture I found upon the great facility, with which the government raises men, compared to the violent methods made use of in King William's and Queen Anne's time. Indeed I am sensible, that when the great ease, with which the government raises money, and the low interest it pays, have been urged in the House of Commons, as evident proofs of a flourishing trade, and plenty of cash, it has constantly been answered by a gentleman, who understands these matters better than any body else, that they are rather proofs of a want of trade, and that people do not know what to do with their money. In the same manner it may be answered, that the great facility, with which the government raises soldiers, is not owing so much to the great plenty of men, as to the want of employment: which it is possible may really be the case.

But where certainty may be had, it is trifling to talk of appearances and conjectures. For a century now past, the English way of philosophising (and all the rest of the world is come into it) is not to sit down in one's study, and form an hypothesis, and then strive to wrest all nature to it; but to look abroad into the world, and see how nature works; and then to build upon certain matter of fact. In compliance with this noble method, I have done all
in

in my power: I have examined the regifters of feveral neighbouring parifhes, and fend you the fubftance of three of the moft perfect ones. Indeed, I could have added feveral others; but as they feem to have been now and then neglected, I did not care to truft to them. However, this I can fafely deduce from them; *viz.* that what I have here fent will be a proper ftandard for thefe parts: and if other gentlemen would take the like pains (and it is next to nothing) in four or five parifhes in each county, and in every great town, we might perceive, by one caft of the eye, whether our people are in an ebbing or flowing ftate. I have not fet down the burials, as that would but have embarraffed the table; and the increafe will appear very well without them. However, upon an average of all the parifhes I have examined, the proportion of the burials to the baptifms is as 83 to 149,4.

	Lamborn.	Welford.	Shefford.	Total.
From 1614 to 1623 incluf.	327	67	69	463
1624 to 1633	401	62	64	527
1634 to 1643	391	119	86	596
1662 to 1671	441	146	93	680
1672 to 1681	380	132	108	620
1682 to 1691	451	201	112	764
1692 to 1701	366	134	88	588
1702 to 1711	387	137	84	608
1712 to 1721	422	171	97	690
1722 to 1731	483	156	106	745
1732 to 1741	578	205	128	911
1742 to 1751	566	253	137	956
1752 to 1756	349	120	64	533

This table stands in need of no remarks: it speaks loud enough of itself, that our people increase in a very rapid manner. All I shall take the liberty of observing from it is, that all the registers I have looked over seem to resent the wretched policy of King Charles II. who submitted himself and kingdom too much to a powerful neighbour: and that our civil war had no effect upon our numbers, in comparison to our foreign wars.

I trust, that the very ingenious author of the *politico-arithmetical* letters, I have all along had my eye upon, will take no offence, if I recommend an article or two advanced by him to be reconsidered; which, if pursued, might perhaps induce some small errors in government.

The first is, That all ways to increase our people would be for the public welfare, even the naturalizeing of foreigners: whereas, if I remember right, all political writers lay it down as a maxim, that numbers of people without employment are a burden and disease to the body politic; and where there is full employment, there the people multiply of course. So that we should not measure the happiness of the nation by the number of mouths, but by the number of hands. Nay, if we were to import a quantity of foreigners, we must immediately re-export them, as we actually did in the case of the Palatines and Saltzburghers. Indeed, I cannot deny, but that if the new-comers were to bring new trades with them, they would be welcome: tho' I apprehend it is not an easy matter to find out many new manufactures. I can at present think of nothing but the cambrick business;

business; and that, with a little encouragement, might be established in either Scotland or Ireland, without the importation of strangers.

The next thing I propose to be ruminated is the assertion, That our commerce at sea is one cause of the decay of our fencible men: which sounds in my ear like saying, that if we had less trade, we should have more people. And if this is the purport of it, I am afraid it is a paradox, literally so called.

That emigrations to our colonies do lessen our numbers in appearance, is beyond dispute: but then it is only in appearance: for if employment begets people, the filling our plantations must increase us beyond imagination, it having been made out, if I misremember not, that every man rightly occupied in America finds employment for three persons in Old England. But then care should be taken, that the planters were generally employed in raising rough materials; and that every thing imported there were manufactured by ourselves; because, if we settle colonies, and then supply them with East-India stuffs and foreign linens, it is neither better nor worse than being at a vast expence to maintain other people's poor.

I cannot conclude without begging leave to observe, that this gentleman's doctrine is, from beginning to end, to say the best of it, ill timed. We are contending with our hereditary enemy, the most powerful prince in the world, not for superiority, but for independence, *pro aris et focis*. And, at such a time as this, to be told, that we are but little better than half peopled, and the few we have

dwindling

dwindling away every day, is indeed very difcourageing: whereas, on the contrary, I do not balance one moment to declare it, as my fixt perfuafion, that we can fpare 100,000 brifk young fellows, and ftill be the moft populous flourifhing nation in Europe.

I am,
    Reverend Sir,
      Your affectionate Brother,
        and very humble Servant,
           Richard Forfter.

LVIII. *A Letter to the Right Honourable the Earl of* Macclesfield, *Prefident of the* Royal Society, *from the* Rev. William Brakenridge, *D. D. F. R. S. containing an Anfwer to the Account of the Numbers and Increafe of the People of England, by the Rev. Mr.* Forfter.

My Lord,

Read Mar. 16, 1758.

AS I endeavoured, at a former meeting of the Society, to anfwer extempore fome objections offered by a Gentleman in the country, to what I have wrote concerning the number of people in England; I now prefume to fend you what I faid then in writing, with fome farther reflections. And this fubject I never intended to have meddled with any more; but as I seem to be called upon, to defend what I have formerly wrote, I hope I shall be excused if I briefly attempt it. Your Lordship, I know, and our illustrious Body only desire a fair representation of facts, which is the ground of all philosophical inquiries; and therefore I shall endeavour to do this, as far as I can, without regarding any hypothesis.

My design, when I first entered on this subject, was to discover whether our people were in an increasing or decreasing state, with regard to their numbers; which I thought of great importance to be known, because of its influence on the affairs of Government, in determining our strength, in settling of taxes, and directing us in the œconomy and imployment of our people. Now, in order to proceed in this inquiry, it was evident to me, that if the number of houses were exactly known, the number of people would be nearly ascertained. And therefore I attended to this, to find out the number of houses, as the only thing that could with any certainty help us to judge of this matter. And accordingly, being resolved to depend only upon the most sure, and general observations, I applied to a public office, where I thought I might possibly get at their number. And I there found, that from the last survey that was made, since the year 1750, there were 690,700 houses in England and Wales that paid the window-tax, and the two-shilling duty on houses; besides cottages that paid nothing. By cottages are understood those who neither pay to church or poor, and are, by act of parliament in 1747, in consideration of the poverty of the people, declared to be exempted both from the

tax

tax and the two-shillings duty; and they only remain not accurately known, to ascertain the whole number of houses. However, they are so far known, that from all the accounts that are hitherto given in, they do not appear to be so many as 300,000; and from what I myself have seen, in the books of that office, I should think they were not much above 200,000; for in some places, that I was perfectly acquainted with, I found many of the day labourers rated to the two-shillings duty, and there did not appear to be one house in ten omitted. And therefore, if there are not 300,000 cottages, as seems plain to me, there cannot be a million of houses in the whole in England and Wales; and the rated houses are to the cottages more than two to one; of both which, according to the returns made, there is now about one in seventeen or 58,800 empty throughout the kingdom. But if we were to allow, that there are a million of houses in the whole; which is more than the Gentlemen in the above mentioned office believe, and then deduct those that are empty, there could not be above 941,200 inhabited houses; and consequently supposing six to a house, about 5,647,200 people, or near about five millions and an half; which at the utmost, is what I insist on to be the real number.

But now the Gentleman, who objects to my calculations, thinks, that I have made the number of houses too few, and that in the whole there are above 1,400,000 houses, of which he imagines there are more than 700,000 cottages; for he supposes them to be more than the rated houses; and from thence he infers, that there are about seven millions and an half of people, in England and Wales; which I wish, with all my heart, was the true number: But I am so far from thinking that I have under-rated them, that I suspect I have rather made them more than they are. However, this controversy will soon be determined, there being now orders given, as I am informed, to all the Officers concerned in the window-tax, to make an exact return of all the cottages, as well as the rated houses, in each of their several districts. In the mean time, the Gentleman and I differ in this, that he supposes above 400,000 cottages more than I can possibly imagine.

Let us now see upon what grounds, and by what method of reasoning he determines his numbers. He makes a division of the 690,000 taxed houses into three classes, placing 200,000 of them in the open country and villages, and 200,000 in the market and inferior towns, and the next, *viz.* 290,000, in the the cities and great towns; for which division he has nothing to direct him; no proof, nor even probability. And as it is a mere arbitrary supposition, all reasoning and calculations founded upon it are nothing to the purpose, and the number of houses or people comptued from thence must be false or uncertain. But yet, upon this supposition, as if it was absolutely certain, he goes on to compute the houses and people in each division.

As to the first, he says he has counted all the houses in nine contiguous parishes in Berkshire, in which he has found the whole number to be 588, and those charged to the duty to be only 177; and therefore the cottages are to the rated houses as 411 to 177, or above two to one. And from this he assumes, that the whole number of houses thro' the villages and open country in England will be

[469]

be to the cottages nearly in the fame proportion. But here I am furprifed, that he fhould reafon in fo loofe and an inaccurate a manner. For, as there may be 7000 parifhes in the villages and open country, to infer from the numbers in nine of them that are contiguous, and that all of them together do not make a very large parifh, many being much larger as to the number of houfes, and where there may be particular circumftances; I fay, to infer from them what the proportion will be in all parifhes, in the villages and open country, is the fame way of reafoning as to fay, becaufe the poor in one parifh are in fuch a proportion, therefore they are fo in 1000 parifhes, or thro' four or five counties: whereas it is plain, that the proportion differs almoft in every parifh, and in every county; and the fum of all muft be added together, before we can know what the real proportion is. And nothing can be inferred from the circumftances of a few parifhes, or even of a County, what the proportion will be in the whole. And yet, from fuch precarious and vague reafoning he prefumes to compute, that there are above 460,000 cottages in the villages and open country; having affumed, without any hefitation, that there are 200,000 rated houfes in that extent. Such reafoning is unufual in philofophcal inquiries.

In like manner the Gentleman reafons very inaccurately about his fecond divifion, containing the leffer market and country towns, having fuppofed in them 200,000 taxed houfes: For from one inftance of the market town of Langborne, having found the whole number of houfes to be to the cottages as 445 to 229, or the rated houfes to the cottages as 216 to 229, he fuppofes the like proportion in all the market

ket towns. That is, tho' there be perhaps above 300 market towns in England, he supposes each of them has the same proportion of the poor in it as the single town of Langborne; which is unreasonable to imagine. For every one of them may have a diferent proportion, according to the various circumstances of their trade and situation. But yet from this strange and uncertain way of reasoning, without any induction, and from one instance among 300 cases at least, he concludes by proportion, that there are 388,646 houses in the country market towns, of which there are 188,646 cottages, besides those in the cities and great towns.

In the next place, as to his third class, the cities and great towns, he allows, that my proportion may be among them, *viz.* that the rated houses are to the cottages as 690,000 to 200,000, or 69 to 20: For he thinks, that it cannot be any-where but in the most flourishing places. And therefore, as he has arbitrarily placed 260,000 taxed houses in them, he computes that they must contain 84,058 cottages. But he has given no proof, that my proportion is only in the most flourishing places, besides these few instances that he has produced; which are nothing to form any general conclusion upon. For if we were to be directed by a few cases, we might think that there were much fewer cottages than I have allowed. There are some parishes, in which there are none at all. In the great parishes of St. James's and St George's Westminster, in which there are about 7000 houses, there are none: in the country parish of Chiselherst in Kent, where there are above 100 houses, there are but three: and in many parishes there is not one in 20. So that from particular instances, there is nothing to be concluded. But in all Middlesex, London, Westminster, and Southwark included, in which the poor are as numerous as in most places in the kingdom, because of the numbers of labouring people that flock hither for imployment, there is nearly the same proportion that I have assigned. For from a late survey in that district, as I am informed, there are 87,614 houses in the whole, and of these 19,324 cottages, and 4810 empty. Which indeed shews, that we are not so populous, in and near the metropolis, as is commonly supposed, and much less than I had calculated in my first letter: For from this account, if it be true, there are not above 530,000 people in that compass; of which, within the bills of mortality, there die about 25,000 yearly; that is, not less than one in 20.

As to what the Gentleman mentions concerning the militia, he seems to be much mistaken. For if the proportion be as he says, that one in 45 is levied, this directly proves the number of people in England and Wales to be about five millions and an half, according to my calculation; because the electors or balloters are the fencible men, or those able to carry arms. And if the whole levy be 32,000, then 45 multiplied by 32,000 will give 1,440,000 for all the fencible men in England. But Dr. Halley has clearly shewn, that the fencible men are one quarter of the whole people, children included; and therefore, four times 1,440,000, or 5,760,000, will be the whole number of the people; which is nearly what I have made them.

And thus, having seen how he has established his numbers in opposition to me, let us now, in the next place,

place, confider what he has faid with regard to the increafe of our people. He fays, whether the kingdom is really in a declining or increafing ftate, is a problem not to be folved by calculation: And yet he himfelf can guefs by appearances, that it has greatly increafed within thefe 40 years. But, by his good leave I muft tell him, that it is a problem in political arithmetic to be folved from fome *data*, as well as others. If the number of people be nearly found, and the general proportion of births to burials, at an average, thro' the kingdom be known, with the annual loffes of our fencible men, at a moderate computation; from thefe *data*, I fay, any one, who underftands numbers, will eafily determine whether we are increafing or decreafing. And accordingly, I have fhewn, that the annual increment of our fencible men is not much above 8000, which number is confumed by our annual loffes; and therefore we are not in an increafing ftate. For the whole number of people muft always be in proportion to the fencible men; fo that, if there is no increafe of them, there can be none upon the whole.

It is true, I am the firft who ventured upon a folution of this queftion; but when I confider what I have done, I cannot fee but that the principles upon which I reafoned are right. The *data* are, I think, exact enough to difcover our ftate. And Dr. Halley's rule to compute the fencible men, where our loffes are to be reckoned, is undoubtedly true. So that if there is any difficulty, it is in fixing the general proportion between births and burials, thro' the kingdom, *viz.* 112 to 100; which I have taken from Dr. Derham, who had collected many obfervations; being

a greater

a greater proportion than Sir William Petty allowed.
And which if it is thought too small, it is to be considered, that within the bills of mortality the births are much under the burials as 4 to 5; and in some of the great towns there are fewer births than burials, and in others they are nearly equal; so that these reduce the proportion that arises from the villages and open country.

But if we were to make a calculation from the births and burials, only in the villages and open country; which Dr. Derham has found to be at an average as 117 to 100, or nearly as 7 to 6; and suppose this to obtain all over Britain and Ireland, in the towns as well as the country, which is surely more than the truth; we shall then find, that the annual increment cannot be more than 9000 fencible men; which corroborates my former estimate. For, to compute it by the principles I have formerly endeavoured to establish; let the number of our people in Britain and Ireland be eight millions and an half, that is, five and an half in England and three millions in Scotland and Ireland; because some Irish Gentlemen have assured me, from some facts, that there is half a million more in their country than I formerly allowed; for I did not pretend to calculate them; and then the annual number of the dead, in Britain and Ireland, being one in 40, will be about 212,500; which will be to the births as, 100 to 117: And therefore the births must be 248,625, and the increase 36,125; of which the fourth part is about 9000 for the fencible men, which I am persuaded is more than the real number.

Now let any one compute our losses in the moderate way that I have done, and he will easily see, that they cannot be lefs than this number; and confequently we are far from increafing. And indeed it is evident from the number of empty houfes thro' the kingdom, mentioned above, *viz.* one in feventeen, or 58,000, and one in twelve of thofe that are taxed within the bills of mortality. For it is impoffible, if we were increafing, that there could be fo many empty; And therefore the appearance of fo much building is only the effect of our luxury, requiring larger, more convenient, and more elegant houfes, and not caufed by our increafe.

However, the Gentleman objects to all this, and fays, that he has examined the Regifters of fome neighbouring parifhes, and particularly of three that are perfect; and he finds, that the burials are to the baptifms as 83 to 149; which may poffibly be the cafe, as I myfelf have known it in one parifh in the Ifle of Wight, where the place is healthy, and people generally marry. But does he imagine that this proportion is general all over England? If fo, we fhould increafe in a rapid manner indeed! for then we fhould double our people in 35 years, if it were not for our loffes; which no reafonable man will venture to fay. He does not reflect, that in many country places, from their bad fituation, there is very little increafe, and in fome towns none at all, and in others a decreafe, continually fupplied from the neighbouring country. Within the bills of mortality there are annually 5000 burials more than the births; and confequently, to maintain our numbers here, there muft be a yearly fupply of 5000; which deftroys the whole increafe of fix or feven counties. And Dr. Derham found, from the accounts he had of country parifhes,
that

that in general among them the proportion of births to burials was not greater than 117 to 100, as we mentioned above; fo that nothing can be concluded from particular healthy places. The queftion is, what is the refult upon the whole thro' the kingdom? what is the general proportion of the births to burials, from which the increafe is to be eftimated? and which Sir William Petty fays is 111 to 100, and Dr. Derham as 112 to 100. See if he can difprove thefe numbers by putting together all the different accounts from every corner, among the towns as well as the country; and if he cannot, to argue only from a few inftances is nothing to the purpofe; for where there there is a multitude of different cafes, they muft all be confidered, to arrive at the general truth. But even in the particulars he mentions, he has not completed his argument; for, to make it conclufive, he fhould have fhewn, that, within thefe laft forty years, the time, he thinks, of our great increafe, in thofe parifhes the number of houfes or people were increafed, in proportion almoft as the births were above the burials, as 149 to 83: and if that cannot be made to appear, it is plain, that, for all he has faid, the annual increafe may be conftantly confumed by our loffes.

And now the worthy Gentleman having endeavoured to fhew, from the cafe of a few parifhes in the country, that we are in an increafing ftate, he proceeds to give me his ferious advice in two particulars:

Firft, That I would reconfider a propofition advanced by me, That all reafonable ways of increafing our people, even to the naturalizing of foreigners, would be for the public welfare. In anſwer to which kind admonition I muſt ſay, that I have often conſiderd the thing, as far as I can; and I think this may be eaſily ſhewn againſt any political writer, That it is the intereſt of a government, when they have powerful and dangerous neighbours, to increaſe their people by all reaſonable means, even to the inviting of foreigners, ſo far as the natural produce of the country can ſuſtain them; and that it is the fault or weakneſs of an adminiſtration not to be able to employ them. And in Britain, where they can have the aſſiſtance of the produce of ſo many large and fruitful countries of their own in America, I will venture to ſay, that it is an error in their policy, not to endeavour to increaſe their people; by which they might be more formidable, and perhaps ſtronger than their grand Enemy. The preſent King of Pruſſia has ſhewn the utility of this within his dominions; by which he has been enabled to make ſuch a figure in Europe.

The *ſecond* thing he admoniſhes me to reconſider is, That I have ſuppoſed our commerce to be one cauſe of the loſs of our fencible men. And who in the world doubts of it, but himſelf! Do ſhipwrecks, the diſaſters and inclemency of the ſea, the ſcurvy, *&c.* beget people? But he will ſay, without theſe we could not have trade, which employs great numbers of our people; and therefore, what we loſe, we may gain another way. And juſt ſo he may ſay of our wars, that occaſion the deſtruction of ſo many of our people, that they are no loſs to us; for we gain by them in their conſequences, in ſecuring of our liberties and property, and by which

our

our trade is preserved and promoted. But notwithstanding this, can it be said, that war does not diminish our fencible men! The truth is, trade increases riches, and gives more of the conveniencies of life, and brings luxury along with it; but it does not necessarily breed people: For we see in those countries where they have little trade, the people increase much faster than they do with us, as appears from the Bills of mortality in Prussia; where the general proportion of the births to the burials is greater than it is here, *viz.* 4 to 3; and by which the people might double in 84 years, if it were not for their losses. *(Vid. Phil. Transf. vol.* xxxvi.) Which great increase, by the way, easily accounts for those vast swarms of people that came from thence and the adjacent countries in former ages, and over run all Europe. And therefore it is not so terrible a paradox, as he imagines, that possibly where there is much less trade the people may increase faster; for luxury and other vices, that come with trade, do not promote an increase.

And now, as he has been so good as to give me his advice, I will return the favour, and desire him to reconsider the method of reasoning by induction; which may possibly help him to escape some paralogisms, in arguing upon these subjects. And I would likewise recommend it to him to inquire diligently, whether the number of our houses in England be increased these last sixty years; which, according to his reasoning, ought at least to be doubled: For if there is no increase of the houses, there can be none of the people.

To conclude: He adds, that my doctrine, from

beginning to end, to say the best of it, is ill-timed, when we are contending with our hereditary enemy, *pro aris & focis*. But here his zeal hurries him on, that he does not look to the dates of my Letters. For the first three were read before the Society, and ordered to be printed, long before the war was proclaimed; and as for the last, it is only a supplement to the rest; in which I have shewn, that France, by the bad œconomy of her people, is not in an increasing state; which, I think, is a comfortable hearing. But supposing they had been all printed during the war: What then? Is a fact to be concealed that, if discovered, may be useful to prevent errors in government, and rectify our notions of the œconomy of our people? What advantage can our enemies make of such a discovery? Will it encourage them to imagine that we shall be easier subdued, when they know, by the most moderate computation, we have at least two millions of fencible men in our British islands. Enough, surely, to resist them in all their attempts! But I doubt we are not so deficient in our numbers as in public virtue, without which the greatest multitude may be easily overcome.

And thus, my Lord, I have endeavoured to answer what this Gentleman has wrote in his second Letter; for I pass over the first, as it does not seem to contain any more in opposition to me, than what I have here considered. And upon the whole I cannot see, that he has said any thing to invalidate what I have formerly advanced. If I could discover it, I should be very ready to acknowlege my error.

I am

I am sensible I have made this reply too long; but I trust your usual benevolence to all our worthy Members will excuse me, who shall always esteem it an honour to be,

   My Lord,

    Your Lordship's

Sion-College, Most obedient
March 16. 1758.

     and faithful Servant,

      Wm. Brakenridge.

END of PART I. VOL. L.

AN ANSWER
TO THE
Rev. Dr. *Brakenridge*'s
LETTER, &c.

HAVING been defired by a worthy Gentleman to confider an Effay, written by the Reverend Doctor *Brakenridge*, Minifter of St. *Michael Baffifhaw*, and Librarian of *Sion College*, tending to prove that the Number of Inhabitants within the Bills of Mortality for *London* and *Weftminfter*, are of late Years greatly diminifhed; I have confidered it accordingly, and upon the Iffue, find more Objections to offer than Compliments to pay the learned Doctor upon it: Curiofity which he affigns for the Motive of his Enquiry, will hardly excufe him for publifhing it, if founded upon Truth, more efpecially by the Channel of the *Royal Society*, by which it was fure to be communicated to all the Learned in *Europe*. If we are really in the confumptive Way he would have the World believe, the Secret ought to have been kept as much in the dark as poffible, we were fhrunk abundantly too much in the Opinion of our Neighbours before; and to be the Expofers of our Decays, are Wantonneffes the moft inexcufable. But fhould the Doctor's whole Hypothefis prove only a melancholy Dream, what Excufe will he make for printing and publifhing fuch Trafh, or what Amends can he make his Country for fuch a Mifreprefentation of it? Not inclined to fee Things in fo difcouraging a Light, I fhall endeavour to give this learned Gentleman a categorical Anfwer, and fubmit the Determination to the Public, defiring the refpectable Corps of Reviewers, Critical-Reviewers, Magazine, and Literary Magazine-Writers, to give their Opinion, either for the Doctor or me, as feemeth beft to their profound unnerring Judgment. I place both Performances before them, giving, as I ought, the Precedency to the Doctor's, defiring no other Favour than this, that not being a Writer by Profeffion, nor ever gained by Writing, Defects of Method or Stile, may not be conftrued into Defects of Matter or Argument.

A

A LETTER
FROM THE
Rev. Dr. *Brakenridge*, F. R. S.

DATED,

November 20, 1754,

Concerning the Number of Inhabitants within the London *Bills of Mortality.*

AS I have lately had the Curiosity to consider the Number of Inhabitants in *London* and *Westminster*, whether they increase or decrease . . . .

I have consulted the yearly Bills of Mortality for the last fifty Years, which I imagine will be sufficient for my Purpose; and from them I have extracted all the Numbers of the Baptisms and Burials, both within the Walls of *London*, and at large within the Bills; for I thought that within the City Walls, where the Number of Houses is nearly known, the Baptisms and Burials might be very useful to reason upon, con-

[4]

cerning the whole Inhabitants within and without. And becaufe it may be furer to compute from a Number of Years taken at an Average, than from the Numbers in any one Year, as they ftand in the Bills; I have taken the Sums of the Numbers, for each five Years of the fifty, and then the fifth Part of each of thefe Sums; which will, at a Medium, be the Number for any particular Year. And in like Manner, I have taken the Sums of the Numbers for each ten Years, and the tenth Part of each of the Sums will be the Number for each Year at an Average. And the Numbers fo found will appear thus:

Years.	Baptifms.	Burials	Baptifms.	Burials.
1704 — 8	1870	2553	15867	22103
1709 — 13	1805	2551	15288	21701
1714 — 18	1890	2706	17586	24641
1719 — 23	1871	2719	18360	26978
1724 — 28	1829	2727	18442	27670
1729 — 33	1578	2532	17452	26267
1734 — 38	1406	2242	16762	26165
1739 — 43	1221	2397	15034	28219
1744 — 48	1062	1989	14402	23884
1749 — 53	1087	1790	14850	22006
1704 — 13	1837	2552	15577	21602
1714 — 23	1880	2712	18073	25809
1724 — 33	1703	2647	17920	27168
1734 — 43	1313	2320	15898	27192
1744 — 53	1074	1890	14626	22945

Where the Numbers are ranged in five Columns: the firft denotes the Years; the fecond

cond and third, the Baptisms and Burials within the City Walls; and the third and fourth shew the Baptisms and Burials at large, within the Bills. Thus, for Instance, 22945 is the Number of Burials, at a Medium, for any of the ten Years within the Bills, from 1744 to 1753 inclusive. And in like Manner, 1221 is the Number of Baptisms for any Year, at an Average for five Years, from 1739 to 1743 inclusive, and so of others. The Numbers above the Line are computed for five Years, and those below for ten.

In the Burials it is always to be considered, that they are perhaps 2000 more, than what the Bills represent them. For there are Burying-Grounds belonging to the Protestant Dissenters, the *Quakers*, and the *Jews*; of which there is no Account taken, and that are very considerable. In the first of which in *Bunhill-Fields*, I have been informed, there are about 400 Burials in the Year, and in the others, together, there may be about 400 more; which Sum of 800 comes, we may suppose, from all Parts within the Bills. But I think the one half, *viz.* 400, must at least come within the City; where there are most Protestant Dissenters and *Jews:* so that

400

400 may always be added to the Burials, within the City. It is likewise to be remembered, that both from within and without the City, a great many Burials go into the Country, of which there is no Notice taken. But from what I have observed, if we were to suppose that there are 1200 in the Whole carried out into the Country, over and above the 800 mentioned above, in the Burying-Grounds; I should imagine that to be the utmost. And therefore in our Calculations we shall suppose 2000 Burials yearly, more than in the Bills at large. And which, whether we are exact enough or not in the Supposition, will by no means hinder us to discover the Increase or Decrease of the People.

It is next to be observed, that in the Bills, the Baptisms are always about two fifth Parts at least less than the Burials, with the Numbers added to them above-mentioned; and that this Difference within the City seems continually to increase, so that it is much greater now than it was some Years ago; which appears plainly to arise from two Causes; the Number of Dissenters of various Denominations, and the Multitude of
People

People that live unmarried. But I think it is rather owing to the laſt: for in *London* and *Weſtminſter* the one half of the People at leaſt live ſingle, that are above twenty-one Years of Age; which muſt prevent almoſt as many more Births, that might be reaſonably expected. And this is not mere Conjecture, I have had ſome Proof from a particular Detail given me of one Pariſh within the City; where the greater Part of thoſe that are above that Age are ſingle. In the natural State of Mankind it ſeems plain, that the Number of Births ſhould be greater than the Burials, and I believe that in many Pariſhes in the Country they are near double. I found it ſo in the Iſle of *Wight*, where I lived ſome Time, and had an Opportunity to ſee the Regiſters; for there the Births were generally near double. And even in *London*, before the great Fire 1666, it appears from ſome Pariſh Regiſters, that the Baptiſms were near about equal to the Burials, and never afterwards: the Reaſon of which I do not underſtand, unleſs it be that more People were then married, and that from that Time there was a greater Confluence of Strangers;

Strangers; for there certainly were more Diffenters at that Time, than ever after.

It is farther to be obferved, that in the Bills from the Year 1704 to the Year 1728, without the City both the Number of Chriftenings and Burials continually increafed; and that from that Time to 1743, they continued nearly the fame; but after 1743 they gradually decreafed till this Time; which plainly fhews, that the Inhabitants were increafing till about the Year 1728; and that from thence to 1743, they remained in the fame State nearly; but that afterwards during the laft ten Years, till 1753, they were conftantly diminifhing. For it is evident that the Number of the Inhabitants muft always be in Proportion to the Number of Births and Burials confidered together. And hence it appears, that the Cities of *London* and *Weftminfter* were in the moft flourifhing State, with Regard to Numbers, from 1728 to 1743, and that they are now paft their Height, and in the fame State, they were in the Year 1708; and the firft Decreafe feems to have been at the Beginning of the laft *French* War, which was in the Year 1744. Within the City Walls the Number of the

In-

Inhabitants do not seem to fluctuate in the same Periods of Time, as without; for the most numerous State of the City, appears to have been from the Year 1718 to the Year 1728, and then after that they have been continually decreasing; so that when they were most numerous within the Walls, they were not then arrived at the Height without; and when they were in the highest State without, they were diminishing in the City. Perhaps the vast Number of New Buildings within the Liberties of *Westminster*, may have in Part caused this Diminution. And as from the Year 1718, within the City, the Christenings have been so remarkably decreasing, that they are now but three fifths of what they were at that Time, and the Burials are likewise diminished above one fourth in the last five Years; this seems to shew that the Inhabitants within the City Walls must be near one fourth fewer, than they were in the Year 1718.

Now in order to calculate the Number of Inhabitants, it will be necessary to observe, that in a Year in *London* there generally dies one Person in thirty. This Sir *William Petty* has long ago observed; and I have found it to be be near the Truth, upon confulting my Parifh Regifter. For in the Parifh of *Baſſiſhaw, London*, there are not above 800 People, as appears from an Account that I had lately given me: and the Burials for the laſt ten Years, in the whole amount to 262; which at a Medium gives 26 for one Year, which is the thirtieth Part of 800 nearly. In fome Parifhes in *London* there die more than in this Proportion, as in St. *Giles's Cripplegate*; and in others in the out Parts of the Town there die fewer, but, I believe in general it will hold true, in and about the City. In the Town of *Breſlaw* in *Germany*, from which Dr. *Halley* formed his famous Table for the Probabilities of Life, their die about two in fixty-nine, that is, lefs than one in thirty-four; as is plain from an eaſy Computation. But there certainly die more than in that Proportion within the *London* Bills; for it appears that one third at leaſt of the Children die under two Years of Age; whereas at *Breſlaw* there die under that Age only one fifth; and therefore the Difference being two-fifteenths, or four-thirtieths, there die four in thirty more at *London* than at *Breſlaw*, under two Years of Age.

In

In the Country the Case is very different; for there does not die above one in fifty, in healthy Places. Sir *William Petty* has likewise observed this, and I have found it true. For in the Parish of *Newchurch* in the Isle of *Wight*, where I resided some Time, there are about 900 People, and there does not die at a Medium above eighteen yearly; which is one in fifty exactly. And I believe this will be found to be nearly the same, in most of the Counties in *Britain*; where the People do not live in great Towns; which shews the great Difference between the Effects of the Air, in *London* and the Country.

If then it be allowed, that in *London* and *Westminster* there dies one in thirty, it will be very easy to make a Calculation of the whole Number of the People nearly, that are within the Bills. For if we take the Number of the Burials at an Average for some Years, and multiply that by 30, the Product must be the Number of the People. Thus if we take the Number of the Burials at large within the Bills, for any one of the last ten Years at a Medium, from 1744 to to 1753 inclusive, to be 22945, and add to this 2000 for those Burials omitted in the

Bills, as is supposed above, the Total will be 24945, all the Burials within the Limits of the Bills, for one Year at 1753, and then multiply this by 30, the Product 748350 will be the whole Number of the People nearly, at present. But if we take 27192, the Number of Burials at a Medium, for any one of the ten Years preceeding 1743, inclusive, and add to this 2000 as above, the whole of the Burials at that Time within the Bills will be 29192, which being multiplied by 30, gives 875760 for the Number of the People at the Year 1743. And therefore the Inhabitants are fewer now than they were in 1743 by 127000. I have taken the Numbers at a Medium, for ten Years, to avoid any Uncertainty that might arise about a Computation for a single Year.

If we were to try the same Calculation, by taking the Burials, at a Medium, only for five Years to 1753, and also for five Years to 1743 inclusive, the Difference will be greater. For the Numbers at these two Times will be 720180, and 906570, of which the Difference is 186390; so that the People would appear fewer at 1753 than they were in 1743, by 186000. But this is not so much

to

to be depended upon as the Numbers above; becaufe there were two extraordinary Bills at 1740 and 1741 : or if we fhould imagine that there might not more die at *London* than at *Breflaw*, that is, one in thirty-four, ftill the Difference would be greater than we found at firft. For taking the Burials at an Average for ten Years, at 1753 and 1743, as above, the Numbers would at thefe two Times be 848130 and 992528, of which the Difference is 144398; fo that it feems plain, if the Bills are to be depended upon, that there is a Decreafe of the People fince 1743 of above an hundred thoufand, and that at prefent the Number is about 74000. And this Decreafe has been annually continued, for if we try the Thing farther, at the Diftance of five Years, and take at a Medium for five Years, the Burials for 1753 and 1748, the Numbers will come out 720180 and 776520; of which the Difference is 56340, the Number decreafed for the laft five Years.

 There is another Way of computing from the Number of Houfes; but I think this not fo certain as the other. For here are two Difficulties, to afcertain the Number of

Houfes

Houses, and to fix on the Number of Persons for each House. As to the last, Sir *William Petty* thought we might allow eight Persons to a House; which I have found to be a Mistake. I have made an Experiment of it, and got an exact Account of the Numbers in each House in a certain Parish in *London*; and I find that they exactly come to six in a House, empty and full together, for there is seldom above one in twenty empty. And as in that Parish the People are in a middle Condition, and some of them have a Number of Servants; it may be presumed they are in a middle State with regard to Numbers between the very great Families and those in the lowest Rank. This is also confirmed, if we allow, as above, one in thirty to die yearly in *London*. For within the City Walls there were 11857 Houses in the 97 Parishes, as appears from Mr. *Smart*'s Account, which was supposed to be very accurate at that Time: but since he published that in the 1741, there are not so many Houses within the City Walls; for in many Parishes there are Houses greatly enlarged, some rebuilt in Place of two or three, and Warehouses made of others. I know some

Parishes

Parishes in which there is one in twenty fewer than in his Time. In others perhaps there is no Alteration. But I think they must, at an Average, be diminished three in an hundred, at least; and consequently there are about 354 fewer, and the Number of Houses within the City Walls is about 11503, which being multiplied by 6, gives 69018, for the Number of Inhabitants; which is nearly equal to the Burials 2290 multiplied by 30, or 68700; taking the Burials at a Medium for ten Years, and adding 400 as above.

The Number of Houses within the Bills may then be nearly come at, from the Number of Burials. For if we take the Number of Burials for the last ten Years at an Average, within the City to be 1890, and add 400, which makes 2290, we may say, if 2290 comes from 11503 Houses, then the whole Number 24945 of Burials within the Bills, having allowed 2000 as above, must come from 125302 Houses. And there cannot be fewer; for there are more Burials within the City, in proportion to the Baptisms, than in the Out-parishes; and therefore more Burials in proportion to the

Number of Houses; which shews that the Number of Houses cannot be less than 125302; which being multiplied by 6, will give 751812, for the Number of People for this present Time; and it is nearly equal to the Number 748350 found above. So that the Numbers produced from these two Methods being almost equal, this is some farther Proof that our Supposition of six Persons to a House, empty and full, is near to the Truth. But if we suppose, that the Number of Houses within the Walls is now the same, as in Mr. *Smart*'s Time, 11857; then all the Houses within the Bills will be 129158, and the Number of People 774948 greater than 748350, found above, by 26598, which is not much in such Calculations.

Sir *William Petty* likewise says, that he was informed there were 84000 Houses, tenanted within the Bills, in the Year 1682, in which he wrote; and if so, the Number of Houses seem to be increased near one third since that Time. And according to our Way of computing, to suppose six to a House, empty and full, there could not be more than 504000 People at that Time; which

which is less than the Number we found above for the present Time, 748350, by 244350. But now instead of increasing, we are decreasing; for since the Year 1743 the Inhabitants have been annually diminished; by which it appears, that this great City is past its Heighth, and is rather upon the Decline with regard to Numbers. And hence we see how far Sir *William* was mistaken, who imagined that it might increase continually till the Year 1800; when the Number of People would be five Millions, that is, near seven Times as many as they are at present.

Now to account for this Decrease there may be various Conjectures: I think three Causes may be assigned, that may all operate jointly. One may be the vicious Custom that has prevailed of late Years, among the lower People, of drinking spirituous Liquors; another, the fashionable Humour of living single, that daily increases; and a third may be the great Increase of Trade in the Northern Parts of *Great Britain*, that keeps the People there employed at home, that they have no Occasion as formerly to come hither

D for

for Business; and it were to be wished, that this Cause was the most prevailing. But whatever be the Cause, it seems plain to me, that it could not be the late *French* War, as some imagine. For by what was shewn above, there has been a Decrease of 56000 since the Year 1749, after the Peace: but if the War had been the Cause, there ought rather to have been an Increase after it. And as in the Whole, we could not have lost more than 150000, in the War by Land and Sea, of which there was not one fifth, or 30000, taken from about the City; this can never account for 64000, the Decrease before the Year 1748. In the former War, between 1702 and 1711, the City never decreased, but continually increased: from which one would imagine, that the last War could not diminish its Numbers.

Nor can this Decrease in the Bills be accounted for, from a greater Number than formerly leaving the Town in Summer; because it does not appear that there is a greater Number of such, than was ten Years ago. And if it could be allowed that the Number was greater, it can never be thought that it

can

can amount to 120000 more than in the Year 1743.

It is true this Decrease may appear surprising to some, when they see the Number of new Buildings in *Westminster* continually increasing; but then, on the other Hand, it is likewise to be considered, that there is a great Number of Houses enlarged, or rebuilt, in Place of two or three others, as mentioned above; and others falling in, and empty, about the Eastern Parts of the City: so that for the last twenty Years the Inhabitants seem only to be moving, from the Eastern to the Western Parts of the Town, and not increasing.

Whether the Doctor's Curiosity was well founded or not, is the Question; that it is not is my Opinion, his Premises having no Solidity, the whole Hypothesis can be no more, nor better, than building a Cathedral in the Air.

The Doctor supposes but 2000 annual Buryings among the Dissenters, &c. buried within the Bills of Mortality, including the Bodies carried into the Country: Whereas *Maitland*,

Maitland, in his Survey of *London*, has set down One Thousand more; and in my Opinion even that latter Reckoning is not large enough. It is certain that more People of Quality and Gentry, with their Families, reside within the Bills of Mortality during the Winter Season now, than in former Times; and of these, most that die in Town are interred in the Country. The Churchyards of *Paddington* and *Pancras* have been enlarged, one new Burying-Place has been made at *Marybon*, and there are two in *Pancras*, (these Parishes are without the Bills) where Clergymen attend in the Evenings to read the Service of Interments. The calculating by Burials is therefore so uncertain, as to render it only conjectural.

Then, why Baptisms are two fifths less than the Burials may be accounted for thus: The Children of *Papists, Jews, Greeks, Lutherans, Moravians, Anabaptists*, and other Dissenters, that use not Baptism according to the Rites and Ceremonies of the Church of *England*. Persons of Quality, Gentry, and many more, seldom register the Births of their Offspring. Where the Number of lusty Batchelors is large, many are the merry-
begotten

begotten Babes: On thefe Occafions, if the Father is an honeft Fellow and a true Church of *England-Man*, the new-born Infant is baptized by an indigent Prieft, and the Father provides for the Child: But the *Diffenters*, *Papifts*, *Jews*, and other Sects fend their Baftards to the *Foundling Hofpital*; if they are not admitted, there are Men and Women, that for a certain Sum of Money will take them, and the Fathers never hear what becomes of their Children afterwards; thefe, it may be fuppofed, are never baptized, except fuch as are taken into the Hofpital. Female Servants and poor Single Wenches, when pregnant, are compelled by the Parifh-Officers to name and fwear to the Begetters of the Children in their Bodies, who are forthwith taken up by Warrants; if a nominated Father is poor he muft run-away, marry the Girl, or be fent to *Bridewell*, when apprehended. Men of known Subftance are treated in another Manner; the Parifh-Officers go civilly to them, and after a Treat or two the Affair is fettled, the Fornicator pays at the leaft Ten Pounds, and receives a Difcharge; but if the firft nominated Father cannot be found, the big-bellied Woman

man muſt nominate another, and ſwear that he is the Father; and ſometimes it happens that two or three Perſons pay each the uſual Demand for one Child. I knew a young Woman who ſwore her great Belly to ſix Gentlemen, living in ſo many different Pariſhes. There always was, ever will, and muſt be, great Numbers of unmarried Men above the Age of twenty-one, in and about *London*; becauſe not many Apprentices are out of their Servitude at that Time of Life, and would be ruined by forfeiting Indentures, if married before free. Premature Marriages commonly ruin young Gentlemen, and others deſigned for the Law, or that are ſtationed in public or private Offices; few Maſters will keep married Servants in their Houſes, &c. It is true that Marriages promote Chriſtenings and Burials; the two firſt occaſion Mirth and good Cheer, the laſt ſome Mourning Perquiſites, all three Surplice Fees; therefore the Clergy have cauſe to promote Matrimony, and inveigh againſt Celibacy: But what would become of our famous Univerſities, the Prieſthood and Church of *England*, if the Students were to have Yoke-Fellows at twenty-one. Moſt ſober People

of

of both Sexes fay, that very many couple too soon, and before they are of sufficient Ability to provide for Children, who frequently fall upon the Parishes for their Support. Certainly, the Doctor knows that in Country Parishes there are very few *Dissenters*, and that all the Children, whose Parents go to Church, have them baptized, though they live but one or two Days; whereas in and about *London* a prodigious Number of Infants are cruelly murdered unchristened, by those Infernals, called Nurses; these detestable Monsters throw a Spoonful of Gin, Spirits of Wine, or Hungary-Water down a Child's Throat, which instantly strangles the Babe; when the Searchers come to inspect the Body, and enquire what Distemper caused the Death, it is answered, Convulsions, this occasions the Article of Convulsions in the Bills of Mortality so much to exceed all others. The Price of destroying and interring a Child is but Two Guineas; and these are the Causes that near a Third die under the Age of Two Years, and not unlikely under two Months.

I have been informed by a Man now living, that the Officers of one Parish in *Westminster*, received Money for more than

Five

Five Hundred Baſtards, and reared but One out of the whole Number. How ſurprizing and ſhocking muſt this diſmal Relation appear, to all that are not hardened in Sin? Will it not ſtrike every one, but the Cauſers and Perpetrators with Dread and Horror? Let it be conſidered what a heinous and deteſtable Crime Child-murder is, in the Sight of the Almighty, and how much it ought to be abhorred and prevented by all good People. To put an End therefore to ſuch a Courſe of Inhumanity accompanied with Perjuries and Impoſitions of all Sorts: Let the parochial Clergy within the Mortality Bills, the Veſtries, and ſuch Pariſh Officers, who have more regard for the Salvation of their Souls, than pampering and ſurfeiting their Bodies by Gluttony and Drunkenneſs, apply to the Governors of the *Foundling Hoſpital* for the Reception of all the Baſtard Children they receive Money for, ſending the Ten Pounds with each Child. Again, Foreigners rarely ſettled in *London* before the Revolution of the Edict of *Nantz* in the latter End of *Charles* the Second's Reign, (except the *Walloons* in the Days of Queen *Elizabeth*) but then the Proteſtants of *France* firſt came

to

to fix themselves and Families in *London*, and many other Cities and Towns in *England* and *Ireland*; and since the glorious Revolution, *Germans, Dutch, Danes, Swedes,* and Multitudes more of *French* settled their Habitations in *London*, the Descendants of whom are undeniably become very numerous and prosperous. Now, few of these, as I apprehend, communicate with the Church of *England,* and as I also know that many new Meeting Houses have been erected within my Memory for *Presbyterians*, I cannot conclude with the Doctor, that there were more *Dissenters* in *London*, before the great Fire in 1666, than at any Time since. The *Independants, Anabaptists, Moravians, Methodists,* &c. &c. together with the *Scotch, French, Germans, Danes,* and *Swedes,* who all have their Meetings, Chapels and Churches. Besides, the *Papists,* who were then inconsiderable, are now grown very numerous; and that the same my be said of *Quakers* and *Jews*: I cannot therefore conclude with the Doctor, that there were more *Dissenters* in *London* before the great Fire in 1666, than at any Time since.

Then as to the Account of Christenings and Burials, as published in the Bills of Mortality is too uncertain to form a true Judgment upon. I have obferved in the weekly Bills, one, two, and fometimes three Parifhes, of the ten, that compofe the City and Liberty of *Weftminfter*, had only Cyphers againft their Names; and in the laft I looked upon, no Burials were fet down for St. *George*'s in the Liberty of *Weftminfter*, nor St. *Bride*'s by *Fleet-Street*.

London within the Walls, it is true, is not altogether fo populous as heretofore; the chief Reafon of which may be, the great Number of Shopkeepers fet up in *Weftminfter* and other Parts about the City: But if in lieu of a fourth Part, the Doctor had mentioned the fortieth, it would have been fufficient for the Decreafe, befides; the leffening of Chriftenings by the parochial Clergy, may poffibly be, though I hope not, that many Infants receive Baptifm from the Nonjuring Clergymen, and Popifh Priefts, who are not regiftered; and many of the Diffenting Minifters keep Regifters; it is well known the *Anabaptifts, Quakers, Jews*, and fome other Sects, have no Chriftenings at all. This Subject has been a Topic for Difcourfe and Altercation more than fifty Years to my Knowledge;

Knowledge; though the Judgment I always formed upon it was, that as many were born in the Bills of Mortality, as died; but that one third of the Inhabitants not being of the Church of *England,* only two Thirds of the Children born were set down in the Bills; not to repeat what has been said of the Infants destroyed, and others born of Church of *England* Parents, who die before Baptism. Then in regard to Burials, let it be considered that of late Years many Hospitals and Infirmaries have been enlarged, and new erected for curing the Sick and Maimed; besides Workhouses, that cloath and feed Old and Young, who would perish for Want if not so provided for. The *Foundling Hospital* saves annually Abundance of Lives; and the Lying-in Hospitals for poor Women, these preserve both Mothers and Infants, and are as useful and necessary Charities as any in the Nation. I have heard however but of four, two in the Liberty of *Westminster,* one in *London,* and the *Middlesex Hospital.* It is to be hoped and desired, that the Rich will communicate to the Poor, and the Parts without these Hospitals will have them. The *Lock Hospitals* cure Abundance of unfortunate People. Inoculation for the Small-Pox, and the Hofpital for curing that Diftemper both Ways; Dr. *James*'s Powder, which is a certain Remedy for Fevers, if taken in Time: the charitable Difpofition of fome Phyficians, Surgeons, and Apothecaries, who at certain appointed Times and Places, (as appears by Advertifements) give their Advice *gratis* to all Comers; to thefe may be added the great Improvements made in Chemiftry, Pharmacy, and chirurgical Operations. I fay all thefe Particulars contribute to preferve the Lives of many Thoufands every Year, and confequently ferve to confute the Doctor. The Doctor muft be egregioufly miftaken, yet again, in fuppofing *Weftminfter* was in the moft flourifhing State, with Regard to Numbers in 1743, becaufe nothing is, or can be more certain, than that in every Year fince, many good Houfes have been erected on new Foundations, old ones pulled down, and better rebuilt to occupy the Ground they ftood upon. I was lately informed that there were only fourteen Houfes empty in the City of *Weftminfter*, and I know not why the Doctor made no Obfervation refpecting the Buildings on the north Side of the great Street from St. *Giles*'s

Giles's Pound, almoſt home to the Barrier, on the north-eaſt Side of *Hyde Park*; true it is they are not included in the Bills of Mortality, but deſerve to be eſteemed a Part of *London* or *Weſtminſter*, more than *Iſlington* or *Hackney*; nor ought it to be forgot, that the *Foundling* and *Middleſex Hoſpitals*, are in the Pariſhes of *Marybone* and *Pancras*.

Sir *William Petty* was an ingenious Gentleman, but ſometimes erroneous in his Calculations; I have no Objection to offer on his Obſervation, or rather Suppoſition, that one out of thirty-one, depart this Life annually. Dr. *Halley*'s Tables have been admired and commended by all that have ſeen and were capable of underſtanding them; but the Reaſon why more Children die proportionably to Births in *London* than in *Breſlaw*, is becauſe the Mothers ſuckle their Babes in *Breſlaw*, and that there are no Pariſh or other Nurſes there to deſtroy the Innocents with Impunity.

Every Man in and near *London*, cannot avoid ſeeing and knowing that new Buildings are erected every Year in all the out Parts of the Mortality Bills, as alſo in the Pariſhes of *Marybone* and *Pancras*, and that in all Places when the Leaſes expire, the old Houſes are pulled

pulled down, and rebuilt in a better Manner, handsome without, and commodious within; that notwithstanding so many new Buildings, Tenants are not wanting for Houses, but Houses for Tenants, and the Price of Lodgings enhanced in most Streets; albeit the Doctor has insinuated, and attempted, by Arguments to me appearing frivolous, and by Calculations of no Validity, to prove the Decrease of Inhabitants in the Bills of Mortality; I do firmly believe, that taking in *Pancras* and *Marybone*, the Houses and Inhabitants, have increased as much in the last fourteen Years, as in any Term of Time that can be mentioned. And to manifest the Calculations and Mediums, the Doctor has produced, are no more to be depended upon than Salivating without Mercury. I will suppose that there are some Men in the City of *London* worth one hundred thousand Pounds a Man, and others worth Nothing; now no one will deny or contradict either of these Positions. The Medium between one hundred thousand Pounds and nothing, is fifty thousand Pounds; therefore the Citizens one with the other according to such Reasoning as his, are

worth

worth fifty thousand Pounds a Piece; but although this Calculation and Medium is clearly proved by Figures, I do not defire the gentle Readers to give their Affent and Confent, before they are fatisfied of the Truth, by all the Housekeepers within the Walls of *London*, Males and Females.

Now the Doctor has made three different Calculations upon Suppofitions, to prove the Diminution of People in *London* and *Westminster*, and yet all of them deferve no more Regard, nor are of more Significancy than my Calculation and Medium before-recited; fuppofing however, but not allowing, that the Number of Inhabitants are fo leffened as the Doctor would have us believe, what is become of one hundred and twenty thoufand People? Certainly they did not die in the Bills of Mortality, for if it had been true, the Bills muft have amounted to near ten thoufand more annually, than they did in the laft fourteen Years? Again, was this extravagant Calculation well founded, by the Doctor's own Account, twenty thoufand Houfes muft have been deferted, or funk into Ruins, and the Pavements in Abundance of Streets overfpread with Grafs and Weeds;

Weeds; but the contrary is so notorious, that I cannot believe the Doctor or any other Person will pretend, that the old Streets are less frequented, that the Concourse of People, or Number of Carriages are less at this Time, than in 1743, from which Year the pretended Decay commenced in the Doctor's Dreams. But was the Fact otherwise, it might be answered, that People have more Streets to walk in, and that *Westminster-Bridge* to the *Borough*, and both Sides the River, from *London-Bridge* down to *Deptford* and *Greenwich*; the new Roads from *Bethnal-Green* to *Shoreditch*, from thence to *Old-Street*, *Islington*, and *Paddington* prevents Multitudes of Carriages, Horses, &c. from passing through the City of *London*.

My own Opinion, after repeated Inquiries, is, that seven Persons may be allowed for Houses, one with the other; Lodgers included; and if there are many empty Tenements in the City, they must stand in bad Situations, or be out of Repair; for we seldom see many Bills on the Doors in passing through the Streets.

I also think the Enlargement of Buildings may make an Addition to the Number of Inhabi-

Inhabitants, not leſſen them; ſome miſerable Fabricks have been demoliſhed, and ſubſtantial Ware houſes ſupplied their Places, and in a few Streets, one good Habitation now ſtands, where two or three paultry ones were before; but then as theſe new Houſes are larger than the old, undoubtedly each contains a greater Family than one of thoſe demoliſhed; ſo that Alterations of that Nature will add very little to ſupport the Doctor's Argument; then granting the Number of Houſes within the Walls, to be decreaſed three hundred fifty and four, and reducing the Number of Inhabitants to ſix Perſons for every Houſe, the Amount is no more than two thouſand one hundred and twenty-four; and in his loweſt Eſtimate he ſuppoſes, the preſent Inhabitants of the ninety-ſix Pariſhes within the Walls, to be ſixty-eight thouſand ſeven hundred; which Reckoning is ſo far from tallying with his former Calculation, that the ſaid Inhabitants were decreaſed a fourth Part, that comes it very near my own (*viz.*) a fortieth.

The Subſtance of the next Paragraph, I apprehend has been already anſwered.

Whether Sir *William Petty* came near Exactnefs, in refpect to the Number of Houfes in 1682, is infignificant to the Doctor's Scheme, of pretending to prove the Decreafe of Inhabitants: but having compared Mr. *Morgan*'s large Map made in the Reign of *Charles* the Second, with the late one by Mr. *Rocque*, it feems to me, that the Increafe of Houfes is more than a Third; in the Writings of fome Authors of thofe Days, the Number of Inhabitants was computed at five hundred Thoufand; I cannot, I will not affent to the Doctor's pofitive Declaration, that the Inhabitants are now, and have been decreafing fince 1743, for the Reafons before produced, by which the Readers will fee that Dr. *Brakenridge* is as much miftaken in the decreafing, as Sir *William Petty* was of increafing; Sir *William*'s Calculations are deftitute of Mediums, which in this Way of Writing, may defervedly be efteemed as ufeful as Curves in Geometry. Sir *William* muft certainly be delirious, when he penned his Calculation, that *London* in the Year 1800 would contain five Millions of People. There never was, nor ever will be any Situation for a City, where

fo

so many Inhabitants could live: As I think it ridiculous for any Man to pretend, that he can by any Method know the exact Number of Souls in *London*, my Conjecture is, that including *Marybone* and *Pancras* there may be near nine hundred thousand, and that *London* is not arrived to its greatest State, but will increase above forty Years longer, and then may contain about a Million, the Buildings in St. *George*'s between the great Western and *Oxford* Roads, are almost finished, those in *Marybone* are briskly carrying on, and will continue before a Bridge is built over the *Thames* at *Black-Fryars*, then a Cessation will ensue, to building on the north Side of the Town, and St. *George's Fields* in all Probability will be regularly laid out for Streets, and built upon.

To account for a Decrease, when no such Misfortune has come to pass, is laying down false Premises; consequently, Conclusions upon such Premises, must be absurd, and favour more of *Bethlem College* than *Sion*. The Doctor assigns for his imaginary Decrease of Inhabitants three Causes, *viz*. the vicious Custom of drinking spirituous Liquors among the lower People, living single, and the great

Increase of Trade in the Northern Parts of *Great Britain*, the lower People in late Years have not drank spirituous Liquors so freely, as they did before the good Regulations, and Qualifications for selling them, were settled by Parliament, the additional Excise has raised the Price, Improvements in the Distillery have rendered the home-made Distillations as wholesome as the imported; we do not see the hundredth Part of poor Wretches drunk in the Streets since the said Regulations and Qualifications as before, Marriages at present are not so expeditiously dispatched, as when People scarcely known to one another, could be joined together, without Banns or Licence; more Men marry too soon, than defer that interesting Affair too late, the Reasons have been above given. The greater the Births are in every Part of *South Britain* is advantageous to *London*, because it is a Circumstance that furnishes the City and Suburbs with the more industrious and useful People. *London* cannot but be enlarged and increased by a Conflux of Inhabitants from all the different Parts of *Great Britain*. *Ireland* also greatly assists in filling the Capital; the Revenues of the Nobility and Gentry

try of that Kingdom, being exceedingly augmented since the Accession of the present Royal Family to the Throne of *Great Britain*, enables many of them to reside here, in good Houses with handsome Equipages. Merchants and Shopkeepers from the same Country, Journeymen in all Trades, Labourers at Buildings, Venders of Things in the Streets, and Villages round about, with *Irish* Servants, make a considerable Number of the present Inhabitants.

Foreigners from all Protestant Countries, and too many Papists come to *London* continually, some as Servants, others to follow the Employments they were bred to, not above one in twenty of Shop and Alehouse-keepers, Journeymen, and Labourers, living in the Bills of Mortality, were either born or served their Apprenticeships in Town; the Sugar-Refiners employ, for the most part, *Hamburghers*. It is very probable that two Thirds of the grown Persons at any Time in *London* came from distant Parts. Arguments to prove a Decrease of the Inhabitants in *London*, may be compared to the Decay of Woollen Manufactures in this Kingdom, which

have

have been increased a full Third since the Revolution.

The late War with *France* affected *London* inconsiderably in the Decrease of People, not a hundredth Part of the Soldiers and Sailors, who lost their Lives in that War, being born within the Bills of Mortality. The precise Decrease of fifty-six thousand since 1749, and sixty-four thousand before, is grosly absurd and void of Truth. As new Buildings were vigorously promoted during the last War, and the Houses filled as soon as finished, there can remain no Doubt with sensible Men, of the Multiplication of Inhabitants, the Time that War lasted, faster than in all Queen *Anne*'s Reign, the new Buildings then erected being more numerous, and considerable, which I am capable of demonstrating upon View.

The Paragraph before the last is too trivial and insignificant to merit Regard.

The Conclusion of the Performance appears to my Understanding weak; the learned Author's Decrease cannot be surprising, because not sudden; it commenced in 1743, or 1744, and continued to 1755. This same Decrease, if true, must inevitably have

have leſſened the public Revenues in every Branch, and ruined many thouſand Families, by ſinking their Rents; but as no ſuch Information has yet been given by the Hoſt of Writers, that ſerve their Country with ſo much Zeal and Diligence, no Credit can be given to ſuch an Account. The major Part of the Buildings in the Bills of Mortality being Leaſholds, erected for certain Years, many Leaſes terminate annually; when they are near expiring, the Houſes commonly want repairing or rebuilding, many Landlords will not be at any Charge, before they obtain Renewals, which is the Occaſion that ſome Houſes become deſerted and empty. I am very certain that *London* is flouriſhing at this Juncture, and ſee no Cauſe to ſuppoſe that two Pariſhes without the Walls, have decreaſed in People ſince 1743. I deny, that the Inhabitants move from the Eaſtern to the Weſtern Parts of the Town, the Latitude Weſt of *Temple-Bar*, is not proper for thoſe born or bred, to the Eaſt of *Aldgate*, the Occupations and Manner of Life being very different, the one from the other. For the laſt twenty Years (ſays the Doctor) the Inhabitants ſeem only moving, not increaſing.

creafing. I cannot conceive what could induce the very learned Gentleman, in his hard ftudied Letter, to inform his Readers in the very laft Line, that the Inhabitants were not increafing, when he before affirmed, and attempted to prove, they had decreafed one hundred and twenty thoufand, and were daily decreafing.

FINIS.

THE MAIN DISPUTE

Republished in 1973 by Gregg International Publishers Limited
Westmead, Farnborough, Hants., England

Received April 20.

XVI. *Observations on the* Expectations *of Lives, the Increase of Mankind, the Influence of great Towns on Population, and particularly the State of* London *with respect to Healthfulness and Number of Inhabitants. In a Letter from Mr.* Richard Price, *F. R. S. to* Benjamin Franklin, *Esq; LL. D. and F. R. S.*

Dear Sir,

Read April 27 and May 4, 1769.

I BEG leave to submit to your perusal the following observations. If you think them of any importance, I shall be obliged to you for communicating them to the Royal Society. You will find that the chief subject of them is the present state of the city of London, with respect to healthfulness and number of inhabitants, as far as it can be collected from the bills of mortality. This is a subject that has been considered by others; but the proper method of calculating from the bills has not, I think, been sufficiently explained.

No competent judgment can be formed of the following observations, without a clear notion of what the writers on *Life Annuities* and *Reverſions* have called the *Expectation of Life*. Perhaps this is not in common properly underſtood; and Mr. De Moivre's manner of expreſſing himſelf about it is very liable to be miſtaken.

The moſt obvious ſenſe of the *expectation* of a given life is, " That particular number of years " which a life of a given age has an equal chance " of enjoying." This is properly the time that a perſon may reaſonably *expect* to live; for the chances *againſt* his living longer are greater than thoſe *for* it; and, therefore, he cannot entertain an *expectation* of living longer, conſiſtently with probability. This period does not coincide with what the writers on Annuities call the *expectation of life*, except on the ſuppoſition of an uniform decreaſe in the probabilities of life, as Mr. Simpſon has obſerved in his *Select Exerciſes*, p. 273.——It is neceſſary to add, that, even on this ſuppoſition, it does not coincide with what is called the *expectation of life* in any caſe of joint lives. Thus, two joint lives of 40 have an even chance, according to Mr. De Moivre's hypotheſis *, of conti-

---

* Mr. De Moivre's hypotheſis, here referred to, ſuppoſes (as is well known to thoſe who have ſtudied the ſubject of Life Annuities) an equal decrement of human life through all its ſtages. That is, it ſuppoſes that out of any given number alive at a given age, the ſame number will die every year till they are all dead. Thus; 86 Mr. De Moivre makes the utmoſt probable extent of life. The number of years which any given life wants of 86 he calls the *complement* of that life.——56, therefore, is the *complement* of 30; and ſuppoſing 56 perſons alive at this age, *one* will die every year till, in 56 years, they will be all dead. The like will happen to 46 at 40, to 36 at 50, and ſo on, for all other ages. This is an

nuing

nuing together only 13½ years. But the *expectation* of two equal joint lives being (according to the same hypothesis) always a *third* of the *common complement*, it is in this case 15⅓ years. It is necessary, therefore, to observe, that there is another sense of this phrase which ought to be carefully distinguished from that now mentioned. It may signify " The *mean conti-* " *nuance* of any given *single, joint,* or *surviving* lives, " according to any given table of observations:" that is, the number of years which, taking them one with another, they actually enjoy, and may be considered as sure of enjoying, those who live or survive *beyond* that period, enjoying as much *more* time in proportion to their number, as those who *fall short* of it enjoy *less*. Thus, Supposing 46 persons alive, all 40 years of age, and that, according to Mr. De Moivre's *hypothesis*, one will die every year till they are all dead in 46 years, half 46 or 23 will be their *expectation of life:* that is; The number of years enjoyed by them all will be just the same as if every one of them had lived 23 years, and then died; so that, supposing no interest of money, there would be no difference in value between annuities payable for life to every single person in such a set, and equal annuities payable to another equal set of persons of the same common age, supposed to be all sure of living just 23 years and no more.

excellent *hypothesis*. It eases exceedingly the labour of calculating the values of lives. It is remarkably agreeable to Dr. Halley's Table of Observations; and, as far as it implies an equal decrement of life, is, in a great measure, confirmed by other Tables.

In like manner; the *third* of 46 years, or 15 years and 4 months, is the *expectation* of two joint lives both 40; and this is also the *expectation* of the survivor. That is; supposing a set of marriages between persons all 40, they will, one with another, last just this time, and the survivors will last the same time; and annuities payable during the continuance of such marriages would, supposing no interest of money, be of exactly the same value with annuities to begin at the extinction of such marriages, and to be paid, during life, to the survivors. In adding together the years which any great number of such marriages and their survivorships have lasted, the sums would be found to be equal.

One is naturally led to understand the *expectation* of life in the first of the senses now explained, when, by Mr. Simpson and Mr. De Moivre, it is called, *the number of years which, upon an equality of chance, a person may expect to enjoy;* or, *the time which a person of a given age may justly expect to continue in being*; and, in the last sense, when it is called, *the share of life due to a person**. But, as in reality it is always used in the last of these senses, the former language should not be applied to it: and it is in this last sense that it coincides with the *sums* of the *present* probabilities that any given single or joint lives shall attain to the end of the 1st, 2d, 3d, &c. *moments* from this time to the end of their possible existence; or, in the case of survivorships, with the sum of the probabilities that

---

* See Mr. De Moivre on *Annuities*, p. 65, &c. 4th edition, and Mr. Simpson's Select Exercises, p. 255, 273.

there

there shall be a survivor at the end of the 1st, 2d, 3d, &c. *moments*, from this time to the end of the possible existence of survivorship. This coincidence every one conversant in these subjects must see, upon reflecting, that both these senses give the true present value of a life-annuity secured by land, without interest of money*.

* The *sum* of the probabilities that any given lives will attain to the end of the 1st, 2d, 3d, &c. *years* from the present time to the utmost extremity of life (for instance, $\frac{45}{46} + \frac{44}{46} + \frac{43}{46}$, &c. to $\frac{1}{46} = 22\frac{1}{2}$ for lives of 40, by the *hypothesis*) may be called their *expectation*, or the number of payments due to them, as *yearly annuitants*. The sum of the probabilities that they will attain to the end of the 1st, 2d, 3d, &c. *half years* (or, in the particular case specified, $\frac{91}{92} + \frac{90}{92} + \frac{89}{92} + \frac{8.8}{92}$, &c. $= \frac{91}{2}$ *half years*, or $22\frac{3}{4}$ *years*) is their expectation as *half yearly annuitants*. And the sums just mentioned of the probabilities of their attaining to the end of the 1st, 2d, 3d, &c. *moments* (equal in the same particular case to 23 years) is properly their *expectation of life*, or their *expectation* as annuitants secured by land.

Mr. De Moivre has concealed the demonstrations of the rules he has given for finding these *expectations* of life, and only intimated, in general, that he discovered them by a calculation deduced from the method of fluxions, p. 66, of his *Treatise on Annuities*. It will, perhaps, be agreeable to some to see how easily they are deduced in this method upon the hypothesis of an equal decrement of life.

Let $\dot{x}$ stand for a moment of time and n the *complement* of any assigned life. Then $\frac{n-\dot{x}}{n}$, $\frac{n-2\dot{x}}{n}$, $\frac{n-3\dot{x}}{n}$, &c. will be the *present* probabilities of its continuing to the end of the 1st, 2d, 3d, &c. moments; and $\frac{n-x}{n}$ the probability of its continuing to the end of x time. $\frac{n-x}{n} \times \dot{x}$ will therefore be the *fluxion* of the sum of the probabilities, or of an *area* representing this sum, whose

This

This period in *joint* lives, I have obferved, is *never*

ordinates are $\frac{n-x}{n}$, and *axis* x.——The *fluent* of this expreffion, or $x - \frac{x^2}{2n}$ is the fum itfelf for the time x; and this, when $x = n$, becomes $\frac{1}{2}n$, and gives the *expectation* of the affigned life, or the fum of all the probabilities juft mentioned for its whole poffible duration.——In like manner: Since $\frac{\overline{n-x}^2}{n^2}$ is the probability that two equal joint lives will continue x time $\frac{\overline{n-x}^2}{n^2} \times \dot{x}$ will be the *fluxion* of the fum of the probabilities. The *fluent* is $x - \frac{x^2}{n} + \frac{x^3}{3n^2}$, which when $n = x$ is $\frac{n}{3}$ the expectation of two equal joint lives.——Again: Since $\frac{n-x}{n} \times \frac{2x}{n}$ is the probability that there will be a furvivor of two equal joint lives at the end of x time, $\frac{n-x}{n} \times \frac{2x}{n} \times \dot{x}$ will be the *fluxion* of the fum of the probabilities; and the *fluent*, or $\frac{x^2}{n} - \frac{2x^3}{3x^2}$ is (when $x = n$) $\frac{1}{3}n$, or the *expectation* of furvivorfhip between two equal lives, which therefore appears to be equal to the *expectation* of their joint continuance. The expectation of two *unequal* joint lives found in the fame way is $\frac{m}{2} - \frac{m^2}{6n}$, m being the *complement* of the oldeft life, and n the *complement* of the youngeft. The whole *expectation* of furvivorfhip is $\frac{n}{2} - \frac{m}{2} + \frac{m^2}{3n}$. The expectation of furvivorfhip on the part of the oldeft is, $\frac{m^2}{6n}$; and the expectation on the part of the youngeft is, $\frac{n}{2} - \frac{m}{2} + \frac{m^2}{6n}$. It is eafy to apply this inveftigation to any number of joint lives, and to all cafes of furvivorfhip.

I have above endeavoured to fhew diftinctly how the *expectations* of *fingle* lives may be found, agreeably to any Table of Obfervations, without having recourfe to any principles, except fuch as are plain and common.

the

[95]

the fame with the period which they have an equal hance of enjoying; and in fingle lives, I have obferved, they are the fame only on the fuppofition of an uniform decreafe in the probabilities of life. If this decreafe, inftead of being always uniform, is *accelerated* in the laft ftages of life, the former period, in fingle lives, will be *lefs* than the latter; if *retarded*, it will be *greater*.

It is neceffary to add, that the number expreffing the former period, multiplied by the number of fingle or joint lives whofe expectation it is added annually to a fociety or town, gives the whole number living together, to which fuch an annual addition would in time grow. Thus; fince 19, or the third of 57, is the *expectation* of two joint lives whofe common age is 29, or common *complement* 57, twenty marriages every year between perfons of this age would, in 57 years, grow to 20 times 19, or 380 marriages always exifting together. The number of *furvivors* alfo arifing from thefe marriages, and always living together, would, in twice 57 years, increafe to the fame number. And, fince the *expectation* of a fingle life is always half its *complement*, in 57 years likewife 20 fingle perfons aged 29, added annually to a town, would increafe to 20 times 28.5 or 570; and when arrived at this number, the deaths every year will juft equal the acceffions, and no further increafe be poffible.

It appears from hence, that the particular proportion that becomes extinct every year, out of the whole number conftantly exifting together of fingle or joint lives, muft, wherever this number undergoes no

variation,

variation, be exactly the same with the *expectation* of those lives at the time when their existence commenced. Thus; was it found that a 19th part of all the marriages among any body of men, whose numbers do not vary, are dissolved every year by the deaths of either the husband or wife, it would appear that 19 was, at the time they were contracted, the *expectation* of these marriages. In like manner; was it found in a society, limited to a fixed number of members, that a 28th part dies annually out of the whole number of members, it would appear that 28 was their common expectation of life at the time they entered. So likewise; were it found in any town or district, where the number of births and burials are equal, that a 20th or 30th part of the inhabitants die annually, it would appear that 20 or 30 was the *expectation* of a child just born in that town or district. These *expectations*, therefore, for all *single* lives, are easily found by a *Table of Observations*, shewing the number that die annually at all ages, out of a given number alive at those ages; and the general rule for this purpose is " to divide " the sum of all the living in the Table at the age " whose expectation is required, and at all greater " ages, by the sum of all that die annually at " that age, and above it; or, which is the same, by " the number in the Table of the living at that age; " and half subtracted from the quotient will be the " required *expectation*." Thus, in Dr. Halley's Table, the sum of all the living at 20 and upwards is 20,724. The number living at that age is 598; and the former number divided by the latter, and half

half unity * subtracted from the quotient, gives 34.15 for the *expectation* of 20. The expectation of the same life by Mr. *Simpson's* Table, formed from the bills of mortality of London, is 28.9.

These observations bring me to the principal point which I have had all along in view. They suggest to us an easy method of finding the number of inhabitants in a place from a *Table of Observations*, or the *bills of mortality* for that place, supposing the yearly births and burials equal. "Find by the "Table, in the way just described, the *expectation* "of an infant just born, and this, multiplied by the "number of yearly births, will be the number of "inhabitants." At *Breslaw*, according to Dr. Halley's Table †, though half die under 16, and therefore an infant just born has an *equal chance* of living only 16 years, yet his *expectation*, found by the rule I have given, is near 28 years; and this, multiplied by 1238 the number born annually, gives 34,664,

---

* This subtraction is necessary, because the *divisor* ought to be made as much greater than the number dying annually given in the Table, as the *expectation*, with $\frac{1}{2}$ unity added, is greater than the *expectation*, on account of the number that will die, in the course of the year, out of those who are continually added, in order to preserve the number of the living the same.

In other words: If we conceive the *recruit* necessary to supply the *waste* of every year to be made always at the *end* of the year, the *dividend* ought to be the *medium* between the numbers living at the *beginning* and the *end* of the year; that is, it ought to be taken *less* than the sum of the living in the Table at and above the given age, by *half* the number that die in the year; the effect of which *diminution* will be the same with the *subtraction* I have directed.

† Vid. Lowthorp's Abridgment of the Philosophical Transactions, vol. III. p. 669.

the number of inhabitants. In like manner; it appears from Mr. Simpson's Table, that, though an infant just born in London has not an *equal chance* of living 3 years, his *expectation* is 20 years; and this number, multiplied by the yearly births, would give the number of inhabitants in London, were the births and burials equal. The medium of the yearly births, for the last 10 years, has been 15,710. This number, multiplied by 20, is 314,200; which is the number of inhabitants that there would be in London, according to the bills, were the yearly burials no more than equal to the births: that is, were it to support itself in its number of inhabitants without any supply from the country. But for the last 10 years, the burials have, at an average, been 22,956, and exceeded the christenings 7,246. This is, therefore, at present, the yearly addition of people to London from other parts of the kingdom, by whom it is kept up. Suppose them to be all, one with another, persons who have, when they remove to London, an *expectation* of life equal to 30 years. That is; suppose them to be all of the age of 18 or 20, a supposition certainly far beyond the truth. From hence will arise, according to what has been before observed, an addition of 30 multiplied by 7,246, that is 217,380 inhabitants. This number, added to the former, makes 531,580; and this, I think, at most, would be the number of inhabitants in London were the bills perfect. But it is certain that they give the number of births and burials too little. There are many burying-places that are never brought into the bills. Many also emigrate to the navy and army and country; and these ought to be added to the

number

number of deaths. What the deficiencies arising from hence are, cannot be determined. Suppose them equivalent to 6000 every year in the births, and 6000 in the burials. This would make an addition of 20 times 6000 or 120,000 to the last number, and the whole number of inhabitants would be 651,580. If the burials are deficient only two thirds of this number, or 4000, and the births the whole of it; 20 multiplied by 6000, must be added to 314,290 on account of the defects in the births: and, since the excess of the burials above the births will then be only 5,246; 30 multiplied by 5,246 or 157,380, will be the number to be added on this account; and the sum, or number of inhabitants, will be 591,580. But if, on the contrary, the burials are deficient 6000, and the births only 4000; 80,000 must be added to 314,290, on account of the deficiencies in the births; and 30 multiplied by 9,246, on account of the excess of the burials above the births, and the whole number of inhabitants will be 671,580.

Every supposition in these calculations seems to me too high. *Emigrants* from London are, in particular, allowed the same *expectation* of continuance in London with those who are born in it, or who come to it in the firmest part of life, and never afterwards leave it; whereas it is not credible that the former *expectation* should be so much as half the latter. But I have a further reason for thinking that this calculation gives too high numbers, which has with me irresistible weight. It has been seen that the number of inhabitants comes out less on the supposition, that the defects in the christenings are greater than those in the burials. Now it seems evident that this is really the case; and, as it is a fact not attended to, I will here endeavour to explain distinctly the reason which proves it.

The proportion of the number of births in London, to the number who live to be 10 years of age, is, by the bills, 16 to 5. Any one may find this to be true, by subtracting the *annual medium* of those who have died under 10, for some years past, from the *annual medium* of births for the same number of years.——Now, tho', without doubt, London is very fatal to children, yet it is incredible that it should be so fatal as this implies. The *bills*, therefore, very probably, give the number of those who die under 10 too great in proportion to the number of births; and there can be no other cause of this, than a greater deficiency in the *births* than in the *burials*. Were the deficiencies in both equal, that is, were the *burials*, in proportion to their number, just as deficient as the *births* are in proportion to *their* number, the proportion of those who reach 10 years of age to the number born would be right in the *bills*, let the deficiencies themselves be ever so considerable. On the contrary, were the deficiencies in the *burials* greater than in the *births*, this proportion would be given too great; and it is only when the former are least that this proportion can be given too little.——Thus; let the number of annual *burials* be 23,000; of *births* 15,700; and the number dying annually under 10, 10,800. Then 4,900 will reach 10 of 15,700 born annually; that is, 5 out of 16.——Were there no deficiencies in the *burials*, and were it fact that only *half* die under 10, it would follow, that there was an annual

annual deficiency equal to 4,900 subtracted from 10,800, or 5,900 in the *births*.———Were the *births* a third part too little, and the *burials* also a third part too little, the true number of *births, burials,* and of *children dying under* 10, would be 20,933———30,666, and 14,400; and, therefore, the number that would live to 10 years of age would be 6,533 out of 20,933, or 5 of 16 as before———Were the *births* a third part, and the *burials* so much as two-fifths wrong, the number of *births, burials,* and children dying under 10 would be 20,933———32,200 and 15,120; and, therefore, the number that would live to 10 would be 5,813 out of 20,933, or 5 out of 18——— Were the *births* a 3d part wrong, and the *burials* but a 6th, the foregoing numbers would be 20,933——— 26,833———12,600; and, therefore, the number that would live to 10 would be 8,333 out of 20,933, or 5 out of 12.56: and this proportion seems as low as is consistent with any degree of probability. It is somewhat less than the proportion in Mr. Simpson's Table of *London Observations*, and near *one half* less than the proportion in the Table of *Observations* for Breslaw, where it appears that above 9 of 16 live to be 10, and that *one half* live to be 16. The deficiencies, therefore, in the *births* cannot be much less than double those in the *burials* *; and the least numbers I have given

---

* One obvious reason of this fact is, that *none* of the *births* among *Jews, Quakers, Papists,* and the *three denominations of Dissenters* are included in the bills, whereas *many* of their *burials* are. It is further to be attended to, that the abortive and still-born, amounting to about 600 annually, are included in the burials, but never in the births. If we add these to the christen-

muſt, probably, be neareſt to the true number of inhabitants. However, ſhould any one, after all, think that it is not improbable that only 5 of 16 ſhould live in London to be 10 years of age, or that above *two thirds* die under this age, the conſequence of admitting this will ſtill be, that the foregoing calculation has been carried too high. For it will from hence follow, that the *expectation* of a child juſt born in London cannot be ſo much as I have taken it. This *expectation* is 20, on the ſuppoſition that half die under 3 years of age, and that 5 of 16 live to be 29 years of age, agreeably to Mr. Simpſon's Table. But if it is indeed true, that *half* die under 2 years of age, and 5 of 16 under 10, agreeably to the *bills*, this expectation muſt be leſs than 20, and all the numbers before given will be conſiderably reduced.

Upon the whole: I am forced to conclude from theſe obſervations, that the ſecond number I have given, or 651,580, though ſhort of the number of inhabitants commonly ſuppoſed in London, is, very probably, *greater*, but cannot be much *leſs*, than the true number. Indeed, it is in general evident, that in caſes of this kind numbers are very much overrated. The ingenious Dr. Brakenridge *, 14 years ago, when the bills were lower than they are now, from the number of houſes, and allowing ſix to a houſe, made the number of inhabitants 751,800. But his method of determining the num-

---

ings, preſerving the burials the ſame, the proportion of the born, according to the bills, who have reached ten for the laſt ſixteen years, will be very nearly one *third* inſtead of *five ſixteenths*.

* Vid. Phil. Tranſact. vol. XLVIII.

ber of houses is too precarious; and, besides, six to a house is, probably *, too large an allowance. Many families now have two houses to live in. The magistrates of Norwich, in 1752, took an exact account of both the number of houses and individuals in that city. † The number of houses was 7,139, and of

* If this is true, Dr. Brakenridge has also over-rated the number of people in England. The number of houses rated to the window tax he had, he says, been certainly informed was 690,000. The number of cottages not rated was not, he adds, accurately known; but from the accounts given in it appeared, that they could not amount to above 200,000; and, allowing 6 to a house, this would make the number of people in England 5,340,000. But if 5 to a house should be a juster allowance, the number will be 4,450,000. The number of people in Scotland he reckons 1,500 000, and in Ireland 1,000,000.—See a Letter to George Lewis Scott, Esq; Phil. Transact. vol. XLIX. p. 877. 1756.

† Vid. Gentleman's Magazine for 1752, and Dr. Short's *Comparative history of the increase of mankind*, p. 38. In page 58 of this last work the author says, that, in order to be fully satisfied about the number of persons to be allowed to a family, he procured the true number of families and individuals in 14 market towns, some of them considerable for trade and populousness; and that in them were 20,371 families, and 97,611 individuals, or but little more than $4\frac{3}{4}$ to a family. He adds, that, in order to find the difference in this respect between towns of trade and country parishes, he procured from divers parts of the kingdom the exact number of *families* and *individuals* in 65 country parishes. The number of *families* was 17,208; *individuals* 76,284; or not quite $4\frac{1}{2}$ to a family.—In the place I have just referred to, in the Gentleman's Magazine, there is an account of the number of *houses* and *inhabitants* in Oxford exclusive of the colleges, and in Wolverhampton, Coventry, and Birmingham, for 1750. The number of persons to a house was, by this account, $4\frac{4}{5}$ in the two former towns, and $5\frac{3}{4}$ in the two latter. It seems, therefore, to appear that 5 persons to a house is an allowance large enough for London, and too large for England in general.

individuals 36,169, which gives nearly 5 to a houfe.
—— Another method which Dr. Brakenridge took to determine the number of inhabitants in London was from the annual number of burials, adding 2000 to the bills for omiffions, and fuppofing a 30th part to die every year. In order to prove this to be a moderate fuppofition he obferves that, according to Dr. Halley's Obfervations, a 34th part die every year at Breflaw. But this obfervation was made too inadvertently. The number of annual burials there, according to Dr. Halley's account, was 1174, and the number of inhabitants, as deduced by him from his Table, was 34,000, and therefore a 29th part died every year. Befides; any one may find, that in reality the Table is conftructed on the fuppofition, that the whole number born, or 1238, die every year; from whence it will follow that a 28th part died every year. *Dr. Brakenridge, therefore, had he attended to this, would have ftated a 24th part as the proportion that dies in London every year, and this would have taken off 150,000 from the number he has given. But even this muft be lefs than the juft proportion. For let three fourths of all who either die in London or migrate from it, be fuch as have been born in London; and let the reft be perfons who have removed to London from the country or from foreign nations.

---

* Care fhould be taken, in confidering Dr. Halley's Table, not to take the firft number in it, or 1000, for fo many juft born. 1238, he tells us, was the annual medium of births, and 1000 is the number he fuppofes all living at one year and under. It was inattention to this that led Dr. Brakenridge to his miftake.

The *expectation* of the former, it has been shewn, cannot exceed 20 years, and 30 years have been allowed to the latter. One with another, then, they will have an *expectation* of $22\frac{1}{2}$ years. That is, one of $22\frac{1}{2}$ will die every year. *And, consequently,

* The whole number of inhabitants in Rome, in the year 1761, was 157,452; of whom 90,239 were males, and 67,213 females. And the annual medium of births, for 3 years from 1759 to 1761, was 5,167, and of burials 7,153. According to this account, therefore, a 22d part of the inhabitants die in Rome every year. See Dr. Short's *Comparative History of the increase and decrease of mankind in England and several countries abroad*, p. 59, 60.——In Berlin, as the same author relates, p. 69, in six years, from 1734 to 1740, the annual medium of births was 3,504, of burials 3,639, and the number of inhabitants was 68,197; males 32,990, and females 35,207. A 19th part, therefore, of the inhabitants of Berlin are buried every year. As numbers taken by actual survey are generally too little, suppose, in the present instance, an error committed in reckoning the number of inhabitants, equal to a 10th of the whole number, or to the whole number of children under 5; and suppose likewise no omissions in the burials. The consequence will be, that about 1 in 21 are buried at Berlin every year.——At Dublin, in the year 1695, the number of inhabitants was found, by an exact survey, to be 40,508 (see Philos. Transactions, N° 261). I find no account of the annual burials just at that time; but from 1661 to 1681, the medium had been 1613; and from 1715 to 1728 it was 2123. There can, therefore, be no material error in supposing that in 1695 it was 1800; and this makes 1 in 22 to die annually.——In 1745 the number of *families* in the same city appeared, by an exact account laid before the Lord Mayor, to be 9,214. It is probable, this number of families did not consist of more than 50,000 individuals. Suppose them, however, 55,000; and, as at this time the medium of annual burials appears to have been 2,360, 1 in 23 died annually: see Dr. Short's *Comparative History*, p. 15, and *New Observations*, p. 228.——I know not how far these facts may be depended on. If they come at all near the truth, they demonstrate that I have been very moderate in making

[106]

fuppofing the annual recruit from the country to be 7000, the number of *births* 3 times 7000 or 21,000, and the *burials* and *migrations* 28,000 (which feem to be all high fuppofitions), the number of inhabitants will be $22\frac{1}{2}$ multiplied by 28,000, or 630,000.

I will juft mention here one other inftance of exaggeration on the prefent fubject.

Mr. Corbyn Morris, in his *Obfervations on the paft* only 1 in $22\frac{1}{2}$, including emigrants, to die in London annually.——In 1631 the number of people in the *city and liberties* of London was taken, by order of the Privy Council, and found to be 130,178.——This account was taken five years after a plague that had fwept off near a quarter of the inhabitants; and when, therefore, the town being full of recruits in the vigour of life, the medium of annual burials muft have been lower than ufual, and the births higher. Could, therefore, the medium of annual burials at that time, within the walls and in the 16 parifhes without the walls, be fettled, exclufive of thofe who died in fuch parts of the 16 parifhes without the walls, as are not in the *liberties*, the proportion dying annually obtained from hence might be depended on, as rather lefs than the common and juft proportion. But this medium cannot be difcovered with any accuracy. Graunt eftimates that two thirds of thefe 16 parifhes are within the *liberties*; and, if this is right, the medium of annual burials in the *city and liberties* in 1631, was 5,500, and 1 in $23\frac{3}{4}$ died annually; or, making a fmall allowance for deficiencies in the bills, 1 in 22.——Mr. Maitland, in his Hiftory of London, vol. II. p. 744, by a laborious, but too unfatisfactory, inveftigation, reduces this proportion to 1 in $24\frac{1}{2}$; and on the fuppofitions, that this is the true proportion dying annually, *at all times*, in London, and that the deficiencies in the burials amount to 3,038 annually, he determines that the number of inhabitants within the bills was 725,903 in the year 1737.

The number of burials not brought to account in the bills is, probably, now much greater than either Dr. Brakenridge or Mr. Maitland fuppofe it. I have reckoned it fo high as 6000, in order to include emigrants, and alfo to be more fure of not falling below the truth.

growth

growth and present state of the city of London, published in 1751, supposes that no more than a 60th part of the inhabitants of London, who are above 20, die every year, and from hence he determines that the number of inhabitants was near a million. In this supposition there was an error of at least one half. According to Dr. Halley's Table, it has been shewn, that a 34th part of all at 20 and upwards, die every year at Breslaw. In London, a 29th part, according to Mr. Simpson's Table, and also according to all other Tables of London Observations. And in *Scotland* it has been found for many years, that of 974 ministers and professors whose ages are 27 and upwards, a 33d part have died every year. Had, therefore, Mr. Morris stated a 30th part of all above 20 as dying annually in London, he would have gone beyond the truth, and his conclusion would have been 400,000 less than it is.

Dr. Brakenridge observed, that the number of inhabitants, at the time he calculated, was 127,000 less than it had been. The bills have lately advanced, but still they are much below what they were from 1717 to 1743. The medium of the annual *births*, for 20 years, from 1716 to 1736, was 18,000, and of *burials* 26,529; and by calculating from hence on all the same suppositions with those which made 651,580 to be the present number of inhabitants in London, it will be found that the number then was 735,840, or 84,260 greater than the number at present. London, therefore, for the last 30 years, has been decreasing; and though now it is increasing again, yet there is reason to think that the additions lately made to the number of buildings round it, are owing, in a great measure, to the increase of luxury, and the inhabitants requiring more room to live upon*.

It should be remembered, that the number of inhabitants in London is now so much less as I have made it, than it was 40 years ago, on the supposition that the proportion of the omissions in the *births* to those in the *burials* was the same then that it is now. But it appears that this is not the fact.——From 1728, the year when the ages of the dead was first given in the *bills*, to 1742, near five-sixths of those who were born died under 10, according to the *bills*.—— From 1742 to 1752 three quarters; and ever since 1752 this proportion has stood nearly as it is now, or at somewhat more than two-thirds. The omissions in the *births*, therefore, compared with those in the *burials* were greater formerly; and this must render the difference between the number of inhabitants now and formerly less considerable than it may seem to be from the face of the bills. One reason why the proportion of the amounts of the *births* and *burials* in the bills comes now nearer than it did to

---

* The medium of annual burials in the 97 parishes within the walls was,

From 1655 to 1664, ——	3264
From 1680 to 1690, ——	3139
From 1730 to 1740, ——	2316
From 1758 to 1768, ——	1620

This account proves, that though, since 1655, London has doubled its inhabitants, yet, *within the walls*, they have decreased; and so rapidly for the last 30 years as to be now reduced to one half.——The like may be observed of the 17 parishes immediately without the walls. Since 1730 these parishes have been decreasing so fast, that the *annual burials* in

the true proportion, may, perhaps, be that the number of Diſſenters is conſiderably leſſened. The Foundling Hoſpital alſo may have contributed a little to this event, by leſſening the number given in the bills as having died under 10, without taking off any from the *births;* for all that die in this hoſpital are buried at *Pancraſs* church, which is not within the *bills.* See the preface to a collection of the yearly bills of mortality from 1657 to 1758 incluſive, p. 15.

I will add, that it is probable that London is now become leſs fatal to children than it was; and that this is a further circumſtance which muſt reduce the difference I have mentioned; and which is likewiſe neceſſary to be joined to the greater deficiencies in the births, in order to account for the very ſmall proportion of children who ſurvived 10 years of age, during the two firſt of the periods I have ſpecified. Since 1752, London has been thrown more open. The cuſtom of keeping country-houſes, and of ſending children to be nurſed in the country, has prevailed more. But, particularly, the deſtructive uſe of ſpirituous liquors among the poor has been checked.

I have ſhewn that in London, even in its preſent

them have ſunk from 8,672 to 5,432, and are now lower than they were before the year 1660. In Weſtminſter, on the contrary, and the 23 out-pariſhes in Middleſex and Surrey, the *annual burials* have, ſince 1660, advanced from about 4000 to 16,000.——Theſe facts prove that the inhabitants of London are now much leſs crowded together than they were. It appears, in particular, that *within the walls* the inhabitants take as much room to live upon as double their number did formerly.——The very ſame concluſions may be drawn from an examination of the *chriſtenings.*

ſtate,

state, and according to the most moderate computation, half the number born die under *three* years of age; and I have observed that at Breslaw half live to 16. At Edinburgh, if I may judge from such of its bills as I have seen, almost as great a proportion of children die as even in London. But it appears from *Graunt's* * accurate account of the births, weddings, and burials in three country parishes for 90 years; and also, with abundant evidence, from Dr. Short's collection of observations in his *Comparative History*, and his treatise entitled, *New Observations on Town and Country Bills of Mortality* †; that in country villages and parishes, the major part live to mature age, and even to marry. So great is the difference, especially to children, between living in great towns and in the country. But nothing can place this observation in a more striking light than the curious account given by Dr. Thomas Heberden, and published in the Philosophical Trans-

---

* See *Natural and Political Observations on the Bills of Mortality*, by Captain John Graunt, F. R. S.

† The public is much obliged to this author for the pains he has taken in collecting observations on the mortality and increase of mankind, in different countries and situations. In his New Observations, p. 309, he mentions an ingenious parish clerk, in the country, who, by a particular account which he took, found that of 314, who had been baptized in his parish in one year, 80, or nearly a quarter part, died under four years of age. Forty-six died the first year; thirteen the second; sixteen the third; and five the fourth. After four, life grows more stable, and at ten acquires its greatest stability; and in this case it cannot be reckoned that above a 10th, or, at most, an 8th more than the quarter that died under four, would die under age; and therefore, probably, near two-thirds arrived at maturity.

actions

actions (vol. LVII. p. 461), *of the increase and mortality of the inhabitants of the island of Madeira.* In this island, it seems, the weddings have been to the births, for 8 years, from 1759 to 1766, as 10 to 46.8; and to the burials as 10 to 27.5. Double these proportions, therefore, or the proportion of 20 to 46.8, and of 20 to 27.5 are the proportions of the number marrying annually, to the number born and the number dying. Let 1 marriage in 10 be a 2d or 3d marriage on the side of either the man or the woman, and 10 marriages will imply 19 individuals who have grown up to maturity, and lived to marry once or oftener; and the proportion of the number marrying annually the first time, to the number dying annually, will be 19 to 27.5, or near 3 to 4. It may seem to follow from hence, that in this island near three-fourths of those who die have been married, and, consequently, that not many more than a *quarter* of the inhabitants die in childhood and celibacy; and this would be a just conclusion were there no increase, or had the births and burials been equal. But it must be remembered, that the general effect of an increase, while it is going on in a country, is to render the proportion of persons marrying annually to the annual deaths *greater*, and to the annual births *less* than the true proportion marrying out of any given number born. This proportion generally lies between the other two proportions, but always nearest to the first *; and, in the present case, it is sufficiently evident that it cannot be much less than two-thirds.

---

* In a country where there is no increase or decrease of the inhabitants, and where also life, in its first periods, is so stable,

In London, then, *half* die under three years of age, and in Madeira about *two-thirds* of all who are

and marriage fo much encouraged, as that half all who are born live to be married, the *annual* births and burials muft be equal; and alfo *quadruple* the number of weddings, after allowing for 2d and 3d marriages. Suppofe in thefe circumftances (every thing elfe remaining the fame) the *probabilities of life*, during its firft ftages, to be improved. In this cafe, more than *half* the born will live to be married, and an increafe will take place. The births will exceed the burials, and both fall below *quadruple* the weddings; or, which is the fame, below *double* the number annually married.——Suppofe next (the *probabilities of life* and the *encouragement to marriage* remaining the fame) the *prolificknefs* only of the marriages to be improved. In this cafe it is plain, that an increafe alfo will take place; but the *annual* births and burials, inftead of being lefs, will now both rife above *quadruple* the weddings, and therefore the proportion of the born to that part of the born who marry (being by fuppofition two to one) will be lefs than the proportion of either the *annual* births or the *annual* burials to the number marrying *annually*.——Suppofe again (the *encouragement to marriage* remaining the fame) that the *probabilities of life* and the *prolificknefs of marriages* are both improved. In this cafe, a more rapid increafe will take place; or a greater excefs of the births above the burials; but at the fame time they will keep nearer to *quadruple* the weddings, than if the latter caufe only had operated, and produced the fame increafe.——I fhould be too minute and tedious, were I to explain thefe obfervations at large. It follows from them, that, in every country or fituation where, for a courfe of years, the *burials* have been either *equal to* or *lefs* than the *births*, and both under *quadruple* the marriages; and alfo that wherever the burials are *lefs* than quadruple the annual marriages, and at the fame time the births *greater*, there the major part of all that are born live to marry. In the inftance which I have confidered above, and which occafions this note, the annual births are fo much *greater* than *quadruple* the marriages, and at the fame time the annual burials fo much *lefs*, that the proportion that lives to marry of thofe who are born can fcarcely be much lefs than I have faid, or two-thirds.

born

born live to be married. Agreeably to this, it appears alſo from the account I have referred to, that the *expectation* of a child juſt born in Madeira is about 39 years, or near double the expectation of a child juſt born in London. For the number of inhabitants was found, by a ſurvey made in the beginning of the year 1767, to be 64,614. The annual medium of *burials* had been, for eight years, 1293; of *births* 2201. The number of inhabitants, divided by the annual medium of *burials*, gives 49.89, or the *expectation* nearly of a child juſt born, ſuppoſing the *births* had been 1293, and conſtantly equal to the *burials*, the number of inhabitants remaining the ſame. And the ſame number, divided by the annual

I have ſhewn how the allowance is to be made for 2d and 3d marriages; but it is not ſo conſiderable as to be of any particular conſequence; and, beſides, it is, in part, compenſated by the natural children which are included in the births, and which raiſe the proportion of the births to the weddings higher than it ought to be, and therefore bring it nearer to the true proportion of the number born *annually*, to thoſe who marry annually, after deducting thoſe who marry a 2d or 3d time.

In drawing concluſions from the proportion of *annual* births and burials in different ſituations, ſome writers on the increaſe of mankind have not given due attention to the difference in theſe proportions ariſing from the different circumſtances of increaſe or decreaſe among a people. One inſtance of this I have now mentioned; and one further inſtance of it is neceſſary to be mentioned. The proportion of *annual* births to weddings has been conſidered as giving the true number of children derived from each marriage, taking all marriages one with another. But this is true only when, for many years, the births and burials have kept nearly equal. Where there is an exceſs of the births occaſioning an increaſe, the proportion of *annual* births to weddings muſt be leſs than the proportion of children derived from each marriage; and the contrary muſt take place where there is a decreaſe.

Q medium

medium of *births*, gives 29.35, or the *expectation* of a child just born, supposing the burials 2201, the number of births and of inhabitants remaining the same; and the true *expectation* of life must be somewhere near the mean between 49.89 and 29.35.

Again: A 50th part of the inhabitants of Madeira, it appears, die annually. In London, I have shewn, that above twice this proportion dies annually. In smaller towns a smaller proportion dies, and the births also come nearer to the burials. At Breslaw, I have observed, that, by Dr. Halley's Table, a 28th part dies annually; and the annual medium of births, for a complete century, from 1633 to 1734, has been 1089; of burials 1256. * At Norwich, the annual medium of births, dissenters included, for four years, from 1751 to 1754, was 1150; of burials 1214. And as the number of inhabitants was at that time 36,169 (see pag. 103), a 30th part of the inhabitants died annually. In general, there seems reason to think that in towns (allowing for particular advantages of situation, trade, police, cleanliness, and openness, which some towns may have), the excess of the burials above the births and the annual deaths are more or less as the towns are greater or smaller. In London itself, about 160 years ago, when it was scarcely a fourth part of its present bulk, the births were nearly equal to the burials.

* Vid. Dr. Short's *Comparative History*, p. 63. And the *Abridgment of the Philosophical Transactions*, vol. VII. part iv. p. 46. During the five years on which Dr. Halley has founded his Table, or from 1687 to 1691, the births happened a little to exceed the burials.

[115]

But in country parishes and villages the births almost always exceed the burials; and I believe it seldom happens that so many as a 30th, or much more than a 40th part of the inhabitants die annually*. In the four provinces of New England there is a very rapid increase of the inhabitants: but, notwithstanding this, at Boston, the capital, the inhabitants would decrease were there no supply from the country: for, if the account I have seen is just, from 1731 to 1762, the burials have all along exceeded the births†. So remarkably do towns, in consequence of their unfavourableness to health, and the luxury which generally prevails in them, check the increase of countries.

---

* In 1738 there was an account taken of the number of families and inhabitants in the Prussian dominions. The number of inhabitants was 2,138,465. The medium of annual births, weddings, and burials was nearly 84,000; 21,000, and 55,481. Near a 40th part, therefore, died every year. Vid. Dr. Snort's *Comparative History*, p. 69, and *Abridgment of the Philosophical Transactions*, ibid.——The proportion of weddings and burials to the births shews that, in these countries, there was a quick increase, notwithstanding the waste in the cities.——In the year 1733 a survey was taken of the inhabitants of the parish of *Stoke Damerel* in *Devonshire*, and the number of men, women, and children, was found to be 3361.——The *christenings* for the year were 122——the *weddings* 28——*burials* 62.——No more, therefore, than the 54th part of the inhabitants died in the year.—— In part of this year an epidemical fever prevailed in the parish. See Martyn's *Abridgment of the Philof. Transactions*, vol. IX. p. 325.—— According to Graunt's account of a parish in *Hampshire*, not reckoned, he says, remarkably healthful, a 50th part of the inhabitants had died annually for 90 years. *Natural and Political Observations, &c.* Chap. xii.

† See a particular account of the births and burials in this town from 1731 to 1752 in the *Gentleman's Magazine* for 1753, p. 413.

Healthfulness and Prolifickness are, probably, causes of increase seldom separated. In conformity to this observation, it appears from comparing the births and weddings, in countries and towns where registers of them have been kept, that in the former, marriages, one with another, seldom produce less than four children each; generally between four and five, and sometimes above five. But in towns seldom above four; generally between three and four; and sometimes under three *.

I have sometimes heard the great number of old people in London mentioned to prove its favourableness to health and long life. But no observation can be much more erroneous. There ought, in reality, to be more old people in London, in proportion to the number of inhabitants, than in any smaller towns, because at least one quarter of its inhabitants are persons who come into it, from the country, in the most robust part of life, and with a much greater probability of attaining old age, than if they had come into it in the weakness of infancy. But, notwithstanding this advantage, there are much fewer persons who attain to great ages in London than in any other place where observations have been made.——— At Vienna, of 22,704 who died in the four years

---

* Any one may see what evidence there is for this, by consulting the accounts in Dr. Short's two books already quoted; and in the *Abridgment of the Philosophical Transactions*, vol. VII. part iv. p. 46.—In considering these accounts, it should not be forgotten that allowances must be made for the different circumstances of increase or decrease in a place, agreeably to the observation at the end of the note in pag. 113.

1717,

1717, 1718, 1724, 1725*, 109 reached 90 years, that is, 48 in 10,000. But in London, for the laſt 30 years, only 35 of the ſame number have reached this age.——At Breſlaw it appears, by Dr. Halley's Table, that 41 of 1238 born, or a 30th part, live to be 80 years of age.——In the pariſh of *All-ſaints* in Northampton †, an account has been kept for many years of the ages at which all die; and, I find, that of 1377, who died there in 13 years, 59 have lived to be 80, or a 23d part.—— According to Mr. Kerſſeboom's Table of Obſervations, publiſhed at the end of the laſt edition of Mr. De Moivre's Treatiſe on the Doctrine of Chances, a 14th part of all that are born live to be 80; and, had we any obſervations in *country* pariſhes, this, probably, would not appear to be too high a proportion ‡. But in London, for the laſt 30 years, only 25 of every 1000

---

* Vid. Abridgment of the Philoſophical Tranſactions, vol. VII. part iv. p. 46. —— It appears alſo that more than three-fifths of all who died in theſe years at Vienna were boys and girls, by whom, I ſuppoſe, are meant perſons under 16. About the ſame proportion dies under 16 at Berlin.

† In this town, as in moſt other towns of any magnitude, the births, including Diſſenters, fall ſhort of the burials; and the greater part die under age.

‡ This, however, will appear itſelf inconſiderable, when compared with the following account: "In 1761, the burials in "the diſtrict of Chriſtiana, in Norway, amounted to 6,929, and "the chriſtenings to 11,024. Among thoſe who died, 394, or "1 in 18, had lived to the age of 90; 63 to the age of 100, and "ſeven to the age of 101.——In the dioceſe of Bergen, the per- "ſons who died amounted only to 2,580, of whom 18 lived to "the age of 100; one woman to the age of 104, and another "woman to the age of 108." See the *Annual Regiſter* for 1761, p. 191.

who have died, have lived to be 80, or a 40th part; which may be eafily difcovered by dividing the fum of all who have died during thefe years at all ages, by the fum of all who have died above 80.

Among the peculiar evils to which great towns are fubject, I might further mention the PLAGUE. Before the year 1666 this dreadful calamity laid London almoft wafte once in every 15 or 20 years; and there is no reafon to think that it was not generally bred within itfelf. A moft happy alteration has taken place, which, perhaps, in part, is owing to the greater advantages of cleanlinefs and opennefs, which London has enjoyed fince it was rebuilt, and which lately have been very wifely improved.

The facts I have now taken notice of are fo important that, I think, they deferve more attention than has been hitherto beftowed upon them. Every one knows that the ftrength of a ftate confifts in the number of people. The encouragement of population, therefore, ought to be one of the firft objects of policy in every ftate; and fome of the worft enemies of population are the luxury, the licentioufnefs, and debility produced and propagated by great towns.

I have obferved that London is now* increafing. But it appears that, in truth, this is an event more to be dreaded than defired. The more London in-

---

* This increafe is greater than the bills fhew, on account of the omiffion in them of the two parifhes which have been moft encreafed by new buildings; I mean *Marybone* and *Pancrafs* parifhes. The former of thefe parifhes is, I fuppofe, now one of the largeft in London.

creases, the more the rest of the kingdom must be deserted; the fewer hands must be left for agriculture; and, consequently, the less must be the plenty and the higher the price of all the means of subsistence.
——*Moderate* towns, being seats of refinement, emulation, and arts, may be public advantages. But *great* towns, long before they grow to half the bulk of London, become checks on population of too hurtful a nature, nurseries of debauchery and voluptuousness; and, in many respects, greater evils than can be compensated by any advantages *.

---

* The mean annual *births*, *weddings*, and *burials* in the following towns, for some years before 1768, were nearly,

	Births.	Weddings.	Burials.
At Paris,	19,200	4,300	19,500
Vienna,	5,600	—	6,800
Amsterdam,	4,500	2,400	7,600
Copenhagen,	2,700	868	3,100

In the Paris bills there is, I am informed, an omission of all that die in the *Foundling Hospital*, amounting to above 2000 annually. The excess, therefore, of the burials above the births is greater than the bills shew. This excess, however, is much less than could have been expected in so large a town. I am not sure to what cause this ought to be ascribed; but I cannot wonder at it, if it be indeed true, that a fifth of all born in Paris are sent to the *Foundling Hospital*, and that a third of the inhabitants die in *hospitals*, and also that all married men are excused from serving in the militia, from whence draughts are made for the army. These are encouragements to marriage and population, which no other city enjoys; and it is strange that in this kingdom some policy of the same kind with that last mentioned should not be pursued.——A further singularity in the state of Paris is, that the births in it are above four times the weddings, nothing like which is the case in any other town whose bills I have seen. It may seem, therefore, that here, as well as in the most healthful

Dr. Heberden

Dr. Heberden obferves that, in Madeira, the inhabitants double their own number in 84 years. But

and increafing country parifhes, each marriage produces more than four children; but this is a conclufion which, in the prefent cafe, cannot be depended on. It fhould be confidered that, probably, fome who leave the country to fettle at Paris, come to it already married; and that no fmall proportion of the births may be illegitimate. Thefe caufes, however, may only balance the allowance to be made for the fecond and third marriages among the annual weddings; and, if it is indeed fact, that the people at Paris are fo prolific as they appear to be in the bills, it will only prove more ftrongly that, like other great towns, it is very unfavourable to health; for the more prolific a people are, the greater muft be the mortality among them if they do not increafe.
―――――Let us fuppofe the true number of deaths at Paris, including emigrants and fuch as die in the *Foundling Hofpital*, to be 21,000; the number married annually 2 × 4,300 or 8,600; and the births, as before, 19,200. 1,900 then will be the number of annual recruits from the country. Of thefe let only 1,200 be fuppofed to marry: and 8,600 leffened by 1,200, or 7,400, will be the number of thofe born at Paris who marry annually; and 11,800, or above *three-fifths* will be the number dying in childhood and celibacy. This, though it gives an unfavourable reprefentation of Paris when compared with the country, makes it appear to advantage when compared with fome other great towns. I am not fufficiently informed of the ftate of Paris to know how near this calculation comes to the truth. Every fuch doubt would be removed, were the ages of the dead given in the Paris bills. It is much to be wifhed this was done. The births and burials here come fo near to one another, that there can fcarcely be a properer place for fuch bills; and a Table of Obfervations might be formed from them that would give the values of lives much more exactly than the London Tables.

I cannot help adding that, excepting the omiffion I have mentioned in the burials, the Paris bills are complete; but it is well known that the London bills are extremely otherwife. London, therefore, muft be much larger in comparifon of Paris than it appears to be in the bills.

this (as you, Sir, well know) is a very flow increafe compared with that which takes place among our colonies in AMERICA. In the back fettlements, where the inhabitants apply themfelves entirely to agriculture, and luxury is not known, they double their own number in 15 years; and all through the northern colonies in 25 years*. This is an inftance of increafe fo rapid as to have fcarcely any parallel. The births in thefe countries muft exceed the burials much more than in Madeira, and a greater proportion of the born muft reach maturity.——In 1738, the number of inhabitants in New Jerfey was taken by order of the government, and found to be 47,369. Seven years afterwards the number of inhabitants was again taken, and found to be increafed, by procreation only, above 14,000, and very near one *half* of the inhabitants were found to be under †16 years of age. In 22 years, therefore, they muft have doubled their own number, and the births muft have exceeded the burials 2000 annually. As the increafe here is much quicker than in Madeira, we may be fure that a fmaller proportion of the inhabitants muft die annually. Let us, however, fuppofe it the fame, or a 50th part. This will make the annual burials

---

* See a difcourfe on *Chriftian union*, by Dr. Styles, Bofton, 1761, p. 103. 109, &c.——See alfo *The intereft of Great Britain confidered with regard to her Colonies, together with Obfervations concerning the increafe of mankind, peopling of countries*, &c. p. 35. 2d edit. London, 1761.

* According to Dr. Halley's Table the number of the living under 16 is but a *third* of all the living at all ages; and this may be nearly the cafe in all places which juft fupport themfelves in the number of their inhabitants, and neither increafe or decreafe.

to have been, during thefe feven years, 1000, and the annual births 3000, or an 18th part of the inhabitants.———Similar obfervations may be made on the much quicker increafe in Rhode Ifland, as related in the preface to Dr. Birch's *collection of the bills of mortality*, and alfo in the valuable pamphlet, laft quoted, on *the intereft of Great Britain with regard to her colonies*, p. 36.———What a prodigious difference muft there be between the vigour and the happinefs of human life in fuch fituations, and in fuch a place as London?———The original number of perfons who, in 1643, had fettled in New England, was 21,200. Ever fince it is reckoned, that more have left them than have gone to them[*]. In the year 1760 they were increafed to half a million. They have, therefore, all along doubled their own number in 25 years; and, if they continue to increafe at the fame rate, they will, 70 years hence, in New England alone, be four millions; and in all North America above twice the number of inhabitants in Great-Britain [†].———But I am wandering

---

[*] See Dr. Styles's pamphlet juft quoted, p. 110, &c.

[†] The rate of increafe, fuppofing the procreative powers the fame, depends on two caufes: The "encouragement to mar-"riage;" and the "*expectation* of a child juft born." When one of thefe is given, the increafe will be always in proportion to the other. That is; As much *greater* or *lefs* as the *ratio* is of the numbers who reach maturity, and of thofe who marry to the number born, fo much *quicker* or *flower* will be the increafe.——— Let us fuppofe the operation of thefe caufes fuch as to produce an annual excefs of the *births* above the *burials* equal to a 36th part of the whole number of inhabitants. It may feem to follow from hence, that the inhabitants would double their own number in 36 years; and thus fome have calculated. But the truth is, that they would double their own number in much lefs time.

from

from my purpose in this letter. The point I had chiefly in view, was, the present state of London as

Every addition to the number of inhabitants from the births produces a proportionably greater number of births, and a greater excess of these above the burials; and if we suppose the excess to increase annually at the same rate with the inhabitants, or so as to preserve the *ratio* of it to the number of inhabitants always the same, and call this *ratio* $\frac{1}{r}$, the period of doubling will be the *quotient* produced by dividing the logarithm of 2 by the *difference* between the logarithms of $r + 1$ and r, as might be easily demonstrated. In the present case, r being 36, and $r + 1$ being 37, the period of doubling comes out 25 years. If r is taken equal to 22, the period of doubling will be 15 years.—— But it is certain that this ratio may, in many situations, be greater than $\frac{1}{22}$; and, instead of remaining the same, or becoming less, it may *increase*, the consequence of which will be, that the period of doubling will be shorter than this rule gives it.——According to Dr. Halley's Table, the number of persons between 20 and 42 years of age is a third part of the whole number living at all ages. The prolific part, therefore, of a country may very well be a 4th of the whole number of inhabitants; and supposing four of these, or every other marriage between persons all under 42, to produce *one* birth every year, the annual number of births will be a 16th part of the whole number of people; and, therefore, supposing the burials to be a 48th part, the annual excess of the births above the burials will be a 24th part, and the period of doubling 17 years.——The number of inhabitants in New England was, as I have said from Dr. Stiles's pamphlet, half a million in 1760. If they have gone on increasing at the same rate ever since, they must be now 640,000; and it seems to appear that in fact they are now more than this number. For, since I have writ the above observations, I have seen a particular account, grounded chiefly on surveys lately taken with a view to taxation and for other purposes, of the number of males, between 16 and 60, in the four provinces. According to this account, the number of such males is 218,000. The whole number of people, therefore, between 16 and 60, supposing 14 males to 13 females, must be nearly

to healthfulnefs, number of inhabitants, and its influence on population. The obfervations I have made may, perhaps, help to fhew how the moft is to be made of the lights afforded by the London bills, and ferve as a fpecimen of the proper method of calculating from them. It is indeed extremely to be wifhed that they were lefs imperfect than they are, and extended further. More parifhes round London might be taken into them; and, by an eafy improvement in the parifh regifters now kept, they might be

420,000. In order to be more fure of avoiding excefs, I will call them only 400,000. In Dr. Halley's Table the proportion of all the living under 16 and above 60, to the reft of the living, is 13.33 to 20; and this will make the number of people now living in the four provinces of New England to be 666,000. But, on account of the rapid increafe, this proportion muft be confiderably greater in New England, than that given by Dr. Halley's Table. In New Jerfey, I have faid the number of people under 16 was found to be almoft equal to the number above 16. Suppofe, however, that in New England, where the increafe is fomewhat flower, the proportion I have mentioned is only 16 to 20, and then the whole number of people will be 720,000.

I cannot conclude this note without adding a remark to remove an objection which may occur to fome in reading Dr. Heberden's account of Madeira, to which I have referred. In that account 5945 is given as the number of children under feven in the ifland, at the beginning of the year 1767. The medium of annual births, for eight years, had been 2201; of burials 1293. In fix years, therefore, 13,206 muft have been born; and if, at the end of fix years, no more than 5945 of thefe were alive, 1210 muft have died every year. That is; almoft all the burials in the ifland, for fix years, muft have been burials of children under feven years of age. This is plainly incredible; and, therefore, it feems certain, that the number of children under feven years of age muft, through fome miftake, be given, in that account, 3000 or 4000 too little.

extended

extended through all the parishes and towns in the kingdom. The advantages arising from hence would be very considerable. It would give the precise law according to which human life wastes in its different stages, and thus supply the necessary *data* for computing accurately the values of all *life-annuities* and *reversions*. It would, likewise, shew the different degrees of healthfulness of different situations, mark the progress of population from year to year, keep always in view the number of people in the kingdom, and, in many other respects, furnish instruction of the greatest importance to the state. Mr. De Moivre, at the end of his book on the doctrine of chances, has recommended a general regulation of this kind; and observed, particularly, that at least it is to be wished, that an account was taken, at proper intervals, of all the living in the kingdom, with their ages and occupations; which would, in some degree, answer most of the purposes I have mentioned.——But, dear Sir, I am sensible it is high time to finish these remarks. I have been carried in them far beyond the limits I at first intended. I always think with pleasure and gratitude of your friendship. The world owes to you many important discoveries; and your name must live as long as there is any knowledge of philosophy among mankind. That your happiness in this, and every other respect, may continually increase, is the sincere wish of,

SIR,

Your much obliged,
and very humble servant,

Richard Price.

Newington-Green,
April 3, 1769.

XVII. *Dissertatio*

Reply to Dr. Price.

To the Printer *of the* St. James's Chronicle.

SIR,

THE Rev. Dr. *Price*, in his very ingenious *Obſervations on reverſionary payments,* has drawn ſuch a picture of the declining population of this kingdom, as muſt alarm and terrify all well-wiſhers to their country, and much exhilerate the ſpirits of our neighbours. This *opinion,* for I can call it nothing elſe, is publiſhed in a work, the principal part of which conſiſts of a chain of demonſtrative proofs; the author being remarkably attentive not to advance any aſſertions in his calculations of the value of reverſions, &c. without giving the poſitive facts on which he builds; and at the ſame time, being a gentleman of conſiderable literary reputation, whatever is found in his book muſt carry a much greater weight than the ſame ſentiments would have if found in inferior company. The conſequence is, that the idea of our depopulation will become more general;
clamours

clamours about engrossing farms, and the high prices of provisions, will be more riotous; and the old worn-out declamations against luxury be again common in the mouths of our politicians. It is not only an author's readers that converse about his sentiments; the discourse is retailed among numbers. *The kingdom is depopulated!* Who says it is depopulated? *Why Dr. Price, who has written so excellently on reversions.* Immediately the assertion spreads, and connected with the idea of being as clearly proved as any other assertion in his book. *Engrossing farms depopulates the kingdom.* This is supposed to be proved as satisfactorily as the *value of joint lives for a given number of years.*

But here, Sir, I beg leave to observe, by way of consolation to my countrymen, that a very great distinction is to be made in the doctor's book. The positive assertions he has ventured on the number of the people, engrossing farms, &c. are by no means attended with any but conjectural proofs; no positive ones; that is, he offers us such and such *opinions*, supported by *arguments*; which, if you approve, you may accept; and if not, reject. But this is not the case with the other parts of his work; he there commands your assent by facts; not solicits it by arguments founded on suppositions.

The following are the propositions which Dr. *Price* labours to establish:

I. That the number of the people is fallen a million and a half since 1685.

II. That the present number is four millions and a half.

III. That the depopulation is partly owing to the engrossing of farms.

From an attentive perusal of the work, I can find no other data from whence these conclusions can be drawn than the following:

1. The number of houses calculated from the hearth books by *Davenant*, were, at the restoration, - - - 1,230,000

In 1685, ditto	1,300,000
In 1690, ditto	1,319,215

2. The number in 1759 *(from Confiderations on Trade and Finances)* — 986,482
   In 1766, ditto — 980,692

3. Individuals per houfe at *Norwich*, found to be in 1752 — 5
   Ditto in *Oxford* (exclufive of the colleges) and at *Wolverhampton* — $4\frac{4}{5}$
   Ditto in *Birmingham* and *Coventry* — $5\frac{3}{4}$
   Ditto in *Shrewfbury* — $4\frac{1}{3}$
   Ditto in *Holy-Crofs* — $4\frac{1}{3}$
   Ditto in *Northampton*, *Manchefter* and *Liverpool* — $4\frac{3}{4}$
   Ditto in *Ackworth*, *Newbury* and *Speen* — 4
   Ditto in *Calne* — $4\frac{1}{2}$
   Ditto in *Altringham* — $4\frac{1}{7}$
   Ditto in *St. Michael's*, *Chefter* — $4\frac{5}{6}$
   Ditto in *Leeds* (partly conjectured) — 5

4. Individuals *per* Family in 14 Market-Towns *(from Dr. Short.)* Little more than — $4\frac{3}{4}$
   Ditto in 65 country parifhes; not quite — $4\frac{1}{2}$
   Ditto in *Leeds* — $4\frac{1}{5}$

Upon thefe authorities I fhall obferve, that the number of houfes given by *Davenant* is not from an actual enumeration, (for none was ever yet made) but *calculated* from the hearth tax. This may be juft; but reafons are not wanting to think the contrary.

Here it is to be obferved, that Dr. *Halley* calculated them (fee *Houghton's Hufbandry*) from the fame authority, in 1691, at 1,175,951, which agrees fo badly with that of 1690, as to make a prodigious error in one account, and fhews how extremely fallible the authority is.

Dr. *Brakenridge* gives the number, in 1710, to be 911,310, which is lefs than at prefent. It is to be noted, that Dr. *Price* takes no notice of thefe accounts. It may be faid, that Dr. *Brakenridge* does not mention the office whence he got the lift, but his character

is

NUMBER OF THE PEOPLE.

is too well established to suppose him utterly mistaken.

If the lists from which the Doctor calculates be true, the number of houses in 1766 were less by 249,308 than in 1660.

The list of 1691 gives 56,826 more houses in *Yorkshire, Middlesex, London, Kent, Essex, Surry,* and *Sussex,* for that year, than for 1758, which is simply impossible. (*See Three Tracts on Corn Trade.*) From hence is to be seen what credit is to be given to the calculations of the last century.

Let us compare the two periods.

	£.
Customs at the Revolution, produced	*1,015,000
At present, above	2,000,000
The excise at the Revolution	† 666,383
At present	4,600,000
Total of imports and exports in 1668	‡ 10,000,000
In 1763	26,651,854
Rental of the kingdom in Sir *William Petty*'s time, after the Restoration	**9,000,000
At present	20,000,000
Years purchase of land then ‡‡	17½
At present	33½
Interest of money from 1660 to 1690,	£.7 6 6
From 1730 to 1760	3 13 6

Agriculture needs no comparison.

In the name of common sense, if the kingdom contained in the former period a million and a half of souls more than in the latter, about what were they employed?

Does the Doctor imagine, that the superiority of all these circumstances can indicate a *less* numerous people, by a *quarter,* than in the former period? If Dr. *Price* can conceive these circumstances to exist, and at the same time mark a population inferior to that of 1660, I must say, by the same rule, that the most

---

* *Davenant's Essay on Ways and Means,* 1695, p. 36.   † Ib. p. 36.
‡ *Davenant's Works,* Vol. II. p. 15.
** *Petty's Political Arithmetic,* p. 151.   ‡‡ Ibid.

moſt populous age of *Britain* muſt have been the reign of the Conqueror.

In the next place, reſpecting the preſent liſt, it is ſuppoſed (and I apprehend juſtly) that theſe are much the moſt accurate ever taken; but I muſt remark, that a gentleman (equally eminent for his abilities, his eloquence, and his accurate inveſtigation of theſe affairs) has informed me, that by taking particular accounts of ſeveral pariſhes, the inhabitants, houſes, births, &c. he finds the number of houſes falſely reported to government in 1759, &c. being in *every inſtance* FEWER than the real number. This is extremely probable to be univerſal; and of which the Doctor might have taken a hint, from the great difference between the number of houſes in *London*, as appears in the pariſh books, and from *Maitland's* accurate and laborious examination. This circumſtance is *eſſential*: It deſtroys the foundation of all the arguments to prove our depopulation, at one ſtroke.

Laſtly, as to the number per houſe:—Suppoſe the houſes 980,692, and the average

5 to a Houſe,	as at *Norwich*, the total is	4,903,460
5	as at *Leeds*,	4,903,460
4⅘	as at *Oxford*,	4,717,320
4⅘	as at *Wolverhampton*,	4,717,320
5¾	as at *Birmingham*,	5,638,979
5¾	as at *Coventry*,	5,638,979
4⅓	as at *Shrewſbury*,	4,249,665
4⅓	as at *Holy Croſs*,	4,249,665
4¾	as at *Northampton*,	4,658,287
4¾	as at *Mancheſter*,	4,658,287
4¾	as at *Liverpool*,	4,658,287
4	as at *Ackworth*,	3,922,768
4	as at *Newbury*,	3,922,768
4	as at *Speen*,	3,922,768
4½	as at *Calne*,	4,413,114
4⅐	as at *Altringham*,	4,062,867
4⅚	as at *St. M. Cheſter*,	4,740,008
Average,		4,587,000

At *Oxford*, the Colleges are rejected—at *Ackworth*, the Hofpital—and at *Calne*, the Poor-houfe: Thefe omiffions are named; nor have we any information that fimilar deductions are not elfewhere ufed. But upon what principles can fuch a calculation be made? As the application of the facts is to know the general average not *per* family, but *per* houfe, the largeft feminaries of people ought to be included, or the refult cannot come near the truth. This is fo apparent, that it muft ftrike every one at firft fight. Yet does Dr. *Price determine* the general number by the average of the particulars, after all fuch buildings are rejected. So that a houfe with a family of ten, two of whom are at college, is called eight, yet the college no where included—And the fame with hofpitals, poor-houfes, &c. This is fuch a method of calculating as I cannot comprehend—for in it 2 and 2 do not make 4.

No parifh at *London* is included, where the numbers *per* houfe muft certainly be more confiderable, though perhaps more than a tenth of the total are there *. No place in which any great nobleman or rich commoner refides.—What allowance is made for all the body of feamen? the army, which in 1759 was above 100,000; alfo the men fought off by the war, but which peace foon recruits? The number taken *per* houfe of only one family, we find 4,587,000: To thefe are to be added the fuperiority of *London* and its

---

* It deferves notice, that Dr. *Price* procured an account of part of *Pancras* parifh, wherein the numbers are above feven to a houfe; which is explained away by faying many were lodgers.

Within the Bills there were in 1737, 95,968 houfes, *Pancras* and *Marybone* not included; call it only 100,000, and if they are claffed in whatever probable manner you may fix on, the number will turn out greater than the Doctor's idea.

20,000	at	12	240,000
20,000	at	10	200,000
20,000	at	8	160,000
20,000	at	6	120,000
20,000	at	5	100,000
			820,000

its environs to 4½ *per* houfe; the inhabitants of all colleges, fchools, hofpitals, poor-houfes, and prifons; all foldiers and feamen; all perfons without fettled habitations, &c. You are farther to add the deficiencies in the lift of houfes, which *cannot* exceed, and which *may* fall fhort, as we know it does, and reckon for thefe the *real* average *per* houfe. And when all thefe circumftances are confidered, the reader, it is apprehended, will not approve of the pofitive expreffion ufed by our author. "Four millions and a half are *probably* too large an allowance; five millions *certainly* fo," (Page 60 of *Supplement*.) To what purpofe fuch an affertion can be ventured, unfupported by facts, unlefs to convince the world that *the nation is ruined*, I know not.

As to the number of individuals *per family*, it is in this enquiry ufelefs, unlefs it was proved that every houfe contains but one; which is impoffible to prove. But I fhould be glad to know, whether an hofpital, a prifon, a college, a fchool, &c. were reckoned as families? The author takes no notice (except in the cafe of *Leeds*) of the difference between *houfe* and *family*; fo that we have no certain fatisfaction on this head.

Laftly, Sir, I come to the caufe of this imaginary depopulation, which the Doctor attributes chiefly to *engroffing farms*. I will offer no *reafons* in fupport of that which I have already *proved*. From a comparifon of the population of 250 farms, containing more than feventy thoufand acres, I have fhewn that farms of above 500 acres are in population fuperior to fmaller ones, as 8¼ to 6½ (*Six Months Tour*, vol. iv. p. 192, 251, 253, 267). I will change my opinion when a longer lift, taken with more care and impartiality, is produced, that proves a contrary fact. And I have there given the reafons why it is impoffible the fact fhould be otherwife.

Attributing the high price of provifions *(Supplement,* p. 19) to any caufes that can be remedied by government, muft have an extreme bad effect on the

minds

minds of the people; it is like all we hear about jobbers, badgers, foreftallers, &c. It is a miftake to fuppofe, that large farms can have any fuch effects, unlefs the foil, when well cultivated, yields lefs food than when full of beggary and weeds.

The Doctor from M. *Muret* fpeaks alfo of laying arable lands to grafs, as a caufe of depopulation. This has nothing to do with the fize of farms. This *Swifs* writer fpeaks alfo of engroffing farms; but the author fhould recollect an effential difference between *England* and *Switzerland* in this refpect. In the latter, the fmall farms M. *Muret* fpeaks of, are generally fmall eftates, that is, the property of the farmer. I find this in almoft every page of the *Berne Memoires*; but this is a direct exception to fmall farms. It is poffible (but this again is a point which wants proof) that fmall farms *in property*, may be favourable to population; for the farmer may afford a much better culture than that miferable one univerfally feen on them when rent is paid.

No part of this fubject will admit of general, random affertions; exceptions muft be made, or a writer can only miflead.

If the prices of provifions be high, it muft be owing to the cheapnefs of money, or a natural fcarcity; but the people never recur to natural caufes; they always drefs up a phantom among their neighbours, and call it jobber, badger, butcher, or what not, to whom they attribute every evil under the fun. But who will be fo hardy as to affert that provifions are dear? What do you mean by dearnefs? Would you have wheat at the fame price when a kingdom has thirty millions of fpecie as when it had but twenty; or when it has twenty, the fame as when it had ten? Before you talk of the comparative dearnefs of two periods, prove to me, that the quantity of fpecie in both is equal. For want of attending to this circumftance, the people are blown up into difcontent, by writings which cannot poffibly have any good effect. If my commodity

is

is wheat, and I pay for moſt of my conſumption double the price of 80 years ago (and juſtly too; owing to the different value of money) ought I not to receive double the price for my wheat?

But the truth is, the prices of commodities muſt always vary according to the variations of *demand* for them; and the *quantity* that is brought to market to anſwer that demand. If the people either increaſe in numbers, or conſume more, or a better ſort of food than formerly, in either caſe the demand increaſes and prices muſt riſe: If on the contrary, the demand continues the ſame, but the quantity is leſs, the ſame effect muſt follow. If the people decreaſe, or eat leſs, or a worſe ſort of food than formerly, and the ſame quantity is brought to market, then prices muſt certainly fall. In all which caſes, whatever is found to be the price of a commodity, OUGHT TO BE the price of that commodity; ſince it is evidently regulated by the variations in the demand, and the quantity which ſupplies it. Nothing, therefore, can be more pernicious, and at the ſame time futile, than to attempt to regulate that by laws, rules, ſtatutes, and proclamations, which regulates itſelf by the vibrations in the market. And I do not comprehend, how a country can greatly increaſe in wealth, through induſtry, without the *quantity of wealth* having a conſiderable effect in theſe vibrations. (*But for a contrary opinion, ſee Sir James Steuart*, vol. i. p. 394).

To return to population—I have lately taken great pains in procuring liſts for ſatisfying me on this head. —I ſhall continue to collect them, and doubt not being able to convince the publick, as far as any authority, except directly numbering the people, will allow, that the numbers, ſo far from declining, advance conſiderably; which may be ſeen by the great increaſe of births in very many places ſince the Reſtauration. The gentleman I mentioned above has made ſimilar reſearches, and the event is with him univerſally the ſame. Dr. *Price*, though he has been so conversant in such registers, takes not the least notice of this; from which I conjecture, that he also might find it thus.

But whether the people are increasing or not, it is certainly of high importance to know the real and the whole truth; this can only be gained by numbering them. I published last year, *Proposals to the Legislature*, for that purpose; and since opinions still continue so contrary, the necessity of that measure is greater than ever.

It is my being an enemy to all writings that can increase the groundless discontents of the people concerning the rates of provisions, &c. or convert into the melancholy prospect of a ruined nation the unparalleled prosperity of this great and populous kingdom, that has urged me, Sir, to trouble you with this letter; and by no means a fondness for contradiction: I honour the abilities of the author from whose opinion in one point I differ; and my aim, believe me, is nothing but the acquisition of real facts.

I am, Sir, your's, &c.
ARTHUR YOUNG.
North Mims, March 28, 1772.

LETTERS
TO THE
EARL OF CARLISLE,
FROM
WILLIAM EDEN, Esq.

Republished in 1973 by Gregg International Publishers Limited
Westmead, Farnborough, Hants., England

Greenwich, Jan. 17th, 1780.

SEEING occasion to make some additions to the preceding Letters, I have once more the honour of addressing myself to your Lordship; and shall proceed, without regard to formal method, or other connection than that in which the Remarks to be submitted to you present themselves to my mind.

When an Englishman submits himself by name to the public observation, as a writer on the prevailing weaknesses and inherent virtues, the apparent embarrassments and possible exertions, the misfortunes and resources of his country and his cotemporaries; he ought to be aware, that he is stepping out of his ordinary sphere into a perilous path:—He ought to know, that integrity of motives, though a good protection in the wilds of poetry against wolves and lions, is a very vulnerable armour in the field of politics.—He must know, if he knows any thing, that, amidst the various characters of which a free, active, and enlightened nation is composed; amidst the multiplicity of pursuits, caprices, concurrences, and disconnections, by which those characters are influenced, every public effort stands exposed to much public misconstruction.—I have somewhere seen an account of a Mongall chief, who was so desirous to attract observation, that he built a large bridge on the summit of a mountain, near the road leading from Petersburg to Pekin, in the hope that all passengers would ask the name of so strange an architect.—The ambition was innocent, and might probably be gratified in Mongalia, without producing a single witticism, or one mortifying remark.—But, at this end of Europe, names are not so cheaply circulated; and it must be some better motive than mere vanity, which can induce any prudent man to obtrude himself even into a printed title-page. He may wish to support the example of those, who have attempted, at different periods, to rescue political discussions from anonymous licentiousness; his motives and principle

of

of action may be the defire of public approbation directed to the end of public profperity; but he muft forthwith be prepared either to encounter, or to bear, all the conftitutional petulance, fplenetic difparagement, and malevolent invectives, as well of thofe who cannot, as of thofe who will not, underftand him.

There are fome men, who think that the ceremonies fubfequent to conviction are the only important and enviable part of a judge's office:—The truth is, their faculties, incompetent to any rational or argumentative deductions, naturally lead them rather to decide than to examine: and they pronounce judgment, therefore, without fcruple, though they are utterly unable to go through the preliminaries of a trial. Thefe men are gentle readers, and mercilefs critics.

Others again are fo formed, that their favourite fubjects in painting are, the flaying of Marfyas, the plague at Athens, the maffacre of the Innocents, and the martyrdom of St. Lawrence.

"——The surly spirit Melancholy
"Curdles their blood, and makes it heavy
"thick:"

——when men of this disposition apply themselves to political subjects, they receive every cheering communication with an austere coldness bordering on disgust, and treat every inventory of prosperous or promising circumstances as the fiction of an irregular brain.

Last, and least worthy to be mentioned, there will be some characters, in the mass of mankind, so incurably perverted, so inveterately warped (whether from natural defect, or by their own industry, is immaterial), that they reject even all semblance of candour, and every pretension to moderation. Estimating others by themselves, they ascribe all generous exertions to interested motives, and construe the language of plain sense into the inventions of a designing heart: holding themselves forward in all the glaring parade of assumed, and perhaps real, superiority of talents, they can twist and torture their faculties, in order to bear down the honest efforts

efforts of humbler minds. These men are governed by a spirit of political intolerance, and will bear no creed of national salvation, unless the bulle, which prescribes it, is issued by themselves. With a bigotted and proscriptive spirit, they can construe every overture of union into an act of hostility; with a solemn and pompous plausibility, they can convert every demonstration of resource into an admission of distress. It is their system to cover the naked simplicity of truth under shreds and patches of borrowed declamation; to substitute silly sarcasms in the place of solid reasoning; and to convert public discussions into mean personalities.

Such were the speculations of my mind when I first launched this publication into the world; and I now feel a pleasure in confessing that they have proved groundless, or at most have been verified in instances, either so insignificant, or so explicable, that they do not merit to be farther mentioned or regarded —I feel a pride too in recollecting, that I have told serious and unflattering truths to my cotemporaries of every party and denomination; that those truths have

had

had a quick and extensive circulation, both in Great Britain and in Ireland; and that they have been received with general candour, and with an indulgence much beyond what I could have claimed in justice, or even in favour.—The impression of what I have farther said may, and perhaps ought, to be perishable and transient:—Before, however, it is consigned to oblivion, and whilst it continues to draw an existence from the interests of the day, I wish to avail myself of suggestions, received both through public and private channels, which deserve respect and attention.—It was strictly true, that I wrote without the advantage of official intercourse or official information.—The intelligent and liberal communications, as well of friends, as of others whom I am not fortunate enough to call by that name, will now enable me to explain and enforce some material points; and this I shall do, without any mixture of controversy, which, in every shape and sense, I desire to avoid.

It is related of the Spartan Cleomenes, that, on some occasion of a long and laboured speech being addressed to him, in order to engage his concurrence in a great war, he gave this answer: "The exordium entirely escaped "my attention; nor have I any recollection of "the reasonings which followed it; and as for "the conclusion, I feel no disposition to adopt "it."—I feared, and indeed foresaw, that the first Letter in this collection would meet with a similar fate on the part of those to whom it relates.—In lamenting the predominancy of party spirit, and the disunion of able men, it was the honest wish of my mind to enforce the importance of joining the compacted weight of national talents, and national virtues, to the velocity and energy of the executive power:—But it required only a superficial view of the age and country in which we live, to know, that when popular divisions act and operate with a certain degree of permanence and effect, there must have been found and solid materials in the first composition of each; and that those materials must have cemented by habit and the course of years. Opposite bodies of men, practised in struggles and competitions, may become at

length

length so utterly irreconcileable in their views, passions, sentiments, and whole system of conduct, that though a pressure of circumstances may disperse or annihilate the one or both, no possible event can unite them to each other.

If, however, there is reason to lament, that the exertions of this country must still continue, from the want of a general co-operation, to be in some degree retarded in their course and weakened in their effect; there is, on the other hand, good reason to hope, that the war, which called for that co-operation, is, in the progress of events, become less formidable. The truth is, the contentions of empires, and the transactions of extensive wars, exhibit, only on a larger theatre, all the reverses, disappointments, and uncertainties, which are seen among individuals at a gaming-table. The house of Bourbon seized the hour of our embarrassments, and came upon us like an armed man in the night, in the hope of crushing us for ever: they came with all the greatness of collected strength, with the confidence of certain victory, with the foretaste of an early triumph. We were for a time a time in the crisis so well described by the Roman Poet;

Ad confligendum venientibus undique Pœnis,
Omnia quum belli trepido concussa tumultu
Horrida contremuere sub altis ætheris auris;
In dubioque fuit sub utrorum regna cadendum
Omnibus humanis esset terrâque marique.

But the balance of power (hitherto the *perpetuum mobile* of politics) still remains suspended; it is still a doubt whether the combined enterprize of France and Spain will, in the result, enable them to pass the just and proper boundaries of their ambition. The faith of nations, indeed, has sustained a shock, which is hereafter likely to introduce the dangerous and destructive system of an armed peace throughout Europe: nor is it possible that a conduct so baneful to the general interests of mankind, should not, in due season, draw the attention and interference of other established empires.— In the mean time, the events of the war are thus far glorious to Great Britain, and in the whole not favourable to her enemies. That providence,

dence, which over-rules human machinations by secret and undiscovered springs, does not always give the race to the swift, nor the battle to the strong: Its blessings, however, conveyed as they are through second and subordinate instruments, are to be sought by the diligent use of our own faculties; and we are to expect the divine protection only in proportion as we exert ourselves, in a just cause, to deserve it.

Under these, or similar impressions, I offered, in my second Letter to your Lordship, every consideration that occurred to me upon the circumstances and conduct of this war. I do not now wish to retract, nor am I able to enforce any thing therein stated.—But, as the exertions to be made, depend, both for their extent and duration, on the national resources, which form the subject of the third Letter; and as that Letter goes into the discussion of ponderous and complicated interests and accounts, I shall here avail myself of such farther information as I may possess. Nor can it be cause of severe reprehension, if in such variety of matter I should have fallen into some inaccuracies, both of expression preffion and of fact;—fo far as I am aware of any fuch, I now mean to correct them.

When I ftated *(a)* that our taxes are not hitherto found to cramp the maintenance of the poorer clafs, fo as to diminifh the ufeful population of the country, and that this ifland, under all her burthens, does not exhibit any fymptom of internal decay; I confefs that I confidered the notion of any progreffive decreafe in the numbers of the people as a phantom *(b)*, which has in all ages haunted the joylefs imaginations of fome fpeculative men, but which has not at prefent any folid exiftence.—And accordingly, I founded feveral other remarks *(c)* upon the old-fafhioned eftimate of eight millions of inhabitants within Great Britain.—Dr. Price's *Obfervations on the Populoufnefs of England and Wales* had at this time efcaped my notice; but, like his other works, it deferves the ferious attention of every man, who wifhes to examine the circumftances of thefe kingdoms, though he may neither ad-

(a) P. 109, 110.   *(b)* P. 8.
(c) P. 82. 199. 113, &c.

mit all the premises, nor consequently adopt all the conclusions.

Questions respecting the populousness of different districts of the earth, at different periods of time, may lead to endless researches of curiosity and amusement; but they are valuable only in proportion as they produce discussions to ascertain the causes of the decrease and increase of the species, that mankind in general may derive profit from the intelligence; or so far as they enable particular nations to form a due estimate of their own actual situation, and the virtues or defects of their government.—With regard to natural causes, it is not found that there has been any universal difference discernible among the human species in the history or experience of ages subsequent to the deluge. But particular national causes, so far as they can be supposed to operate, afford some presumptions in favour of modern population.—This country has not been afflicted by pestilence within the memory of man; and the discovery of inoculation has averted the malignity of another
disease,

disease, which was sometimes nearly as fatal as a pestilence.

We are to look then to another class of causes, which operate very differently in different societies. These are, the constitution and circumstances of the respective government, the manners of the people, war, and emigration. But, after having fatigued ourselves with disquisitions under each of these heads, we shall find, that, like many other questions of general policy, they may be supported by plausible arguments either way, and even by contradictory examples drawn from the supposed experience, and pretended records of nations. On the one hand, it will not be disputed, that civil liberty is favourable to industry and to agriculture, to marriage and increase. On the other, it may be asserted, that the populousness of France, and of other monarchies, appears to advance in larger proportions than that of freer nations; and the despotic empires of China or Japan may be pointed out as the most populous districts in the known world.—Again, it may be said, that simplicity of living, few inequalities of property, ty, smallness of farms, and cheapness of provisions, are favourable to population:—But to this it may be answered, that, though these apparent advantages exist only in the first rudiments of society; yet they are amply compensated in the advanced stages of civilization, when the aggrandizement of individuals, and the active and refined demands of luxury draw forth the exertions of ingenuity and industry, and promote that facility of subsistence, by which the increase of mankind is best encouraged.—It may indeed be true, that large and crouded cities occasion an annual waste and consumption of mankind, and exact a continual recruit from the country; but it will be stated, as some compensation, that the neighbourhood of such devouring cities is always well peopled, and possibly more productive than in proportion to the demand.—Still it may be said, that the increase of public debts and of taxes, by occasioning an extreme difficulty of subsistence, may alone press fatally on the populousness of the freest country under heaven; but we might fairly reply, that a possible cause does not imply

an

an exifting effect; and that the particular effects here alluded to certainly do not exift. Whilft we fee, in every corner of the kingdom, the progreffive improvements of barren waftes into productive fields, it may be prefumed, that more food being raifed, there are more people to confume it.——Even wars and emigrations, though caufing the actual expenditure of a certain number taken from the particular fociety, may be argued not to depopulate in proportion to that expenditure. For here too there is infenfibly fome reproduction created by the demand.—It is known from hiftory that particular nations, under a regular and conftant wafte of war, regularly increafed and multiplied. And, with refpect to emigrations, we are affured, that thofe provinces in Spain, which fend the largeft numbers of their people to South America, continue the moft populous;—nor can it efcape notice, in other ftates, that many, who emigrate, would have perifhed unproductive in the parent foil, though they profper with little exertion in another country, and become fources of new commerce, wealth, and popu-

lation

lation to the world.——In fhort, the compenfations of fuppofed difadvantages, in every human predicament, as well of nations as of individuals, are mixed and manifold; and thus it is, that firft appearances, in great branches of political fcience, are often fo deceitful, and always fo difputable, that it is impoffible to truft to the conclufions, which ingenuity and acutenefs may find in general caufes and abftract reafonings. The lights are fo fcattered, that a well intentioned mind may naturally take either fide, or at leaft will check all hafty determination.

Enquiries then concerning the caufes of population muft not rafhly be admitted to prove any thing, farther than they are fupported by facts. It is a fact of no decifive confequence, which fhews only, that a particular village, diftrict, or even a whole country, is more thinly peopled than heretofore. It may be anfwered, that the inhabitants of towns in general appear to have increafed in a greater proportion, than thofe of villages and cottages have decreafed; it may be fhewn, that emigrations from one part of the kingdom to the other, are often the

fore-

fore-runners of population to the whole country. We fee waftes grow into villages, other villages into towns, and towns exceeding the boundaries of cities; and thefe again flourifhing, and augmenting in ftrength, people, and opulence. We are not then to infer a general depopulation from partial inftances. The moft decifive fact would be an actual enumeration of the whole people at ftated periods; but, as enumerations are perhaps impracticable in great ftates, and in truth have not been attempted with regard to the country and periods now in queftion, recourfe muft be had to inductions from the comparifon of collateral circumftances at different times: It is with this view probably that Dr. Price, though he lays much ftrefs at the fame time on many of the general reafonings above mentioned, ftates upon inferences drawn from Davenant's account of the Hearth Books, that the number of houfes in England and Wales has decreafed near one fourth fince the Revolution; whence he concludes, that the decreafe of inhabitants has been proportionable, and profeffes to fhew, that it has made a rapid progrefs during the laft twenty years.

These positions are maintained by other remarks selected from the bills of mortality and the excise books, which apparently afford presumptive arguments in favour of the point to which they are brought, but which, I am persuaded, would have been stated with much more hesitation, if there had been competent and fuller information within reach; I shall attempt at least to shew, among other matters in the separate note *(d)* annexed, that the selection of different periods from the same documents would equally imply an increased and progressive population.

The existing strength of a nation does not so much depend on the multitude of its inhabitants, as on the manner in which they are employed; yet it surely is of consequence not to admit, except on manifest proof, that the populousness of Great Britain is rapidly approaching to the level of that of Naples; and therefore I have been tempted to dwell upon a subject, which, however dry, cannot be unimportant.—I should not indeed have said so much in reference to a writer of less eminence than Dr. Price; but his

(d) See Appendix, No. VI.

conclusions,

conclusions, even when drawn from a misapprehension or misinformation, are so ingeniously stated, that they make an impression, which in such a case he certainly would not wish. Having rendered this due acknowledgment to his abilities, I owe a farther tribute to that liberality of mind with which he has communicated to me the knowledge of some of my own errors, at the same time that he differed from me, as to the principal positions, which I had wished to establish.

Much remains to be said respecting the state of our population, and the presumptions to be collected from all the circumstances of our apparent strength and real exertions. But this would draw me from other considerations, and is in truth a subject, with respect to which mankind have differed, and will continue to differ in every period and in every country, where they have no actual enumerations to put an end to uncertainty and to force assent. We have seen, in our own time, a very able and learned dispute between Mr. Hume and Mr. Wallace on the populousness of ancient nations. The disposition of men has generally inclined towards the melancholy

choly side of the question. Diodorus Siculus, who wrote in the age of Julius Cæsar, observes, that we must not form a notion of the populousness of ancient times from the desolation and emptiness which, in his days, prevailed in the world; and Montesquieu, speaking of Gaul from Cæsar's Commentaries, and of the supposed populousness of Rome, and other places, according to classical accounts, concludes with a remark, that in our days the world has hardly a tenth part of the number of inhabitants, which it formerly had. Mr. Hume, in quoting the first of these passages, observes, that " the humour
" of blaming the present and admiring the past
" is strongly rooted in human nature, and has
" an influence even on persons endued with the
" profoundest judgment and most extensive
" learning."

In these times an empire is certainly not to be peopled, like the fields of Pyrrha or of Cadmus, with pebbles and dragons teeth. The population of modern states depends much on national virtues and wise institutions; and though we should avoid the extravagant and visionary prosperity of the Athenian, who persuaded himself, that every

ship,

ſhip, which entered the Piræum, came freighted with his property from a fortunate voyage; it is reaſonable on the other hand to reject, except on the compulſion of clear and firm proofs, any poſitions tending to depreciate the ſuppoſed ſtrength of our country, and of the ſprings which move it.

Sir William Petty's mixed education, and courſe of life, did not difpoſe him to involve plain ſenſe in refined expreſſion; but his natural wiſdom, and chearfulneſs, led him to doubt and to controvert the gloomy ſpeculations, current among his cotemporaries, relative to " the ſinking
" of rents, the decay of trade and commerce, the
" poverty and depopulation of the kingdom, and
" the riſing omnipotence of France." " Theſe,
" with other diſmal ſuggeſtions, ſays he, I had
" rather ſtifle than repeat:" " They affect the
" minds of ſome to the prejudice of all."—"An ill
" opinion of their own concernments renders men
" languid and ineffectual in their endeavours."—
" Upon this conſideration, as a member of the
" commonwealth, next to knowing the preciſe
" truth, in what condition the common intereſt
" ſtands,

"stands, I wou'd in all doubtful cases think
"the best, and consequently not despair, without
"strong and manifest reasons; carefully examin-
"ing whatever tends to lessen my hopes of the
"public welfare."—

"That some are poorer than others ever was
"and ever will be, and that many are naturally
"querulous and envious, is an evil as old as
"the world.

"These general observations, and that men
"eat, and drink, and laugh, as they used to
"do, have encouraged me to try, if I could
"also comfort others; being satisfied myself,
"that the interest and affairs of England are in
"no deplorable condition."

No. VI.

Pandere res alta terra et caligine merfas.—

THE Obfervations on the Population of England and Wales fhew *(a)*, that according to the returns of the furveyors of the houfe and window duties the number of houfes were,

In 1759 — 986,482
    1765 — 980,692
    1777 — 952,734;—

They next proceed to ftate, upon the authority of Davenant, that the total of houfes in 1690 was, 1,319,215:—from thefe premifes it is inferred *(b)*, that " our people have decreafed fince 1690 near *a quarter*;" and that the depopulation in the laft twenty years has been progreffive.—

It fhould perhaps have been added, that Dr. Halley, whofe authority is at leaft as good as Davenant's, eftimates the number of houfes in 1691 at 1,175,951. They both argued from the Hearth Books, over which oblivion has fomewhere contrived to fpread her cobwebs; for I cannot learn, after a ftrict fearch by gentlemen

(a) Obfervations, p. 288. *(b)* Ib. p. 293.

peculiarly able to make it, that there is now any trace of thofe books either in the Tax-office or Exchequer. We want the lights therefore which might be collected from the original materials of information; we know however from the Statutes, that the tax was impofed not upon houfes, but upon every fire-hearth, or ftove, in every houfe, to be paid by the owners or occupiers. Two entries then were required, one of the owners or occupiers charged, and the other of the hearths rated.——Davenant accordingly *(c)* prints two columns, the one intitled, " Number of Houfes " in each County according to the Hearth Books " of Lady-day 1690—Total 1,319,215:" The other, " Number of Hearths in each County " according to the Books of Lady-day 1690— " Total 2,563,527." It is believed, but we cannot decide, that thefe numbers, whatever they may import, were founded on conjectural eftimates, and not on actual enumerations. But under Dr. Price's conftruction of the firft column when compared with the fecond, it would follow that there were lefs than two fire-hearths or ftoves upon an average to every houfe in the kingdom. The firft then feems to be an account not of houfes but of families. It is plain that Davenant

(c) Effay upon Ways and Means, edit. 1695, p. 76.

understands

understands it in this sense, and that by the word *houses* in the title of his Account referred to by Dr. Price, he means *households* not *tenements*; for he says *(d)* in the same publication, "And though it appears from the Books of Hearth-money, that there are not above 1,300,000 *families* in England; and allowing six persons to a *house* one with another, which is the common way of computing, not quite eight millions of people; and though (as likewise appears by the Hearth Books) there are 500,000 poor *families* in the nation, living in cottages, who contribute little to the common support; yet the 800,000 remaining *families* would be able to carry on the present business a great while longer, and perhaps till France is weary of it."—Davenant is countenanced in this plain explanation of his own sense, by the account of the produce of the tax so far as it can be relied on: The amount of the tax, on an average, as it was delivered to the House of Commons on the day of presenting the King's message which consented to the repeal, was 200,000 *l.* which at 2 *s.* per hearth gives 2,000,000; there remains therefore 563,527 hearths for the "500,000 families living in cottages, whom Davenant repeatedly states to have contributed little towards the common support." Dr. Price

(d) Observations, p. 34.

seems to have anticipated this objection, by attempting to shew that the number of persons in a family are equal upon an average taken in particular places to the number in a house. But in the estimates which support that position, and which at best must be uncertain, due attention has not been paid to the numbers in schools, colleges, hospitals, prisons, barracks, shipping, dock-yards, and other public buildings.

According to Dr. Price's construction of Davenant's Paper, the number of houses in London, Westminster, and Middlesex, in 1690, was 111,215; and the houses in the same places, with the addition of Southwark, are supposed, by the latest accounts, not to exceed 91,000: a difference totally discountenanced by every account, and every map of London and the environs! We might indeed try it by the usual criterion of the Bills of Mortality;—thus, the number of houses, in 1690, in London, Westminster, and Middlesex, according to the expression used in Davenant, was 111,215; the number of houses for the same district, with the addition of Southwark, in 1757, according to an actual survey, was only 87,614: yet for fifteen years, ending in (e) 1690, the annual average

---

(e) The annual average burials for the fifteen years subsequent to 1690 were only 20,877.

burials within the Bills of Mortality, were 21,657; and for fifteen years, ending in 1757, they were 22,762; exclusive of the great increase in Marybone and Pancras, if the number of deaths in those two parishes could be learned, and added respectively to the two periods here compared —It is also beyond a doubt, that London was become much healthier in the latter period than in the former.—It is true, indeed, that, in the former period, there were only 134 parishes within the Bills, and, in the latter, 147; but this objection would not furnish any adequate explanation, even if it were not known that the extension of the Bills of Mortality has arisen only from the spreading out of buildings, crouded formerly within the walls (f), but now upon a larger space. The dilemma then is, that, during a considerable period, when we are

(f) The medium of annual burials in the 97 parishes within the walls, was from

1650	to	1660	—	3123
1680	to	1690	—	3139
1730	to	1740	—	2316

But the medium of annual burials within the whole Bills of Mortality was, for the

First Period	—	12,886
Second Period	—	22,362
Third Period	—	26,492

to suppose the inhabitants ¼th more in number, we are to admit that the annual burials were $\frac{1}{20}$th less, and yet that the condition of the people was more unhealthy.

As a farther proof of the modern depopulation of London, it is mentioned *(g)*, that the annual average of burials in London from 1774 to 1778 inclusive, was 20,835; but that the average for five years before 1690 was 22,742.—Here we find a colourable evidence; but it is furnished by the use of a particular period. The average of twenty years ending in 1690, was 20,733. The average of ten years ending 1700, was 20,770.— The average of seventeen years ending in 1690, was 21,371.—Now in comparing the least favourable of those periods with the present times, we shall find that the average of 17 years ending in 1778, happens to have been 22,765.—The average of eleven years ending in 1772, was 23,743—and for five years ending in 1766, it was 24,562,—and, though Dr. Price supposes our depopulation to have made a great progress during the last twenty years, it will be found, that, for five years, ending in 1761, this average was only 19,877.—London seems indeed to have been most crouded during the period from 1720

(g) Observations, p. 281.

to 1745, when the annual average of burials was above 26,000; but this too is in a great meafure accounted for, when we recollect again, how much the town has, within the laft thirty-five years, expanded itfelf into the parifhes of Marybone and Pancras, which are not within the Bills.—The prefent queftion, however, is, whether London appears to be now lefs populous than it was in 1690; and, if we ufe the old-fafhioned mode of calculation, to which we might be entitled in comparing the two periods, we fhould, as authorized by Sir William Petty, multiply 22,765 (the average burials of the laft 17 years) by 30 (a fuppofed proportion of lives to burials) which would give 682,950 people. But I am convinced, by another work *(h)* of Dr. Price's, that this mode of computation is extremely erroneous; and it feems but too probable that the annual number of deaths in London is much greater than in the proportion of 1 to 30.—I mean, however, only to compare our very imperfect data, in fuppofed facts, fo far as they are known; I do not wifh to propofe any conclufion without much better premifes than any which the very wretched ftate of this branch of national police can furnifh. " In the

(h) On Reverfionary Payments, p. 198, &c.

"year 1603, fays Mr. Anderfon *(i)*, the weekly
"Bills of Mortality, at London, began to be
"regularly kept, as in our days; yet many of
"thofe Bills, in earlier times, have been loft;
"and even the Bills in their modern condition
"afford us but an imperfect conjecture of the
"magnitude of London, as comprehending only,
"or moftly, the chriftenings and burials of thofe
"of the eftablifhed church; though the Diffenters
"of all denominations form a numerous body
"of people. Thofe alfo who are buried in St.
"Paul's cathedral, in the abbey church at Weft-
"minfter, in the Temple church, the Rolls chapel,
"Lincoln's Inn chapel, the Chapter Houfe, the
"Tower of London church, and fome other parts,
"are faid to be entirely omitted." Exclufive of
thefe, and other defects, which are anxioufly defcribed in Maitland, all who are carried into the
country to be buried are alfo omitted, and the very
populous parifhes of Marybone and Pancras are
not yet included in the Bills.——In fhort, if I
could bring myfelf to that difpofition, which
fometimes leads us, firft to frame a conclufion,
and then to look for premifes, I could fuggeft
many reafons to imply an increafed population;
but, wifhing merely to refift the negative, and

(i) Deduction of Commerce, ii. p. 461.

having no wiſh with ſuch materials to attempt the affirmative propoſition, I ſhall only add a ſhort remark on the ſuggeſtion of a late apparent decreaſe.

The number of houſes in England and Wales by the Surveyors returns was,

In 1759 — 986,482
  1765 — 980,692
  1777 — 952,734:

But I find on enquiry that the total of houſes returned as charged and chargeable were,

In 1759 — 704,053
  1765 — 704,544
  1777 — 708,833:

And though of the laſt mentioned number 7,360 were afterwards diſcharged on appeal, it appears clearly that the houſes brought into charge were more in 1777 than in 1759. The apparent diminution of the total number is in the cottages not liable on account of poverty, with reſpect to which, it is notorious and avowed, that the Surveyors returns are conjectural and very defective. Nor indeed is there much regularity in their returns of houſes liable to duty;—for example, the houſes returned as charged and chargeable in 1750 were 729,048; and in 1756 only 690,702; but in 1759 they were again 704,544.—The Surveyors have lately received

an

an order to make strict returns of all houses every third year; it will however be difficult to enforce it to any purpose of the kind now in question.

Here then I shall dismiss a subject which, though it contains matters of curiosity and relative importance, is involved in endless conjecture and uncertainty. I expect to shew that it is equally unavailable to have recourse to the Excise.

It is certainly true, as expressed in the *Observations*, that " the gross annual produce of the
" hereditary and temporary Excise for three
" years ending in 1689 was, as appears from the
" Excise books, 740,147 *l.*; and its gross annual
" produce, for four years, ending in 1768,
" only 527,991 *l*. It had decreased, therefore,
" 212,156 *l.* per ann.; deducting, however,
" 112,156 *l.* for the duties on low wines and
" spirits (which duties, about 70,000 *l.* per ann.,
" were in 1736 carried to the aggregate fund)
" and for the use of the spirituous liquors and
" wine, which may have affected the consumption of beer, there will still remain a diminution unaccounted for, and amounting to
" 100,000 *l.* a year."

This instance, if unexplained, would warrant the inference meant to be conveyed by it.

it. In the firft place, however, there is not any mention made of the large allowance given to brewers by the alteration of meafure which took place after the Revolution, and which made an immediate and perceptible difference in the grofs annual produce of the Excife. The coffee duty was alfo taken from the Excife in 1690, and fubjected to the Cuftoms: But, without infifting on thefe points, or on the decreafed confumption which may have been occafioned by fubfequent additional duties, the very fame medium of proof, if different periods are felected, will afford ftronger prefumptions of a great increafed population. For example;—the grofs annual produce of the hereditary and temporary Excife for three years, ending in 1695, was 484,183 *l.*, and its grofs annual produce for four years, ending July 5th, 1774, was 520,623 *l.*—Again, the annual produce of the fame branch of Revenue, for three years, ending in 1698, was 464,142 *l.*; and for four years, ending in 1778, it was 554,460 *l.*—I have not, in either of thefe inftances, deducted from the produce of the two early periods the 112,156 *l.* per ann. above mentioned: my argument, though entitled to thofe advantages, does not want them. It affords, *prima facie*, a prefumption of a regular, increafed population.

The

The *Observations* proceed in the following words: " In conformity to this fact, it appears
" that there has been a proportionable diminu-
" tion in the quantity of beer brewed for fale
" and in the number of victuallers;—for three
" years ending in 1689 the annual average of
" ſtrong barrels brewed for fale, was 5,055,870.
" The average of ſmall barrels, was 2,582,248.
" ——For three years ending in 1768 the former
" average was 3,925,131; the latter, 1,886,760.
" —The average of common victuallers in the
" whole kingdom for the former three years,
" was 47,343; for the latter three years, 34,867.
" ——This laſt fact ſeems of particular conſe-
" quence," &c.

Here again a reference to different periods will prove the inverſe of every propoſition.—Thus, for three years ending 1700, the annual average of ſtrong barrels brewed for fale, was 3,074,256; the average of ſmall barrels, was 1,966,065; but for three years ending 1762, the former average was 4,244,783—the latter was, 2,073,197; the average of common victuallers in the whole kingdom for the former three years, was 37,170; for the latter three years, 39,803.——We differ only in the choice of inſtances, and any perſon who finds his leiſure as unimportant as mine, and who will take the trouble of examining the Excife Books, will obferve, that the periods which I have adduced are not felected with any particular induftry and attention. The four years ending in 1768, are almoft the loweft period for Excife produce that can be found in modern times; and it cannot be forgotten, that during that period the fcarcity of grain and high price of provifions were fuch as to excite dangerous tumults, and occafion an exertion of prerogative, for which the Legiflature paffed an Act of Indemnity:—the three years ending in 1689, were as remarkable in the oppofite extreme, and indeed unparalleled in any inftance prior or fubfequent. If, however, we lengthen even that favourite period, the refult will be different: Thus, the average annual produce of the hereditary and temporary Excife for fifteen years, ending in 1702, and including the period ending in 1689, was 549,175 *l*. That of four unfavourable years in the prefent century, was 527,991 *l*., to which muft be added, the duty on fpirits and low wines, 70,000 *l*. Total, 597,991 *l*.—The fame average produce for four years immediately preceding Dr. Price's publication, was 554,460 *l*. to which, in like manner, muft be added, the duty on fpirits and low wines, 70,000 *l*.—Total 624,460 *l*.

I do not mean to draw any conclusion; I have endeavoured only to shew, that, with equal plausibility, and by similar modes of proof, it is easy, from such dark materials, to produce opposite inferences; and it surely is neither unfair nor unreasonable to presume that each inference is inconclusive and fallible :—

Imus obscuri solâ sub nocte per umbram
Perque domos Ditis vacuas, et inania regna.
Quale per incertam lunam, sub luce malignâ,
Est iter in sylvis : ubi cœlum condidit umbrâ
Jupiter, et rebus nox abstulit atra colorem.

AN ESSAY ON THE POPULATION OF ENGLAND,

From the REVOLUTION to the present Time.

WITH

AN APPENDIX,

CONTAINING

REMARKS on the Account of the Population, Trade, and Resources of the Kingdom, in Mr. EDEN's Letters to Lord CARLISLE.

THE SECOND EDITION,
With CORRECTIONS and ADDITIONS.

By RICHARD PRICE, D.D. F.R.S.

LONDON:
Printed for T. CADELL, in the Strand.
M.DCC.LXXX.

Republished in 1973 by Gregg International Publishers Limited
Westmead, Farnborough, Hants., England

PREFACE.

THE following Essay was published last summer, at the end of Mr. Morgan's Treatise on the *Doctrine of Annuities and Assurances on Lives and Survivorships.*——Mr. Eden having, in his Fifth Letter to Lord Carlisle, made several objections to it, I now offer it to the Public in a separate tract, with an *Appendix* containing a reply to his objections.——At the end of the *Appendix* are added a few observations on Mr. Eden's account of the trade and resources of the kingdom. I feel myself deeply impressed with a conviction

viction of the importance of these observations; but at the same time, I know that I may be under the influence of those improper byasses to which Mr. Eden ascribes the apprehensions which many now entertain of the public danger. I therefore refer all I have said to the candid attention of those who may chuse to consider it, wishing them to pay no more regard to it than the evidence which will be laid before them shall render unavoidable.

May 8, 1780.

ADVERTISEMENT

TO THE

SECOND EDITION.

I THINK it neceffary to inform the Reader, that the principal corrections in this edition will be found in the account of the navy-debt, p. 78; and that the only additions of any confequence are the notes in p. 31, 67, and 73; the accounts of our trade, in p. 83, &c.; and the paragraph in the laft page relating to the gold coin.

June 27th, 1780.

CONTENTS.

Accounts of the number of houses in London *and* Middlesex, *at different periods, with observations* — p. 1, &c.

Accounts of the number of houses in ENGLAND *and* WALES *at different periods, with observations* — — — p. 9, &c.

Progress of depopulation, with facts confirming it — — p. 17, &c.

Causes of our depopulation - p. 29, &c.

State of population in other countries, Sweden, Naples, France, &c. - p. 30, &c.

APPENDIX, *containing remarks on Mr.* Eden's *account of the population, trade, and resources of the kingdom* — p. 36, &c.

State and fluctuations of London *from the Restoration* — — p. 55, &c.

Present state of the kingdom with respect to its trade and resources — p. 64, &c.

Comparison of the expence of the last *war with the expence of the* present *war* p. 70, &c.

CONCLUSION — — p. 73, &c.

ACCOUNTS *of the navy-debt, loan, unfunded debt, &c. in* 1762 *and* 1780 p. 77, &c.

Accounts of trade — — p. 83, &c.

Distribution of a hundred knights for the counties of England, &c. — p. 87

OBSERVATIONS

ON

The POPULATION of ENGLAND and WALES.

IT will be proper to introduce thefe obfervations with the following accounts of LONDON and MIDDLESEX.

Number of Houfes in LONDON, SOUTHWARK, WESTMINSTER, *and the* COUNTY OF MIDDLESEX, *in the Year* 1777; *from the Accounts of the Surveyors of the Houfe and Window Duties.*

Houfes charged in 1777, having 25 windows and upwards — —	12,560
Houfes charged, having lefs than 25 windows — — — —	61,080
Total of houfes charged — —	73,640
Uninhabited houfes chargeable —	3,368
Total of houfes charged and chargeable — — — —	77,008
Cottages not charged by reafon of poverty — — —	13,562
Total of houfes — —	90,570

Number

Number of Houses in London, Southwark, Westminster, *and the* County of Middlesex, *from the Survey mentioned by Dr.* Brackenridge *in a Paper read to the Royal Society in March* 1758, *and published in the Philosophical Transactions, vol.* 50, *p.* 471.

Houses charged to the house and window tax in 1757 — —	63,486
Houses uninhabited — —	4,810
Total of houses charged and chargeable — —	68,290
Cottages — —	19,324
Total of houses, including cottages — —	87,614

REMARKS.

These accounts shew, that the number of houses in *London, Westminster, Southwark,* and *all Middlesex* had, in the course of about 20 years preceding 1758, increased 2,956 in the whole; but that the houses excused on account of poverty had decreased 5,762; from whence it follows, that the houses *charged* and *chargeable* had increased 8,718. —It should be considered, that most probably this is less than the real increase of the best sort of houses; for the decrease of the cottages proves, that the meanest of the houses * which pay the tax must likewise have decreased; and this decrease is to be added to 8,718, in order to obtain the whole increase of the best houses; for it is obvious that, if the best houses had not increased as much as the worst decreased, the total of houses, instead of being greater in 1777, must have been less.—Perhaps, therefore, we shall reckon moderately enough if we reckon an increase within the last 20 years of 10,000 substantial houses in and about *London*; and this is a number that falls little short of the whole number of houses in *Liverpool* and *Manchester*.

The increase of buildings in *London* has for several years been the object of general

* That is, houses paying the house duty of 3s. only. The number of these houses in 1777 was 5,738; but I have no account of it for any preceding year. It will appear presently, that taking *England* in the gross, there has been a great decrease in these houses; and this makes it almost certain they must have decreased in *Middlesex*. —The decrease of cottages, or houses excused, since 1757, is the more remarkable, because the house and window duties have been increased since that year by three different acts of parliament, the first in 1758, the second in 1762, and the third in 1766.

obfervation. It deferves particular notice that it is derived entirely from the increafe of luxury; an evil which, while it flatters, never fails to deftroy. It has been fhewn from authentic accounts, that the decreafe of the lower people in *London* and *Middlefex* has kept pace with the increafe of buildings. The annual deaths alfo in the Bills of Mortality have for many years been decreafing, and are now near 6,000 *per annum* lefs than they were fifty years ago. In particular; it is obfervable with refpect to that part of *London* which lies within the city walls, that, though always filled with houfes, the births and burials, and, confequently, the inhabitants *, have decreafed ONE HALF.—The juft account of this muft be, that thofe who cannot now fatisfy themfelves without whole houfes, or, perhaps, two or three houfes, to live in, ufed formerly to be fatisfied with lodgings, or with parts of houfes.

The number of *houfes* in *London, Weft-minfter*, and all *Middlefex*, in 1690, was

---

* See a particular account of this fact in my Obfervations on Reverfionary Payments, page 190, 3d edit.

111,215,

111,215, according to Dr. *Davenant*'s account from the hearth-books *.

I will only further obferve concerning the preceding accounts, that they demonftrate that the number of inhabitants in London has been greatly over-rated. They have been fometimes eftimated at a million. In an Effay on the State of London, on Population, &c. in the Treatife on Reverfionary Payments, I offered evidence, which I thought little fhort of demonftration, to prove that they fell fhort of 651,000. But it now appears that, allowing 6 to a houfe, and including the whole county of Middlefex, their number in 1777 was only 543,420.

That fix to a houfe for London, and five to a houfe for all England, is too large an allowance, will be proved by the following recital of facts.

---

* See Dr. Davenant's works, vol. 1ft, page 38. This number does not include *Southwark*.——The average of burials for five years in *London* before the prefent year, or 1780, was 20779. The average for five years before 1690 was 22,742; that is, confiderably greater than it has been for the laft five years, though twelve parifhes, now the moft populous, were not then included in the Bills.

Observations on the Population

	Houses, Families	Inhabitants,	To a house, To a family
In Nottingham, according to a survey in Sept. 1779, exclusive of 294 in hospitals and workhouses	3,267 / 3,556	17,417	5 1/1, 4 4/5
Norwich, according to a survey in 1752	7,139	36,169	5.
Shrewsbury, by a survey in 1750	3,078	13,328	4 1/3
Northampton, by a survey in 1746	1,083	5,136	4 3/4
The parish of Ackworth, Yorkshire, in 1767	184	728	4.
Newbury, Berkshire, in 1768	930	3,732	4.
Speen, adjoining to Newbury, in 1768	303	1,200	4.
Aldwinckle, Northamptonshire, in 1772	96	402	4 1/5
The parish of Holy Cross, near Shrewsbury, in 1760	242	1,050	4 1/3
Altringham, Cheshire, in 1772	248	1,029	4 1/7
The Parish of St. Michael's, Chester, in 1772	127	618	4 5/6
The town and parish of Bala, North-Wales, in 1774	401	1,723	4 3/10
Fifty-nine Dutch villages mentioned by Struyk	12,005	45,888	3 5/6
Birmingham, in 1770	6,025	30,804	5 1/3
Liverpool, in 1773, including 400 in the Poor-house	6,340	34,407	5 2/5

of England and Wales. 7

In Manchester and Salford, in 1773	Houses	4,338	Inhabitants, 27,246	$6\frac{1}{4}$.
Leeds, in 1775	Families	4,096	17,121 — To a family	$4\frac{1}{5}$.
The District of Vaud in Switzerland	Families	25,778	112,951	$4\frac{3}{5}$.
Chester, in 1774	Families	3,428	14,713	$4\frac{3}{10}$.
Rome, in 1770	Families	37,449	158,442	$4\frac{1}{4}$.
Calne, Wiltshire	Families	776	3,467	$4\frac{2}{7}$.
Liverpool	Families	8,002	34,407	$4\frac{3}{10}$.
Manchester	Families	6,416	27,246	$4\frac{2}{5}$.
Bolton in Lancashire, in 1773, including Little Bolton	Houses	1,178	5,339 — To a house,	$4\frac{1}{2}$.
Bury in Lancashire, in 1772	Houses	463	2,090	$4\frac{1}{5}$.
The parish of Bala in North-Wales, in 1774	Houses	401	1,723	$4\frac{3}{10}$.
Chippenham, Wilts, in 1773	Houses	483	2,407	5.
Brenhill, near Calne, in Wiltshire	Houses	218	1,206	$5\frac{1}{2}$.
The Island of Sicily (see end of 2d vol. of Brydone's Travels)	Houses	268,120	1,123,163	$4\frac{1}{5}$.
Fourteen market towns mentioned by Dr. Short, Comparative History, page 58	Families	20,371	97,611 — To a family	$4\frac{3}{4}$.
Sixty-five country parishes, ibid.	Families	17,208	76,284	$4\frac{2}{5}$.

In

Observations on the Population

In the Parish of *Skelton*, Yorkshire, in 1777	— Houses	139 — Inhabitants,	506 — To a house, $4\frac{1}{5}$.
The town and parish of Wycombe, Bucks	— Families	500	2,461 — To a family, $4\frac{9}{10}$.
Worsley, Barton, Pendleton, Pendlebury, and Clifton, Lancashire, in 1778	— Families	1,685	9,117 — $5\frac{2}{5}$.
Parish of St. Cuthbert, Edinburgh, in 1743 (see Maitland's History of Edinburgh, page 171)	— Families	2,370	9,731 — $4\frac{1}{10}$.
In a number of small towns and parishes in the Generalities of Auvergne, Lyon, and Rouen, in France (see *Recherches sur la Population, par* M. Messance, pages 8, 26, and 62)	— Families	24,931	99,332 — $4\frac{1}{10}$.
Parish of Manchester, exclusive of the town, in 1774	— Families — Houses	2,525 2,412	13,786 — $5\frac{1}{5}$. 13,786 — To a house, $5\frac{7}{10}$.
Parish in the city of London (see Phil. Tract. part 2d, page 796)			— 6 to a house.

of England and Wales.

Number of Houses in England and Wales, from the Returns of the Surveyors of the House and Window Duties in 1761 *and* 1777.

	In 1761.	In 1777.
Houses charged, having 25 windows and upwards	*32,595	32,595
Houses having 21, 22, 23 and 24 windows	12,404	14,623
Total of houses having more than 20 windows	44,999	47,218
Houses having from 12 to 20 windows	88,494	98,756
Total of houses having more than 11 windows	133,493	145,974
Houses having 8, 9, 10, and 11 windows	102,525	117,857
Total of houses having more than 7 windows	236,018	263,831

* In the returns for 1761 this number is wanting. I have, therefore, supposed it the same that it was found to be in 1777. But the truth is, that it must have been less, as will appear presently.

This return has been given by Mr. Grenville in his *Considerations on the Trade and Finances of the Kingdom*, as made in 1766; but I have been informed from the tax-office that it was made in 1761.

Increase

	In 1761.	In 1777.
Increase in 1777 of houses having from 8 to 24 windows		27,813
Houses charged having 7 windows — —*	....	—131,950
Total of houses paying the window-tax —	236,018	395,781
Houses paying only the house tax of 3s. —	442,897	286,296
Total of houses charged	678,915	682,077
Increase in 1777 of houses charged — —		3,162
Houses uninhabited, but chargeable — —	†25,628	19,396
Total of houses charged and chargeable —	704,543	701,473

* The number of houses in 1761, having exactly seven windows, was 400,273; but by the law, as it then stood, all such houses were exempted from the window tax. In 1766 the tax was extended to these houses; and the consequence was, that near two thirds of them were reduced to houses having only six windows.

† The decrease which may be here observed in the number of empty, but chargeable, houses, is an effect which could not but attend the greater demand for houses which produced the increase between 1761 and 1777, of houses having more than seven windows.

of England and Wales.

	In 1761.	In 1777.
Decrease in 1777 of houses charged and chargeable	—	3,070
Cottages excused on account of poverty only	276,149	251,261*
Total of houses charged, chargeable, and excused	980,692	952,734
Decrease of houses charged, chargeable, and excused, from 1765 to 1777	—	27,958
To this decrease add the increase of houses having from 8 to 24 windows, or	—	27,813

And the total will shew, that the number of houses not having *eight* windows was 55,771 less, in 1777, than it had been in 1761.

Again; from 27,813, the increase in 1777 of houses having from 8 to 24 windows, subtract 3,162, the increase of houses charged, having less than 25 windows; and it will appear, that in the houses charged, having 7 windows or less, there has been in the same period a decrease of 24,651 houses.

---

* Of these cottages, 7360 *had* been charged, but were *dis*charged by appeal in 1777.

——But

————But this is by no means the whole decrease of houses of this sort. The increase of houses having more than 24 windows ought to be added; but the number of such houses not having been given in the return for 1761, it does not appear what this increase has been. It seems, however, past doubt, that there must have been such an increase, because all other houses having more than seven windows had increased.

NUMBER OF HOUSES IN ENGLAND AND WALES *in* 1759, *from the Return of the Surveyors of the House and Window Duties.*

Houses charged in 1759 — —	679,149
Uninhabited houses in 1759 chargeable — — — —	24,904
Houses excused on account of poverty only — — —	282,429
Total of houses in 1759 —	986,482
———————————in 1761, *see p.* 11.	980,692
———————————in 1777, *see p.* 11.	952,734
Diminished in 18 years from 1759 — — — —	33,748
Number of houses charged in 1756 — — —	690,702

of England and Wales.

Number of houses charged and
  chargeable in 1750 * — — 729,048
Deduct 25,000, and the charged
  houses in 1750 will be — 704,048
Total of houses according to the
  Hearth-books of Lady-day,
  1690 † — — — 1.319,215
Total of houses from the
  Hearth-books in 1666 ‡ — 1.230,000

---

* In the former edition of this essay, I had, on the authority of Dr. *Brackenridge,* (in the Philosophical Transactions, vol. 49, part 1st, p. 270,) given this as a return in 1710; but I have lately been informed from the tax office that it was made in 1750, and that it includes the chargeable houses.

† This account is given on the authority of Dr. Davenant. See his works, vol. 1st, page 38, where the number of houses, and also of hearths, is given separately for each county.—In page 136 he says, that "the hearth-tax had given a view *certain enough* of the number of families in the kingdom."

‡ See Tindall's Continuation of Rapin's History, vol. 1st, page 53.—Dr. Davenant says, that from 1666 to 1688 there had been about 70,000 new foundations laid. See his works, vol. 1st, page 370.—It is probable that the civil war in the time of King Charles the First, and the emigrations which then took place, lessened the number of people in the kingdom; and therefore, in Queen *Elizabeth's* time, or about the *Reformation,* the number of inhabitants in *England* might have been greater than it was even at the *Revolution,* agreeably to the facts mentioned at the end of my *Appeal to the Public on the Subject of the National Debt,* page 87, &c.

OBSERVATIONS *on the foregoing Accounts.*

Firſt. The firſt of theſe accounts makes the number of houſes in England and Wales in 1777 to be 952,734. Let it, however, be ſtated at a MILLION. Five perſons to a houſe is too large an allowance, as appears from the accounts in page 6, &c. It follows, therefore, that the number of inhabitants in *England* and *Wales* muſt be ſhort of FIVE MILLIONS.

In the kingdom of SWEDEN the number of inhabitants was 2.446,394, in 1763.— In the kingdom of NAPLES (one of the *Two Sicilies*) it was 4.311,503, in 1777.— In all FRANCE, 25.741,320, in 1772 *.

Theſe

---

* The account here given of *Sweden* is taken from actual ſurveys of the kingdom in 1757, 1760, and 1763. In the firſt of theſe years the inhabitants, of all ages, were found to be 2.323,195; in the ſecond 2.367,498; in the third, 2.446,394. See a Memoir by M. Wargentin in the 15th vol. of the Collection Academique, printed at Paris, 1772. The account of the kingdom of *Naples* is alſo given from ſurveys made there every year, and publiſhed in the Court Calendars.—In 1766, the number of inhabitants was 3.771,234; in 1772, 4.040,680; in 1777, 4.311,503.

The Intendants of provinces in *France* were, in 1770, 1771, and 1772, ordered to make returns of the number of deaths, births, and marriages in their reſpective diſtricts.

These facts shew, in a striking light, the superiority which arts, commerce, science, industry, and liberty give to a people.

ENGLAND

districts. The annual average of deaths for these three years was 780,040. See a Treatise *On the Legiflation and Commerce of Corn*, printed at Paris in 1775, and translated into English, and published in London in 1776, page 42.—I have been assured by the ingenious author, now the Director-general of the finances of *France*, that this account may be depended on as rather below the truth; and it affords a decisive proof that the number of inhabitants in France cannot be less than that stated above, or 25.741,320, which is the product of the average of deaths multiplied by 33. That this is the least multiplier which ought to be used will appear undeniably from the following facts.——In *Sweden*, the average of deaths for 9 years ending in 1763, was 69,125, or a 35th part and two-fifths nearly of the inhabitants. See M. Wargentin's Memoir just referred to.—In the kingdom of *Naples*, the average of deaths for 5 years before 1778, was 115,412, or a 37th and a third of the inhabitants.—These facts (and many others of the same kind may be found in the Treatise on Reversionary Payments, page 200) convince me that the average of annual deaths in *France* might have been multiplied by 35 instead of 33, and this would have brought out the number of inhabitants 27.301,400.—The same conclusion nearly may be drawn from the births in *France*, the average of which for five years ending in 1774, was 928,918. See *Recherches fur la Population de la France, par M. Moheau*, printed at Paris in 1778, page 147.—In *Sweden*, the average of annual births for 9 years, ending in 1763, was 90,240, or a 27th part and a tenth of the inhabitants.—In the kingdom

ENGLAND does not confift of many more inhabitants than the kingdom of NAPLES; but in refpect of dignity, weight and force, the kingdom of NAPLES, compared with it, is *nothing*. Not long ago, this little ifland, with its dependencies, like the ftate of ATHENS formerly among the *Greeks*, was the arbiter of EUROPE, and more than a match for all the three kingdoms I have mentioned, with SPAIN added to them.

Secondly. The great difparity between the numbers of people in the higher and the lower ranks of life feems to deferve particular obfervation, as it may be collected from the foregoing accounts. Families living in houfes having *feven* windows or lefs, muft confift of perfons in the loweft ftations; and yet the number of thefe houfes was 688,903 in 1777. Add to thefe fuch of

---

dom of *Naples*, the average of annual births for 5 years, ending in 1777, was 166,808, or a 25th part and four-fifths of the inhabitants. The medium is $26\frac{1}{2}$, which multiplied by 928,918, gives 24.616,327.——But it is certain, that a greater multiplier than $26\frac{1}{2}$ ought to be ufed in this cafe, becaufe the births exceed the deaths confiderably lefs in *France* than in either *Sweden* or *Naples*.—Upon the whole, therefore, I reckon that it appears with fufficient evidence that the inhabitants of *France* may very moderately be ftated at the number I have given.

the

the lowest people as live in the remaining 263,603 houses; and it will appear, that the people of property and opulence in the state, compared with the rest, are indeed a very small body. And yet their number is *now* greater in this country than it ever was; and, very probably, it is much greater in this country than in any other *.——It is proper to add, that this observation shews us distinctly why no taxes in a state can be very productive which do not reach the lower as well as higher ranks of people.

But, thirdly, What requires most to be attended to is the certain evidence which the preceding accounts give of the progress of depopulation in this kingdom.—The number of houses in ENGLAND and WALES

---

* In ENGLAND, the houses having more than *seven* windows are above a *fourth* of all the houses. In SCOTLAND, the number of houses having more than *five* windows, and paying the house and window duties, was, in 1777, only 16,206; and consequently could not be above a *fifteenth* of all the houses.—Agreeably to this poverty, the people of SCOTLAND, though more than a *fifth* of *Britain*, do not contribute more than a *fiftieth* to the revenue.—And it is also remarkable that of 4,876,171*l.* gold coin deficient between six and three grains, and brought in by the proclamation in 1774, to be recoined, only 52,984*l.* was brought from SCOTLAND. The sum brought in from IRELAND, in consequence of the same proclamation, was 394,201*l.*

was at the REVOLUTION 1.319,215. The number of houses now is not a *million*. Our people, therefore, since that æra, have decreased near a *quarter*.—This appears distinctly, as far as Dr. Davenant's account is to be depended on *. The following facts and observations will confirm this account, and furnish us with some additional evidence on this subject.

First. It appears, that there has been a very great decrease, since the Revolution, in the produce of a tax called the *hereditary and temporary excise*. This excise (almost the only one that existed before the Revolution) consists chiefly of 2*s*. 6*d.* per barrel on all strong beer or ale above 6*s.* the barrel, and 6*d.* on every barrel of ale sold at 6*s.* or less; and also a duty of 2*s.* 6*d.* per hogshead on cyder and perry; a duty on mead, strong waters, and low wines and spirits. The gross annual produce of this tax for three years, ending at 1689, was (as appears from the Excise books) 740.147*l.*

---

* Some may suspect that Dr. *Davenant* has, by mistake, taken from the Hearth-books the number of *houses* in the kingdom, when he ought to have taken the number of *families*. But this is improbable; and if true, will make no great difference, as may be inferred from the accounts in page 6, &c.

—Its gross annual produce for four years, ending in 1768, was 527,991*l*. It has decreased, therefore, 212,156*l*. *per annum.* One of the reasons of this decrease has been, that in 1736 the duties on low wines and spirits (amounting then to 70,000*l. per ann.*) were taken from the Hereditary and Temporary Excise, and carried to the Aggregate Fund. Deduct*, therefore, 70,000*l.* from 212,156*l.*; and the real decrease will be 142,156*l.* And this decrease will appear more remarkable, when it is considered how much less the currency and wealth of the kingdom were before the Revolution than they are now.——It may be said, that more wine is now drank; but this, being confined to the higher classes of people, makes no great difference.—It may with more reason be objected, that the lower people drink now greater quantities of spirituous liquors, and therefore less ale. With respect to this, it seems sufficient to observe,

* This is too great a deduction; for the use of spirituous liquors was in 1736 so much increased, that it became necessary to restrain it by additional duties.—The produce of that part of this Hereditary and Temporary Excise which consists of the tax upon beer only, was 674,387*l.* in 1688; and 694,476*l.* in 1689. See Dr. Davenant's works, vol. 1st, page 175.

that it appears from the Excife Books that the ufe of fpirituous liquors never funk the produce of this excife more than about 40,000 *l.* in a year; and that fince 1751 it has been fo much checked by new regulations, additional duties, and other caufes, that moft probably it does not prevail much more now than it did at the Revolution. After allowing, therefore, for the operation of this caufe *, (and alfo for the increafed ufe of wine) there will remain a diminution unaccounted for, of at leaft 100,000 *l. per annum.*

In conformity to this fact, it appears that there has been a proportionable diminution in the quantity of beer brewed for fale, and in the number of victuallers.——For three years, ended in 1689, the annual average of

---

* The following facts will confirm what is here faid, and fhew the progrefs of gin-drinking in the kingdom.—The ufe of fpirituous liquors prevailed moft in 1750 and 1751; and the *annual* average of fpirits drawn from malted corn, cyder, melaffes, and brewers' wafh in thofe two years was 11,326,976 gallons.—In 1752 and 1753 it was 7,500,000 gallons.—In 1767 and 1768 it had funk to 3,663,568 gallons.——In 1730 and 1731, it was 6,658,788 gallons.—In 1692 and 1693, it was 2,329,487 gallons.

In 1767 and 1768 the annual average of excifeable brandy imported was 1,612,631 gallons.—In 1688 and 1689, it was 1,713,974.

ftrong

strong barrels brewed for sale was 5.055,870. The average of small barrels was 2.582,248.—For three years, ended in 1768, the former * average was 3.925,131; the latter 1.886,760.—The average of common victuallers in the whole kingdom for the former three years † was 47,343; for the latter three years, 34,867.——This last fact seems of particular consequence, because victuallers in both periods include all that keep houses for selling any strong liquors;

* It is natural to suspect that this decreased consumption of beer must have been owing to the increase of the taxes upon it. But this does not appear; for in 1761, (after an addition in 1760 of 3 d. per bushel to the duty on malt) an addition was made to this tax of 3 s. per barrel, and yet it produced in the following years rather more in proportion than it did before.—The quantity likewise of strong beer brewed for sale increased a little afterwards; though these two additions were so considerable as to bring into the revenue near 900,000 l. *per annum*. In 24 years from 1740 to 1764, the taxes were more than doubled, and yet at the end of this term there was hardly a single tax which did not produce more than ever.

† For 10 years before the check given to the use of spirituous liquors in 1751, the victuallers in the kingdom amounted to near 48,000, though the quantity of strong beer brewed annually for sale was then less than it has been for the last 15 years. This, I suppose, must have been owing to the vast numbers of shops for selling gin, which, during that period, were opened every where.

and becaufe alfo there is reafon to believe, that the private brewery *, of which no account is taken, was greater formerly than it is now.—I cannot help adding, as a farther fact, indicating a particular degree of populoufnefs at the Revolution, that King William wanting, in 1689, to raife 23 new regiments for the war in Ireland, the levies were completed in fix weeks. See Sir John Dalrymple's Memoirs of Great Britain, vol. 1ft, page 384.—But what is moft of all decifive in the prefent queftion is, the depopulation which has certainly taken place *lately* in this kingdom.

---

* The number of common brewers in the whole kingdom in 1687 and 1689 was 776; in 1767 and 1768 it was increafed to 1083. One reafon of this muft be, that fewer victuallers and private people now brew their own beer.—It is remarkable, that the number of brewers in London *decreafed* during the fame period from 187 to 157; and alfo that the quantity of fmall and ftrong beer brewed for fale *decreafed* from 1.958,859 to 1.533,242 gallons. And this feems to confirm what has been already fuggefted, that even London is lefs populous now than it was at the Revolution. See page 4.

This decreafe was gradual and flow till 1726. After 1726 it became confiderable; and for fome years before 1750, the quantity of beer confumed in London was about 100,000 gallons *per annum* lefs than it is now, in confequence, undoubtedly, of the exceffive ufe of fpirituous liquors which then took place in *London* more than any where elfe.

From the preceding accounts it appears, that between the years 1761 and 1777 a destruction has taken place of at least 55,771 houses having less than 8 windows; which is equal to the loss of above a *quarter of a million* of those inhabitants who furnish recruits for our navy and army, and trading ships; and who, therefore, constitute the main strength of the kingdom.

I am not sensible that any thing can be objected to the evidence from which this conclusion has been drawn, except that there is an uncertainty in the returns of the cottages, because the surveyors, though directed to include them in their returns, take their number with less accuracy, no duty being paid for them. But it should be observed,

First, That this uncertainty does not at all affect the evidence for the diminution of houses *charged* having less than eight windows, and of which exact accounts are kept.

Secondly, The returns of the cottages, have not, I suppose, been made with less care for 1777 than for 1761; and it is the difference only on which the conclusion I have drawn depends.

But, thirdly, The diminution which there has certainly been in the houses
charged

charged having lefs than eight windows, proves undeniably, that there muft have been a proportionable decreafe in the cottages not charged.

Between the years 1759 and 1761 there appears in the returns a diminution of only 234 in the houfes charged. But it fhould be remembered, that the higher fort of houfes having increafed between 1761 and 1777, the caufes (which will be explained prefently) of that increafe muft probably have begun to operate fooner, and checked the decreafe, which (as may be diftinctly feen in the *Poftfcript*) had been going forward before that period.

Before 1759 it appears that the houfes *charged* had diminifhed 25,899 in nine years; and that fince 1759, houfes having lefs than eight windows have diminifhed 61,561 in *eighteen* years. Thefe are facts which fhew plainly, that the depopulation fince the Revolution cannot have been lefs than it is ftated in page 18.

The Honourable Mr. Grenville, in a pamphlet entitled *Confiderations on the Trade and Finances of the Kingdom*, after giving the fame account with that here given of the houfes in *England* and *Wales* in 1759 and 1761, expreffes the utmoft furprize at the proofs of depopulation which it afforded, and obferves, " that the deftruction of " 5790 houfes in fo fhort a fpace as * *eight* " *years*, is fuch a fymptom of diftrefs as " requires every attention to check the pro- " grefs of the evil.—Relief to the landed " intereft is now (he adds) no longer the " concern of individuals only who are to " receive that relief, but is become an im- " portant national concern."—What would he have faid, had he known that the depopulation which fhocked him was proceeding fo rapidly as I have fhewn; that no attention would be given to it; that the public burdens, inftead of being leffened, would increafe; and that he himfelf had laid the foundation of fuch an increafe of them as would, in a few years, bring the nation to the brink of ruin?

The increafe in the higher claffes of houfes has been for fome time obvious to every one. It may be imagined, that this implies fuch an increafe of people in the middle and higher ranks of life, as makes

* It fhould be remembered here, that the return which I have given in p. 9, &c. for 1761, was underftood by Mr. *Grenville* to have been a return for 1766.

amends

amends for the depopulation among the lowest ranks. But the truth is, that no such conclusion can be drawn. One of the principal causes of this increase has been that very evil which has destroyed the common people; or the increase of luxury. This, I think, has been demonstrated, by the account I have given of London *. See page

---

* The following circumstance may perhaps deserve some notice here.—By the new regulations of the window-tax in 1776, particular inducements were given to divide buildings deemed *single* houses, but holding *several* families, into houses having only one family in each; and this, as well as luxury, may have contributed to increase the number of houses without increasing the number of inhabitants.

For instance. By dividing a house having 30 windows, and containing *three* families, into *three* houses or tenements, having ten windows, and one family in each house, only 9 s. *per annum* would have been saved before 1766; but since the alteration in the tax that year, 1 l. 14 s. *per annum* may be got by such a division.——In like manner. By dividing such a house into two houses, having one family in each, and 15 windows, 3 s. *per annum* would have been *lost* before 1766; but now 15 s. *per annum* may be *saved* by it.

N. B.—Before 1766, houses having from eight to eleven windows paid 1 s. per window; and houses having more than eleven windows paid 1 s. 6 d. per window, besides 3 s. for the house.—By the new regulations in 1766, besides the old duty of 3 s. for every house, all

houses

page 4. It muſt, however, be acknowledged, that in many of our towns, and particularly our manufacturing towns, there has been a great increaſe of people as well as of houſes; but it ſhould be conſidered, that it has been derived from the depopulation of country pariſhes and villages, the inhabitants of which, by removing to theſe towns, and many of them thriving there, and living in better houſes, have increaſed the number of ſuch houſes at the expence of meaner houſes. This increaſe of people, therefore, in our towns has either quickened depopulation; or, if not, it muſt have been owing entirely to the increaſe of trade. From the accounts of the exports at the Cuſtom-houſe it appears, that * for ſome years before

---

houſes having ſeven windows pay 2 d. per window. Houſes having 8, 9, &c. to 13 windows, pay reſpectively 6 d.—8 d.—10 d. &c. to 1 s. 4 d. per window.—Houſes having from 14 to 19 windows pay 1 s. 6 d. per window. —Houſes having 20, 21, &c. to 24 windows, pay 1 s. 7 d. —1 s. 8 d. &c. to 1 s. 11 d.—Houſes having above 24 windows, pay 2 s. per window.

* See *The Additional Obſervations on Civil Liberty*, page 113. The annual average of exports for four years ending in 1764, was 15.793,158 *l*.—In 1773, the average for nine years had ſunk to 14.814,074 *l*. But the imports had increaſed from 10.110,870 *l*. to 11.996,769 *l*.—The decay

fore 1765 they were at the higheſt, and that they have ſince decreaſed. This decreaſe, however, has been more than compenſated by the increaſe of our *home-conſumption*, occaſioned by a vaſt increaſe † of luxury; and this, though it has operated fatally among the body of the lower people, has, in one way, contributed to retard the progreſs of depopulation; I mean, by furniſhing an increaſe of employment, and conſequently of the means of ſubſiſtence, for our manufacturers and artizans. But though depopulation has been thus checked, yet it has proceeded rapidly; and if we aſcribe one half

---

decay of foreign trade may farther be underſtood from hence. In 1764, the drawbacks on exportation amounted to 2.264,820*l*.—The average for ten years after 1764 was 1.843,404*l*.—but in 1776 they ſunk to 1.544,300*l*. —In 1777, to 932,860*l*.—In 1778, to 868,600*l*.

† The following account will ſhew how great this increaſe has been.—The *net annual* amount of all the exciſe duties for two years, ending 1768, was 4.431,075*l*. For two years, ending in 1773, it was 4.712,265*l*.—For two years, ending in 1777, it was above FIVE MILLIONS, after deducting the new taxes for 1776 and 1777.—The great increaſe of our importations, while the exportations have decreaſed, as mentioned in the laſt note, is another certain proof of the increaſe of luxury; and has probably been the means of turning the balance of trade againſt us. See *Additional Obſervations on Civil Liberty*, p. 116, &c.

of the increase in the higher classes of houses to this cause (or a real increase of people) and the other half to luxury, as before explained, we shall, I think, reckon very moderately; and it will appear, that in eighteen years near 200,000 of our common people have been lost.

I will only observe farther, that since the Revolution, most of the causes of depopulation have prevailed so much as to render it an evil which could not but happen. The causes I mean are—the increase of our navy and army, and the constant supply of men necessary to keep them up—a devouring capital, too large for the body that supports it *—the three long and destructive continental wars in which we have been involved—the migrations to our settlements abroad, and particularly to the East and West Indies—the engrossing of farms—the high price of provisions—but above all, the increase of luxury, and of our public taxes and debts.

I have given a particular account of these causes of depopulation in the Supplement to

---

* PARIS cannot contain so much as a *fiftieth* part of the inhabitants of *France*. LONDON contains a *ninth* of the inhabitants of *England*; and consumes *annually* about 7,000 persons, who remove into it from the country every year, but without increasing it.

the Observations on Reversionary Payments, page 371, third edition.—I will here only observe, that the depopulation they have produced is the more mortifying, because it seems, in some degree, peculiar to this nation.—In FRANCE, (in the principality of *Dombes,* the diocese of *Vaison,* and the six generalities of *Auvergne*, Lyon, Rouen, Bourgogne, Provence,* and *Alençon,* containing 2152 parishes) the average of annual births before 1764 had increased in 60 years from 54,827 to 59,894, or in the proportion of 100 to 109.—The average for five years of annual births in the whole kingdom of *France,* (as mentioned in the note, page 15) had been 928,918, in 1774, of which 479,649 were males, and 449,269 females.— The average of deaths, as mentioned in the same note, had been 780,040 for *three* years, ending in 1772. But Mr. MOHEAU has given the average for *five* years, ending in 1774 †; and it was 793,931. The annual

---

* See *Recherches sur la Population,* printed at Paris in 1766, page 274, and page 19, &c. See also on this subject M. MOHEAU's *Recherches & Considerations sur la Population de la France,* printed at Paris in 1778; where, in page 276, &c. the account of the increase of the generalities of Auvergne, Lyon, and Rouen is continued to 1774.

† MOHEAU's *Recherches,* &c. page 65.—The average of marriages was 192,180.

excess

excess of the births above the deaths was, therefore, 134,987; or near a *seventh* of the births; and this is probably an excess which in *France* more than counterbalances the destruction occasioned by emigration, war, and the sea-service.

The increase in SWEDEN and the kingdom of NAPLES has been distinctly mentioned in the note just referred to.

In the English colonies in NORTH AMERICA there has for many years been an increase scarcely ever before known among mankind *.

Thus unhappily distinguished are we in this country. Nor will it appear wonder-

---

* An account of this increase may be found in my Treatise on Reversionary Payments, p. 206, &c. 3d. edit. Another account of it is given in an important tract just published, and entitled, *A Memorial humbly addressed to the Sovereigns of Europe on the Present State of Affairs between the Old and New World*; where the following facts are stated as authentic:

In Massachusett's Bay the inhabitants increased from 94,000 in 1722, to 300,000 in 1773
In Connecticut from 129,994 in 1756, to 257,356 in 1774
In New-York from 96,776 in 1756, to 182,251 in 1774
In Virginia from 173,316 in 1756, to 300,000 in 1774
In South Carolina from 64,000 in 1750, to 115,000 in 1770
In Rhode-Island from 15,302 in 1730, to 28,439 in $174\frac{8}{9}$
In Philadelphia the houses in 1749 were 2076. In 1769 they were 4474.

ful, when we confider how unhappily we are diftinguifhed by fome of the worft caufes of depopulation; and with what particular force they have been operating for the laft *twenty* years. At prefent we are finking under new incumbrances and difficulties. The moft valuable of our dependencies are loft. Another foreign war is begun. Trade is declining; our ftrength is wafting; and at the fame time, that load of debts which has preffed fo heavily on our population, is increafing fafter than ever.—Never, certainly, were the refources of a ftate fo anticipated and mortgaged*—Never before did imprudence and extravagance bring a great kingdom into fuch peril.

"Our

---

* The terms of the loan for the prefent year will throw fome light on what is here faid.—A 3 *per cent.* ftock has been fold at 40 *per cent.* difcount, to which has been annexed an annuity of $3\frac{3}{4}$ *per cent.* for 29 years, at ten years purchafe, but really worth (when the 3 *per cents.* are at 40 *per cent.* difcount) $15\frac{14}{100}$ years purchafe.—The public, therefore, befides fubjecting itfelf to the neceffity of paying at redemption 40*l.* more than it has received for every 100*l.* ftock, has given a prefent premium on the fhort annuity of near 33 *per cent.* And even on thefe terms, (with the profits of a lottery added) only *feven millions* could be got, though above ten millions and a half (including 2.176,000*l.* increafe of navy debt in in 1778) were wanted for defraying the neceffary expences, exclufive of the ufual vote of credit for a million.—Thefe deficiencies

"Our late delusions (says Mr. Hume *) have much exceeded any thing known in history, not even excepting those of the Crusades. For there is no arithmetical demonstration that the road to the Holy Land is not the road to Paradise; as there is, that the endless increase of national debt is the direct road to national ruin. ——So egregious, indeed, has been our folly, that we have even lost all title to compassion under the numberless calamities that are waiting us."

deficiencies must be made good; and at least *eleven* or *twelve millions* more borrowed at the beginning of the next year, for which, very probably, if the war continues and spreads, a higher interest and still higher premiums must be given.—The national debt is now considerably greater than it was in 1776, when Mr. *Hume* wrote the words quoted in the next page; and it is advancing fast towards *two hundred millions*. It may signify little how a nation, in such circumstances, borrows money; but I am mistaken if I have not (in the *Supplement* to the Additional Observations on Civil Liberty) proposed regulations by which the loan of this year might have been procured at an interest of 5 (or, at most, $5\frac{1}{2}$) *per cent*. and consequently an expence of 100,000*l. per annum* for 29 years saved; which saving, properly applied, might have discharged, in 28 years, either the capital of *five millions* bearing *four* per cent. interest created in 1777, or a *larger* capital in the *three* per cents.

* See History of England, vol. 5th, page 475.

POSTSCRIPT.

The Favour of a Friend has lately procured for me, from the Tax-Office, the following Particulars in the Returns for 1756 *and* 1759, *mentioned in Page* 24.

	In 1756.	In 1759.
Houses *charged* having *less* than 10 windows	482,533	475,147
Houses *charged* having from 10 to 14 windows	105,153	103,610
Houses *charged* having from 15 to 19 windows	55,457	53,193
Houses *charged* having 20 windows or *more*	47,559	47,199
Total	690,702	679,149

This account scarcely needs a comment. A comparison of it with the *returns* in page 9, &c. for 1761 and 1777, will shew distinctly, that *before* 1759, houses of all sorts were decreasing; but that afterwards an increase (produced by increased trade and

and luxury, as explained page 25, &c.) begun among the *higher* classes of houses, which soon became considerable; but was all along accompanied with a decrease much more considerable in those inferior classes of houses which constitute near *four fifths* of all the houses in the kingdom.

APPENDIX.

IN the preceding Essay I have offered a good deal of evidence to prove that, while other countries are increasing, this country, in consequence of the causes of depopulation which have unhappily distinguished it, has for many years been decreasing. This is a fact so melancholy, that every person who loves this country must wish that the evidence for it could be fairly overthrown. Mr. Eden, in his fifth letter to Lord Carlisle, has made many objections to this evidence; and his means of information, as well as abilities, are such as entitle all that he says to particular attention.

My design in this Appendix is to give a brief account of his arguments; and, with all the respect due to him, to offer my reasons for not being convinced by them.

In p. 10, &c. it has been shewn from the accounts in the tax-office, that between the years 1761 and 1777 the number of houses

APPENDIX.

in the kingdom having lefs than eight windows had decreafed 55,771. This evidence feems to be direct and full, and it is the evidence on which I have laid the principal ftrefs. The objections which Mr. Eden has made to it, are the two following.

Firft, He obferves, that the account in the tax-office of the number of cottages excufed on account of poverty are uncertain and defective. To this I have, in page 23, &c. given an anfwer, which appears to me clear and decifive.

Secondly, He intimates a doubt whether the returns made of even the charged houfes can be relied on; and the reafon he affigns is the irregularity in the following returns. " The houfes, he fays, returned as *charged* " and *chargeable* in 1750 were 729,048, " and in 1756 only 690,702, but in 1759 " they were 704,544."* But Mr. Eden has here fallen into an incorrectnefs of confiderable confequence. The number for 1756 confifts of the *charged* houfes only. Adding, therefore, 25,000 for the *chargeable* or *uninhabited* houfes, thefe three returns (with thofe for 1761 and 1777) will be as follows:

* See the Fifth Letter to Lord Carlifle, page 65.

Charged and chargeable
houfes in — — 1750—729,048*
1756—715,702
1759—704,053
1761—704,543
1777—701,473

There is no irregularity in thefe returns, which gives them any appearance of incredibility. On the contrary they afford as ftrong a proof of progreffive depopulation as actual furveys can give. The decreafe, which appears before 1759, muft have been occafioned in part by the fhocking havock, which had been made for many years among the lower people by the ufe of fpirituous liquors, and the progrefs of which has been ftated in the note, p. 20. After this year the number of the beft fort of charged houfes began to increafe; but at the fame time the houfes excufed, or paying only the 3 s. duty, went on to decreafe fo faft as to over-balance that increafe. The chief reafon of this increafe I have, in page 26, ftated to be

* In the Tax-office accounts this is called, " the total " number of houfes in the refpective counties, *chargeable* " with the duties on houfes and windows." And the number for 1756 is called, " the number of houfes in " England, &c. *charged* with the duties, &c."

luxury;

luxury*; and of this we have a diftinct proof in the returns for London, where, though the increafe of new buildings has been fo great as to overbalance a decreafe of 5,762 in the houfes excufed, yet the number of inhabitants, if we may judge from the bills of mortality, has diminifhed. But of this more will be faid prefently.

The decreafe of cottages has for many years been an object of general obfervation. It is an effect which could not but arife from the inclofing of common fields, the engroffing of farms, the high price of provifions, the raifing of rents, and that inequality in the divifion of property, which has lately prevailed among us more than ever.

I will juft mention here the following facts.

In 1689 the houfes in the kingdom called cottages, and having only *one* hearth, and which, therefore, I fuppofe, anfwer to the houfes now denominated *cottages*, were — —	†554,631
The houfes denominated cottages in 1777, were —	‡251,261

---

* Promoted and accelerated by an influx of *wealth*, during this period, from the EAST-INDIES.
† See Dr. Davenant's works, Vol. II. p. 203.
‡ See p. 10.

In 1686 the whole expence of maintaining the poor was — *665,362*l*.
In 1778 this expence (exclusive of 137,656*l*. for county rates, &c.) amounted to — †1.556,804*l*.
In 1777 no less than 7,360 houses, which had been brought into charge, were discharged by appeal on account of poverty.

These facts seem to me to indicate a growing distress among the lower people, which did not take place formerly. They also lead us to carry our views as high as the *Revolution* for the commencement of depopulation among us. In the preceding Essay I have given a particular account of the evidence which has determined me to believe this to be the truth; and it is against this evidence that Mr. Eden has chiefly directed his objections.

First. He is unwilling to allow Dr. Davenant's authority in this instance; and in opposition to it observes, that Dr. Halley (whose authority, he says, is at least equal to Dr. Davenant's) estimated the number of houses in 1691 to be 1.175,951. Mr. Eden

---

* See Dr. Davenant's works, Vol. I. p. 39.

† See abstract of the returns made by the overseers of the poor, in pursuance of an act passed in the 16th year of his present majesty's reign.

may, perhaps, have good reasons for ascribing this estimate to Dr. Halley; but I wish he had said what they are. All I can find is, that it is given in a collection on *Trade and Husbandry* published by Mr. Houghton, in weekly numbers, in 1693 *. But it is not said from what authority it was taken, nor in what year it was made; and it is given among other accounts, most of which are too vague and conjectural. Till, therefore, I am better informed, I must think that it deserves no particular regard. And as to Dr. Davenant, it is proper to observe, that on such a subject as this there can scarcely be an equal authority; that his account is derived from materials which might have

---

* See Houghton's *Husbandry and Trade improved*, Vol. I. N°. 26, for Saturday, Feb. 3, 169$\frac{2}{3}$.——In N°. 24, Mr. Houghton has mentioned an assistance which he had received from Dr. Halley, and published a letter from him written ten years before, containing an account of a method of computing, within a million or two, the number of acres in all England. But Mr. Houghton has said nothing that implies he had received his account of the number of houses in England from Dr. Halley.—Dr. Davenant's account from the hearth-books was published three years afterwards, in his Treatise on *Ways and Means*, and is frequently referred to in some of his subsequent treatises; but he never takes notice of Mr. Houghton's account, which, therefore, I suppose, was not much regarded.

furnished

furnished him with the particular information which he gives on this subject; and that in the writings which followed that in which he gives this account (and particularly in his Observations on the People of England, published in 1699) he frequently refers to it, and reasons upon it, as an information of importance in political arithmetic, about which there was no reason to doubt *.

Secondly. It is farther objected by Mr. Eden, that Dr. Davenant meant to give the number of *families*, and not of *houses*. I have already in the note, page 18, taken notice of this objection. He that will consider the table in page 6 †, must see that in most places

---

* " The wealth of a whole people is a great matter
" to consider; but in time it may be compassed, especially when there is such a footing to fix our reasonings upon, as is the *certain* knowledge of the numbers
" of the people, which it is hoped some abler head will
" hereafter so improve as to make all points, relating to
" the strength and power of England, much clearer than
" they seem at present." Davenant's works, Vol. I. page 373.—Of the hearth money, he says, in page 136,
" that it had given a view certain enough of the number
" of families in the kingdom, which was the very
" ground-work in political speculations."—And that
" the accounts of it were fairly kept and stated, and had
" been under exact management."

† The numbers in this table are given from actual surveys. It cannot therefore be proper to call them, as Mr.

APPENDIX. 43

places there is very little difference between the number of *houses* and *families*; and, consequently, that, supposing Dr. Davenant to mean families, their number now in the kingdom must be far short of their number at the Revolution. But Dr. Davenant, at the head of the table which contains the particulars of this account †, calls it the number of *houses*. In reasoning upon it afterwards he generally does the same; and in his ‡ account of Mr. King's observations (which

---

Eden does, *estimates*, and to represent them as uncertain? Mr. Eden objects farther to this table, that due attention has not been given in it to the numbers in schools, docks, hospitals, and prisons.

This remark is wrong as far as it respects *schools*. As for *prisons*, *hospitals*, and *docks*, the numbers in them are little or nothing to the whole kingdom. In 1779 the number of persons confined in prisons and houses of correction, including all debtors, felons, and petty offenders, was 4,375, according to an accurate account, which the public owes to the unexampled benevolence of Mr. Howard. See the State of the Gaols, page 449. 8vo. edit.

† See his works, Vol. I. page 29.

‡ Mr. Eden quotes the following passage to prove that Dr. Davenant meant *families* and not *houses*. " Though
" it appears from the books of hearth-money, that there
" are not above 1.300,000 *families* in England; and, al-
" lowing six persons to a *house*, one with another, which
" is the common way of computing, not quite eight
" millions of people; and though (as likewise appears
" from the hearth-books) there are 500,000 poor fami-

(which he represents as more to be relied on than any thing that had been done in political arithmetic, and which appear indeed to have been the result of particular enquiry united to great sagacity) he makes the number of families to be 1.349,586; the number of persons to a family $4\frac{1}{17}$, and the number of people in the kingdom 5.500,000.—The truth is, that Dr. Davenant considered the number of houses and families as so nearly the same, that he did not think it ne-

"lies in the nation, living in cottages, who contribute lit-
"tle to the common support, yet, &c." Dr. Davenant's Essay on Ways and Means, published in 1695. (See his works, vol. I. p. 27.) It is evident that he makes use in this passage of round numbers without aiming at accuracy, or chusing to distinguish between houses and families. But afterwards, in the same tract, page 53, he speaks with more precision, and in a manner that demonstrates he meant *houses* and not *families*. "If," says he, "111,215 "houses in and about London, with no more ground "than what they stand upon, are in rent one million and "a half *per annum*, it is hardly possible but that the "1.208,000 houses in the country, with all the land "about them, and all the benefits that attend land, must "be in rent 13.500,000*l*."—Dr. Davenant's allowance of six to a family deserves no regard, for it is certainly wrong; and he was himself afterwards (as observed above) better instructed by Mr. King's Observations, published in 1699 in an Essay *on the probable method of making a people gainers by the balance of trade*. See his Works, Vol. II. page 185, &c.

APPENDIX. 45

ceffary to be careful in diftinguifhing between them.

I have in page 18, &c. as a collateral evidence in this queftion, given an account of the decreafe in the produce of the temporary and hereditary excife upon beer fince the Revolution.—Mr. Eden objects to this,

Firft, That there was an alteration of the meafure at the Revolution which diminifhed the produce of this excife, and alfo that a duty on coffee had formed a part of it which was then taken off. The alteration in the meafure is mentioned by Dr. Davenant (fee his Works, Vol. I. page 185, &c.) and its effect in diminifhing the excife eftimated at 20,000*l. per annum*. As for the duty on coffee, it was only 4*d.* a gallon *, and therefore fo trifling as not to deferve notice. Neither of thefe caufes therefore can account for the decreafe ftated in page 19th, and their effect has been counterbalanced by an exorbitant deduction of 70,000*l.* which I have made from the produce of this excife at the Revolution, on account of its including then a duty on low wines and fpirits, which was taken from it in 1736. The average of the grofs annual produce of this excife for

---

* This duty is now three fhillings per pound, and produces about 30,000*l. per annum*.

three years ending in 1689 was 740,147*l.* of which the excife on beer alone produced 679,590*l.* *. The difference is 60,550*l.* and confifted not only of duties on low wines and fpirits, but alfo on mead, cyder, perry, chocolate, fherbet, and beer and cyder imported. Had, therefore, a deduction of only 40,000*l.* been made, I fhould probably have exceeded the truth, and the decreafe would have appeared 30,000*l.* more than I have made it.

Mr. Eden has objected farther, that though the conclufion I have drawn is countenanced by a comparifon of the produce of this excife at prefent with its produce at the Revolution, yet a different conclufion may be drawn by comparing it with the produce of the fame excife at feveral periods fince the Revolution. This is Mr. Eden's principal argument, and the following table will reprefent it in its greateft force †.

---

* See Davenant's Works, Vol. I. page 175.

† It muft be remembered here, that this table gives the GROSS ANNUAL PRODUCE of the *hereditary and temporary* excife, with a deduction from it (on account of the duties on low wines and fpirits) of 40,000*l.* 'till 1710; of 50,000*l.* for the two years ending at 1719; and of 70,000*l.* for the two years ending at 1736.

Three

	£.
Three years ending at 1689	700,147
Two years ending at — 1695	438,573
* 1699	381,886
1703	473,799
1710	449,666
1719	509,370
1736	515,400
† 1746	495,749
1753	527,091
1761	575,280
For four years ending at 1768	527,991
1774	520,613
1778	554,460

It may be observed in this account, that during King William's wars the produce of this excise sunk greatly, that it rose at the subsequent peace, that it sunk again a little during Queen Ann's wars, and that ever since it has been rising except about the time when gin-drinking was most prevalent, but

* I have taken the whole of this account from the Excise books, except the average for the four years ending in 1774 and 1778, which I have copied from Mr. Eden's fifth letter, page 67.

† The fall in 1745 and 1746 might also be owing to the shock given the nation by the rebellion in those years. This was a shock that was very near proving fatal to public credit

but that it has always kept far below what it was at the Revolution.

The quantity of *beer* brewed for fale at thefe different periods, and the number of *victuallers* in the kingdom, correfpond in a great meafure to this account. The remarkable excefs in all thefe inftances, which took place at the Revolution, when joined to the evidence arifing from Dr. *Davenant*'s account of the number of *houfes* or *families*, appeared to me to afford a very ftriking proof

---

credit. In order, at the beginning of 1746, to raife two millions on the land-tax, fubfcriptions (as had been ufually practifed in preceding years) had been opened in the city. But only half a million could be procured. In this diftrefs the BANK was applied to, but fuch was the alarm which had taken place, that it could then fcarcely fupport its own credit. In order, therefore, to enable it to lend a *million* to government, this fum in *Exchequer-bills* was converted into *Bank-ftock*, and a call of 10 *per cent*. made on the proprietors as the payment for fo much ftock at *par*, one half to be paid in two months, and the Ladyday dividend to be reckoned a part of payment. But even on thefe advantageous terms the payments could not be eafily made, and it became neceffary to allow the proprietors farther time. In April the rebellion was crufhed, and foon afterwards the pannic occafioned by it ceafed entirely and credit recovered its former vigour. The three *per cents*. in particular, which when the rebels were at *Derby* had been as low as 60, rofe before Auguft to 89, and continued between this price and 82 during the whole remainder of the war.

of

APPENDIX.

of an excefs likewife of populoufnefs at that period. Nor did I think it neceffary to take notice of the fudden fall exhibited in the preceding table, becaufe I thought there were fuch particular and obvious reafons for it, as rendered it a circumftance not neceffary to be mentioned in this enquiry.—Since, however, Mr. Eden has laid great ftrefs upon it, and even intimated that it affords an argument for an increafed population, it is neceffary I fhould enter into an explanation of it.

Every one knows, that the productivenefs of taxes depends chiefly on the quantity of money in a kingdom. A fmaller number of people will be able to pay more in taxes than a greater number, if they are better fupplied with a circulating medium. During King William's wars, the trade of the kingdom funk; all the public fecurities, which fhould have circulated as money, loft their credit; and the greateft part of the current coin was either miferably clipped, or fent away to pay armies and fubfidies in foreign countries. In 1694 the Bank was eftablifhed; but for feveral years continued fo weak, as to be incapable of giving the public much affiftance by fupplying it with a fubftitute for coin.——In thefe circumftances it was impoffible that the people
fhould

should be able to make their usual payments. The taxes, therefore, fell near one half; and government became distrest to a degree of which we have now no conception *.

In the subsequent peace trade revived, and began to bring in silver and gold. Those public securities which had been a dead stock, recovered activity, and the taxes of course became less deficient.——But the war in Queen Ann's time soon renewed the former distresses, and the taxes again sunk.

From the Accession to 1764 trade increased fast, and brought in a large favourable balance.

* Tallies and malt-tickets were in 1696 discounted at several rates from 25 to 50 *per cent*.——In 1694 and 1695 the annual import of brandy, which had been 1.713,974 gallons, was only 54,081.——The whole revenue, which in 1689 had been 2.001,855*l*. was in 1693 only 1.570,318*l*. though new duties had been added which produced 466,203*l*. See Dr. Davenant's Works, Vol. I. p. 20.

The Bank Account (as delivered to the House of Commons on Dec. 4, 1696) stood as follows:

	£.	s.
DEBTOR to sundry persons for sealed bills standing out — —	893,800	
For notes for running cash —	764,196	10
To money borrowed in *Holland* —	300,000	
To interest due on Bank-bills standing out — — —	17,876	
Balance — — —	125,315	2
	2.101,187	12

CREDITOR

APPENDIX. 51

lance. Public credit acquired vigour, and foreigners threw in great sums into our funds. The BANK at the same time increased its emissions; and so powerfully did it co-operate with an increasing trade and flourishing credit, that in the two last wars, notwithstanding the treasure they carried out and the additional taxes they occasioned, none of that distress took place (except for a few months at the end of 1745, and the beginning of 1746), which had been felt in the two former wars.

Since 1764 there is reason to apprehend that an unhappy change has taken place, and that the balance of payment between us and the rest of the world has been turned against us, by the increase of luxury, our quarrels with

	£.	s.
CREDITOR by tallies on several parliamentary securities — —	1.784,576	16
By half a year's deficiency of the fund of 100,000*l*. — — —	50,000	
By cash, pawns, mortgages, &c. —	266,610	16
	2.101,187	12

In Queen *Ann's* war the *Bank* had got out of this state of infancy; but still it was so far from being very strong, that the apprehension of an attempt to invade *Scotland* in 1708, produced a run upon it that might have ruined it, had not Lord Godolphin, the Duke of Marlborough, and other great men, offered considerable sums to support it; and had not also the Directors increased the interest of their sealed bills from 3 to 6 *per cent.* and made a call upon the proprietors of 20 *per cent.*

the Colonies, and the payments due to foreigners from our funds. But the increase of our paper circulation has concealed this change, and counteracted its effects; and now so abundantly are we supplied from this source, that we find ourselves able to sustain a load of taxes, which at the beginning of this century would have at once overwhelmed us *———Still, however, and though much better supplied than ever with the means of paying taxes, we find that the hereditary and temporary excise produces near a *quarter* less than it did before the Revolution.—Others may think as they please; but I cannot see that this is fairly to be accounted for on any other supposition than that the common people, who chiefly pay this tax, are diminished in number.

Mr. Eden, as a farther objection to this evidence, chuses to compare the present produce of this tax, not with its average produce for *three* years, but for *fifteen* years

---

* This account has been given more at large in the *Additional Observations on Civil Liberty*, Part III. Sect. I. p. 113, &c. It is natural to infer from it, the usefulness of banks of circulation; and they are, without doubt, attended with great temporary conveniencies; but they give a complexion rather florid than healthy; and, by subjecting a kingdom (as Dr. Davenant speaks) to *apoplectic* disorders, may prove in the end the greatest of evils.

before the Revolution; and from this comparison it appears that there is no considerable difference, the former average having been 554,000*l.* and the latter 520,000*l.*

―――But nothing can be juſtly inferred from ſuch a compariſon. The kingdom, in conſequence of recovering tranquility after the diſtractions of the civil war, made a quick progreſs in all kinds of improvement. Between the *Reſtoration* and *Revolution*, an addition of 70,000 was made to the number of ſmaller houſes in the kingdom. Ten millions and a half in bullion (an overflowing produced by foreign trade) was carried to the mint to be coined, and the current ſpecie increaſed to eighteen millions and a half *.―――Theſe, and ſeveral other par-

* " As to plate, it may be ſafely affirmed, that there
" was more wrought for uſe in families from 1666 to
" 1688, than had been fabricated for 200 years before.
" —As to inhabitants, ſuch as are verſed in political
" arithmetic have ſufficient grounds to believe that the
" people of England were about 300,000 more in 1688,
" than they were in 1665, notwithſtanding the laſt great
" plague.―――As to the common people, there is no
" country in the world where the inferior rank of men
" were better clothed and fed, and more at their eaſe.—
" —As to buildings, during that time, not only many
" ſtately edifices have been erected, but farm-houſes
" have been kept up; and beſides, from the books of
" hearth-money, and for other reaſons, it appears, that
" of ſmaller tenements from 1666 to 1688, there have
" been

particulars of the same kind, are stated by Dr. Davenant, in his discourses on the revenue and trade of the kingdom, published in 1698.——With respect to this tax in particular, he shews that its produce, during this period, had been always on the increase; partly in consequence of an increase of people and of money; and partly in consequence of improvements in the methods of collecting it. When it was granted to Charles the IId. as a compensation for the profits of the court of wards and tenures by knight-service, it was not understood; and the people, being then not ha-

" been about 70,000 new foundations laid, &c. &c."
Davenant's Works, Vol. I. p. 370, &c. In p. 374, &c. this author computes that the stock of the kingdom was more than half doubled between 1666 and 1688. " Not " long ago, he says, (referring to King William's " war) we must have been impotent for the war, but " that it has been all the while and is still supported by " a stock formerly gathered, and not yet exhausted."— How far he thought this stock diminished by Queen Ann's war, appears from the following words in a report he made in 1711 to the commissioners for stating the public accounts :—" It is plain to all who are not " resolved to shut their eyes, that we have nine mil- " lions less in coin than we had in 1688." Davenant's Works, Vol. V. p. 451. This must have soon crippled the kingdom, had it depended entirely on its coin; but the BANK had then acquired some strength; and trade also, notwithstanding the war, was on the increase.

bituated

bituated to taxes, paid it reluctantly. At first it was farmed, and a considerable part lost by improper management. But for some years before the Revolution, the kingdom had been reconciled to it, and the collection of it had been brought under more strict and regular management.—Dr. Davenant shews, that this likewise was the case with the tax upon hearths. When first granted to King Charles the IId. it produced no more than 100,000*l. per ann.*; but it grew from time to time, till at the Revolution it came to yield net 240,000*l. per ann.**—In such instances, and, in general, in all cases where an increase or decrease takes place, it is evidently improper to argue from any averages for long terms.

I have observed in the preceding essay, that there is reason to believe, that even LONDON was more populous at the Revolution, than it is now. The number of houses in the bills of mortality, as given from the hearth-books by Sir William Petty in 1687; and in *London, Middlesex,* and *Westminster,* as given by Dr. Davenant in 1690; compared with the accounts now kept by the surveyors of the house duties, gives a direct and posi-

* See Dr. Davenant's works, Vol. I. p. 209.

tive proof of this *. And it is confirmed by a comparison of the annual average of burials within the bills of mortality, for *five* years before the Revolution, with the average for the same number of years at present. See the Note, p. 5.——Mr. Eden has objected only to the last of these arguments; and, in order to overthrow it, he compares the annual average of burials for *fifteen* years before the Revolutions (which was 21,657), with the annual average for *seventeen* years ending in 1778, which was 22,763.—Here a remark just made must be repeated. This is one of the cases in which averages for long terms prove nothing. LONDON, after

---

* " The number of houses in London appears by the
" register to be 105,315; whereunto adding $\frac{1}{10}$ part, or
" 10,531 as the least number of double families that
" can be supposed in London, the total of families will
" be 115,846." Essays on Political Arithmetic by Sir William Petty, published in 1687, p. 74.——" By cer-
" tificate from the hearth-office, I find the houses *within*
" *the bills of mortality* to be 105,315." Ibid, p. 79.—
This agrees with Dr. *Davenant*, who from the same hearth-office gives 111,215 as the number of houses in London, *Westminster*, and *Middlesex*, on Lady-day, 1690. See his Works, Vol. I. p. 39.——Mr. Maitland tells us, that he took, with incredible pains, the number of houses in London in 1737, and found them to be 95,968. He also then took an account of the omissions in the burials, which he found to be 3,038, including the burials in Marybone and Pancras parishes. See his History of London, Vol. II. p. 744.

APPENDIX. 57

the fire in 1666, rose from its ruins with great improvements, and increased very fast; and, at the beginning of the period for which Mr. Eden's average is taken, two of the principal parishes in Westminster, namely, St. *James* and St. *Anne*, were not included in the bills.—On the contrary, during the second period, LONDON appears to have been decreasing. For five years, at the beginning of it, or from 1762 to 1766, the annual average of burials was 25,084. For the five years ending in 1772, it was 22,950; and for five years ending in 1778, it was 20,835.—It is, therefore, only the average at the end of these two periods, that furnishes any evidence in the present question.

It is again objected, that *Pancras* and *Marybone*, two of the most populous parishes in London, are not included in the bills.—In answer to this, it is enough to say, that there were at the Revolution twelve * other parishes omitted; and that

---

* These parishes were St. John Wapping, added to the bills in 1698.—St. Mary le Strand, added in 1726.—St. George Hanover-Square, Christ Church Spitalfields, St. George Ratcliffe-Highway, and St. George the Martyr, added in 1729.—St. Ann, Limehouse, in 1730.—St. George, Bloomsbury, and St. John, Westminster, in 1731.—St. John, Southwark, and St. Luke, Old-Street, in 1733.—St. Matthew, Bethnal-Green, in 1746.

these

these omissions, together with the omissions of the burials among Dissenters, must, probably, have occasioned *then* much greater deficiencies in the bills than exist *now*. In these twelve parishes there were buried, in the years immediately succeeding those in which they were taken into the bills, 5000 annually. In *Pancras* and *Marybone*, the annual burials for ten years, ending in 1772, were 1041. See *Treatise on Reversionary Payments*, p. 204, 3d Edit.—It is, therefore, of little consequence in the present enquiry, that these two parishes are out of the bills. The increase of buildings has, by no means, been confined to *them*. It has extended itself to most of the principal parishes *within* the bills; and yet the number of burials is considerably lower than it was when this increase begun. The increase, therefore, has been merely an increase of buildings, arising from luxury; and this has been distinctly exhibited to us in that part of London which lies within the walls, where, though the number of houses cannot be much less, the burials have sunk gradually from 3139 (the annual medium at the Revolution) to 1428, the annual medium for five years ending in 1779.

It has been farther observed, that London is healthier now than it was. See fifth Letter to Lord Carlisle, p. 61. This probably

bably may have had some effect in diminishing the burials; but it could not produce a diminution of any consequence, compared with that which has taken place. London is not now, in this respect, very different from what it was seventeen years ago; and yet, even within this period, the burials have fallen near a fifth. The rate of mortality, or the value of lives in London, (that is, its healthiness) is determined with precision, by tables of observation formed from the proportions of the numbers dying at all ages. See Observations on *Reversionary Payments*, Chap. III. Essay IV.—But these tables, whether they are formed from the bills as they are *at present*, or as they were *fifty years ago*, will give the values of lives nearly the same; but yet very different from the values of lives determined, in the same method, from registers of mortality in small towns, and country parishes and villages. The truth seems to be, that though London must be healthier now, than it was when the inhabitants were more crowded together; yet the principal causes which shorten life in great towns, (namely, the irregular modes of living and the foulness of the air) having continued much the same, the law according to which life wastes, and the values of lives in London, have not sensibly varied.

It is also objected, that the bills are very erroneous—but the observation just made, demonstrates that they are not erroneous in the degree which is often supposed. Were they so, the values of lives deduced from them would be continually varying, which is not the case. They are, indeed, *defective*; but in consequence of a *great decrease* of Dissenters, they are less so than they used to be.

The fluctuation of London from the RESTORATION to the present time, may, in some measure, be collected from the following table:

Annual medium of burials for five years ending in 1664, when, besides other omissions, 17 parishes, including *Marybone* and *Pancras*, were omitted in the bills — — —	17,019
Annual medium for 5 years ending at 1689, 14 parishes omitted	22,742
Annual medium for 5 years ending at 1698, or at the conclusion of King William's war, 13 parishes omitted — —	20,487

Annual

Annual medium for 5 years, ending

                      in 1715—22,177
              *   in 1725—26,512
Three parishes omitted in 1739—26,039
Marybone and Pancras
only omitted   —   in 1748—23,884
                     in 1760—19,839
                     in 1765—23,992
                     in 1770—22,688
                     in 1777—21,087
                     in 1779—20,743

I have

---

* With this table, let the following account of the quantity of coals imported to London be compared.

                                            Chaldrons.

Annual medium for 3 years, ending in 1715—382,629
                                in 1725—460,138
                                in 1739—469,786
                                in 1748—476,902
                                in 1760—500,343
                                in 1765—584,856
                                in 1770—621,477
                                in 1777—683,457
                        Single year 1778—637,744

It appears, from hence, that between 1760 and 1777, the confumption of coals in London increafed fo faft, as at laft to exceed the confumption *fifty years* ago near one half, though the burials were then near 6000 *per ann.* more than they have been lately. It is remarkable, that this great increafe in the confumption of coals, happened at the very period when from other evidence (the increafe of buildings, increafed produce of the taxes, &c.) it appears, that luxury became particularly prevalent in

the

I have chosen to bring these particulars to view, because they may help to illustrate some of the preceding observations. Were we to judge from the splendid shew which the new buildings round London make, we could not avoid believing, that there never was a time when it was so populous. But splendour and refinement have never favoured population. The state in which mankind increase most, is that in which they lead simple lives, are most on an equality, and least acquainted with artificial wants. Luxury in Society renders it a rank soil, which favours the growth only of noxious plants and weeds.—In p. 29, I have mentioned this, among the other causes, which have produced the destruction which has

the nation.—The late improvements in agriculture, the cultivation of barren wastes, &c. have been mentioned to prove that our population has increased; but this is the same kind of argument with the increase of buildings and of the consumption of coals in London, for the increase of London.

It may deserve to be further mentioned here, that the increase of coaches has kept pace with the increase of the consumption of coals in London; for the annual medium of the duty of 1*l.* per wheel on carriages, for two years ending 1750, was 56,091*l.*—In 1761, the same medium was 62,513*l.*—In 1768, it was increased to 75,132*l.*—And in 1778, to 94,002*l.*

taken

taken place among our people. But Mr. Eden seems to think, that none of these causes have any great effect; and, if he is right, a country may be growing populous, in which they all operate to a degree scarcely ever before known in any country. It would be to little purpose to enter into a discussion of this subject. I will, therefore, only observe, that due attention has never been given to one of the causes I have mentioned; I mean, the very disproportionate size of our capital. Towns in general, and great towns in particular, do more towards obstructing the increase of mankind, than all plagues, famines, and wars; and they have been generally largest in the declining periods of states. I have often thought, with pity and surprise, of the zeal with which Sir William Petty, and after him Mr. Maitland, contended in opposition to some French writers for the superiority of London to Paris, or any other city in the world. They did not consider, that they were only maintaining that England had a greater evil in it than any other kingdom.

In offering these remarks, I have no other intention, than to contribute the little in my power to inform the nation of its true state.

ftate. I think this, in the prefent inftance, of particular importance; for if, indeed, there has been fuch a progreffive decreafe in the numbers of our people as the facts on which I have infifted feem to prove, the worft internal evils are operating among us; and all poffible means ought to be employed to remove them.

I hope I fhall not do wrong, if, with views of the fame kind, I take this opportunity to mention a few more particulars, in which my ideas of our fituation differ from Mr. Eden's.

He is unwilling to allow that we have any one mark of decay upon us. The *lofs of trade*, and *diminifhed refources*, as well as a *decreafe of population*, he enumerates among *the chimeras which haunt the joylefs imaginations of fome fpeculative men among us.* ——I fhall think it ftrange if, after perufing the foregoing remarks, any one can think this a cenfure juftly applicable to thofe who think our population has declined. That our trade alfo has declined, can fcarcely be doubted, by thofe who will recollect, that we have loft the *Mediterranean*, the *African*, the *Spanifh*, a confiderable part of the *Irifh*, and, above all, the *North American* trade.

I muft

APPENDIX. 65

I muſt add, that the *Newfoundland* fiſhery in particular (our great nurſery of ſeamen, and the very trade which we have endeavoured to extend by deſtroying the *New-England* fiſhery) is ſo much diminiſhed, as to be in the way to total and irreparable ruin.

Mr. Eden's chief argument for the proſperous ſtate of our trade, is taken from the productiveneſs of the Cuſtoms for the laſt year. The truth is, that the annual payments into the Exchequer from the Cuſtoms, which, for five years before 1776, were 2.521,768*l.* had fallen in 1776 to 2.460,402*l.* in 1777 to 2.199,105*l.* and in 1778 to 2.131,458*l.*; but that, in 1779, they had riſen to 2.502.273*l.* The cauſes of the advance in the laſt year were, the addition of 5 *per cent.* to all the cuſtoms, a new tax upon wines in 1778, an extraordinary importation of Portugal wines in 1779, and particularly, the captures of our privateers, and the importation from the northern countries of naval ſtores, which, when imported from the colonies, *leſſened* the revenue by *bounties*, but now *increaſe* it by the payment of high duties. The laſt of theſe cauſes, though it helps the revenue, has plainly the moſt pernicious operation; and, in general, it may be obſerved, that the cuſtoms being drawn from our importations, their moſt flourishing state is consistent with a state of public affairs the most threatening.—During the last peace, the annual produce of the customs increased near *half a million*; but this increase has been the effect of a most unfavourable change in the state of our trade; a change, which, since the commencement of our disputes with the colonies, has been growing every year more and more conspicuous and alarming. To speak more plainly; while luxury has been keeping up our importations, and increasing the revenue, our exportations have been decreasing to such a degree, as to make our trade an evil, which supplies artificial wants, and feeds vice and extravagance at the expence of the treasure and strength of the kingdom. A proper attention to the following table will illustrate and prove these assertions.

Annual average of	Imports.	Exports.	Excess.
in 1738 and 1739	7.634,166	10.892,430	3.258,264
1747 and 1748	7.626,582	11.896,741	4.270,159
1756 and 1757	8.607,460	12.977,962	4.370,502
1761 and 1762	9.207,069	15.250,000	6.043,000
1770 and 1771	12.519,466	15.713,899	3.194,434
1774 and 1775	13.412,030	15.559,350	2.147,320
1776	11.696,754	13.729,731	2.032,977
1777	11.841,577	12.653,363	0.811,786

Of the imports and exports in 1778 and 1779, I know no more than what Mr. Eden has told the public, " that in January last

" the accounts of them were not adjusted;
" but that there was good reason to believe
" that their average might be safely esti-
" mated by the account for 1777." Fifth
Letter to Lord Carlisle, p. 25. *

There are several melancholy truths which must force themselves on the reflection of those, who will compare the latter part of this table with the former part; but my present views allow me only to point out the demonstration it affords of the deplorable effects of this war. It appears, that both our exportations and importations have been diminished; but the former so much more than the latter, as to produce a *certainty* that we are now carrying on a losing trade. It is universally known, that the Custom-House entries give the importations *less*, and the exportations *greater*, than they are. The single article of smuggled tea (amounting, according to the estimate mentioned by Mr. Eden †, to a million *per annum*) when added to the imports, will

---

* Since the former edition of this tract, I have learnt that the *imports* for 1778 were 10.086,536*l.*; and the *exports* 11.507,525*l.* ——The latter, in 1774, were 15.916,343*l.*; and the average for four years ending in 1774 was *sixteen millions*. The exports, therefore, have decreased *four millions and a half*. An account of this decrease in some of the chief branches of our trade will be given at the end of the Appendix.

† Fifth Letter to Lord Carlisle, p. 36.

make them almoſt equal to the exports. How greatly then would they exceed the exports, were all other ſmuggled articles added?—Nothing can be more pernicious, than ſuch a ſtate of trade to a kingdom which has ſuch a debt to ſupport as we have, and a tribute of about a million and a half *per annum* to pay to foreigners.—What renders this a conſideration yet more mortifying is, that it appears from the preceding table, that during the wars which begun in 1740 and 1755, our trade went on uniformly increaſing; and that at the end of the laſt war in particular, it was riſen to its higheſt pitch, and muſt have brought in a very large favourable balance, which contributed to replace the treaſure carried out, kept money at a moderate intereſt, and enabled government to proſecute the war with vigour, and to finiſh it with dignity and honour. The reverſe, in every reſpect, is true of the *preſent* war. It appears, that the firſt approaches of it have operated on our trade like the graſp of death; and that now, inſtead of bringing *in*, as our trade uſed to do, a conſtant ſupply of treaſure in return for our manufactures, it is continually carrying *out* our treaſure, and uniting with the demands of foreigners from our funds, and the expence of of armies in distant countries, in draining and impoverishing us *.

It will be asked, how it comes to pass, that a state of affairs so detrimental, is not more felt in a diminution of the revenue; in an unfavourable course of foreign exchanges; and in a scarcity of cash, attended with difficulties in raising money by public loans?——The answer to this enquiry is obvious. Distress has not yet forced us to any great retrenchment of luxury; and the exertions of the war, the profits of contracts, and the successes of our cruisers, have enriched many individuals, and occasioned an extraordinary expenditure, which has kept up the revenue. Remittances of balances due to our merchants withdrawing from trade; the sale of French sugars, and other prize goods abroad; and the subscriptions of foreigners to our loans, have prevented the course of exchange from becoming unfavourable. The high interest given by government for money, draws all that can be collected of it from trade, and land and private securities. But above all;

* Mr. Eden, in his Fifth Letter to Lord Carlisle, p. 24. has acknowledged, that our export trade has suffered a great diminution; and he seems to think this an effect which could not but arise from the present war. But why, in our two former wars, did just the contrary effect take place?

our paper credit fupplying us with the moft* convenient kind of money, we can fpare our coin, which is now become an incumbrance generally avoided, and of ufe only to make up odd fums, and to carry on fmall traffic.

But to proceed to fome obfervations of a different nature.

The laft war was attended with an expence which far outwent the experience of all former wars; but it produced an increafe of commerce and of territory, which raifed the kingdom to a fituation of dignity and eminence which aftonifhed and alarmed *Europe*. The effect of the prefent war on the dignity of the kingdom, and the extent of its territories, I leave to the forrowful reflexion of the reader. My prefent purpofe is only to contraft, in a few particulars, the *expence* of it with the expence of the laft war.

At the end of 1762 (the laft and moft expenfive year of the laft war) the navy-debt, including tranfport fervice, was 5.929,124*l*. and the increafe of it within the year, 2.157,148*l*.—At the end of 1779,

* In the courfe of the year, from Lady-day 1780 to Lady-day 1781, TWENTY-FIVE MILLIONS AND A HALF, confifting of the loan, the taxes, the lottery, and the vote of credit, will be paid into the *Exchequer*. This, though a fum which, *in coin*, did it exift in the nation, could be conveyed to the Exchequer only in carts, will be taken thither in pocket-books.

the

the navy-debt was 8.357,877. The increase of it within the year was 3.178,877; and its increase in the present year (1780) will not probably be much less than three millions and a half *.

In 1762 the extraordinaries of the army amounted to 3.080,000*l*.—In 1779, they amounted to 3.418,000*l*. †

In 1762, the public borrowed TWELVE MILLIONS at an interest of FOUR AND A HALF *per cent.* ‡.—In the present year the public has borrowed TWELVE MILLIONS, but at an interest of SIX *per cent.*

The whole expence, ordinary and extraordinary, of 1762, was TWENTY MILLIONS

* See Note A at the end.

† These extraordinaries, from Christmas 1761, to Feb. 19, 1763, that is, for a year and 55 days, were 3.540,005*l*. including the vote of credit. Deduct 460,000*l*. for 55 days, and the remainder, or 3.080,000*l*. will be the extraordinaries for 1762. See Public Accounts of Services and Grants, by Sir CHARLES WHITWORTH, p. 68.

A million was granted in 1762 (and also in the preceding year) towards paying for bread, forage, &c. for the combined army under Prince FERDINAND. But this, if I am not mistaken, was a grant or allowance for a service to be performed in the year in which the grant was made and provided for in the supplies of that year. It cannot, therefore, be reckoned an *extraordinary*, which is an exceeding of grants for specific services; or a debt contracted without the consent of parliament, and provided for in the supplies of some subsequent year.

‡ See Note B.

AND

AND A HALF *.—The whole expence of this year, exclusive of the interest of the public debts, will be TWENTY-THREE MILLIONS AND A HALF.

The unfunded debt at the end of the last war was FIFTEEN MILLIONS AND A HALF †.—The unfunded debt at Christmas next will be TWENTY-ONE MILLIONS AND A HALF.

The last war increased the national debt near SEVENTY-ONE MILLIONS AND A HALF ‡.—The present war has already made a further addition to it of SIXTY-FOUR MILLIONS; and at Christmas next will make it up nearly to a HUNDRED AND NINETY-SIX MILLIONS.

It should be remembered, that this war is but *beginning*; that it will probably last for *years*, as Mr. Eden intimates; and that the more years it continues, the greater the expence of every year will become. To what then is the expence of it likely to grow; and HOW LONG SHALL WE BE ABLE TO BEAR IT?—This very dark prospect will be

---

* See Note C. In these sums is included the deficiencies of the new taxes, and of the land and malt-tax, which, in 1762, amounted to 393,567 *l.*; but in 1779 to near a million.

† See Note D.

‡ See Additional Observations on Civil Liberty, Part III. Sect. II. p. 147. See also Note E.

rendered

rendered darker, if we consider how much we were loaded before the war begun, and that we are entering into it with almost all the burdens of former wars upon us.

It is often said, that the great men in opposition want to force themselves into power. But it is scarcely possible they should be so foolish.—Involved in a most expensive and hazardous contest with two of the first powers in *Europe*—surrounding nations *hostile* to us in a degree which leaves us without a *friend*, or even a *well-wisher* * among them — a consider-

---

* " The mother country now rises to offensive war against all these combined powers; not only without an ally, but almost without a *well-wisher*, from the extraordinary jealousy her greatness had inspired." See An Account of some Particulars relative to the meeting at York, on Thursday, Dec. 30, 1779. By Leonard Smelt, Esq;—We have a recent proof of this in the confederacy now forming among the neutral powers of *Europe*, for the purpose of establishing a new maritime code of laws, and making the ocean *free*; or, in other words, for rendering themselves general carriers of goods and stores for our enemies, and depriving us of our long boasted empire of the sea.—" Powers (says *Montesquieu*) established on commerce may subsist long in *mediocrity*; but are not durable in *grandeur*.——They raise themselves imperceptibly; but when they become so great as to draw attention and to signalize themselves, they excite jealousy; and all other powers will endeavour to deprive such a nation of a superiority which it has acquired, as it were, by surprize."—*Causes of the Rise and Fall of the Roman Empire*, Chap. iv.——*Montesquieu*

considerable part of our strength torn from us, and converted against us—our resources mortgaged beyond the hope or possibility of redemption—a debasing and wasteful luxury destroying public virtue, and producing a dissipation and venality in *private* life, and an extravagance in the expenditure of *public* money, which were † never equalled —and, at the same time, a monstrous debt pressing us, and increasing rapidly, without any other support than a frail credit, which the first disaster or panic may break.—— In SUCH CIRCUMSTANCES, wonderful must be that ambition which can render the management of our affairs an object of contention.—No enemy of our present ministers can wish them a greater punishment, than their *continuance* in power to conduct the war a few years, must prove. —Mr. Eden, indeed, thinks they are able

had a particular view in this observation to *Carthage*; and he introduces it with another observation worth mentioning. " The *Spaniards*, he says, had been op-
" pressed under the government of Carthage. This
" made them regard the *Romans*, when they entered
" *Spain*, as their deliverers; the consideration of which,
" and of the vast sums the Carthaginians spent in the
" war under which they sunk, may convince us that
" injustice is always the worst policy."

† See a striking representation of this extravagance in a pamphlet lately published, and entitled, Facts addressed to Landholders, stockholders, merchants, farmers, manufacturers, &c.

to extricate us. At a juncture of unparalleled embarrassment and danger, he has undertaken to give us comfort. He exhorts us, taking things as we find them, to prosecute the war with vigour, assuring us that we have not upon us any symptoms of decay which should discourage us; that we can bear much more, and have still sufficient resources left *.

—— Entertaining other apprehensions, I have taken another course.—The difference between us is great; but there is one circumstance attending it, which, if I have been misled, will relieve me.—My representations will not be much regarded; or if they should, they can do harm only by putting the nation too much on its guard, and leading it to measures for recovering peace, and preserving its independence, which the necessity of its affairs does *not* require.

* In enumerating these resources, Mr. Eden (in his Four Letters, p. 101) has proposed one (mortgaging the peace revenue) to which we cannot have recourse, without the dissolution of all government; and expressed himself, I think, with too much doubt about *another* (the reduction of places, pensions, emoluments of office, &c.) to which the general expectation of the kingdom is directed; a resource with which our enemies are making war against us, in a manner that threatens us more than all their armies and navies; and which, while it bore a part of the expence of the war, would help to secure our liberties, and to *restore* the constitution.

—On the contrary, Mr. Eden's weight in the state, and his abilities and character, command attention; and the counsel he gives will be followed. Should it, therefore, happen that he is wrong, and that our situation is perilous in the degree I have represented, he has been urging us towards a precipice, and the consequences may prove fatal. —In this respect, we are like two persons observing a friend who totters under a burden plunging into a deep water, one of whom, believing that he is not in a condition to combat danger, calls upon him to come back: and the other, believing the contrary, advises him to go on. If he takes the former advice, he will, at worst, be only over-cautious. But if he takes the latter advice, and should find himself deceived, he will lose his life.

After all. Did I apprehend that we were in a situation which admitted of no retreat, I should, however I might lament the misconduct which has brought us to it, think myself bound to be silent. But our circumstances are not, I hope, so desperate. A retreat is, probably, still practicable by the same measure which would *certainly* have saved us not long ago—I mean, by withdrawing from that country where all our troubles have originated; and yielding to the

the colonies that blessing, which we are employing our armies to force from them, but which every country values above all blessings, and the loss of which we ourselves are now deprecating as the greatest calamity that can happen to us.

ACCOUNTS referred to in the preceding APPENDIX.

(A) *Calculation of the Increase of the Navy Debt in 1780, and of its probable Amount at the end of the year.*

FROM accounts laid before the House of Commons, it appears, that on the 30th of Sept. 1779, the navy-debt was 7.262,415*l*.; and on the 31st of December following, 8.357,877*l*. It increased, therefore, in three months, 1.095,462*l*.; or at the rate of 4.381,848*l*. in a year. From this increase, deduct a *million and a half* ordered to be paid off, and included in the grants for this year. The remainder (or 2.881,848*l*.) added to 8.357,877*l*. will give 11.239,725*l*. the amount of the navy-debt at Christmas next; supposing it to increase this year as it did in the last quarter of the last year.

It deserves to be farther mentioned, that the navy-debt having increased 1.379,153*l*. in 1777—2.175,487*l*. in 1778—and 3.178,877*l*. in 1779, it seems not unreasonable to expect that it may increase above four millions in 1780.

Again; the Parliament has ordered for the service of this year 85,000 seamen, which makes the number to be maintained 15,000 *more* than it ever was; and will therefore produce a proportionably greater increase of debt.

I mentioned these facts in the former edition of this tract, as evidences to prove that the amount and increase of the navy-debt at *Christmas* next will not be less than the sums now stated. But I have lately found reason to suspect, that the number of seamen in service this year will not in reality be greater than it was last year, and that the pay provided for the *additional* number will be only

only an *additional* fupply for maintaining the fame number of feamen; and therefore, inftead of accelerating, may retard the increafe of the navy-debt. For this reafon, and to avoid the danger of exaggeration, I *now* chufe to ftate the amount and increafe of this debt at *Chriftmas* next, at a *million* lefs than the fums given at the beginning of this note; that is, the *amount* at 10.239,725*l*. inftead of 11.239,725*l*. and the *increafe* at 3.381,848*l*. inftead of 4,381,848*l*.

(B) *Calculation of the different Rates of Intereft at which Government borrowed Twelve Millions in* 1762 *and* 1780.

In 1762 the public gave for TWELVE MILLIONS in money,

	£.
Firft, Twelve millions three *per cent.* ftock, worth, reckoning intereft at 4½ *per cent.* or the 3 *per cents* at 66⅔ — —	8.000,000
2. A fhort annuity of 120,000*l.* for 19 years, worth, at the fame rate of intereft, 12⅗ years purchafe — —	1.512,000
3. A long annuity for 98 years of 120,000*l.* worth, at the fame rate of intereft, 21 9/16 years purchafe — —	2.628,000
4. Commencement of intereft before the completion of payment, and difcount (amounting to 46,539*l.*) for prompt payment — — —	200,000
	12.340,000

N. B. This loan was fettled in Dec. 1761, and the intereft upon it began from Jan. 5th following. The value of this ftock and the premiums annexed, at 5 *per cent.* is 11.219,000*l.* or 6½ *per cent. lefs* than the money paid for them.

In

In 1780 the public has given for TWELVE MILLIONS in money,

	£.
1. Twelve millions 4 *per cent.* stock, worth, reckoning interest at 6 *per cent.* —	8.000,000
2. A long annuity for 80 years of 217,500*l.* worth, reckoning interest at 6 *per cent.* 16½ years purchase, or — — See *Smart*'s Tables, or Table II. at the end of the *Treatise on Reversionary Payments*.	3.588,750
3. Commencement of interest before payment, discounts for prompt payment, and profits of a lottery — —	450,000
Total —	12.038,750

N. B. This loan was settled in March 1780, but the interest upon it began from Jan. 5th preceding. The value of this stock, and the premiums annexed, is, at 5 *per cent.* 14.313,000*l.* or 19¼ *per cent. more* than the money paid, besides a larger profit at redemption.

(C) *Comparison of the whole Expence of* 1762, *with the whole Expence of* 1780.

	£.
Supplies in 1762, including 1.500.000*l.* old exchequer bills, vote of credit for 1761, and the new vote for 1762.—See Public Accounts of Services and Grants, by Sir Charles Whitworth — —	18,625,046
Add the increase of navy-debt within the year, beyond the debt discharged *	322,123
Add the value of the *premium* given to the lenders of twelve millions. See last note	4.140,000
	23.087,169
Deduct old Exchequer bills renewed, and the vote of credit for 1761 —	2.500,000
Remains the expence of the year —	20.587,169

---

* Navy-debt on the 31st of Dec. 1762	—	5.929,124
Ditto, Dec. 1761	—	5.607,001
Difference	—	£. 0.322,123

Supplies

	£.
Supplies in 1780, exclusive of the vote of credit for 1779 *	19,678,250
Add vote of credit for 1780	1,000,000
Add the increase of navy-debt beyond 1,500,000 *l.* included in the supplies. See note (A)	1,881,848
Add the value (at 5 *per cent.*) of the *premium* given to the lenders of twelve millions. See note (E)	4,263,000
	26,823,098
Deduct Exchequer bills renewed	3,400,000
Remains expence of the year, exclusive of the interest of the public debts	23,423,098

(D) *Comparison of the Unfunded Debt at the end of the last war, with the Unfunded Debt at the end of the present year; supposing the war not to be continued beyond it.*

	£.
Navy-debt at Christmas 1780. See note (A)	10,239,725
Exchequer bills	3,400,000
Extraordinaries of the army, reckoned not to exceed those in 1779	3,418,000
Extraordinaries of the ordnance, reckoned likewise not to exceed those in 1779	591,000
Anticipation of the sinking fund	500,000
Calling home troops †, and many expences which cannot immediately cease with the operations of war	3,500,000
Total of unfunded debt at Christmas next	21,648,725
Unfunded debt at the end of the last war	15,639,793

See Additional Observations on Civil Liberty, p. 145.

* This was the amount of these supplies, as they were stated in March last by Lord North in opening the budget.

† This is the sum which was borrowed in 1763 for discharging these expences; and it is included in the unfunded debt at the end of the last war, as here stated. The preliminaries of the last peace were signed at Paris, Nov. 3, 1762.— The navy in 1763 consisted of 14,000 sailors more; and the army in British pay (for near a *third* of the year) of 82,000 men more, than the ordinary peace establishment.

(E) *Calculation of the amount of the National Debt, supposing the war not to be continued beyond the present year.*

	£.
Amount of the national debt in 1775, exclusive of the unfunded debt.—See Additional Observations on Civil Liberty, Part III. Sect. II.	132.343,051
Added in 1776, 1777, 1778 and 1779 — See Facts addressed to the Landholders, &c. Chap. II.	26,487,500
Four per cent. stock, created in 1780 *	12,000,000
Long annuity 1780 of 217,500*l.* for 80 years, which, though sold to the subscribers to the loan in 1780, at $16\frac{1}{2}$ years purchase, is worth, when money is at 5 *per cent.* $19\frac{3}{5}$ years purchase	4.263,000
Unfunded debt. See last Note	21.657,725
	196.751,276

* For this stock only *eight millions* were received (See note B); but the public is bound to return for it *twelve millions*. Such are our methods of borrowing.

ADDITIONAL ACCOUNTS.

IN P. 61, I have given an account of the annual importation of coals into London. In 1776 it was 697,608 chaldrons, and had increased gradually near 200,000 chaldrons in 17 years. In 1777 it was 692,034 chaldrons. In 1778 it was 637,744; and I am just now informed that in 1779 it was 590,765. In the two last years, therefore, it has decreased considerably, in consequence *perhaps* of some check which the decline of trade and the difficulties of the times have given to luxury.

ACCOUNTS referred to in Page 67.

AFRICA.

	Imports.	Exports.
In 1775	£. 67,328	£. 786,168
1776	99,674	470,779
1777	62,740	239,218
1778	81,951	154,086

IRELAND.

	Imports.	Exports.
In 1775	£. 1.486,325	£. 2.169,608
1776	1.516,532	2.178,227
1777	1.502,893	1.931,800
1778	1.360,688	1.470,671

HOLLAND.

HOLLAND.

	Imports.	Exports.
In 1775	£. 513,561	£. 1.887,400
1776	381,098	1.427,396
1777	581,632	1.080,644
1778	346,357	1.390,174

TURKEY.

	Imports.	Exports.
In 1775	£. 168,882	£. 226,997
1776	249,738	215,756
1777	225,586	177,214
1778	148,919	50,128

ITALY.

	Imports.	Exports.
In 1775	£. 818,171	£. 1.003,528
1776	910,354	873,448
1777	774,099	846,160
1778	395,742	555,532

ANTIGUA.

	Imports.	Exports.
In 1775	£. 353,563	£. 168,092
1776	297,535	169,436
1777	134,068	114,028
1778	160,635	107,344

JAMAICA.

	Imports.	Exports.
In 1775	£. 1.653,735	£. 786,728
1776	1.359,033	632,315
1777	1.303,289	536,574
1778	1.372,677	486,870

GRENADES.

	Imports.	Exports.
In 1775	£. 486,035	£. 139,946
1776	370,884	163,366
1777	360,088	95,209
1778	374,689	85,829

St. VINCENTS.

	Imports.	Exports.
In 1775	£. 164,199	£. 69,246
1776	135,919	45,993
1777	130,195	40,230
1778	112,252	25,914

DOMINICA.

	Imports.	Exports.
In 1775	£. 185,131	£. 62,945
1776	257,775	64,697
1777	177,397	47,230
1778	162,408	31,813

PORTUGAL.

	Imports.	Exports.
In 1775	£. 367,893	£. 632,989
1776	372,439	530,784
1777	382,708	554,449
1778	340,576	430,936

The Imports in this trade for the laſt 50 years have varied little; but the exports before 1765 uſed to be more than double thoſe here given.

GERMANY.

	Imports.	Exports.
In 1775	£. 660,763	£. 1,545,014
1776	666,080	1,460,776
1777	709,599	1,323,419
1778	588,198	1,214,929

FRANCE.

	Imports.	Exports.
In 1775	£. 67,481	£. 258,157
1776	56,865	178,319
1777	71,495	139,802
1778	23,260	29,411

SPAIN.

	Imports.	Exports.
In 1775	£. 564,386	£. 1.205,215
1776	561,071	1.191,477
1777	533,641	843,075
1778	415,702	980,352

The *Exports* to NOVA SCOTIA, for 1776, 1777, and 1778, were 245,036*l.* 934,164*l.* and 332,156*l.*; the *Imports* 6,529*l.* 8,030*l.* and 5,329*l.*———NEW-YORK, the *Exports* for the fame years refpectively were . . . . .*l.* 57,294*l.* 26,449*l.*; the *Imports* 2,318*l.* 8,429*l.* 16,192*l.* ——FLORIDA, *Exports* 174,175*l.* 137,607*l.* 64,165*l.* the *Imports* 30,628*l.* 48,322*l.* 48,236*l.*———This is all that, in thefe three years, remained of a trade with the colonies, which, before the America war, brought in (exclufive of the trade to *Canada*) a favourable balance of above a *million and a half* annually; the annual medium of *Exports* for four years ending in 1774, having been 3.039,042*l.*; and of *Imports* 1.354,563*l.*

The Reader is defired to correct the account in P. 66. of the Imports and Exports for 1777, which fhould have been as follows:

Imports £. 11.721,327—Exports £. 12.632,522——
Excefs, £. 911,194.

THE

[87]

THE addition of a hundred knights to reprefent the counties in parliament being a meafure now much talked of, I have, by the defire of fome friends, framed the following table for fhewing, as nearly as the nature of the cafe will allow, the additional number to which the population and confequence of each county would entitle it, were fuch a meafure carried into execution.

After allowing for SCOTLAND eight knights, becaufe in the fame proportion to a hundred that 45 is to 558, there would remain for ENGLAND and WALES *ninety-two*, out of which number

Middlefex, including LONDON and Weftminfter, would be entitled to	10
Yorkfhire	8
Norfolk	3
Devonfhire	3
Lancafhire	3
Suffolk	3
Surrey and Southwark	3
Somerfetfhire	3
Lincolnfhire	3
Kent	3
Effex	3
Gloucefterfhire	3
Wiltfhire, Worcefterfhire, Warwickfhire, Suffex, Hampfhire, Staffordfhire, Salop, Northamptonfhire, Cornwall, Chefhire, Durham, and Northumberland — two each	24
Leicefterfhire, Berkfhire, Bucks, Cambridgefhire, Bedfordfhire, Cumberland, Derbyfhire, Dorfetfhire, Herefordfhire, Hertfordfhire, Huntingdonfhire, Nottinghamfhire, Oxfordfhire, Monmouthfhire, Glamorganfhire, and five other Welch counties — one each	20
Rutlandfhire, Weftmoreland, and fix Welch counties	0
	92

This diftribution was propofed in the former edition of this Tract. I have been fince favoured with fome remarks upon it, and I am fenfible that it may be liable to objections. I ftill think it, however, a proper diftribution; and, therefore, have chofen to continue it.

I shall take this opportunity to add, for the information of those who may have attended to the account of the gold coin in the *Introduction* to the two Tracts on Civil Liberty, p. 31, and in the Second Tract (Part II. Sect. I.) that about two millions of the coin brought in by the proclamations in 1773, 1774, and 1776, were purchased and melted into bars by the Bank; and that Mr. Eden says, (in his Fifth Letter, p. 40.) this sum is not included in the total (or 15.563,593*l.*) brought to account under those proclamations.

F I N I S.

AN

INQUIRY

INTO THE

Present State of Population in England and Wales;

AND THE PROPORTION

Which the present Number of Inhabitants bears to the Number at former Periods.

BY

WILLIAM WALES, F. R. S.

And Master of the Royal Mathematical School in Christ's Hospital.

LONDON,
Printed by G. BIGG, Denmark Court, Strand,
For C. NOURSE, in the Strand.
M,DCC,LXXXI.

Republished in 1973 by Gregg International Publishers Limited
Westmead, Farnborough, Hants., England

AN

INQUIRY into the PRESENT STATE

OF

POPULATION IN ENGLAND.

THE subject of the following sheets is obviously of such great concern to every one who has the prosperity of his country at heart, that if the importance of the subject were alone a sufficient apology for a man's printing his thoughts on it, I should want none for making them public. But I have always thought that the more important any subject was, the more careful every man ought to be that he publishes nothing relating to it which may not answer some useful purpose; much more ought he to be careful that what he publishes may not be productive of a bad one.

one: and, from considerations, like these, I am very unwilling to hazard my reputation, small the stock of it may be, without endeavouring to point out which way I think this publication may be useful.

Truth ought at all times to be the object of our researches; but it is a truth, notorious even to a proverb, that it ought not, at all times, to be made public. And surely, at no time whatsoever could publications, which tend to depress the spirit of the nation, be more improperly introduced than now, when we are surrounded by numerous and powerful enemies, through whom we must fight our way, or sink into the most humiliating state of insignificancy, or perhaps contempt, amongst the nations of Europe. But if publications of this nature, stampt with the authority of persons of great respect and influence, be built on partial or false information, it becomes the duty of every member of society to use his utmost endeavours to stop the effects of such misrepresentations. And those gentlemen, who have written with good intentions, will be pleased to see truth established on either side of the question in so respectable a branch of human knowledge; and, as fellow subjects, must receive great satisfaction

tion in difcovering that the ftate of population, at this period, and that part of our refources which depend on it, are not fo bad as they had been led to conceive them.

I was firft induced to fet on foot this inquiry, by reading the ingenious Effay on the fame fubject which was publifhed at the end of *Mr. Morgan's* Book on Affurances, in the Spring of the year 1779. The ftate of the kingdom, there laid before us, is fo deplorable, that I think it muft affect every one who reads it. I foon difcovered that no very material objections could be made to the calculations in that performance; and the objections which have hitherto been made to it, only fhew that the author is not to be confuted on the ground which he has chofen to ftand on. But it was no lefs evident to me, that the returns which are made by the window-furveyors are by no means fufficient to fupport calculations of this nature, even where the chargeable houfes are returned with the greateft exactnefs. Cottages are feldom returned; and but in fome places when they are demanded, as was the cafe in the year 1777: and, where they are returned, it is generally from conjecture, or from fome old duplicate, which was, perhaps, the conjecture of 20 or 30 years before. I am very credibly informed, that the true number of the cottages were purpofely withheld in fome parts of Yorkfhire, Nottinghamfhire, and others of the midland counties; and it is very likely in more places than thefe, through an apprehenfion that they were then required with a view of extending the tax on windows, or forming a new one. And to a fufpicion of this nature I attribute the obftruction which I met with, in my endeavours to collect the number of houfes, which will be mentioned bye and bye.

With refpect to the calculations, which are founded on the encreafe or decreafe of the excife and cuftoms, it may juftly be faid, that a man muft fee and know but little of what paffes in the kingdom, at this time, who is not aware that the pernicious practice of fmuggling is carried to too great a length, not to be moft feverely felt in thefe two articles of the revenue; and, therefore, that no dependance can be placed in calculations founded on them.

Convinced, as I was, that no dependance could be placed on calculations, founded on either of the two confiderations which have been difcuffed above, and that a tolerable

degree

degree of exactness could be expected only from an actual survey, made on the spot, by persons in no wise interested in this affair, or any others which have the least connection with it, or with any article of the revenue; I began to consider in what way authentic information, of this kind, though of a more limited extent, might be procured. I observed that the advocates for a depopulation suppose that the destruction has fallen chiefly, and of late years, wholly upon the cottages; and that it was allowed, on all hands, that the principal manufacturing and trading towns have *increased*; and some of them, as Manchester, Leeds, Birmingham, Seffield, Liverpool, and Bristol, most amazingly. It was moreover obvious, that many cottages would not be found in large towns where there are no manufactures; consequently the desolation must have happened chiefly in small country towns and villages; in which places I knew it would be very easy for a person, who lived on the spot, to inform himself exactly of the present number of houses; and, if he had spent his whole time in the place, to recollect every material alteration which had been made in it for thirty or forty years past.

In consequence of these considerations, I addressed the following queries to every acquaintance which I had in the country, as well as to every other person that I could get recommended to.

1. The number of houses which there are now in the township, or village.

2. The number of houses there were in it about the year 1750.

3. The number of houses which have been built since that time, where none stood before.

4. The number of houses which have been suffered to decay, and become uninhabitable since 1750; in the place of which none have yet been rebuilt.

5. By how many the total number of houses have been lessened by putting two, or more, into one.

6. By how many the total number of houses have been increased by separating large old houses into smaller ones.

7. The number of houses that are assessed to the window tax.

8. Whether, in the several surveys that have been made, but especially in 1777, the surveyor returned the number of houses which were *not* assessed, as well as those which were.

Lastly,

Laſtly, To take the opinion of two or three ſenſible perſons, who have lived the whole time in the village, &c. whether, ſince that period, the number of the inhabitants has increaſed or decreaſed.

To theſe letters I had many anſwers, and ſome procured me the information which I wanted, as will be ſeen farther on. But it would be almoſt incredible, were I to relate the oppoſition which this ſcheme of numbering the houſes met with. My friends, in ſome parts of the country, were aſſailed, not only with perſuaſions, but by threatenings of every kind; ſuch as loſs of employment, proſecutions, and even blows. The letters which I have received from ſome of them are ſo extraordinary, that, I confeſs, I ſhould almoſt have doubted the truth of them, if I had not experienced the ſame treatment myſelf, in ſome places, during a tour that I made laſt ſummer on this buſineſs. In a large manufacturing town, in the Weſt Riding of Yorkſhire, I was beſet by a crowd of women, who had taken an alarm from the nature of my inquiries, and perhaps, eſcaped, the fate of *Orpheus*, by whiſpering one of the good women, who had ſet upon us, that his Majeſty might poſſibly ſettle ſmall annuities on every

poor

poor man and his wife, who brought up a certain number of children, to be useful members of society. The news flew like wildfire, and I met with no farther opposition there.

I cannot forbear relating another rebuff which I met with in the course of these inquiries, because of the singularity of it. I had written on this subject, to a very intimate friend, a dissenter of the independant church, without receiving any answer to it; but on a second application, rather more pressing, he vouchsafed to write as follows. " Sir, I have received your two letters of the 2d and 15th instant, and, in answer to them, refer you to 1. *Chron. chap.* xxi. *v.* 1." It will be readily imagined that I was not long in looking for my answer, nor without surprise, when I read, " And Satan stood up against Israel, and provoked *David* to number Israel." To this laconic epistle I replied, " that he had not only mistaken persons, but situations; and that he was so far from being in the situation of *David*, and I in that the of Devil, tempting him to number the people, as he supposed, that I was really David's representative, preparing to stop the sword of the destroying Angel which had lately

lately made such a dreadful devastation amongst us. My friend was convinced of his mistake, and has since furnished me with a great variety of the most useful information.

The opposition which I met with in making inquiries of this kind, convinced me that I should never be able to carry them to any great extent; and happening to recollect some hints which I had formerly seen in the Philosophical Transactions, relating to the use which might be made of parish registers for this purpose, I immediately set about making collections of that kind, and soon found that I had now to do with men of more enlarged minds, and of a more liberal way of thinking. I should indeed be greatly wanting, in gratitude, if I did not acknowledge, that I have met with the utmost readiness to assist me wherever I have applied; and I am assured, from my own experience, that a general invitation to the clergy, and the appointment of a proper place for the reception of their communications, would procure materials sufficient to determine this arduous problem, in political arithmetic, with great certainty. Those, therefore, who may find themselves disposed to look on this publication as incomplete, and not sufficient to exhibit a true state of the nation, with regard to the increase or decrease of its inhabitants, will do well to assist in collecting the registers from a greater number of parishes, rather than attempt to contradict what these appear to prove, by arguments drawn from such imperfect data as the returns of the window surveyors; or from accounts which are most glaringly wrong.* What I have given will shew how much a single person, who is disposed to do it, may perform; and I hope yet to be able to add much more.

I shall deliver the materials which I have collected in the order they came to hand; namely, the information I received concerning the number of houses, and the comparisons of those accounts, with the returns made by the window surveyors first,

proceeding

---

* It has been said, from Dr. *Davenant*, who formed his estimate from the Hearth-Books, that the number of houses in *London*, *Westminster*, and all *Middlesex* were 111215, in the year 1690; and that they were no more than 90570, according to the returns of the window-surveyors, in 1777, including also the Borough of *Southwark*. But no unprejudiced person will suppose that there were more *houses* in *London*, *Westminster*, and *Middlesex*, 80 or 90 years ago, than there are, at this time, in *London*, *Westminster*, *Middlesex*, and *Southwark*, whatever the number of *inhabitants* might be at these two periods.

proceeding from the north towards the south; and the abstracts of the parish registers afterwards. But before I say any thing concerning the kingdom in general, I beg leave to state a few circumstances, which relate to the present number of the inhabitants of the city of *London,* as well as to the proportion which that number bears to the number of them at the Revolution, and also to the number at some other periods between these two: because I am persuaded these points have not been properly represented before.

With respect to the former, namely, the absolute number of the inhabitants, I think it an object of small importance, when compared with the other; for whatever their number might be at the time of the Revolution, we are well assured, now at least, that no material inconvenience arose from it; and, consequently, unless that number be greatly altered since, we may presume none can arise from it now: especially if I shew, as I trust I shall, that other parts of the kingdom are not greatly changed for the worse: beside, this point is more difficult to determine than the other, with any tolerable degree of exactness: I am therefore ready to acquiesce in the number, at which they have been stated by the very ingenious *Dr. Price*, in his Essay on this subject, printed in his *Observations on Reversionary Payments*; that is somewhere from 591,580 to 671,580. But I must here observe, that the reason which he gives for thinking both these numbers too high, appears, to me, at least, not well founded. He supposes there is a greater defect in the baptisms than there is in the burials, and supports his opinion by very forcible arguments. On this supposition the number of inhabitants will appear to be less than if we suppose the defect in each equal: he therefore concludes that the number of inhabitants are less. But it may be remarked, that if the births are considerably more defective than the burials, the expectation of life, by which the number of those births is multiplied, will be greater, and especially at this time, when the number of the births approaches so much nearer to the number of the burials than they did at the period, from which Dr. *Price* has deduced the expectation of life which he makes use of; and I cannot help expressing my surprize, that this circumstance should escape the observation of such an able and attentive computor.

But

But to shew that I do not acquiesce in the above conclusion without reason, I shall compute the number of inhabitants two different ways, according to my own notion of things.

1. In the year 1737, *Mr. Maitland*, by a very careful and exact survey, the particulars of which are related in his *History of London*, vol. 2, p. 719, &c. made the number of houses 95,968. I believe we shall not exceed the truth, if we allow that 4032 have been added to that number since his time; and if so, their present number is 100,000. It appears from p. 205 of *Dr. Price's Observations on reversionary payments, 3d edit.* that when a survey of that part of the parish of *Pancras*, which joins to *London*, was taken in March, 1772, there were in it very near 7 persons and one-third to every house. But because a few of those persons, who live in and about *Percy Street* and *Charlotte Street*, may leave town in summer, we will allow that two persons out of every three houses in that part of the parish which was surveyed, leave *London* for half a year; and then the average of persons to a house, for the whole year, will be exactly seven. The same ingenious gentleman mentions another parish in *London*, at p. 8, of his *Essay on the Population of England*, in which

the

the number of persons to a house were 6. Let the medium between this number and the former be taken, which is 6½, and multiplied by 100,000, the number of houses, it will give 650,000 for the number of inhabitants. I am firmly persuaded, that neither the number of houses, nor the number of persons to a house, here given, is too great: the latter I am convinced is not. For notwithstanding *London* has of late years spread itself over much more ground, than it formerly stood on, there is a great number of houses, to my knowledge, which contain two, three, and some even four families each; which any one may be convinced of by examining the parishes of *Clerkenwell, Old Street, Spittlefields, White-chapel,* &c. &c. and it is much to be wished, that many more families than do, had it in their power to indulge themselves in the LUXURY of a single house, were it ever such a small one.

2. It will be shewn presently, that the births, according to the bills of mortality, are now 18698, on a medium, annually, and the burials 22227: they therefore exceed the births by 3529, which is not $\frac{1}{6}$th part. Between the years 1759 and 1768 the burials exceeded the births, according to the bills, by

by more than ¼th part of themselves, and accordingly the *Rev. Dr. Price* formed his tables of the probabilities of lives, in *London*, on a supposition that the burials did exceed the births by one-fourth part,* allowing the overplus to compensate for the greater defect, which may be supposed to be in the births than in the burials brought into the bills. And, according to these tables, the expectation of life, which belongs to a child just born, is somewhat less than twenty years and three quarters. But it has been shewn that the burials do not now exceed the births by one-sixth part; and, probably, when a proper allowance is made for the greater defect in the births than in the burials, the latter may not exceed the former by more than a twelfth or thirteenth part of themselves; and this may be made to appear in the following manner.

Mr. Maitland, in the year 1729, discovered 2620 omissions in the account of burials, given in the bills, rejecting those which were buried in the parishes of *Pancrass* and *Marybone*, which I have brought to account in another place; we cannot add less than 1000 to

---

* See Observations on Reversionary Payments, p. 248, 1st. edit. or p. 253, 3d. edit.

to this number for emigrants, perfons who are carried to a greater diftance than he extended his refearches to, thofe who are not buried at all, and the greater numbers, which are buried out of *London* now than formerly; confequently, the addition to be made to the bills will be now 3620, and the true number of burials 25847. Dr. *Price* ftates the defect in the number of births, above that in the number of burials, at 2000. I do not think that defect now fo great as it was formerly; but the reafons, which the Doctor has given, convince me that it cannot be much lefs: we will fuppofe it 1750, and the whole defect in the births will be 5370, the true number of the births 24068, and the recruits from the country only 1779, or not quite $\frac{1}{14}$th of the burials. If this be a true ftate of the cafe, and it appears to me to be fo, the expectation of a child, juft born, muft be much greater than 20 years and three quarters, and approach very nearly to what it would be, if all that are buried were born in *London*, which expectation, by Dr. *Price*'s 12th table, is upwards of 25 years and three quarters. I I cannot ftop to calculate what it will be exactly, nor does the bufinefs merit it; but I conclude however, that it cannot be much

lefs

less than 24 years; and 24 × 24068 is 577.632, which would be the number of the inhabitants, if all who die in *London*, were born there: but it has been shewn that about 1779 come, every year, to supply the annual loss, occasioned by the excess of the deaths above the births. These, we may suppose, all arrive between the ages of 15 and 45, for after that age, as many retire out of *London*, as come in and settle there; but, because much the greatest part comes in under 25 years of age, and almost the whole before they are 30, it will not be unreasonable to grant that they all come in between 15 and 35; and the medium of the expectations of life, at these two ages, by Mr. *Simpson's* table, at p. 255, of his *Select Exercises*, is 26,7 years; by which multiplying 1779, the product is 47499, for the number to be added to 577.632 on account of recruits from the country, and this makes the number of the inhabitants in *London* 625.131.

The second point, which I wished to discuss before I enter on any calculations, that relate to the kingdom in general, is the proportion which the present number of the inhabitants of *London* bears, to the number of them at the Revolution. In this disquisition I shall confine myself entirely to arguments

D   drawn

drawn from the bills of mortality; which, imperfect as they are, are by far the best, and I believe the only tolerable data, which we have to go upon. But before I proceed farther, I cannot help expressing my surprise, that those who have made this comparison before me, should confine themselves to arguments drawn from the burials alone; whereas, I think, the births must be, of the two, the more certain criterion. Many circumstances, I am convinced, have contributed to render the number of deaths fewer in *London*, than they were formerly, in proportion to the number of people. At the Revolution, *London* stood on little more than half the ground which it occupies at present; of course the inhabitants, supposing them not much more numerous, are not crouded together in the manner they were then, and the air must be purer, and more healthful. Many parts, of the city especially, are made more open by pulling down houses; and all the streets much more airy and wholesome by removing the signs, which in many places, met in the middle of the street, in such a manner as to make it difficult to determine which side of the way they belonged to. The streets are also better, and more

regularly

regularly cleanſed; and, by the addition of ſeveral new works, water is become much more plentiful than it was heretofore; and this has been a great means of contributing, not only to greater cleanlineſs in our houſes, but alſo towards purifying the air by waſhing the filth out of the kennels and common ſhoars. Nothing, I am convinced from much experience, contributes ſo much to health as cleanlineſs; and I am perſuaſed that in the *Reſolution,* we owed more to *Captain Cook's* care, in this reſpect, than every other cauſe put together. Nothing perhaps has contributed ſo much to cleanlineſs in the *City* of *London,* and conſeqeently to the healthfulneſs of it, as ſo many families having quitted lodgings, and living in whole houſes. It is impoſſible to preſerve any tolerable degree of this wholeſome diſcipline in houſes where there are many families; and thoſe who have branded the preſent cuſtom of taking whole houſes with the oprobrious name of *Luxury,* can never have felt the diſagreeble inconveniences of living otherwiſe.

But although I have been able to numerate many reaſons why the burials are fewer than formerly. I do not recollect any cauſes that can add to the number of births, which are not faid to be operating more ftrongly againſt us at this time, than at any former one; and therefore, we might expect to find the number of births in *London*, fewer now than they were at the Revolution, which is not a fact, as will appear from what follows. And notwithſtanding luxury, extravagance, and diffipation are at a very high pitch, it by no means follows that they are carried higher now than they were formerly; or that they are of a more wicked nature, or of a more dangerous tendency. It was always the cuſtom to praiſe the paſt, and ſpeak ill of the preſent times; and, therefore, when I hear gentlemen declaiming in this manner, I am no more convinced of the truth of what they advance, than they are themſelves by the authors who lived in, and wrote with the ſame feverity of the manners of the ages, which it is now the faſhion to extol ſo much. Dreſs is not more expenſive; nor are places of public amuſement more numerous now, than formerly. Exceffive gluttony and drunkenneſs, the groſeſt, and perhaps the moſt pernicious to population of all others, are by no means the leading vices of the preſent age: indeed, there are very few, except amongſt the loweſt of mankind.

mankind, who would not be afhamed to be thought guilty of them. In fhort, when I caft my eye over the feveral purfuits, fafhions, amufements, and vices of the prefent age, and compare them with thofe of former times, as I find them defcribed by the moral writers, who lived in them, I can only conclude that the circuit of thefe things is changed, but not enlarged; and that providence has caft my lot in an age which is as defirable as any that have preceeded it for many generations.

I know it has been urged, that there are fewer Diffenters in London, than there were at the Revolution, and that, on this account, fewer baptifms are omitted in the bills, than were omitted formerly. But after the ftricteft inquiry into this matter, I cannot find that it is fo: on the contrary, it feems to be a general opinion that although fome of the old fects are diminifhed, yet the new ones which have lately rifen up, have more than compenfated for that decreafe, and that Diffenters, including all forts, are, at leaft as numerous now, as at any time fince the Reftoration.

It may alfo be faid, that the births can only meafure the child-bearing part of the inhabitants—not the whole. To this I anfwer,

fwer, those who insist that the number of inhabitants are diminished, contend also that those who marry, and of course are, in general, the child-bearing part of the community, are still more diminished, in proportion to the whole; owing to the contempt which is shewn to the state by people of fashion; by the difficulties which are thrown in the way of providing for a family by bad management in our superiors, excessive taxes, and want of employment; and by the passion for luxury and extravagance which universally prevails at this time. It may therefore be reasonably presumed, that if the child-bearing part of the inhabitants have not suffered a diminution, the whole have not.

There is however one cause why the number of births may be higher now than formerly, without supposing a greater number of people to produce them, although, as far as I know, it has never been adverted to before; and which, with all due submission to the opinions of medical people, is this. Will not every cause which produces a greater degree of mortality, impare the bodily faculties of the living, before it produces death? and, amongst others, the procreative faculties also? if it will, and if there were

were some cause which produced a greater degree of mortality formerly in the City of London than now, as the following tables seem fully to shew, that cause would operate to produce fewer children formerly than are produced now, when that cause appears not to operate so strongly in producing absolute mortality, as it has done before. But I beg leave to observe, that I advance this only as the Roman Catholic Philosophers are glad to do the motion of the Earth, and other heretical opinions; that is, not *per Thesin*, but *per Hypothesin*; and let the advocates for depopulation make the most of it. I proceed to facts.

	Births	Burials	Waste of human Life.
London Bills, from 1686, to 1690.	14843	22391	
Marybone Bills	9	29	
Pancras Bills	18	60	
Middle year of the 5, is 1688.	14870	22480	7620
London Bills, from 1722, to 1726.	18916	27214	
Marybone Bills	88	165	
Pancras Bills	58	133	
Middle year of the 5, is 1724	19062	27512	8450
London Bills, from 1740, to 1744	14650	27254	
Marybone Bills	184	484	
Pancras Bills	36	261	
Middle year of the 5, is 1742	14870	27999	13129
London Bills, from 1743, to 1747	14582	24151	
Marybone Bills	197	495	
Pancras Bills	40	279	
Middle year of the 5, is 1745	14819	24925	10106
London Bills, from 1746, to 1750	14496	25353	
Marybone Bills	213	571	
Pancras Bills	45	304	
Middle year of the 5, is 1748	14754	26228	11474
London Bills, from 1775, to 1779	17456	20743	
Marybone Bills	1008	1145	
Pancras Bills	234	339	
Middle of the 5, is 1777.	18698	22227	3529

This table can need very little comment; for if no foreign caufes intervened, it is plain that the number of people, at any one time, would be to the number of them, at any other, as the number of births at the firft to the number of births at the latter. The number of inhabitants would be alfo as the num- of deaths at the one time, to the number of deaths at the other; and, in this cafe, it would be indifferent, whether we made ufe of the births or the burials; for each of them would give the fame proportion. But as both thefe are liable to be influenced by accidental circumftance, (although, for reafons given above, I think the births lefs than the burials) it may be beft to fuppofe that the proportion between the number of the inhabitants of London, at the Revolution, and their number, now, is compounded of the proportion which the births at that time bore to the births at this, and of the proportion which the deaths, then, bore to the deaths now: that is, that the number of the inhabitants, at that time, were to the number of the inhabitants at this, as the fquare root of 14870×22480 is to the fquare root of 18698×22227; or as 182833 to 2038603; which is as 9 to 10, exceeding near.

But notwithstanding the deductions from the preceeding table are so easy and evident, I am aware that the table itself will, by some, be thought to stand in need of a defence. In forming it, I have brought the births and burials of the parishes of Marybone and Pancras to account; against which, I am persuaded, nothing can be objected. But it has been observed, that " twelve parishes, *now the most populous*, were not included in the " bills at the Revolution, but are now." It might be replied, that admitting this to be the case, which it is not, the populousness of these parishes *now* is wholly out of the question, and only the births and burials which these parishes produced at the Revolution can have any influence on it. But the truth is, the births and burials of every one of these parishes came as regularly, and, I make no doubt, as truly into the bills then as they do now. For it ought to be remembered, that the parishes of Christ-Church, Spittlefields; St. Anne's, Limehouse; St. George's, in the East, and St. Matthew's, Bethnal Green, were all taken out of St. Dustan's, Stepney. That St. John's, Wapping, was taken out of St. Mary's, White-Chapel; St. Luke's, Old-street, out of St. Giles's, Cripplegate; St. George's,

George's, Queen-square, out of St. Andrew's, Holborn; St. George's, Bloomsbury, out of St. Giles' in the Fields; St. James's, Westminster; St. Ann's, Soho; St. George's, Hanover-square; and St. John the Evangelist, out of St. Martin's, in the Fields; and St. John's, Southwark, out of the parish of St. Olaves. The baptisms and burials of these parishes came, therefore, into the bills through the mother churches, until the new ones were consecrated, or made parochial; and it is remarkable, that, in every instance, the baptisms and burials, from the new churches, were inserted, separately, in the bills, the very first month after the separation took place.

The old church of St. Mary le Strand was pulled down in 1549, by *Edward*, Duke of Somerset, uncle and protector to *Edward* the sixth; who made the parishioners a promise that he would build them a new one, but never performed it. They were therefore under the necessity of joining themselves to the parishes of St. Clement Danes, and St. Mary in the Savoy, at which places they baptized and buried until their own church was rebuilt in 1723. The objection, therefore, which has been made on this account is of no weight.

I have only to add farther concerning this table, that the fourth column, entitled "The "waſte of Human Life," and which contains the number of perſons that died annually, at different periods, in this great city, more than were born in it, diſplays, in the moſt forcible manner, the good effects which have ariſen from the improvements and alterations that have been lately made, and from the mode of living which has been adopted by the inhabitants. (See pag. 19.) Surely it muſt afford the moſt pleaſing ſenſations to every friend to mankind, as well as to every one who has the leaſt regard for the intereſts of this country, to obſerve, that inſtead of about 13000, the number of lives which this city devoured annually about the year 1742, little more than 3500 ſuffice now: and, in all probability, half of that number ought to be deducted, on account of the greater defect which there is in the regiſters of the baptiſms, than in the regiſters of the burials; which is a much leſs number than is deſtroyed annually by any other capital city in Europe. It is for the ſake of ſuch as can take pleaſure in a proſpect like this, that I have added the following table, which exhibits, more fully, the ſteps by which this dreadful

mor-

mortality arose to such an alarming height; and how it has gradually diminished, as the late improvements have been made, and the town has been laid open and extended.

A TABLE, shewing the Waste of Human Life within the Bills of Mortality of the City of London, at different Periods, since the great Fire in 1666.

Years inclusive.	Mean Number of Births.	Mean Number of Burials.	Waste of Human Lives.
From 1666 to 1670	11180	17098	5918
From 1671 to 1675	12119	17982	5863
From 1676 to 1680	12532	20252	7720
From 1681 to 1685	14035	22335	8300
From 1686 to 1690	14843	22391	7548
From 1691 to 1695	14528	21534	7006
From 1696 to 1700	15349	20006	4657
From 1701 to 1705	15758	21091	5333
From 1706 to 1710	15485	21832	6347
From 1711 to 1715	16204	22178	5974
From 1717 to 1721	18209	25982	7773
From 1722 to 1726	18916	27214	8298
From 1727 to 1732	17450	26888	9438
From 1733 to 1738	16880	26677	9797
From 1740 to 1744	14650	27254	12604
From 1745 to 1750	14426	24676	10250
From 1751 to 1757	14926	21084	6158
From 1758 to 1763	14978	21757	6779
From 1764 to 1769	16361	23073	6712
From 1770 to 1774	17180	22561	5381
From 1775 to 1779	17456	20743	3287

This Table shews, that before the late improvements were made, and London began to extend itself over more ground, the loss of human lives in it increased and decreased, in a great measure, as the number of of inhabitants increafed or decreafed; but fince that time, notwithftanding the number of inhabitants have obvioufly increafed, the annual lofs of lives has been continually decreafing. It feems farther to fuggeft, that the body politic, as well as the body natural, is endowed with an inherent power of throwing off a difeafe, when it arrives at fuch a ftate as to endanger its exiftence. London, about the year 1740, was become fo full of inhabitants, and they were fo crouded together, as to be intolerable to, and deftructive of one another; and they were abfolutely *driven* to feek refuge in the neighbouring fields.

It muft be obferved, that by the number of inhabitants, I mean the medium of the numbers which are in London at the two feafons of the year, when it is fulleft and moft deferted. What thefe feafons are, and the proportion which the number of people in London, at one of them, bears to the number at the other, may be gathered from the two following tables, which I have more willingly inferted, as they point out fome other curious and ufeful, particulars, which I omit mentioning, becaufe they are foreign to the fubject in hand.

A TABLE

A TABLE of the Number of Christenings in each Month, from the Year 1753, to the Year 1764, both inclusive, collected from the Monthly Bills of Mortality for the City of London.

Year.	Jan.	Feb.	March.	April.	May.	June.	July.	August.	Sept.	October	Novem.	Decem.
1753	1194	1228	1646	1261	1190	1395	1220	1412	1155	1159	1202	1344
1754	1205	1165	1515	1195	1484	1123	1061	1367	1386	1098	1276	1099
1755	1479	1358	1148	1210	1591	1126	1055	1329	1176	1360	1029	1172
1756	1433	1244	795	1480	1167	1091	1337	1072	1108	1343	1181	1419
1757	1068	1179	1158	1359	1101	1053	1267	1023	1302	1192	1067	1321
1758	1096	1134	1387	1102	1131	1340	1082	1014	1553	1154	1146	1311
1759	1183	1081	1371	1130	1107	1324	1005	1320	1005	1132	1310	1088
1760	1231	1526	1264	1127	1038	1029	1118	1377	1180	1404	1221	1232
1761	1574	1373	1353	1283	1126	1125	1181	1165	1003	1581	1207	1227
1762	1468	1384	1384	1527	1190	1083	1245	1050	1010	1190	1133	
1763	1614	1150	1150	1179	1070	1084	1121		1903	1224	1213	1505
1764	1372	1396	1507	1508	1283	1516	1244	1524	1250	1337	1621	1223
Means	1326	1268	1306	1280	1207	1191	1168	1241	1256	1264	1217	1267

(32)

A TABLE of the number of Burials each Month, from the Year 1753, to the Year 1764, both inclusive, collected from the Monthly Bills of Mortality for the City of London.

Year.	Jan.	Feb.	March.	April.	May.	June.	July.	August.	Sept.	October	Nov.	Decem.
1753	1602	1702	1943	1506	1439	1689	1267	1489	1391	1630	1636	2081
1754	1703	1911	2436	1966	2466	1750	1529	1740	1515	1704	2180	1903
1755	2388	2000	1873	1709	1876	1639	1398	1726	1454	1859	1629	1891
1756	2081	1675	1621	1974	1608	1511	1763	1300	1415	2068	1810	2497
1757	2104	2008	1910	2241	1612	1483	1732	1513	1750	1432	1500	1807
1758	1477	1478	1679	1409	1445	1595	1166	1171	1601	1364	1303	1961
1759	1653	1503	1842	1427	1297	1718	1300	1874	1665	1542	2034	1861
1760	1912	2324	1744	1609	1485	1454	1254	1464	1321	1735	1516	1516
1761	1732	1563	1623	1709	1597	1480	1475	1398	1566	2222	1781	1915
1762	2362	2005	1970	2523	2502	1904	2041	1909	1944	2175	1994	2497
1763	3352	2370	1938	1914	1964	2064	2042		3002	1860	1722	2419
1764	2051	1944	2376	1695	1641	2050	1582	1984	1895	1784	2300	1882
Means	2035	1874	1913	1807	1744	1695	1546	1597	1710	1781	1784	1976

I cannot quit this part of my subject without taking notice of a circumstance relating to the Hospital in which I live. *Dr. Price* has very truly said*, that the average number of children in this house, for 30 years, *before* 1770, was 831; and that the number of those who died annually was $11\frac{4}{5}$, or one out of $70\frac{2}{5}$. The average number of children, that have been in the house for the *last* 20 years, has been 851, and the annual deaths have been $10\frac{1}{4}$; or somewhat less than one in 83. For the *last* 10 years, the average number of children has been 894, and the annual number of deaths $8\frac{9}{10}$, or about one in every $100\frac{1}{2}$. When I reflect, that this hospital is situated in the very centre of London, and that there cannot possibly be any error, either in the number of children, or in the number of those which have died; I cannot help considering the above circumstance as a very strong proof,—indeed an irrefragable one, of the greater healthiness of *London* now than formerly. It must be owned, that several openings

---

* See Observations on Reversionary Payments, 3d. edit. p. 255.

openings and improvements have lately been made, by the direction of the Governors, both within the hofpital, and in its neighbourhood, which, it is hoped, may contribute to the greater health of the children in future; but th y have all been made within the compafs of the laſt two years of this period; and in thofe two years the burials have been 18, which is rather above the medium of the laſt ten: thefe improvements have, therefore, had no influence on the numbers given above.

I fhall now proceed to enquire into the ſtate of population in the kingdom at large. And here I muſt obferve, as it had been afferted that the depopulation had proceeded with quicker ſteps in the laſt 20 or 30 years, than it had done before, and as I could not hope to carry my firſt inquiries much farther back than the year 1750, I confined them wholly within that limit: and, indeed, for fome time after I began collecting the regifters of parifhes, I did not extend them to any earlier period. My proof will not, therefore, be fo complete for all the time fince the Revolution, as it will for the time fince that. However, if it appear that there are no

grounds

grounds to suppose the inhabitants have decreased since the year 1750, in which time it is supposed the decrease has been the greatest, but on the contrary, that there has been a very great increase; we may fairly conclude, no very substantial reasons can be brought to prove that such a diminution had place, before that time; and especially, as the facts, which I have collected, tend to prove the contrary.

(36)

Names of the Villages.	No. of Houses in 1780.	New Foundations since 1750.	Decayed and not re-built	Increase or Decr. by alterations.	No. of Houses in 1750.	Increase or Decrease of Inhabitants.
Ayton	183	8	6	+ 3	178	Increased
Bretton	79	12	4	0	71	Increased
Broughton -	85	5	1	+ 5	76	Increased
Coatham -	85	41	2	+ 2	44	Increased
Eston -	65	10	6	+ 13	48	Increased
Hinderwell -	43	6	1	+ 5	33	Increased
Hutton -	139	20	2	+ 8	113	Increased
Kirby -	37	3	2	+ 1	35	Doubtful
Kilton -	24	0	2	0	26	Doubtful
Lackenby -	24	4	4	+ 7	17	Increased
Lazenby -	21	0	3	+ 6	18	Doubtful
Lofthouse -	165	11	20	0	174	Decreased
Lythe -	116	18	13	+ 2	109	Doubtful
Marsk -	114	17	10	+ 9	98	Increased
Newby -	32	3	0	— 2	31	Doubtful
Newton -	34	6	5	0	33	Increased
Normanby -	25	0	0	+ 6	19	Increased
Ormsby -	71	31	12	+ 3	49	Increased
Pinchinthorp	14	2	0	0	12	Doubtful
Plunswick -	60	7	6	0	59	Increased
Potto -	37	0	3	0	40	Decreased
Redcar -	108	23	4	+ 10	79	Increased
Rudby -	14	2	5	0	17	Decreased
Saltburn -	14	8	0	0	6	Increased
Sandsend -	88	8	12	+ 11	81	Increased
Seamour -	52	1	2	— 1	54	Decreased
Skelton -	172	18	3	+ 31	126	Increased
Upleatham -	46	11	0	+ 1	34	Increased
Wilton -	38	0	2	+ 4	36	Doubtful

The

The remarks which I have to make on the above account are, that Plunfwick Redcar, and Saltburn are fifhing towns, and inhabited chiefly by fifhermen and their families. Allum-works have long been eftablifhed at *Lofthoufe*, which now belong to Sir *Laurence Dundas*; but, I believe, they are not carried on with much fpirit. About the year 1763 or 1764, Allum-works were alfo begun at *Skelton*, by *John Hall Stephenfon*, Efq; and carried on for fome time, with great fpirit, which caufed a great influx of inhabitants to that place; but thefe works have been difcontinued for feveral years: there are, however, few or no empty houfes, and it is not fuppofed that many of the inhabitants have left the place on that account. All the other villages in the preceeding lift may, very properly, be called farming villages, as no manufacture of any moment, is carried on in any of them.

The total number of houfes in 1750 was 1716; at prefent the number of houfes is 1985: there appears, therefore, to have been an increafe of 269 families in the laft 30 years; or one-feventh part of the original number, nearly.

According to the beft accounts that I can obtain, the feveral furveyors *aid* return the
number

number of houfes which were not chargeable, as well as thofe which were, in this diftrict in the year 1777: and my correfpondents make the number of thofe, not chargeable, over and above thofe which are inhabited by perfons who receive affiftance from the parifh, and fifhermen, who are exempt from all taxes of that nature, 752. But I muft obferve that fome of the perfons who ought to have been moft ready, and had it undoubtedly moft in their power to affift thefe inquiries, did all they could to prevent and difappoint them: no dependence muft therefore be placed in this part of the account, and my correfpondent fays, that from the beft accounts which he could obtain, he thinks not more than half the number of houfes are charged.

Villages in the Weft-Riding of *Yorkſhire*.						
Names of Villages.	No. of Houfes in 1780.	New Foundations fince 1750.	Decayed and not Re-built.	Increafe or Decr. by Alterations.	No. of houfes in 1750.	Increafe, or decreafe of Inhabitants.
Bolton on Dearn	88	9	0	0	79	Increafed
Brampton	113	16	0	0	97	Increafed
Hoyland	101	10	0	0	91	Increafed
Rawmarſh	204	50	0	0	154	Increaſ. much
Swinton	103	24	0	0	79	Increaſ. much
Thorp	120	18	0	0	102	Increaſed
Wath	115	20	0	0	95	Increaſed
Wentworth	99	12	0	0	87	Increaſed

The number of houses, at present is 943: in the year 1750, they were 784. The increase is very great indeed! And I am assured the increase of the inhabitants is, at least, equal to that of the houses. I have not been able to learn how many are assessed to the window-tax.

These villages are almost wholly employed in agriculture, except that there is a small pottery at Rawmarsh, and a manufacture of the same kind, and a small colliery carried on at Swinton. I shall add, here, a few circumstances, relating to this Riding, which may contribute towards ascertaining the state of the population of this part of the country, either immediately, or at a future period.

1st. The total number of houses, in the two divisions of Agbridge and Morley, as delivered in by Mr. *Woodcock*, surveyor of the windows, in 1761, which was one of the years, when a general survey was required } 17764

By the same gentleman in 1767   20526.

In 1779, Mr. *Cooper*,* the present surveyor, found the total number to be } 21929

Of

---

* It would be ingratitude not to mention the readiness with which this gentlemen gave me such information as was in his power.

Of these 4697 are charged with the window-tax, 8135 with the house duty of 3s.
and 9097 are excused on account of poverty.

Moreover, out of 12832, the chargeable ones, only 56 were empty in July 1779. It may be farther observed, that these two divisions, which contain five market towns, and some of them very capital ones, have very near $\frac{3}{7}$ths of their houses, such as pay neither the window or house tax.

2d. In the year 1750, by a very careful survey, the houses in Wakefield, of every denomination, were found to be 1059. I have been promised the exact number of them at present, as well as of the inhabitants, but have not yet received it.

3d. To the table which Dr. *Price* has given at p. 6. of his Essay on the Population of England, the following accounts of towns, in the neighbourhood of Leeds, may be added. They were taken immediately after the survey of Leeds, which he mentions; and by some of the gentlemen who were concerned in it.

Town

Towns.	Families.	Souls.	To a family.
Armley	359	1715	4 ¾ +
Beeston	192	862	4 ½ —
Bramley	311	1378	4 ⁴⁄₇
Farnley	116	540	4 ⁱ⁵⁄₂₉
Headingly	143	667	4 ⅔
Holbeck	508	2045	4 ¹⁄₃₂
Hunflet	806	3367	4 ⅛ +
Wortley	196	894	4 ⅔ —

		Villages in *Derbyshire*.				
Names of Villages.	Number of houses in 1780.	New Foundations since 1750.	Decayed, and not rebuilt.	Increase or Decr. by Alterations.	Number of houses in 1750.	Increase or decrease of inhabitants
Afton	61	11	8	+ 7	51	Increased
Barrow	41	10	3	+ 1	33	Increased
Breedon	100	37	11	+13	61	Incr. much
Castle Dunning-[ton	305	70	18	+66	187	Incr. much
Caulk	14	2	4	+ 2	14	Doubtful
Ingleby	24	4	5	+ 6	19	Increased
Melbourne	209	97	21	0	133	Incr. much
Milton ᵣ	30	10	7	0	27	Doubtful
Newton	52	8	6	1	49	Decreased
Repton	181	39	10	+12	140	Incr. much
Stanton	26	3	8	+ 2	29	Increased
Stenfon	14	2	1	+ 2	11	Decreased
Swarkftone	37	3	1	+ 3	32	Increased
Ticknall	168	34	10	+ 8	136	Increased
Tonge	36	1	5	+ 5	35	Increased
Twyford	15	1	1	1	14	Decreased
Willfon	35	6	4	+ 3	30	Decreased

The total number of houses in these villages was 1001 about the year 1750, at present they are 1348; so that we may suppose in the last thirty years, there has been an addition of 347 families, which is more than one-third of the original number. I am not informed what number of these houses are assessed to the window tax; but as much the greater part of them are small, and inhabited by poor people, it may be supposed that they are near the proportion which has been shewn to exist amongst the others.

Villages in *Northamptonshire*.

Names of Villages.	Houses in 1780.	Houses in 1760.	Houses in 1750.	Houses with two families.	Houses with three families.	Houses with four families.	Houses charged to window-tax.
Ailseworth	38	38	46	1			24
Ashton	17	17	17				14
Bainton	30	32	32	1	1		23
Barnack	62	62	63	6			54
Castor	78	78	78	7	1		45
Dogsthorp	43	40	40				38
Eastfield and Newark	32	32	32	2			31
Etton	21	21	21				18
Eye	99	96	96	14	1		62
Glinton	63	63	63	6			54
Gunthorp	11	13	13				7
Helpston	65	70	70	7		1	28
Longthorp	36	38	38				23
Marham	12	12	12	3	1	1	8
Maxey	60	60	60	8			48
Norborough	45	46	46	1			38
Paston	18	18	18				10
Peakirk	34	34	34	3			13
Pilsgate	17	18	18		2		13
Southorp	17	17	17				13
Sutton	23	23	24	1			17
Thornhaugh	33	30	30	8			16
Ufford	26	26	26				19
Upton	10	14	15				5
Walton	28	27	27	1			16
Werrington	76	75	75	9			54
Wittering	30	31	31	2			15

G 2 The

This diſtrict contained 1036 houſes about the year 1750 and contains only 1024 now: there has been of courſe a diminution of 12 houſes; and the number which is charged to the window tax, is 706. The inhabitants are wholly employed in agriculture, and adminiſtering to the immediate wants of one another. The gentleman who favoured me with this account, and who has reſided all his life in the neighbourhood, adds as follows.

" Whatever the number of houſes may
" be, the number of the inhabitants has en-
" creaſed. I have many houſes—Indeed
" almoſt the whole of many villages, under
" my care; and whenever a houſe happens
" to be at liberty, I have many applications
" for it. Where I to build more cottages,
" they would ſoon be let; our poor families
" being obliged, frequently, to croud toge-
" ther, two or three families in a cottage,
" becauſe each cannot get one to itſelf. Very
" few landlords chuſe to build, unleſs for
" particular conveniency, becauſe the rents,
" though higher than formerly, do not
" anſwer the expence".

Villages in *Suffolk*.					
Names of Parishes.	Houses in 1780.	Houses with two Families.	Houses with 3 Families.	Total Number of Families.	Increase of Families since 1750.	Houses charged to Window-tax.
Blythford	21	7	1	30	1	20
Bramfield	62	17	2	83	4	59
Henham	15	7	1	22	1	15
Holton	41	19	3	66	8	37
Sotherton	24	6	0	30	0	17
Spexhall	15	2	1	17	0	15
Swilland	21	6	1	29	2	21
Tuddenham	27	4	6	43	6	15
Wangford	47	10	3	63	6	47
Wenhaston	56	23	4	87	13	56
Westerfield	24	7	5	41	1	20
Westhall	45	12	2	61	1	43
Wissett	38	14	1	54	1	36
Witnesham	50	12	8	78	7	38

The total number of families living, at present, in the above 14 parishes, is 704. The increase of families, since 1750, is 51; consequently the number of families, in 1750 was 653: and it is the general opinion of the inhabitants that they have increased considerably, in number, since that time. They are almost wholly employed in agriculture and supplying the wants of one another. I have not been able to discover whether

ther the unchargeable houses were, or were not, returned in 1777; nor how many of the houses in Swilland and Westerfield are charged to the window tax; but if we suppose that forty, out of the 45, are, the total number of houses will be 486, and those which are assessed to the window tax, 438, which is a much greater part of the whole, than I have found in any other part of England; and it is most probably owing to the great number of families which are crouded together into one house, and therefore require many windows.

Parishes in *Sussex:* the Hundred of *Guestling.*

Names of Parishes.	No. of Houses in 1780.	New Foundations since 1750.	Decayed and not rebuilt.	Incr. or decr. by Alterations.	No. of Houses in 1750.	Increase or Decrease of Inhabitants.
Fairlight	63	19	0	5	39	Increased
Guestling	66	12	0	6	48	Increased
Icklesham	63	10	1	10	44	Increased
Pett	31	9	0	9	13	Increased

The number of houses in this hundred, at present, is 223; in 1750, it was 144: we may therefore reckon an increase of 79 families in the last 30 years; or more than half the original number.

The

The parishes of Icklesham and Pett are chiefly rich marsh-land, which has been left by the sea. Fairlight and Guestling are mosty high land, partly arable, and partly grazing: the former has been greatly improved within the last 30 years. The inhabitants are supposed to have increased greatly, and there was not, last Summer, an empty house in the whole hundred of Guestling. I am not informed what number of houses are chargeable to the window tax; but those which are not, were not returned in 1777. In the parish of Guestling, there are 34 houses, which are not charged; and it is supposed that the proportion between the charged and uncharged houses is nearly the same in the other parishes.

Villages in *Somersetshire*.						
Names of Villages.	No. of Houses in 1780.	New Foundations since 1750.	Decayed and not rebuilt.	Incr. or decr. by Alterations.	No. of Houses in 1750.	Increase or Decrease of Inhabitants.
Ashill	55	2	4	0	57	Doubtful.
Clapton	23	0	4	—2	29	Decreased.
Ilminster	283	5	25	—1	304	Decreased.
Wayford	27	0	12	+1	38	Decr. much.

The

The number of houses in these four townships was 428 in the year 1750; at present, they are only 388: we may therefore presume that there is a loss of 40 families, or somewhat more than one-eleventh part of the number that were in them in 1750. The number which are charged to the window-tax is 134, or little more than one-third of the whole number, and the uncharged houses were *not* returned in 1777. Let us now bring into one view the state of all these accounts.

	1750.	1780.
North Riding of Yorkshire,	1716	1985
West Riding of Yorkshire, Agbridge and Morly Divisions, 1761,	17764	21929
Eight Villages in the West Riding,	784	943
Derbyshire,	1001	1348
Northamptonshire,	1036	1024
Suffolk (Families)	653	704
Sussex,	144	223
Somersetshire.	428	388
Total	23526	28544

That is, the present number of houses, in these districts, is to the number which were in them, about the year 1750, as 28,544 is to 23,526; or, as 28 to 23 nearly.

The prospect is here flattering: let us see what farther comfort the Bills of Mortality seem to afford us.

The average annual Number of Baptisms and Burials in various Parishes, about, or soon after the Revolution.

Counties.	Parishes.	Years.	Baptisms	Burials.
Anglesea	Beaumaris	1676 to 1603	16,87	21,78
	Pentraeth	1672—1679	12,85	13,25
Berks	Lamborn	1682—1691	45,10	
	Shefford	1682—1691	11,20	
	Wilford	1682—1691	20,10	
Devon	Axminster	1688—1697	31,50	42,00
Kent	Chalk	1689—1698	3,90	6,00
	Northfleet	1689—1698	11,50	16,50
	Nurstead	1689—1698	10	10
Lancaster	Bowden	1653—1662	57,30	
	Liverpool	1700—1710	212,70	
	Manchester	1720—1724	339,40	336,50
	Middleton	1663—1672	38,80	36,70
	Rochdale	1684—1693	156,70	211,80
	Warrington	1716—1722	140,14	147,00
Leicester	St. Mary's	1720—1726	60,00	54,71
	Norton	1716—1725	3,90	2,90
Northampton	Peterborough	1688—1697	105,10	111,00
Nottingham	Broughton	1690—1699	6,30	4,10
	Kinolton	1720—1730	6,00	8,00
Somerset	Chard	1688—1697	36,30	60,70
	Ilminster	1688—1697	36,60	47,30
	Puckingham	1694—1703	1,90	2,30
	Wayford	1688—1697	3,30	3,60
	Wellington	1688—1697	81,70	70,10
Sussex	Guestling	1687—1696	4,90	4,00
York	Ackworth	1644—1737	14,24	11,24
	Bawtry	1654—1734	16,80	18,57
	Bolton on Dearn	1619—1737	13,14	10,02
	Brodsworth	1692—1735	6,09	5,19
	Darfield	1653—1737	38,84	33,22
	Felkirk	1647—1683	25,06	18,81
	Heath	1654—1739	7,89	6,58
	Hemsworth	1685—1738	14,45	11,68
	Hooton Pagnell	1650—1738	8,67	7,99
	Kirby	1648—1737	20,27	17,26
	Sheffield	1680—1734	169,50	152,37
	Wath	1673—1734	28,13	25,00
Total annual births and deaths in these 38 parishes			1807,24	1518,24

(50)

The average annual Births and Deaths in the same Parishes at present, or very lately.

Counties.	Parishes.	Years.	Baptisms	Burials.
Anglesea	Beaumaris	1764 to 1771	41,00	31,12
	Pentraeth	1764—1771	18,63	11,25
Berks	Lamborn	1752—1756	69,80	
	Shefford	1752—1756	12,80	
	Welford	1752—1756	24,00	
Devon	Axminster	1770—1779	50,60	45,40
Kent	Chalk	1771—1780	6,70	10,00
	Northfleet	1771—1780	33,90	39,00
	Nurstead	1771—1780	2,00	1,10
Lancaster	Bowden	1763—1772	212,70	
	Liverpool	1762—1771	1001,00	
	Manchester	1770—1779	1278,50	994,80
	Middleton	1763—1772	157,70	99,30
	Rochdale	1771—1780	478,70	415,50
	Warrington	1770—1773	337,25	311,75
Leicester	St. Mary	1770—1779	104,30	90,20
	Norton	1770—1779	5,60	2,70
Northampton	Peterborough	1770—1779	121,10	124,00
Nottingham	Broughton	1770—1779	6,80	4,80
	Kinolton	1770—1779	10,40	5,50
Somerset	Chard	1770—1779	49,50	36,50
	Ilminster	1770—1779	42,30	30,80
	Puckenham	1770—1779	4,50	1,70
	Wayford	1770—1779	7,20	4,10
	Wellington	1770—1779	55,90	48,00
Sussex	Guestling	1770—1779	10,80	6,00
York	Ackworth	1757—1767	21,20	15,60
	Bawtry	1770—1779	15,40	21,30
	Bolton on Dearn	1770—1779	19,10	10,80
	Brodsworth	1770—1779	7,00	5,00
	Darfield	1770—1779	39,50	24,60
	Felkirk	1770—1779	30,70	20,10
	Heath	1770—1779	21,90	16,20
	Hemsworth	1770—1779	21,40	13,50
	Hooton Pagnell	1770—1779	11,00	6,30
	Kirby (South)	1770—1779	31,80	19,10
	Sheffield	1770—1779	1046,90	983,30
	Wath	1770—1779	38,22	25,10

Total annual births and deaths in these 38 parishes — 5384,68 | 3537,62

According to the baptisms, the number of people, in these 38 parishes, at present, is to the number which were in them at the Revolution, as 538468 is to 180724: that is, near three times as many as they were then. If we take the burials as a guide, the present number of inhabitants is to the number of them at the Revolution, as 353762 is to 151824, or somewhat more than $2\frac{1}{3}$ times their number at that time. If we take an arithmetical mean between the two, the present number of inhabitants, will be to their number at the Revolution, as 446115 is to 166274: but if a geometrical mean be taken, which some may prefer, they will be only as 436451 to 165644. That is, their present number is somewhat more than $2\frac{2}{3}$ their number at the Revolution.

I shall now proceed to inquire into the proportion, which the present number of inhabitants, in as many parts of England as my materials extend to, bears the number which was in the same places, between the years 1740 and 1750. And here, through the kind assistance of many good friends, I shall be able to take a wider field than I have done above; and such a one as will, I flatter myself, convince most unprejudiced persons, that we have no reason to fear our number is diminished since that time; but, on the contrary, that we are considerably increased.

The

(53)

The Average annual Number of Baptisms and Burials in various Parishes, about the Year 1745.

Counties.	Parishes.	Years.	baptism	Burials
Anglesea	Beaumaris	1710 to 1717	29,5	26,5
	Llanddyfnan	1750—1757	13,9	6,0
	Llanfadurn	1750—1757	7,9	6,2
	Llanvair	1732—1739	8,5	8,4
	Pentraeth	1740—1747	12,5	10,6
Cambridge	Papworth Agnes	1740—1749	2,4	1,3
	Papworth Ever.	1740—1749	4,0	2,2
Cornwall	Breage	1740—1749	65,5	41,1
	Cury	1740—1749	9,1	6,5
	Germoe	1740—1749	8,1	12,6
	Gunwalloe	1740—1749	5,8	3,5
	St. Hillary	1740—1750	49,7	36,3
	St. Martin's	1740—1749	7,4	6,2
	Mawgan	1740—1749	12,9	12,9
	Sithney	1740—1749	29,1	24,9
Devon	Axminster	1742—1749	43,6	38,6
Essex	Arkesden	1740—1749	9,5	8,6
	Clavering	1740—1749	18,2	14,4
	Heydon	1740—1749	6,7	3,9
	Langley	1740—1749	8,4	4,5
	Quendon	1740—1749	3,9	1,9
	Stensted Montfitchet	1740—1750	17,1	14,5
	Ugley	1740—1749	10,2	5,1
	Wendens Ambo	1740—1749	6,9	4,1
Herts	Brent Pelham	1740—1749	5,6	6,1
	Furneux Pelham	1740—1749	13,2	10,0
Huntington	Folksworth	1736—1745	4,2	3,8
	Lutton	1740—1749	4,0	3,7
	Morborne	1740—1749	1,0	0,5
	Yelling	1740—1749	5,1	4,4
Kent	Chalk	1741—1750	6,0	6,4
	Northfleet	1741—1750	27,2	31,9
	Nursted	1741—1750	0,4	0,0

Counties.	Parishes.	Years.	Baptisms.	Burials.
Lancaster	Manchester	1740—1749	643,2	560,7
	Rochdale	1741—1750	330,8	301,4
	Warrington	1736—1745	168,2	158,6
Leicester	Foxton	1740—1749	12,6	9,2
	Lubenham	1740—1749	9,9	7,4
	St. Mary's	1740—1749	66,9	65,4
	Norton	1740—1749	4,4	2,3
	Thedingworth	1740—1749	7,3	5,4
	Thornby	1731—1740	4,8	3,1
Lincoln	Westdeeping	1740—1749	3,9	3,6
	Jallington	1740—1749	6,2	5,7
Norfolk	Brancaster	1750—1759	14,1	9,6
	Docking	1750—1759	9,9	2,8
	Fitcham	1755—1760	8,5	4,3
	Hilborowe	1740—1749	6,5	4,6
	Hillington	1740—1749	5,4	5,4
	Titchwell	1750—1759	3,5	1,8
Northampton	Castor	1740—1749	15,7	17,1
	Clipston	1731—1740	15,2	10,7
	Cottesbrooke	1731—1740	6,5	7,4
	Glinton	1740—1749	9,9	7,3
	Guilsborough	1740—1749	13,4	7,7
	Helpston	1740—1749	8,6	6,9
	Marham	1740—1749	1,3	2,2
	Marston Trussel	1740—1749	5,0	3,4
	Maxey	1740—1749	14,6	15,1
	Naseby	1740—1749	12,8	9,0
	Peterborough	1740—1749	101,5	127,4
	Ravensthorp	1740—1749	12,6	10,7
Nottingham	Broughton Sul-	1741—1750	8,9	7,6
	Carlton [ney	1741—1750	8,4	9,6
	Kinolton	1741—1750	6,0	4,5
Salop	Holy Cross	1751—1760	33,1	29 0
Somerset	Chard	1740—1749	42,0	57,9
	Curry Rivel	1740—1749	24,9	22,8
	Drayton	1740—1749	10,1	10,3
	Ilminster	1740—1749	28,8	39,8
	Puckington	1740—1749	3,3	2,0
	Wayford	1740—1749	6,3	5,0

Counties.	Parishes.	Years.	Baptisms	Burials.
Somerset	Wellington	1740 to 1749	57,5	63,2
Stafford	Alrewas	1741—1750	24.5	16,3
	Barton under Needwood.	1741—1750	19,7	16,2
	Burton on Trent	1741—1750	95,7	76,8
	Elford	1741—1750	6,7	5,3
	Rugeley	1741—1750	43,4	33,6
	Stapenhill	1741—1750	22,1	20,1
	Tatenhall	1741—1750	9,6	7,9
	Walton on Trent	1741—1750	6,5	2,9
	Yoxall	1741—1750	28,8	21,2
Suffolk	Aldham	1740—1749	3,9	4,1
	East-Bergholt	1740—1749	23,2	20,5
	Brockley	1740—1749	7,4	5,2
	Elmset	1740—1749	7,9	8,4
	Groton	1740—1749	12,3	10,3
	Hadleigh	1740—1749	51,2	40,7
	Hawkedon	1740—1749	6,4	3,7
	Kersey	1740—1749	12,4	10,7
	Layham	1740—1749	16,1	7,9
	Lindsey	1740—1749	5,0	4,0
	Reed	1740—1749	3,4	3,2
	Semer	1740—1749	5,7	3,7
	Stratford (St. Mary's)	1740—1749	13,4	12,2
	Somerton	1740—1749	3,3	2,0
	Whatfield	1740—1749	7,1	5,7
	Barrow	1740—1749	15,2	9,1
	Denston	1740—1749	5,9	4,3
	Depden	1740—1749	7,1	4,1
Sussex	Fairlight	1750—1759	5,8	3,6
	Guestling	1740—1749	9,4	5,9
	Hastings All Saints	1750—1755	24,8	24,5
	Hastings St. Clements	1742—1747	30,7	22,5
	Ickletham	1750—1759	7,9	4,1
	Pett	1750—1759	3,8	2,3
	Westfield	1750—1759	16,2	10,3

Counties.	Parishes.	Years.	Baptisms	Burials.
York	Ackworth	1747 to 1757	12,7	10,7
	Adwick de Street	1740—1749	7,3	5,5
	Arkfey	1740—1749	23,8	20,8
	Auftin	1740—1749	9,9	8,4
	Barmborough	1740—1749	8,8	6,5
	Bawtry	1740—1749	15,6	17,5
	Blyth	1740—1749	28,7	19,0
	Bolton on Dearn	1740—1749	13,4	7,7
	Brodfworth	1740—1749	6,7	3,8
	Burgh-wallis	1740—1749	2,2	2,7
	Campfall	1740—1749	34,6	32,6
	Clayton cum Frickley	1740—1749	4,1	3,3
	Crofton	1741—1750	12,3	7,0
	Darfield	1740—1749	37,3	31,0
	Dewfbury	1740—1749	142,0	92,3
	Doncafter	1740—1749	96,6	92,1
	Felkirke	1740—1749	23,3	14,6
	Firbeck	1740—1749	4,8	3,8
	Halifax	1740—1749	266,8	232,6
	Heath	1758—1767	19,8	13,4
	Hemfworth	1740—1749	19,2	15,4
	Hooton Pagnell	1740—1749	10,8	5,4
	Methley	1740—1749	26,0	15,1
	Normanton	1740—1749	20,1	14,8
	Pontefract	1740—1749	110,7	92,8
	Rawmarfh	1740—1749	18,6	13,7
	Rotherham	1740—1749	110,7	96,1
	Scrooby	1740—1749	5,6	4.9
	Sheffield	1740—1749	544,0	498,4
	Skelbrooke	1740—1749	2,2	1,4
	South Kirby	1740—1749	24,0	16,4
	Tadcafter	1740—1749	31,8	27,4
	Thrunfcoe	1740—1749	4 0	3,8
	Wakefield	1741—1750	209,6	185,9
	Wath	1740—1749	32,2	21,4
		Total	4712,0	4067,0

The Average annual Number of Baptifms and Burials in various Parifhes, for Years lately paft.

Counties	Parifhes	Years	Baptifms	Burials
Anglefea	Beaumaris	1764 to 1771	41,0	31,1
	Llandyfnan	1764—1771	19,2	13,5
	Llanfadurn	1764—1771	8,6	8,5
	Llanvair	1764—1771	12,6	9,6
	Pentraeth	1764—1771	18,6	10,0
Cambridge	Papworth Agnes	1770—1779	3,5	1,3
	Papworth Everard	1770—1779	2,0	2,0
Cornwall	Breage	1770—1779	75,0	42,6
	Cury	1770—1779	5,9	5,8
	Germo	1770—1779	17,6	10,5
	Gunwalloe	1770—1779	6,6	3,0
	St. Hillary	1770—1780	66,2	34,6
	St. Martins	1770—1779	8,1	7,7
	Mawgan	1770—1779	17,0	12,8
	Sithney	1770—1779	37,3	19,9
Devon.	Axminfter	1770—1779	50,6	45,4
Effex	Arkefden	1770—1779	9,9	8,5
	Clavering	1770—1779	21,2	12,8
	Heydon	1770—1779	6,7	5,1
	Langley	1770—1779	7,4	2,8
	Quendon	1770—1779	5,1	2,4
	Stenfted Montfitchet	1770—1780	32,4	24,0
	Ugley	1770—1780	10,9	4,9
	Wendens Ambo	1770—1779	6,3	4,4
Herts.	Brent Pelham	1770—1779	5,8	2,3
	Furneux Pelham	1770—1779	15,9	11,2
Huntington	Folkfworth	1770—1779	3,4	2,2
	Lutton	1770—1779	6,3	3,3
	Morborne	1770—1779	1,5	1,5
	Yelling	1770—1779	5,9	3,8
Kent	Chalk	1771—1780	6,7	10,0
	Northfleet	1771—1780	33,9	39,0
	Nurfted	1771—1780	2,0	1,1
Lancafter	Manchefter	1770—1779	1278,5	994,8
	Rochdale	1771—1780	478,7	415,5
	Warrington	1770—1773	337,2	311,8
Leicefter	Foxton	1770—1779	12,8	11,9

Counties	Parishes	Years	Baptisms	Burials
	Lubenham	1770 to 1779	15,9	12,4
	St. Mary's	1770—1779	104,3	90,2
	Norton	1770—1779	5,6	2,7
	Thedingworth	1770—1779	7,0	5,1
	Thornby	1770—1779	4,9	3,5
Lincoln	West Deeping	1770—1779	5,8	4,7
	Jallington	1770—1779	7,4	5,0
Norfolk	Brancaster	1770—1779	17,7	12,2
	Docking	1771—1780	18,1	10,5
	Fitcham	1771—1780	8,5	5,7
	Hilborowe	1771—1780	12,2	6,8
	Hillington	1771—1780	7,1	5,1
	Titchwell	1771—1780	2,5	1,2
Northampton	Castor	1770—1779	18,6	17,0
	Clipston	1770—1779	15,7	12,0
	Cottestbrooke	1770—1779	7,0	5,3
	Glinton	1770—1779	11,0	8,5
	Guilsborough	1770—1779	18,4	14,3
	Helpston	1770—1779	5,8	5,9
	Marham	1770—1779	2,3	2,2
	Marston Truffel	1770—1779	7,2	5,5
	Maxey	1770—1779	13,3	9,2
	Naseby	1770—1779	14,5	11,4
	Peterborough	1770—1779	121,1	124,0
	Ravensworth	1770—1779	14,5	8,7
Nottingham	Broughton Sulney	1770—1779	6,8	4,8
	Carlton	1770—1779	15,9	10,6
	Kinolton	1770—1779	10,4	5,5
Salop	Holy-Cross	1761—1770	38,2	36,5
Somerset	Chard	1770—1779	49,5	36,5
	Curry Rivel	1770—1779	25,8	13,9
	Draton	1770—1779	10,0	5,0
	Ilminster	1770—1779	42,3	30,8
	Puckington	1770—1779	4,5	1,7
	Wayford	1770—1779	7,2	4,1
	Wellington	1770—1779	55,9	48,0
Stafford	Alrewas	1771—1780	29,5	18,3

(59)

Counties.	Parishes.	Years.	Baptisms	Burials.
	Barton under Needwood.	1771—1780	23,0	16,1
	Burton on Trent	1771—1780	141,8	98,1
	Elford	1771—1780	13,1	5,6
	Rugeley	1771—1780	51,2	37,3
	Stapenhall	1771—1780	35,3	16,0
	Tatenhall	1771—1780	15,4	7,8
	Walton on Trent	1771—1780	9,5	4,7
Suffolk	Yoxall	1771—1780	31,3	22,2
	Aldham	1770—1779	6,5	4,1
	East-Bergholt	1770—1779	28,0	22,9
	Brockley	1771—1780	10,0	4,9
	Elmset	1770—1779	11,2	8,8
	Groton	1770—1779	17,7	14,0
	Hadleigh	1770—1779	63,5	63,9
	Hawkedon	1771—1780	5,8	3,8
	Kersey	1770—1779	18,7	15,3
	Layham	1770—1779	20,0	14,3
	Lindsey	1770—1779	6,1	3,8
	Reed	1771—1780	6,1	3,1
	Semer	1770—1779	5,9	4,1
	Stratford (St. Mary's)	1770—1779	14,0	8,5
	Somerton	1771—1780	2,9	2,9
	Whatfield	1770—1779	6,3	4,1
	Barrow	1771—1780	22,7	15,2
	Denston	1771—1780	9,8	5,9
	Depden	1771—1780	7,9	5,0
Sussex	Fairlight	1770—1779	9,6	3,8
	Guestling	1770—1779	10,8	6,0
	Hastings All Saints	1766—1771	31,3	24,7
	Hastings St. Clements	1766—1771	32,2	22,0
	Icklesham	1770—1779	9,7	5,0
	Pett	1770—1779	5,6	2,7
	Westfield	1770—1779	20,8	11,1
York	Ackworth	1757—1767	21,2	15,6

Counties.	Parishes.	Years.	Baptisms	Burials.
York	Adwick de Street	1770 to 1779	10,1	4,3
	Arkfey	1770—1779	28,3	19,2
	Auftin	1770—1779	11,8	7,0
	Barmborough	1770—1779	11,2	5,6
	Bawtry	1770—1779	15,4	21,3
	Blyth	1770—1779	41,7	26,0
	Bolton on Dearn	1770—1779	19,1	10,8
	Brodfworth	1770—1779	7,0	5,0
	Burgh-wallis	1770—1779	3,6	2,4
	Campfall	1770—1779	46,0	27,0
	Clayton cum Frickley	1770—1779	9,8	4,0
	Crofton	1770—1779	13,4	7,6
	Darfield	1770—1779	39,5	24,6
	Dewfbury	1770—1779	232,6	139,3
	Doncafter	1770—1779	144,2	129,6
	Felkirke	1770—1779	30,7	20,1
	Firbeck	1770—1779	6,0	3,7
	Halifax	1770—1779	361,9	342,5
	Heath	1770—1779	21,9	16,2
	Hemfworth	1770—1779	21,4	13,5
	Hooton Pagnell	1770—1779	11,0	6,3
	Methley	1770—1779	30,3	21,9
	Normanton	1770—1779	18,5	12,4
	Pontefract	1770—1779	159,3	123,1
	Rawmarfh	1770—1779	37,2	21,2
	Rotherham	1770—1779	184,1	139,9
	Scrooby	1770—1779	7,2	4,9
	Sheffield	1770—1779	1046,9	983,3
	Skelbrooke	1770—1779	2,3	1,4
	South Kirby	1770—1779	31,8	19,1
	Tadcafter	1770—1779	57,1	36,6
	Thrunfcoe	1770—1779	6,0	3,3
	Wakefield	1770—1779	308,0	221,1
	Wath	1770—1779	38,2	25,1
		Total	7179,1	5689,1

In the former of these periods; namely, from about the years 1740 to the year 1750, the average, annual number of births in the above 142 parishes was 4712; of deaths, 4067, In the latter period; that is, from about the year 1770 to the year 1780, the average, annual number of births was 7179: of deaths 5689. If, therefore, we supose the mean number of the inabitants, in the latter period, to be to the mean number of them, in the former, as the births in the latter are to the births in the former, they will be as 7179 is to 4712; or somewhat more than as 3 to 2. If the deaths be taken to express the proportion between the inhabitants at these two periods, they will be as 5689 is to 4067; or nearly as 7 to 5. If the arithmetical means be taken between the two, as was done before, the proportion will be as 12868 to 8779: if the geometrical mean be taken, the proportion will be as 63908 to 43776; and, in either case, the proportion will be between the former two.

I shall

I shall now add two tables, which have been communicated to me by a gentleman, who collected them some time ago, one of them for ascertaining, in the best manner he could, the effect which the late marriage act had on the population of this kingdom; and the other for comparing the state of Population, in the diocese of *St. David's*, for the first 30 years of the present century, with the state of it in the second 30 years; and also with the years 1761, 1762, 1763, and 1764.

A Table

(63)

A TABLE of the Baptisms in sundry Parishes for ten Years immediately before, and ten Years immediately after the Year 1754; being that Year in which the Marriage-Act took Place.

Counties.	Parishes.	1754 Before.	After.
Brecknock	St. John's Brecon	479	457
Cardigan	Cardigan	265	285
Carmarthen	Abergwilly	292	297
	St. Ishmael's	168	136
	Llandilo-vawr	921	954
	Llandingat and Llatvair-ar-y-bryn	396	501
Devon	Clehanger	62	62
	Oakford	121	114
	Stoodleigh	86	83
Essex	West-Ham	1074	1196
Hants	North Stoneham	143	137
Kent	Blean	110	83
	Chilham	169	201
	Deptford, St. Nicholas	1747	1789
	Fordwich	63	70
	Greenwich	2314	2265
	Harbledown	129	138
	Hardres (Little)	54	57
	Hearn	297	293
	Ickham	89	95
	Molash	82	89
	Rackington	14	24
	St. Stephens	57	65
Middlesex	Chelsea	1132	1094
Pembroke	Haverfordwest St. Mary's	317	288
Wilts	Warminster	990	1031
		11571	11804

The increase in these twenty-six parishes is very small indeed: the mean number of the inhabitants, in the former ten years, being to the mean number of them in the latter, as 11571 is to 11804. The parishes are, it is true, such as no great increase could be expected in, as they are all, Deptford and West-Haverford excepted, without either trade or manufacture; and, moreover, the length of time between the two periods is very short. The table, however, tends to shew that whatever number of parishes are taken, indiscriminately; or for whatever time or length of time, the result will be, that the inhabitants have increased.

A TABLE

A TABLE of the Average, annual number of Baptisms and Burials, in the several Parishes, within the Diocese of St. David's, from 1700 to 1730; from 1730 to 1760, from 1760 to 1763, in the seven first Deaneries, and from 1760 to 1764, in the remaining ones.

Deaneries.	1700—1730		1730—1760		1760—1763 or —4.	
	Births	Bur.	Births	Bur.	Births	Bur.
Melineth	100,1	103,5	187,0	147,8	182,0	168,3
Elvel	75,8	73,0	158,1	118,8	163,0	118,3
Builth	47,6	42,2	92,4	76,1	93,3	66,2
Hay	67,6	60,7	144,3	130,1	161,0	124,0
I. Brecon	49,7	45,5	133,4	114,6	127,7	103,0
II. Brecon	57,7	47,1	107,7	85,6	113,3	104,7
III. Brecon	73,2	70,3	171,5	148,6	177,3	158,3
Gower	120,5	99,8	137,4	118,2	164,8	128,2
Llandiloe	258,8	227,8	257,7	215,6	308,0	266,3
Carmarthen	138,8	127,3	165,3	146,5	226,2	189,0
Kidwelly	109,9	96,5	140,0	106,0	154,7	124,5
Parishes.						
St Mary's West } Haverfordwest }	28,0	10,3	31,4	20,3	28,8	20,0
Narberth	13,5	11,2	10,7	11,9	21,7	23,3
Cardigan	16,0	8,3	23,1	15,1	31,0	9,7
Llandewy	30,8	23,2	30,3	22,9	41,0	28,0
Caron	24,1	17,6	21,6	16,6	22,3	17,5
Llampeter } Pont Stephen }	16,8	13,4	14,0	13,4	13,5	14,3

The total of the average annual births, in the diocese of St. David's, from 1700 to 1730 was 1228,9 : of the deaths (1077,7.) From 1730 to 1760 the births were annually (1825,9) and the deaths 1508,1. From 1760 to 1763, or 1764, the average, annual births were 2029,6: the deaths 1663,6. Hence, taking the births as the measure of the inhabitants, the mean number of them, between the years 1700 and 1730, was to the mean number between the years 1730 and 1760, as 1228,9 to 1825,9; and to the mean number between 1760 and 1763, or 1764, as 1228,9 to 2029,6. If the deaths be taken as the standard, the mean number of the inhabitants, in this diocese, between the years 1700 and 1730, was to the mean number of them between the years 1730 and 1760, as 1077,7 to 1508,1; and to the mean number between 1760 and 1763, or 1764, as 1077,7 to 1663,6. If the arithmetical means be taken, as they were in former instances, the mean number of inhabitants, in the said diocese, between 1700 and 1730 was to the mean number of them between 1730 and 1760, as 1153,3 to 1667,0; and to the mean number of inhabitants between 1760 and 1763, or 1764, as 1153,3 to 1846,6. If the geometrical means be taken, the proportions will be as
1150,8

1150,8 to 1659,4, and as 1150,8 to 1837,5. Either of which is nearly as 2 to 3 in the first proportion, and as 5 to 8 in the latter.

The few following comparisons of actual enumerations are all that have come to my knowledge. No remarks on them can be necessary.

Counties.	Towns.	Year.	Inhabit.	Year	Inhabit.
Chester.	Altringham	in 1750	1000†	in 1772	1029
Lancast.	Manchester	in 1757	19839	in 1773	27246
	Liverpool	in 1700	5714	in 1773	34407
Norfolk.	Norwich	in 1693	28881	in 1752	36196
	Nottingham	in 1740	11000	in 1779	17711
Salop.	Holy Cross	in 1755	1049	in 1770	1046*
Surry.	Farnham‡	in 1741	1716	in 1780	2123
Warwick.	Birmingham	in 1700	15032	in 1770	30804
York.	Ackworth	in 1757	603	in 1767	728
	Leeds	in 1770	16380	in 1775	17121
			101214		168411

It will not be amiss if I bring the foregoing particulars into a narrower point of view.

1st. The number of inhabitants in London, during the last 5 years, were to the number

---

† Somewhat less.
* Between these two years 38 persons had been driven out of the parish by pulling down their houses to build a bridge; there being no other houses to receive them.
‡ These two enumerations were made by Mr *John Clarke* of this place: the former at the request of Dr. *Adee*, of Oxford, who very obligingly communicated the result; and the latter, at my desire, the beginning of the present month of January.

of inhabitants during 5 years about the time of the Revolution, as 203860,3 to 18283,3. That is, as 10 to 9 nearly.

2d. The number of houses, or families, in certain towns, taken indiscriminately, and in a confiderable variety of countries, are now, to the number which was in the fame towns in 1750 as 28544 to 23526: or as 7 to 6 nearly.

3d. The prefent number of inhabitants in 38 parifhes, taken indifcriminately, in different parts of England, according to the regifters of births and burials in thefe parifhes, is to the number which was in the fame thirty-eight parifhes at the Revolution, as 446115 to 166274: or as 8 to 3 nearly.

4th. The prefent number of inhabitants, in 142 parifhes, taken in the fame manner as in the laft article, is to the number which were in the fame parifhes between the years 1740 and 1750, as 12868 to 8779: or as 10 to 7 nearly.

5th. The baptifms in twenty-fix parifhes, for ten years immediately before the year 1754, when compared with the baptifms in the fame twenty-fix parifhes for ten years immediately after 1754, gave the proportion between the number of inhabitants in the latter ten years

years to the mean number of them in the former ten years, as 1157,1 to 1180,4.

6th. According to the baptisms and burials in the diocese of St. David's, the mean number of the inhabitants, between the years 1700 and 1730, was to the mean number of the inhabitants, between the years 1730 and 1760, as 1153,3 to 1667,0: or as 2 to 3 nearly; and to the mean number of the inhabitants which were in the said diocese between the years 1760 and 1763, or 1764, as 1153,3 to 1846,6; or as 5 to 8 nearly.

Lastly. From actual enumerations, the number of inhabitants in ten cities, towns, and villages, at a former period, were 10,1214; at a latter they were 16841 1.

In every instance the places have been taken indiscriminately; that is, just as I could procure them; and I have omitted no place which I could procure: it may, therefore, be fairly concluded that they represent, justly, the state of the Kingdom in general; and this argument cannot be overturned but by producing a greater number of parishes which tend to prove the contrary; or an equal number of facts of a more certain nature.

Although

Although all arguments drawn from conjecture muſt ſubmit to the foregoing matters of fact, yet the following ones appear to me ſo forcible, that I cannot help ſubmitting them to the public. It has been urged that the inhabitants have decreaſed in country towns and villages, becauſe employment has decreaſed in thoſe places, and that the decreaſe of employment has been cauſed by encloſing common fields, and putting ſeveral ſmall farms into one great one. That both theſe circumſtances may have tended to leſſen employment amongſt huſbandmen, in ſome parts of the kingdom, I will not diſpute; but I believe, by no means, in that degree which thoſe, who argue for a decreaſed population, imagine. The farmer, where he is at liberty to act as he thinks proper, will not be governed by conſidering whether his land is open or incloſed, in aſſigning the proportion between arable and grazing grounds, but by the profits which this or that ſtate of his land produces: conſequently, whether land be incloſed or not, the proportion between the quantity of land which is on tillage, and that which is in graſs, will always be determined by the proportion which the price of corn bears to the price of cattle, as it always was.

It

It is true, great quantities of the newly enclofed common fields have been *laid down*; and the reafon is plain. For every acre of common field land that has been enclofed, there have been enclofed two acres of commons, and other wafte grounds; almoft every acre of which has, neceffarily, had the plough thrown into it, in order to cultivate and improve it. The price of corn muft therefore have funk to nothing, and the price of cattle have rifen to an extravagant rate, if other lands had not been laid in to grafs to feed them.

It may be farther obferved, that hitherto, inclofures have been fo far from leffening employment, that they muft have greatly increafed it. The enclofed commons and wafte land, being fo much more in quantity than the common fields which have been taken in; and requiring, at the fame time, fo much more labour, to bring them into order, then it required to work lands, already cultivated, muft greatly have increafed employment. We may add the great increafe of labour in fencing, and dividing both forts of enclofures, as well as the additional employment of keeping them continually in repair, and in cultivating, continually a quantity of

land

land so much greater than was under cultivation before, as well as keeping a confiderable part of that land in a higher ftate of cultivation: it being well-known, and reafonable to fuppofe, that more care and pains are employed in the cultivation of enclofed lands, than on thofe which are not enclofed. In fhort, the whole inconvenience which has arifen from enclofing, and which has given rife to all thefe complaints, is, that where the enclofures have been chiefly, or wholly, of common fields, employment has declined: whilft it has increafed in a much greater proportion, in thofe parts where the enclofures have been chiefly or wholly, waft lands; and, confequently, the people have been obliged to remove from one place to another, after their employment.

With refpect to the engroffing of farms, there can be little doubt, but that it has been a real grievance to many individuals; and fo, likewife, has many other things been, which have proved very advantageous to the kingdom in general. Every confiderable alteration in the internal policy and management of a ftate, whether it be for the better or worfe, in general, muft be a hardfhip to thofe individuals who are obliged, in confequence of it, to feek a new employment; but it does not, therefore,

follow

follow that every such alteration is for the worse. Whether the change, under consideration, has been for the better, or worse, can only be determined by experience, and the observations of men who are judges of, and conversant in these matters. Mr. *Young*, the very ingenious author of many excellent publications on this subject, and who has certainly considered these things as much, and, perhaps, understands them as well as any other person in England, is clearly for large farms; and has advanced such arguments in their favour, as seem difficult to confute : and, to his works, I wish to refer those who chuse to inquire farther into this affair. It is obvious enough, that the division of land into small farms, may be extremely proper at one time, and as highly improper at another. Such a division may also be proper in one state, and not in another. For example, it would be very proper to encourage it in those states where the form of government is feudal, and where they have no manufactures or commerce ; but it seems very absurd to employ more hands than are necessary, in cultivating the ground, in states which depend chiefly on arts, manufactures, and foreign commerce for their support, as is the case with England at

present

present. If that unhappy time should ever arrive when these are lost, farms will naturally subdivide themselves again, and become as small as they have been formerly.

As it is undoubtedly of the utmost importance in every state, to promote population, so nothing contributes to it so much as encouraging marriage amongst all ranks of people; but especially amongst the lower, and middling ones. To this end, the means of providing for a family ought not to be too difficult and laborious: such provision ought, however, to be obtainable by as few ways as possible without labour. It is by wealth, acquired by the slow means of industry, that a kingdom is enriched, because it is then more equally distributed, and the inhabitants become, by that means, more hardy, robust, active, and, I may add, ingenious, quick-sighted, and penetrating; and, of course, more useful. That wealth which flows easily, and suddenly into a kingdom from mines, or by any other means, independant of labour, tends only to render its inhabitants weak, inactive, and timorous. We have a sufficient proof of this in Spain; and I sincerely hope that England will never be possessed of any such ruinous and destructive means of acquiring it.

But

But notwithstanding I think that wealth ought not to be acquired without labour, it certainly should be in every ones power, who endeavours earnestly, to procure it with honesty, and even honour; or, at least, that every one should have a prospect of obtaining a sufficiency to maintain him in ease, when he arrives at old age. Cut off from the pleasing hope of something like this, a man has no spur to industry beyond the cravings of hunger—he becomes dispirited, and unable to exert his faculties, either with that power, or to that extent which he might otherwise have done.

Much has been said by *Doctor Short*, as well as other writers on this subject, in favour of sumptuary laws for promoting population: I believe they would have little effect. There can be no doubt but that such laws would be useful, could we depend on their being properly executed. For example, no father ought to be allowed to disinherit his child, on the score of marriage. I do not say that he ought not to do all in his power to prevent his children from marrying improperly; but there is a wide difference between prevention and punishment.

That cuftom which prevails of giving all, or the major part to the eldeft fon, is pernicious to population, and of courfe to the ftate which fuffers, or encourages it.

Marriages between perfons of difproportioned ages is another very great hindrance to population, and ought abfolutely to be prohibited; or, at leaft, a heavy tax laid on it to eafe, in fome meafure, the burthens of the publick, in other refpects. There are means which might be ufed to come at the ages of moft perfons, and thofe who appear to come within this objection, fhould be obliged to produce the proper proofs.

Some laws of this kind may alfo be very neceffary for the other fex; and efpecially thofe of middling rank; who, when luxury and extravagance, efpecially in drefs, happen to be the reigning paffion of the times, are more apt to run into the extremes of it than men. It muft be owned, however, that men, of the fame rank, do but too much encourage this propenfity, by paying the moft attention to thofe who are moft extravagant in that refpect; although, at the fame time, the dread of the expence, which attends it, prevents their engaging with them in the more intimate connections of marriage; well knowing that

few,

few, who have once given into a rage for drefs, would not rather run the rifk of ruining their hufbands, than yield the palm to another, whom they have been ufed to vie with, in this refpect.

A pamphlet has lately been written, by a perfon for whofe talents and ingenuity I have the greateft refpect, propofing a public *cenfus*. Such a circumftance would certainly be very agreeable to every fpeculative mind, intent on the inquiry after truth, in any branch of natural knowledge; and, perhaps, at fome future time, fuch a project may be put in execution without any fear of bad confequences refulting from it, on any account whatever: at prefent, fuch an inquiry may not be advifeable. Our enemies have always been ufed to eftimate us at feven or eight millions: and, notwithftanding the foregoing facts feem fully to prove that we are more numerous at this time, than at any former one, yet it by no means follows that we amount to that number, even now. If, therefore, fuch an enumeration fhould take place, and we fhould be found fhort of the number which they have been ufed to take us at, they might probably, inftead of reflecting that they have a ftronger adverfary to contend with than formerly,

formerly, only confider that we are weaker than they had imagined, and take frefh courage from that confideration, and efpecially, as fuch an enumeration would determine nothing with refpect to our number at any former time. However, if fuch a proceeding fhould be thought advifeable at this, or any future time, I am clearly of opinion the moft eligible perfons to perform it are the parochial clergy; and, by them, it would be performed in a very few weeks. I have heard the opinions of the miniftres of fome of the moft extenfive parifhes in England, who think it might be done, even in their parifhes, with eafe and certainty, in two months; with the addition of age, fituation and profeffion of each individual.

But the point, which is of moft confequence to us, is to inquire whether we are, at prefent, an increafing, or a decreafing people: and this, I am perfuaded, can only be effected, to any purpofe, by the means which I have been purfuing, and mean to purfue ftill farther. I fhall therefore conclude with requefting, that fuch of the clergy as this little tract may fall into the hands of, will oblige the author with the annual number of baptifms, marriages and burials,

rials, in their refpective parifhes, for ten years, as near the time of the Revolution as poffible; the fame things for ten years between the years 1740 and 1750, and for the ten years ending with 1780, directed for him, in Chrift's Hofpital, London.

THE END.

UNCERTAINTY

OF THE

PRESENT POPULATION

OF

THIS KINGDOM;

DEDUCED FROM A CANDID REVIEW OF
THE ACCOUNTS LATELY GIVEN OF IT

BY

Dr. *PRICE*, *on the one Hand*,

Mr. *EDEN,* Mr. *WALES,* and Mr. *HOWLETT,*
on the Other.

———————

LONDON:

Printed for RICHARDSON and URQUHART, under the
Royal-Exchange. 1781.

Republished in 1973 by Gregg International Publishers Limited
Westmead, Farnborough, Hants., England

UNCERTAINTY

OF THE

PRESENT POPULATION

OF

THIS KINGDOM.

THAT both the abſolute Population of a ſtate, and its continual increaſe, are matters of high political importance, ſeems univerſally acknowledged. The former gives force and ſtrength to repel the attacks of foreign enemies; the latter, while it more effectally ſecures the ſame deſirable end, with reſpect to the united ſociety at large, promotes likewiſe the happineſs of the individuals of which it is compoſed. Every other circumſtance remaining the ſame, the kingdom whoſe people are few is to that in which they are numerous as the

dwarf

dwarf before the giant, by whofe firft malignant grafp he may be inftantly crufhed to death: and the nation whofe numbers are daily *increafing*, refembles, through its every rank and department, the cheerful vigour of youth, continually advancing towards the perfection of manhood; whereas that in which they are perpetually *decreafing* is but too like the growing infirmities of age, when each limb is gradually becoming more weak and feeble, each joint is filling with aches and anguifh, and we every day go more painfully tottering forward, till we ftumble into the grave, and totally difappear.

As thefe things are of confequence in themfelves confidered, fo it is fcarcely of inferior moment that the truth of the cafe, with regard to each, fhould be actually known. The tradefman who neglects to examine and balance his accounts foon finds his affairs embarraffed, and he fuddenly finks into poverty and ruin, while he foolifhly fancies he is rifing faft into wealth and affluence. If we believe ourfelves in perfect health, while really and deeply difeafed, the groundlefs confidence will make us neglect the neceffary means of cure, and may fpeedily render immature diffolution inevitable:

inevitable: if, on the contrary, we imagine ourselves to be dangerously ill when we are truly and intirely well, the fickly apprehenfion will overfpread our days with gloom and wretchednefs, or perhaps effectually bring on the fatal diftemper which before had no exiftence but in difordered imagination. Juft fo with refpect to the fubject we are about to treat.

If, as a kingdom, we confider ourfelves to be numerous, and conftantly growing more fo, while we are really but few, and every day becoming fewer, we may provoke too powerful hoftilities againft us, and precipitate that deftruction which might perhaps have been eafily avoided. If, on the other hand, we admit the gloomy idea that we are a fmall inconfiderable body, for ever dwindling and wafting away, while the reverfe is the fact, it will naturally tend to deprefs our fpirits, to fink us down into a ftate of defpondence and pufillanimity, incite the infolent depredations of our foes, and bring us by degrees to that pitiful condition which we had hitherto only imagined. A true and accurate knowledge in either cafe may happily prevent thefe pernicious effects. Should it be clearly difcovered, that our inhabitants are few, and still greatly diminishing, it may teach us to remove the causes of still further declension; if they are numerous, and yet rapidly augmenting, we may go cheerfully forward in that road of prosperity in which we have hitherto trodden.

It therefore gives me singular pleasure to observe, that this subject has lately engaged so large a share of the public attention; at the same time I cannot but acknowledge, that it is no inconsiderable mortification to me, that nothing has yet been advanced on either side of the question that can claim any full or rational assent. We are still at a loss to determine, with any degree of certainty, whether our population during the present century has been going forwards or backwards, or whether its present actual amount be eight or nine millions, or only between four and five.

On this important topic four persons have employed their researches and their pens, Dr. Price, Mr. Eden, Mr. Wales, and Mr. Howlett. The first of the four has chosen to enforce the gloomy and dispiriting side of the question, which he has done with a degree of acuteness and ingenuity that seemed to produce, if not a full conviction, at least a temporary and silent acquiescence,

acquiescence. The three last have adopted the more bright and flattering idea, which they have supported with so much plausibility, as to have gained a very considerable share of popular belief. For my own part, I must frankly declare I am convinced by neither party; I feel myself compelled to remain in a state of doubt and sceptical suspense. I will endeavour fairly and candidly to state what has been advanced by each of these gentlemen, and I flatter myself the result will be a full confirmation of what I have now remarked, that in the solution of this momentous problem we are still far from certainty, or even satisfactory probability.

I shall not pretend to examine the minuter and subordinate reasonings of these several writers; both because it would exceed the limits I wish to prescribe myself, and because it would in itself be intirely unnecessary. If their leading and principal arguments are overthrown or established, those of inferior rank may be safely omitted.

In this controversy, Dr. Price's *Essay on the Population of England and Wales* appeared the first, and therefore naturally claims our first attention.

The Doctor's grand argument for the depopulation of this kingdom, and upon which he judiciously lays the principal stress, is at once extremely clear, and comprehended in very narrow compass. About the year 1690, as appears from the books of the hearth-tax, the total number of houses in England and Wales was about thirteen hundred thousand; consequently, allowing five persons to a house, the inhabitants amounted to six millions and one-fourth: or supposing by *houses* in this account was meant *families*, as seems upon the whole most probable, and there can be no absolute certainty of the contrary; yet, as the number of *families* and *houses* were then doubtless nearer an equality than at present, the people could not be considerably inferior to six millions. The accuracy of this estimate is satisfactorily confirmed by Mr. King's Observations, published not long after, and which we are assured were the result of particular enquiry, united to great sagacity: from these it appears, making the number of persons to a *family* only $4\frac{1}{13}$, the inhabitants were five millions and a half. Putting both accounts together, it is indubitably clear, that the people at this æra were as near or nearer six millions

tha

than five. But by the returns of the surveyors of the window-lights to the tax-office in the year 1777, the total number of houses in the kingdom, taxed and untaxed, inhabited and uninhabited, charged with the window duty, or 3 s. house-tax, or excused on account of poverty, was little more than nine hundred and fifty thousand; that is, three hundred and fifty thousand less than in the year 1690; and, by the common allowance of five persons to a house, a decrease in our people of considerably more than a million and a half, and an absolute reduction of them to at most between four and five millions. These returns however cannot be supposed perfectly correct and complete; some deficiency must probably have arisen from the inattention and negligence of county or parochial surveyors. The Doctor seems aware of this, and therefore makes an allowance, p. 14. of even a twentieth part of the whole; he admits that near fifty thousand houses may have been omitted in the returns for the whole kingdom, and is willing to state the real total amount at a million. But supposing that five persons to a house is, as the Doctor contends, too great an allowance, it follows that the number of inhabitants in England and Wales must be short of *five millions* *.

This, though not altogether in the words of the Doctor, is, I think, fairly and essentially the whole of his system respecting the present time, compared with the æra of the revolution; and it is in truth so gloomy and dispiriting a one, that every lover of his country cannot but wish to see it *fully* and clearly refuted.

The first person who attempted this was Mr. Eden, excepting only, I believe, some Cursory Observations of Mr. Arthur Young, in his Political Arithmetic. Mr. Eden has taken a view of the subject so general and superficial, that nothing very determinate or satisfactory can be expected. He has urged, indeed, many plausible speculative arguments, as well to refute the Doctor's hypothesis as to shew the great probability of an increased population. Much also he particularly says on the deficiency of the surveyors returns; how little they are to be depended upon, and how totally insuf-

---

* Should we suppose that the inaccuracy in the returns of houses for the hearth-tax in 1690 was as great as in those for the window and house-duty in 1777, the Doctor's argument of Depopulation is but so much the stronger; but the supposition is not made, because utterly improbable.

ficient to afford any ground for certain fatisfactory conclufion; and all this is conveyed with great ingenuity of reafoning, as well as ftrength and elegance of language. But he feems not to have duly confidered, that a very great deficiency in thefe returns was admitted by the Doctor himfelf, and that his fole bufinefs was to prove, by indubitable facts, that this deficiency greatly exceeded 50,000: as he has not even attempted this, nothing important is really accomplifhed. The ear may be pleafed with the mufic and harmony of his periods, and the fancy delighted with the beauty and brillancy of his images; but the underftanding remains without any clear *information*, and the Doctor's fyftem is fo perfectly unimpaired, that he himfelf confidered it as more firmly eftablifhed than ever.

The next attack it met with, was from the hand of Mr. Wales; and let us enquire what *he* has done to effect its overthrow.

With refpect to the main argument, the Surveyors returns, he fays, p. 3. of his *Enquiry into the prefent State of the Population in England and Wales*, that " they are " by no means fufficient to fupport any " calcula-

" calculations of this nature; that cottages
" are seldom returned at all, and that
" when they are, it is generally from con-
" jecture, or from some old duplicate,
" which, perhaps, was the conjecture of
" 20 or 30 years before."

All this is so extremely vague and indeterminate as to merit but little attention. He does not, indeed, seem to have at all distinguished the true nature of the reasoning he had to encounter; which does not suppose a perfect accuracy in the returns, but admits, on the contrary, that they are even exceedingly deficient, not less than nearly the twentieth part of the whole. This, as far as appears, may be perfectly consistent with a total omission of cottages in some places, and with a great degree of negligence in others, both of the parochial and county surveyors; the former may make their returns of cottages from conjecture, or from some old duplicate, the conjecture of 20 or 30 years before; and the latter may take these conjectural duplicates in their hands, and carelessly gallop through each parish without any further concern or more accurate inspection; and yet, after all, the aggregate deficiency for the whole kingdom may not exceed

exceed 50,000, the allowance made by the Doctor. This random way of talk may fatisfy the fuperficial reader, but brings no fatisfaction to the candid enquirer. The matter in difpute muft be determined, not by vague declamation, or fpeculative argument, but by clear and well authenticated facts. And what of this kind does our author produce? He tells us, p. 45, that the total number of houfes in fourteen parifhes in Suffolk was 486, of which 439 were charged with the windowtax; and that in twenty-eight parifhes in Northamptonfhire, p. 43. the total was 1024, and the taxed 704. From this ftatement, as Mr. Wales acknowledges that the *untaxed* houfes are fometimes returned, we cannot tell whether that was not the cafe here, and that though only a *part* were *affeffed*, they were not *all* inferted in the parochial duplicates. However, as the tenour of his argument requires they *fhould not*, I will take it for granted they *were not*. With this idea let us accompany our Author, to Mr. Cooper, Surveyor of the windows for the two divifions of Agbridge and Morley, in the county of York. What information does this gentleman give us? Why, that he

found

found the total number of houses in these two divisions in the year 1779 to be 21929; of which 4697 were charged with the window-tax, 8135, with the Three Shillings house-duty, and 9097 excused on account of poverty. These, we are to understand, were all returned to the tax-office; nor is there the smallest intimation that there were any still behind which were omitted.

These are the facts which Mr. W. produces on the subject of the surveyors returns. Let us put them together and see to what they amount.

	Total No. of Houses.	Returned.
14 Parishes in Suffolk	486	439
28 Parishes in Northamptonshire	1024	704
2 Divisions in Yorkshire	21929	21929
Total	23439	23072
Omitted in the Returns		367

Here we see, that out of 23439 houses, only 367 were left out of the Surveyors returns; which is but about one *sixtieth* part of the whole number. But Dr. Price allows

allows the aggregate deficiency for England and Wales may be 50,000, which is near a *twentieth* part. Now, suppofing the above ftatement to exhibit the average ratio for the kingdom at large (which Mr. W. can have no objection to, as the places are of his own felection) the collective deficiency is about 17,000, and not even a *fixtieth* part. This attack, therefore, inftead of demolifhing the Doctor's fyftem, renders it three times as ftrong as it was before; and, if nothing further could be faid, the idea of depopulation, for the laft ninety years, muft be admitted.

But the Doctor is not content with maintaining, that a great diminution of inhabitants has taken place during this *long* period, but contends that the decline has been peculiarly rapid within the 20 or 30 years laft paft. And his argument for this latter pofition is even more fpecious than for the former. The returns of the window furveyors for 1759, were upwards of 33,000 more than in 1777: and confequently, at the ufual allowance of five perfons to a houfe, there muft have been in the courfe of eighteen years, a lofs of more than 150,000 people. For however inaccurate and deficient the returns

turns may be, there is no reason to suppose the Doctor thinks they were more so in 1777 than in 1759. To this argument Mr. W. has urged nothing by way of refutation or direct reply. If he has fairly however proved the contrary doctrine, that our numbers, instead of being diminished during each period, have been greatly augmented, a direct reply or formal refutation is rendered unnecessary.

To prove this point then, with respect to the latter period, Mr. W. informs us, that in a great number of parishes in the counties of York, Derby, Northampton, Suffolk, Sussex, and Somerset, the total number of houses in the year 1750, was 23526; but that in the year 1780 they were augmented to 28544; that is, they were increased in the course of thirty years, 5018, or a fourth part of their original number. But unfortunately for this augmentation, 4585 of the additional houses are in the county of York, which every body knows, and Dr. Price himself is ready to acknowledge, has acquired an amazing addition of inhabitants within the last thirty years. And what is more unlucky still, this Yorkshire account was taken from the Surveyors returns, which Mr. Wales himself felf had so fully reprobated, as to declare they *were utterly insufficient to support any calculations of this nature.* An argument which thus on the openly declared principles of its author defeats itself, I need not take any great pains to shew the fallacy of. However, allowing Mr. Wales, what he cannot fairly claim, the free use of these returns, when he thinks them favourable to his cause, though he rejects them with such contemptuous disregard when of an opposite appearance, he should be careful to remember, that nearly at the same time that the returns for these two divisions were so greatly *increased,* the collective one for England and Wales was considerably *decreased;* and that therefore the only fair legitimate conclusion was, that other parts of the kingdom must have been diminished but so much the more for the augmentation of these two particular places.

As to the houses from the other counties, which were the accurate enumerations, I suppose, of political or philosophical curiosity, I might, perhaps, properly dismiss them, as not sufficiently numerous to be of any great importance; but that I may

may not be defective in the moſt punctilious reſpect to them, I would beg leave to aſk, was the number of houſes returned by the Surveyors of the window-lights for the ſame pariſhes in the year 1780 *greater*, or *leſs* than in the year 1750? If *leſs*, it would certainly be a full and direct refutation of Dr. Price's moſt plauſible argument of depopulation, for the period now immediately in queſtion. But had this been the caſe, Mr. Wales would not ſurely have omitted to tell us ſo; it would have given him a greater advantage than any he has gained. We are fairly authorized to ſuppoſe, therefore, that it was *greater*, and conſequently the anſwer juſt given to the Yorkſhire account, holds good here; that by how much the more *theſe* returns were *augmented*, by ſo much the greater muſt have been their *diminution* in ſome other quarters.—In the narrow compaſs of my reading, I do not recollect any thing aſſuming the form and appearance of reaſoning, that more dexterouſly and compleatly, in every part and point, encountered and deſtroyed itſelf than this. Candour and fairneſs, however, oblige me to acknowledge, that had theſe houſes a-

mounted

mounted to about eight or ten times the number they do, and had they all been taken from accurate enumerations at the two periods refpectively, in every part of the nation, middle, eaft, weft, north, and fouth indifferently, and comprehended places of every fize and defcription, from the largeft towns to the fmalleft country parifhes, and thefe from each county in due proportion, the refult would have been decifive for the whole kingdom. But as it is, the probability in favour of increafed population, within the period juft mentioned, is from hence abfolutely nothing at all.

To eftablifh the fame pofition, Mr. W. produces the regifters of the annual baptifms and burials from 140 parifhes on an average of ten years for two periods, the firft from about 1740 to 1750, and the fecond from 1770 to 1780, the former in both periods generally inclufive. The medium of births and burials in the firft period, is to that in the laft nearly as two to three; which we are told indicates a proportionable increafe of people. Waving for the prefent my objections to the evidence of Population, deduced from parifh regifters in general, I have only to obferve, with respect to this now before us, that by much the major part of it is taken from the more flourishing parts of Yorkshire and Lancashire, the increased Population of which needed no proof; as it has long been the astonishment of every traveller, even of those who have most loudly complained of the direct contrary being so strikingly visible in other parts of the kingdom.

To evince our great augmentation of numbers since the *Revolution,* Mr. W. produces the annual average of baptisms and burials for ten years at that æra, and lately; and likewise the annual average of baptisms and burials for thirty years, from 1700 to 1730, and from thence to 1760, for the whole diocese of St. David's. The medium of births and burials of all these taken together in the latter period to that in the former, is nearly as fifty-nine to twenty-seven. Admitting this to be satisfactory evidence, it would lead us to conclude, that our inhabitants were more than doubled since the former of the two periods. But to this I have two objections. With respect to the thirty-eight parishes, it appears, that $\frac{6}{7}$ of all their baptisms and burials are from the counties of York and Lancaster,

Lancaster, and such places too as Liverpool, Manchester, Sheffield, &c. and may therefore, for reasons just advanced, be thrown aside as useless. And with regard to the Diocese of St. David's, every one who knows how inaccurately the regifters were kept, and returned towards the commencement of the first period, will not think it improbable, that at least a third part of the parishes were then either totally omitted or extremely defective, and that this circumstance alone may be the source of the apparent increase.

Upon the whole, I cannot think that the success of this Author's attempt has been over-flattering. Where he endeavours to refute Dr. Price's arguments for Depopulation, he only more strongly *confirms* them; and the *positive* evidence he adduces to establish the contrary position, affords at most a very faint and unsatisfactory degree of probability. In itself alone it presents some glimmering hopes, that our Population may be a little advanced; but when opposed to his own and the Doctor's returns of houses, it cannot be allowed to have weight sufficient to counterbalance them.

Let us next enquire what has been done by Mr. Howlett, the fourth and last writer on this subject. This gentleman's performance is intitled, *An Examination of Doctor Price's Essay on the Population of England and Wales, and the Doctrine of a greatly increased Population in this Kingdom established by Facts.* I wish this title may not disappoint us, by promising more than the book performs.

With regard to the Doctor's argument of continued Depopulation during the last twenty years, deduced from the continual decrease in the Surveyors returns, his reply seems indeed quite satisfactory. He not only shews, from some general remarks, that a diminution in the number of houses returned, must probably have taken place without any consequent real decrease of the total number of houses; but produces a table of facts from several parishes, of a continual decrease in the returns, though it was well known that the real number of houses in none of those parishes was diminished, and that in some of them it was actually increased.

As he has directly and fully refuted this part of the Doctor's argument, which, as I observed, is the most specious, we might naturally entertain hopes that the other part, which is less so, would share the same fate.

fate. In this, however, we fhould be fomewhat miftaken. For Mr. H. like his predeceffors, when he combats the proofs of Depopulation fince the year 1690, feems to have forgot the acknowledged deficiency of the returns; his arguments of refutation being intirely levelled againft the idea of their complete and perfect accuracy; an idea never admitted or imagined. This mifapprehenfion, however, as it is rendered of no confequence by the view afterwards taken of the matter in the third part of our Author's pamphlet, where he endeavours to afcertain the abfolute number of our inhabitants, from the proportion between the returned houfes, and thofe that are omitted, and as the whole collectively meets the Doctor's reafoning in every point, I pafs it over. In page 142 of this performance, and in page 2d of the addenda, we have the total number of houfes, and of thofe returned by the Surveyors from upwards of 100 parifhes in different parts of the kingdom, taken, we are told, perfectly at hazard, and without any motive for preference or felection. The proportion of houfes returned to the total number in this collection, appears to be as 19025 to 33096, or nearly as 19 to 33.

33. Affuming this ratio for the whole kingdom, our inhabitants, inftead of being only five millions, would be between eight and nine. If therefore we allow the authenticity of this account, and likewife admit that the number and variety of places from which it is collected, are fufficient to form a fatisfactory average, the Doctor's grand argument of Depopulation is indeed fairly and fully overturned, and the contrary pofition, of the great increafe of our people, as fairly and firmly eftablifhed. But in both thefe points, it appears to me greatly deficient. The variety of places fhould perhaps have been greater, and the number ought moft certainly to have been four times as many. But, admitting that both the one and the other are adequate to the purpofe, I hope Mr. H. will excufe me, if I venture to fufpect the *authenticity* of many of the articles in his tables of total and returned houfes. I do not mean to infinuate that any of his correfpondents have defignedly mifled him, or that, on his own part, he has knowingly made any falfe infertions; but I am ftrongly inclined to believe there has been a mifapprehenfion between them, and that what are called *returned* houfes, were thofe

onl

only that are *taxed,* and that those stiled *totals* were *many,* if not *most* of them, inserted in the *parochial duplicates.* He himself indeed seems apprehensive of it; for he says, at the end of his addenda; "if I have misunderstood the information of any of my correspondents, they will be kind enough to correct me." Does not this imply some uncertainty; some fear and suspicion? That these apprehensions are well grounded, the very proportion, between the houses said to be returned, and the total number, renders extremely probable. For this proportion is not greatly different from that between the number of houses *charged* at the tax-office, and the whole number *returned* there. The total number returned for the year 1777, was about 950,000; of which above 250,000 were excused on account of poverty. That is, the proportion of the houses *charged* was to the whole number *returned* considerably less than as three to four.

Now, admitting that some of the articles in Mr. H's. tables are correct, authentic, and rightly stated, as they probably are; the proportion, with respect to the remainder, would, I fancy, be nearly the same as that now mentioned.

This striking analogy, however, is not my only ground of suspicion. I have discovered, with regard to *one* place, that the fact is really as I have hinted. The number of houses said to be returned in the parish alluded to is 96, the total 198. A correspondent, on whose veracity I can safely depend, assures me, that these 198 are all in the parish duplicate, and that the 96 are those which are *charged* or *assessed*. As Mr. H. has suffered, either *his precipitation* or *his inattention* to mislead him in one instance, and as strong marks of suspicion accompany many of his other articles, he will, I presume, readily excuse me, if I either do not admit his very sanguine and flattering conclusions, without *great caution and considerable deductions*; or if I deny that he has, in particular, here evinced, that our present numbers are between eight and nine millions, or that their increase has been more than one third since the revolution*.

---

* In the Parliamentary Register for the present Session, No. 4. p. 309—13, I find the number of houses taxed in *Shrewsbury, Northampton, Walsall, Chester, Maidstone*, &c. is very nearly the same for each place respectively, as those represented in Mr. Howlett's tables as *returned*; a circumstance which greatly strengthens the above suspicion.

With respect to the proofs of either absolute or relative population derived from parish registers, which are generally deemed so decisive and satisfactory, they appear to me, of all others, the most precarious and uncertain. The degrees of mortality prevalent at different æras; the number of dissentients or separatists from the state religion, the correctness and fidelity with which the registers themselves are kept; must all be well ascertained before their information can be at all depended upon. The varying ratio of mortality *alone* may sometimes render all comparison useless for the purpose in question. When the pestilence raged quite over Europe, and in the course of a year or two, swept almost half its inhabitants into the grave, had the annual average amount of births and deaths for ten or fifteen years been taken, and a judgment thence formed of its actual Population, we must have concluded it to have been vastly greater than it was fifty years before or after; whereas it is indubitably certain that it was on the contrary, prodigiously less. Should we examine the parochial records of mortality in our own country for ten years, in that part of the last century, in which near fifty-
thousand

thousand persons died of the plague in our metropolis alone, and the same dreadful distemper sent death into every quarter of the nation, we should be led to imagine that our inhabitants were more numerous than before or since; as not only the burials were vastly augmented, but, for obvious reasons, the baptisms likewise. But allowing the ratio of mortality at the two periods between which we want to draw a parallel to remain nearly the same, yet a further difficulty still arises from the different number of separatists from the established worship, who are seldom entered in the parochial registers. Carry this research into France. You will, perhaps, find the Protestants not a third part so many as they were at the revolution; and I am strongly inclined to believe, that that increased Population the French writers, with such colour and plausibility, so much boast of, is a mere deception, owing very much, if not entirely, to this circumstance alone. Bring the enquiry back into England; the Papists are incomparably fewer at present than a hundred years ago; and as to the Dissenters, *their* diminution is so great and striking, that it is even among themselves felves a common topic of complaint and lamentation; and with regard to the carelefs inaccuracy with which the regifters were formerly kept, every one that confults them will be immediately convinced.

All thefe objections, more or lefs, together with a great many others, will fairly apply to the whole regifter-evidence given us by Mr. Howlett. To far the greater part of it I have the fame exceptions as thofe already urged againft that of Mr. Wales; it is taken from the northern counties of York, Lancafter, Chefter, Cumberland, and the immediate vicinity of London. The great augmentation of inhabitants in all thefe quarters, efpecially within the laft thirty or forty years, never was queftioned, and in the environs of our capital in particular, it has been fo prodigious, and fo ftrikingly manifeft, as to have been often a fubject of heavy complaint, it being naturally fuppofed to have arifen from the depopulation of the country. Mr. H. p. 153. of his pamphlet, makes a moft oftentatious difplay of the amazingly rapid growth of Population in our northern provinces; and, among other proofs of it, mentions the vaft number of chapels of eafe
to

to the mother church which in the compafs of thirty years have been erected in that part of the kingdom. I muft here beg leave to remark, that this circumftance might have been more prudently concealed, as it has contributed very materially to impair the teftimony of multiplied inhabitants arifing from the regifter extracts. I am affured, by the moft authentic information, that in confequence of this multiplication of chapels, it is no uncommon thing for baptifms, (and fometimes perhaps burials) to be entered twice over; firft in the chapel-regifter, and afterwards, for greater fecurity, in that of the mother church likewife. Hence the aftonifhing excefs of the baptifms over the burials in fome parifhes of thefe counties, even frequently to more than double.

In the extracts brought from Effex, Suffex, Kent, Suffolk, Norfolk, the appearance of increafe is not greater than what may fairly be accounted for, from the probable imperfection of regifters in the firft period, the great diminution of diffenters fince that time, and the different degrees of mortality. This laft circumftance indeed Mr. H. endeavours to fhew is greatly in favour of the prefent time. Candour, however, obliges me to obferve, that the evidence

dence hitherto adduced is much ftronger *againft* than *for* this pofition. The moft fatal of all the diftempers that have vifited our ifland during the prefent century is the fmall-pox. But Mr. H. himfelf acknowledges that this, during the laft ten years, has carried off a much greater proportion of perfons in our capital than it did in the fame compafs of time ninety or a hundred years ago. The accounts produced of an oppofite tenour are from places fo few in number, and fo inconfiderable in fize, that they are but as the *drop of the bucket*, or *the fmall duft of the balance*.

The regifters from the middle and fouthern counties are too few to authorize any conclufions for or againft his hypothefis. The fame may be faid with refpect to the average ratio of men furnifhed to the triennial fervice of the national militia. This mode of computation muft be acknowledged perhaps intirely new, and, as far as appears, it is unexceptionably juft. But the data from which it has been hitherto collected are at once by much too few, and not fufficiently varied to enable us to form any fatiffactory judgment.

Upon the whole, the united collective evidence yet produced, both by Mr. Wales and

Mr.

Mr. Howlett, affords scarcely the slenderest probability in support of their favorite idea of our greatly increased Population during the present century, or since the æra of the revolution. I am informed that both these gentlemen are continuing their researches. In so important an undertaking, I heartily wish them the utmost success, and shall be happy if any thing advanced in this cursory review of their respective performances may in the smallest degree contribute thereto. Every real lover of his country must rejoice to see a full confirmation of the pleasing doctrine of our advanced and still advancing strength; and I think I can answer for even Dr. Price himself, (who certainly has not yet shewn any obstinate or pertinacious adherence to his original sentiments on this subject) will be sincerely delighted to find his own gloomy and dispiriting system completely overthrown. I cannot, however, conclude without again insisting, that register extracts alone, be they ever so numerous, and although they should be even comprehensive of the whole kingdom, will by no means be fully adequate to this purpose, unless either qualified as above suggested, or supported by concurring testimonies of other and different kinds.

That

That I may not be thought too sceptical, or disposed to indulge an absurd degree of incredulity, I shall be perfectly satisfied with the register evidence, even though the several qualifications necessary to render it a complete ground to estimate our relative numbers, should not be fully attainable, provided it nearly corresponds with the deficiency of the surveyors' returns of houses, and with the proportion of men allotted to the triennial service of the national militia. This deficiency and this proportion will indeed be extremely different, not only in different counties, but even in different parts and divisions of the same county. The average, however, arising from the aggregate of correct and well-authenticated information from two or three principal towns, and thirty or forty villages and country-parishes in every province throughout the nation, and taken perfectly at a venture, will ascertain these points with all desirable precision. If the computations fairly formed from these two data mutually agree with each other, and with the register testimony of advanced Population, we may be as fully convinced of our increased numbers, and may be nearly as sure of what is their present actual amount, as from the most

most correct and accurate survey. But if, on the contrary, they all totally differ, and if in particular the deficiency in the surveyors' returns does not exceed *fifty*, or even a *hundred thousand*, we must be forced to admit the painful idea of Depopulation, and shall have nothing to do but to make the best of it.

F I N I S.

OBSERVATIONS

By RICHARD PRICE, D.D. F.R.S.

M.DCC.XCII.

Republished in 1973 by Gregg International Publishers Limited
Westmead, Farnborough, Hants., England

POSTSCRIPT,

CONTAINING

A Review of the Controverſy relating to the State of Population in England *and* Wales *ſince the Revolution.*

THE obſervations, in the preceding Supplement, on the population of this kingdom, are the ſame with thoſe which have been publiſhed in the former editions of this work. A more particular account of the evidence which ſeems to prove a progreſſive decreaſe in our population, has been given in an ESSAY on this ſubject firſt publiſhed at the end of Mr. *Morgan*'s Treatiſe on the *Doctrine of Annuities and Aſſurances on Lives and Survivorſhips,* and ſince republiſhed with the addition of an *Appendix,* containing remarks on Mr. EDEN's objections in his fifth letter to Lord CARLISLE. Theſe publications have been lately followed by others on the ſame ſubject; particularly, Mr. *Wales's Enquiry into the preſent State of*

the

the Population of ENGLAND and WALES; and Mr. *Howlett's* Examination of Dr. *Price's* Eſſay on the Population of *England*; and a pamphlet entitled *The Uncertainty of the preſent Population of this Kingdom, deduced from a candid Review of the Accounts lately given of it by Dr.* PRICE *on the one Hand, and Mr.* EDEN, *Mr.* WALES, *and Mr.* HOWLETT, *on the other.*

In the Preface to the ESSAY juſt mentioned, fearing that I might have expreſſed my conviction too ſtrongly, I referred myſelf to the candour of the Public, and deſired that my aſſertions might not be regarded any farther than they were ſupported by undeniable facts.——The profpect of an increaſing depopulation is ſo diſcouraging, that nothing but the faireſt overbalance of evidence ſhould engage us to admit it. I thought ſuch evidence did exiſt, and, therefore, ſtated it; believing that ſatisfaction ought never to be founded on impoſition, and that by endeavouring to apprize the kingdom of its true ſtate, I might be doing it an important ſervice.———The ingenious Author of the pamphlet laſt mentioned, writes in the character of one who doubts, and wiſhes only to know how things are; but Mr. *Wales* and Mr. *Howlett* zealouſly maintain, in oppoſition to the arguments I have produced, that our population is increaſing faſt. My intention in this *Poſtſcript* is is to give as fair and yet as brief an account as I can of the prefent ftate of this difpute, by reciting the evidence offered on both fides, and making fuch remarks upon it as fhall appear to me neceffary.

The principal evidence to prove that our population has declined, is taken from the comparifon ftated in page 276 of this Volume but more particularly in the ESSAY), between the number of houfes in the kingdom at different periods from the Revolution to the prefent time.

Houfes in *England* and *Wales* at Lady-day 1690 — — } 1,319,215 { including 554,641 having only one hearth.

	Charged and chargeable.	Excufed for poverty.	Total.
Houfes in 1750	729,048	. . .	. . .
in 1759 (a)	704,053	282,429	986,482
in 1761	704,543	276,149	980,692
in 1777	701,473	251,261	952,734

The number of houfes at Lady-day 1690, is ftated diftinctly by Dr. *Davenant* for every county (fee his Works, Vol. I. p. 38); and reprefented by him as an important inftruction derived from the hearth-books then

(*a*) This year was the firft in which an order was given to return the cottages excufed for poverty.——The chargeable or uninhabited houfes in this year, and in 1761 and 1777, were 24,904, 25,628, and 19,396 refpectively. See the Effay on the Population of *England* and *Wales*, printed for Mr. *Cadell*, p. 10 and 12.

exifting,

exifting, and containing accounts fairly kept and ftated. *Ib.* p. 136, 373.

The numbers for the fubfequent years are given from the returns to the tax-office of the furveyors of the houfe and window-duties in every diftrict in the kingdom, made by the order of government in thofe years.

A comparifon of thefe numbers with thofe given by Dr. *Davenant*, affords an evidence which, as far as it can be trufted, is full and decifive.——I know of nothing which has been urged againft Dr. *Davenant*'s account, except that by *houfes* he meant *families*; but it has been obferved, that the difference between the number of *families* and *houfes* in the kingdom, is by no means confiderable enough to account for the excefs in Dr. *Davenant*'s total; and that, were the contrary true, it is evident he muft have meant *houfes*, becaufe he has divided this total into two numbers (namely, 1,208,000 and 111,215) the firft of which he fuppofes to be the number of houfes having *ground* about them; and the fecond, the houfes not having ground about them.

The principal objections which have been made to the other accounts are the following.

Firft; the cottages are included in them, and thefe being excufed, and no account kept of them, the furveyors could not be correct in returning them.

This

POSTSCRIPT.

This is certainly true. But it should be remembered, that the same objection holds against the returns of the cottages made from the hearth-tax; that if in any instance such returns have been made from *conjecture*, they are more likely to exceed the truth, than to fall short of it; and that it is quite incredible that these returns should be so deficient as not to give above two out of five of the true number; or that the cottages of the poor should be almost equal to all the other houses in the kingdom, which must be the case if there has been no decrease.——I have been, however, assured that in some districts, the returns of the cottages have been made from actual surveys, and may be depended on.——And, if in other districts, they have been made carelessly, or perhaps in some not at all, an allowance on this account of an omission of *half* the cottages would still leave the number of houses short of what it was formerly.

According to the returns, the decrease in the cottages has been much more considerable than in the other houses; and, in the interval between the two last returns, amounted to 24,888. Such an authority only as the returns of the cottages, gives no sufficient reason for believing this. But there are two facts which give it credibility. The first is, that acknowledged destruction of cottages which has been the confeconsequence of the increase of large farms. And the other is, that decrease of the houses *charged* having seven windows or less, amounting to 24,651, which took place in the same interval of time. See the account of this decrease in the Essay on the population of *England* and *Wales*, p. 11.———To this nothing has been opposed but a strange objection of Mr. *Howlett*'s, implying, that, on account of the distresses of the poor, it is not possible that these houses and the cottages should decrease together.

The same writer has endeavoured to discredit all the returns to the tax-office, by observing, in p. 60, that they have represented the number of houses as diminished (since 1755) in some places where it is known they have increased. He instances in *Thaxted* in *Essex*, consisting of 350 houses; two parishes in the same county and one in *Kent*, consisting between them of only 206 houses; and *Maidstone*, consisting of 1106 houses. He gives no other proof that these places have not decreased than a bare assertion; and if I may judge from his principal instance (or *Maidstone*), his account of the returns for these places deserves no regard. According to him, the return of the houses for this town in 1777 was 633, and less by 23 than in 1755: Whereas the number returned in that year of inhabited houses only paying the house and window-duties, and
therefore

POSTSCRIPT.

therefore exclusive of all the other houses (which were included in the general return for the county) was 727; as any one may know who can either enquire at the tax-office, or will consult the accounts printed by the House of Commons in 1781.

Mr. *Howlett*, after making this objection to the tax-office accounts, informs the public (p. 62), from the authority of some surveyor of the window duties, that *doubtless* there was no return at all of the cottages in 1777.——It is difficult to account for so gross an error. In the first session of the present parliament, Lord MAHON moved the House of Commons for an account of all the returns to the tax-office of the houses in the kingdom. In consequence of this motion, the general return for 1777 was, among other returns, laid by the commissioners of the tax-office before parliament. This return was afterwards printed, and it distinctly specifies the number of cottages, as well as of other houses, in *every* county; and it is the same with the return for 1777 which I have given at the beginning of this Postscript, but more at large in the Essay on the Population of *England* and *Wales*.

After finding Mr. *Howlett* so mistaken in this and some other instances (*a*), I might, I think, be excused were I to save myself

(*a*) See Vol. I. p. 255, and 258, 259, 260.

the

the trouble of taking any farther notice of him. There are, however, some other mistakes into which he has fallen, still more important and palpable, which in what follows it will be proper to mention.

In this argument, a great deal depends on the proportion of the houses *charged* and *chargeable* and consequently entered in the books of the assessors) to the whole number of houses in the kingdom. The return in 1777 makes this proportion to be as 701,473 to 952,734, or as 3 to 4 nearly. See p. 299. A comparison of this proportion with the like proportion in a great variety of parishes and towns in different parts of the kingdom, ascertained by careful enumerations, would shew how far it deviates from truth, and what addition ought to be made to the excused houses, in order to obtain the whole number of houses.—— I am not possessed of many such accounts. Those which I think most to be depended on are the following.

	Total of Houses.	Houses charged.
Beccles in *Suffolk*	468	297
Bungay	326	220
Henham, Sotherton, Shipmeadow, Weston, and two other parishes in *Suffolk*	135	106
	929	623

Wenhaston

POSTSCRIPT.

	Total of Houses.	Houses charged.
Brought over	929	623
Wenhaston (a) in *Suffolk*	76	73
Southwold, Aldeburgh, Orford, and *Gorleston,* parishes in *Suffolk*	720	563
Remainder of the district in *Suffolk* in which these parishes are	5906	4859
Warrington in *Lancashire,* with its vicinity	1941	558
	9572	6676

(a) Only 56 houses have been reckoned in this parish; but in the office accounts 73 houses are charged, in consequence of the division of several cottages deemed single houses, into two or three separate dwellings, holding so many families.——One of the excused houses in this parish (and also in *Bungay*) is an alms-house, and in this account reckoned but one house, though consisting of several apartments, and therefore capable of being reckoned 5 or 6 houses; and in all accounts of this kind it should be remembered, that some differences will arise, as a house or cottage containing two or more families, having no communication, is reckoned a single or two or more houses.

Weston parish consists only of 21 houses, *Shipmeadow* of 11, *Henham* of 15, and *Sotherton* of 24. It is not conceivable that any parishes should have been always so small; and yet there are multitudes of such parishes in *Suffolk, Norfolk, Northamptonshire, Sussex, Kent,* and some other counties, and some of them provided with large churches. In *Norfolk,* particularly, the dilapidated churches in *some* places, and their disproportionate size in *others,* prove that it must have been formerly more populous. Even NORWICH itself bears evident marks of having been once a much more considerable city.

306   POSTSCRIPT.

	Total of Houses.	Houses charged.
Brought over	9572	6676
Sandwich in *Kent* (a)	578	349
Christleton in *Lancashire*, by an exact survey in 1780	102	72
First totals	10,252	7097
Add *Sudbury* division	7740	4122
Second totals	17,992	11,219

Accounts collected by Mr. *Wales*. See his *Enquiry*, p. 39, 43, 47, &c.

	Total of Houses.	Houses charged.
The two divisions of *Agbridge* and *Morley* in the West-Riding of *Yorkshire*	21,929	12,832
Twenty-eight villages in *Northamptonshire*	1024	706
Westhall, Wangford, Holton, Spexhall, Swilland, Tuddenham, Westerfield, Wisset, Witnesham, Blythford, and *Bramfield*, parishes in *Suffolk*	391	352
	23,344	13,889

(a) According to an accurate account taken by Mr. *Boys* in 1776. The number of inhabitants was 2252, or $3\frac{7}{10}$ to a house; though *three* workhouses containing 33 persons, and *two* hospitals containing 21 persons, are reckoned as only five families.

Ashill,

	Total of Houses.	Houses charged.
Brought over	23,344	13,889
Ashill, Clapton, Ilminster, and *Wayford,* in *Somersetshire*	388	134
Third totals	23,732	14,023
Add the *Second* totals	17,992	11,219
Fourth total	41,724	25,242

If we may judge from the first totals, which are those alone in which from my own enquiry I can confide, and which (including in them a town with its vicinity full of the poorest manufacturers, where the proportion of charged houses is lower than I have found it any where else) may not possibly be an improper guide in this case, the proportion of charged to the whole number of houses will be as 7097 to 10,252. And, since the charged and chargeable houses are known by the returns in 1777 to have been then 701,473, the whole number of houses in the kingdom will come out 1,013,000, or nearly a million, as I have reckoned it. If we add to these totals those for SUDBURY and its neighbourhood, where also (because full of poor manufacturers) the proportion of charged houses is particularly low, the number of houses in the kingdom will come out 1,125,000.———If we judge by by the accounts Mr. *Wales* has collected, this number will come out 1,187,000.—— If we judge by all thefe accounts taken together it will come out 1,159,000.

All thefe determinations fhew a great diminution in the number of houfes fince the *Revolution*; nor (fuppofing Dr. *Davenant*'s account right, or even not *very* wrong) is it poffible to reckon it equal now to what it was then without contradicting all probability.

A confirmation of this might be derived from Mr. *Howlett*'s accounts, could they be trufted. He has (in his Examination of Dr. *Price*'s Effay, p. 139, &c.) given a lift of towns and parifhes in 20 different counties, in which the total of houfes is 29,262 by *enumeration*, and 17,225 by the *returns* of the furveyors. The laft of thefe totals includes in it only the *charged* houfes; and it gives a proportion of thefe to all the houfes in the kingdom, which makes their number 1,191,000. But the truth is, that Mr. *Howlett*'s account of the returns of the furveyors cannot at all be depended on; and the following particulars will abundantly prove this.

The numbers returned for *Beccles*, *Bungay*, *Shipmeadow*, *Mettingham*, and *Homersfield* in *Suffolk*, were in 1780 (*a*), according to him, 169, 260, 7, 21, and 21 for thefe places refpectively.——I am affured, on the

(*a*) There was no return in this year.

contrary,

contrary, that the numbers (when the laſt general return was made in 1777) were 297, 220, 11, 27, and 23 returned as charged; and 171, 106, 0, 3, and 11, returned as *excuſed*.——The numbers returned for *Northampton*, *Maidſtone*, *Cheſter*, and *Shrewſbury*, he makes to be 768, 623, 1227, and 967 reſpectively; whereas it appears, from the accounts printed by the Houſe of Commons in 1781, that the numbers returned to the tax-office for theſe towns in 1777, were, 706, 727, 1244, and 904, excluſive of the *uninhabited*, and *excuſed* houſes which were likewiſe returned, but included in the totals for the counties.

But Mr. *Howlett* has here fallen into a ſtill greater miſtake; for, through haſte or inattention, he has taken the numbers in his liſt (being in reality only the number of houſes *taxed* given very inaccurately) for the whole of the numbers (*a*) *returned*, including *uninhabited* and *excuſed* houſes; and, arguing upon this miſtake, he makes the houſes in the kingdom 1,609,555; which is above a third more than, by computing in his own way,

(*a*) " The number of houſes in Mr. *Howlett*'s liſt ſaid " to be returned for *Tenterden* in *Kent*, is 96, the total " 198. A correſpondent, on whoſe veracity I can de- " pend, aſſures me that theſe 198 houſes are all in the " pariſh duplicate; and that the 96 are thoſe which are " charged."—*Uncertainty of the Population of this Kingdom*, p. 24.

POSTSCRIPT.

he must have found them had he not fallen into this mistake (*a*).

It

(*a*) Mr. *Howlett*, in consequence of thus over-rating the number of houses, and allowing 5 and two-fifths to a house, makes the inhabitants of *England* and *Wales* to be near nine millions. The proportion of inhabitants to houses may be, in some measure, collected from the Table in p. 6th of the Essay on the *Population of England and Wales*, which has been reprinted with some additions at the end of the First Essay in the preceding Volume of this work. To the towns and parishes in that Table I will here add SANDWICH in KENT, where, by an accurate survey in 1776, the houses were found to be 578, and the inhabitants 2252, or $3\frac{9}{15}$ to a house; and also EASTRY in the same county, where, in 1774, the houses were 141, and the inhabitants 656, or $4\frac{1}{3}$ to a house.— The total of houses in that Table, with these added, is 45,217, and of inhabitants 231,842, which makes 5 and an eighth to a house.

Mr. *Howlett* has inserted in his *Examination*, &c. p. 144, the houses and inhabitants in *Birmingham*, *Norwich*, *Manchester*, *Nottingham*, and *Liverpool*, just as I had given them in the Essay on the *Population of England*, &c. but with such additions as to bring out the allowance just mentioned 5 and two-fifths to a house. But had Mr. *Howlett* chosen to add to his own list the *whole* of my list in the Essay, as well as that part of it just mentioned which gives the highest allowance, he would have found (taking 4338 for the number of houses at *Manchester* and *Salford* in 1773, and not 4268 as he makes it) the total of houses to be 41,030, and of inhabitants 244,422; and consequently the allowance to a house not to be so much as five and one-fifth to a house.

Mr. *Howlett's* additions, with SANDWICH and EASTRY, and the additions which have been made (in the Table in the First Volume, p. 298) to the Table in the Essay on the *Population of England and Wales*, will make the total of houses 52,036, and of inhabitants 268,568, and the allowance 5 and a sixth.

Is

POSTSCRIPT.

It is neceffary to obferve, that the method here ufed of deducing the total of houfes

It fhould be confidered, that thefe totals, confifting chiefly of the houfes and inhabitants in five of the moft populous towns in the kingdom, give moft probably a proportion of inhabitants to houfes too high for the kingdom at large. If we throw out BIRMINGHAM and the town of MANCHESTER, the remainder will perhaps make a properer mixture of great and fmall towns and country parifhes; and the totals (or 41,675 and 210,158) will give $5\frac{1}{10}$ to a houfe. If LIVERPOOL is likewife thrown out, the totals will give lefs than 5 to a houfe.

In the Table juft referred to I have given the number of houfes and inhabitants at *Birmingham* from a furvey in 1770; when the houfes were 6025, and the inhabitants 30,804; of whom 15,363 were males, and 15,441 females.——I have lately been informed that, according to a very accurate furvey of *Birmingham* in autumn 1782, the houfes (exclufive of the hamlet of *Deretend*) were then 8125, of which 291 were uninhabited. From the fame account I learn, that the annual average of burials at *Birmingham* (exclufive of *Deretend*) for four years to 1774, was 1116; and for fix years to 1780, was 1342. ——The number of inhabitants in 1770, divided by the *firft* of thefe averages, makes the proportion dying annually at *Birmingham* to be one in $27\frac{3}{5}$; which, being very nearly the fame with the proportion dying annually at *Liverpool* and *Manchefter*, cannot probably be far from right: and this number (or $27\frac{3}{5}$) multiplied by the *fecond* average, makes the inhabitants in 1780 to be 37039. In order, however, to allow for the increafe of *Birmingham*, and to be more fure of finding a number not lefs than the truth, let the burials in 1782 be reckoned 1500, and the proportion dying annually 1 in 28; and it will follow that the inhabitants were then 42,000, and the number of perfons in a houfe $5\frac{1}{5}$, including about 700 in the workhoufe and hofpital.——I am fenfible that this falls below the common eftimates; but I pay no regard, in cafes of this kind, to any eftimates which are not derived from careful furveys.

houses in the kingdom from the proportion (ascertained by surveys) of the houses taxed to

The annual average of births at *Birmingham* was (according to the register) 1408 for 10 years to 1780. The excess of the births above the deaths is plainly owing to that over-proportion of people in the first stages of mature life, which always takes place in towns, in consequence of their being kept up or increased by an influx of people from other places. See the First of the following Essays. That this is the cause of the increase of *Birmingham* is undoubted, for the excess of the births cannot account for a 40th part of the increase; and before it became so rapid as it has been for some time, the burials *exceeded* the births, the annual average of the former having been, if the register deserves any regard, 708; and of the latter, 619.——The same register makes the annual medium of burials for 10 years to 1697 to have been 156, and of births, 150. But this only confirms an observation before made, that the registers in former times were very deficient; for it is not probable, that *Birmingham* was then so small a town; and an old account which I have seen of a survey in 1700 makes it to consist in that year of 2504 houses, and 15032 inhabitants. The register, therefore, did not then give above a third of the births and burials.

In Vol. I. p. 301, I have also given the number of houses and inhabitants at *Maidstone* in *Kent*, from a survey in 1781. I have since learnt, that another survey was made at *Maidstone* in September 1782; and as some instruction may be derived from it, I will here give the results just as I find them in a pamphlet published in this town by Mr. *Howlett*, and entitled, *Observations on the increased Population, Healthiness*, &c. *of the town of Maidstone.*

	Families.	Houses.	Inhabitants.	Males.	Females.	Male servants.
In the town	1037	982	5028	2306	2722	145
In the country	139	133	727	357	370	41
In the *whole* parish	1176	1115	5755	2663	3092	186

POSTSCRIPT.

to the totals of houses in country towns and parishes, must be too favourable; because this

	Female servants.	Women above 70.	Men above 70.	Girls under 15.	Boys under 15.
In the town -	325	161	96	847	776
In the country -	40	9	10	165	144
In the *whole* parish	365	170	106	1012	920

Persons to a house *in* the town —— $5\frac{1}{16}$
In the parish *out* of the town —— —— $5\frac{4}{9}$
Persons to a family *in* the town —— $4\frac{5}{6}$
In the parish *out* of the town —— —— $5\frac{1}{4}$
Proportion of children under 15 to the total of inhabitants *in* the town - } as 100 to 309
In the parish *out* of the town —— as 100 to 235

In the town one in 17 of the women exceeds 70 years of age, and one in 24 of the men; but in the country only one in 41 of the women exceeds this age, and one in 36 of the men.

Annual average (according to the register) in the whole parish for 20 years—

Of births to 1702 130 Of marriages 29 Of burials 132
to 1722 120 — 30 — 118
to 1742 129 — 40 — 144
to 1762 143 — 46 — 140
to 1782 160 — 50 — 148

By a survey in 1695, the inhabitants were 3676.

From these particulars it seems to appear, that *Maidstone*, at the beginning of this century, was a *de*creasing town; but that lately it has been *in*creasing, not by an excess of births, but, like other towns, by drawing supplies from other places. The ratio of the births to the burials, (if it can be depended on) and the great overproportion of persons in mature life in the town, prove this.

The number of females in it turned of 70 is greater than the number of males, partly, because males are

more

this proportion in *London, Southwark,* and all *Middlesex* (containing at least an 8th or more short-lived, but chiefly in this instance because the males, after removing to the town, are taken off again to the navy, army, &c. And the proportion of both males and females turned of 70 in the country is smaller than in the town, because removals from thence are chiefly to the town; and these being also chiefly removals of females, the town is rendered, at every age, much fuller of females than of males.

It is farther observable, that the town, when compared with the country round it, appears to be particularly unfavourable to population, the proportion of children under 15 being much less there than in the country.——The same is remarkable in the country round *Manchester.* See the First of the following Additional Essays.

It seems, indeed, that the consumption of towns tends to promote the population of the country near them; and were they fed with people only from hence, they would not probably be so prejudicial as they are to population. But the fact is, that there are few towns which would not soon come to nothing, did they draw their supplies of people only from the adjacent country. So true is this of *London* in particular, that, notwithstanding this natural tendency of its consumption, there is scarcely a village or parish within ten or twelve miles of it, in which, if we may believe Mr. *Howlett*'s extracts from the registers, the births do not fall considerably short of the burials. See his *Examination,* &c. p. 96, 97, &c.

In a note at the beginning of the First of the following Essays, it appears that the number of houses at MANCHESTER, exclusive of *Salford,* in 1773, was 3446, including 44 empty houses. My friend Dr. *Percival* has just informed me, that at the end of last year (1782) a new and very accurate enumeration of this town (exclusive of *Salford*) was completed, which made the houses then to be 4606. An addition, therefore, has been made to MANCHESTER of 1160 houses within the last ten years.

9th

9th of the kingdom) is, and, for obvious reasons, must be much higher than it is in the other districts of the kingdom. The returns in 1777 make the houses taxed in *London*, *Southwark*, and all *Middlesex* to be 77,008, and the total of houses 90,570; whereas the same returns for the whole kingdom make the former to be 701,473, and the latter 952,734,——I think it worth adding, that from a return for *London* and *Middlesex*, in 1780, and laid before parliament, it appears that the number of empty houses in this part of the kindom had increased, between 1777 and 1780, from 3,381 to 6,810.

The evidence now insisted on, taken from the returns of the surveyors and assessors of the house and window-duties, is the only direct evidence comprehending the whole kingdom with which we are furnished on this subject; and it is so discouraging, that I do not wonder that the advocates for the increase of our population endeavour to discredit it; and I should certainly join them in this, were I less desirous to know things as they are, than to prove them what I wish them.—The care and attention of Mr. *Rose* (now one of the secretaries to the treasury, but lately the secretary of the tax-office), in collecting these returns, cannot, I believe, be doubted; and he who considers that they are founded upon old taxes, and made upon oath, will not be able easily to per-
suade

suade himself that they can be very grosly deficient.

Mr. *Wales*, a writer whose abilities I respect and whose accounts I am not inclined to distrust, has collected several accounts of enumerations of houses *in* or *about* 1750 and 1780, which he thinks afford a presumptive proof of a general increase during that period. I will transcribe his summary of them, p. 48 (*a*).

	Houses in 1750.	Houses in 1780.
North Riding in *Yorkshire*	1716	1985
Eight villages in the *West-Riding*	784	943
Seventeen villages in *Derbyshire*	1001	1348
Twenty-seven villages in *Northamptonshire*	1036	1024
Fourteen parishes in *Suffolk* (families)	653	704
Four parishes in *Sussex*	144	223
Four villages in *Somersetshire*	428	388

Mr. *Wales* has added an account taken from the returns (which in this instance he is willing to trust) of the surveyors for *Agbridge* and *Morley* divisions in the *West-Riding* of *Yorkshire*. From these returns it appears, that in 1761 the houses in these

---

(*a*) In p. 67, there is a comparison of enumerations at different periods of *Manchester, Liverpool, Birmingham, Leeds, Nottingham, Norwich,* and *Farnham,* which shews, what is well-known concerning the four first of these towns, that they have greatly increased.

divisions

divisions were 17,764; that in 1767, they were 20,526; and in 1779, 21,929.

I will add a similar account of a district in the county of *Suffolk*, where

In 1761 { the houses *charged* were   5584
         { the houses *excused* were   1391

                                                    6975

In 1777 { the houses *charged* were   6118
         { the houses *excused* were   1521

                                                    7639

There has undoubtedly been an increase in *Yorkshire*, and perhaps also in *Derbyshire*; but he that will judge of it from the numbers in these accounts will be in danger of being misled: For I understand, that it is in part an *apparent* increase only, owing to the conversion of houses holding two or more families, and *formerly* charged as *single* houses, into apartments having no communication, and therefore *now* charged as so many separate houses.——The inducements to such conversions among the lower ranks of people have been so great since 1761, as to be irresistible. For first, their poverty has increased, and therefore they have found it more necessary to save every needless expence.——And secondly, in 1761 the window-duties were nearly doubled; and houses having 8 or 9 windows, *before* excused, were subjected to the payment of 1*s.* per ann
for

for every window. In 1766 thefe duties were again increafed, and houfes having only *feven* windows were fubjected to them. By dividing, therefore, fingle houfes holding more than one family into feveral tenements having each of them few windows, the tax upon them might be either leffened or entirely avoided (*a*). The decreafe of fmall farms has likewife contributed to this change, by caufing many farm-houfes to be turned into cottages for day-labourers.

Perhaps, thefe have been the only caufes of the increafe of the diftrict in *Suffolk* juft mentioned; and there is reafon to believe that they have been the principal caufes of the increafe in *Agbridge* and *Morley* divifions in *Yorkſhire*. For the returns fhew an increafe in thefe divifions equal to above a 6th of the whole number of houfes in fo fhort a time as fix years, or from 1761 to 1767; but afterwards, or from 1767 to 1779, they do not fhew *half* this increafe in *double* the time. The firſt increafe, therefore, was probably occafioned, as I have obferved, by the alteration in the window-duties in 1761; nor, indeed, could it have any other caufe than either this, or the de-

---

(*a*) In Mr. *Wales*'s accounts of the increafe of houfes in the *North-Riding* of *Yorkſhire*, and in *Derbyſhire*, it appears that a great part of it proceeded from alterations in old houfes; that is, perhaps, from fuch alterations as thofe here meant.

fertion

sertion of other parts of the kingdom; for it was too great and too sudden to be accounted for by an excess of the births above the deaths, which is the only cause that can produce a general and permanent increase.

There is one more source of information on the subject of our population which is of particular importance; I mean, a comparison of the births and burials and marriages at different periods. Such a comparison for the whole kingdom would decide the question I am discussing. But we are far from being furnished with the means of making it. It is, however, the evidence on which the advocates for a progressive increase in our population principally rely; and I shall here give a fair representation of it, with such remarks as a regard to truth will render necessary.

	Baptisms.	Burials.
Annual average of baptisms and burials about or soon after the Revolution, in 33 parishes in ten counties, taken indiscriminately in different parts of England.—See Mr *Wales*'s Enquiry, p. 49. *(a)*	1460	1518

(*a*) In Mr. *Wales*'s list the average of burials corresponding to the births is not given for *Liverpool* and *Bowden* in *Lancashire*, and for *Lamborn*, *Shefford*, and *Wilford* in *Berkshire*; and, therefore, these places are not included in this account.

All

	Baptisms.	Burials.
Annual average in the same parishes for some years before 1780.—*Ib.* p. 50	4064	3537
Annual average of baptisms and burials about the year 1745 in 142 parishes in 21 counties taken indiscriminately.—*Ib.* p. 53.	4712	4067
Annual average in the same parishes between 1770 and 1780.—*Ib.* 57.	7179	5689

Annual average of births and burials in the Deaneries of *Melineth, Elvel, Buillt, Hay,* and *Brecon* in the diocese of St. *David*'s.—*Ibid.* p. 65.

	Baptisms	Burials
From 1700 to 1730	341	325
From 1730 to 1760	715	587
From 1760 to 1763 or 1764	727	580

Annual average in the other parts of the diocese

	Baptisms	Burials
From 1700 to 1730	888	753
From 1730 to 1760	1111	921
From 1760 to 1763 or 1764	1302	1183

Annual average in the whole diocese of St. *David*'s

	Baptisms	Burials
From 1700 to 1730	1229	1078
From 1730 to 1760	1826	1508
From 1760 to 1763 or 1764	2029	1663

All

All thefe accounts have been extracted from the parifh regifters. The deficiencies in thefe regifters, and the careleffnefs with which they are kept, have been often complained of. I wifh, therefore, fomething had been faid to eftablifh their credit ; or at leaft to fhew, that they have been preferved entire, and that they were not *more* deficient formerly than they are now *(a)*. Suppofing them

---

(*a*) May it not be doubted whether at the *Revolution* the parifh regifters had recovered from the confufion into which all church affairs had been thrown in the times of the civil war and commonwealth?——The number of popifh and proteftant diffenters was then probably much greater than it is now.——But the obfervation moft to the prefent purpofe may be, that regifters of mortality are of late origin, and have been for a courfe of years growing more and more into ufe and eftimation. Among the Diffenters in *London* the regiftration of births was, fome years ago, much neglected. At prefent it is more practifed in confequence of notifications of the eftablifhment of a public regifter, which have been read annually from the pulpit. And in the country I fufpect, that people of all denominations are got fo much more into the habit of reckoning it important, as fometimes to regifter in more than one place.

" In 1538 *Henry the Eighth* gave orders that the in-
" cumbent of every parifh fhould keep true and exact re-
" gifters of all chriftenings, weddings, and funerals in
" his diftrict. But this order, in many places, was lit-
" tle regarded till Queen *Elizabeth*, in 1558, gave another
" order for keeping them more exactly. Yet after all
" they were but remifsly kept in many parifhes, and
" often committed only to loofe papers, by which means
" fome were loft, fome rotted away, and others were
" devoured. To remedy thefe evils, orders were given

them correct, they take in but a very inconfiderable part of the kingdom, and chiefly that very part which, it is well known, has increased, but the increase of which must have been, in some measure, occasioned by removals from other parts of the kingdom. The *second* of these accounts is the principal; and, if from the numbers in it are deducted the births and burials in *Manchester*, *Rochdale*, and *Warrington* in *Lancashire*; and in *Shef-*

"in 1559, that all registers should be kept in parchment-books only, and that all preceding ones which could be found, should be transcribed into new books. But no place in *England* slighted these orders so much as *London*; for, except in two or three years of great plagues, we find no bills in *London* till 1604.——But neither country nor city registers, where there has been, or still is any considerable body of dissenters, popish or protestant, are to be much relied on after 1644, when the division in the church first broke out. And even in places where there are no dissenters, registers are little to be regarded on account of several unhappy concurring circumstances, as the negligence or frequent absence of the register-keeper, and the ignorance, poverty, mistakes, and *prejudices* of several of the people."——See the preface to the *New Observations on Town and Country Bills of Mortality*, by Dr. *Short*, p. 9, &c.

In *London* the bills did not include the distempers till 1629; nor the ages till 1728; and still it is well known that they are very defective.

Conclusions drawn from registers of burials, be they ever so exact, are rendered more uncertain than is commonly imagined, by epidemics, and the different degrees of healthiness or sickliness of different years. This may be learnt in some measure from what is related of SWEDEN in p. 146.

field,

field, Wakefield, Hallifax, &c. in *Yorkshire,* the remainder will be, in the first period, 1630 births *per ann.* and 1408 burials; and, in the second 2010 births *per ann.* and 1502 burials, which makes a small increase.

The *first* account overthrows itself by making the burials at the *Revolution* in eleven counties to exceed the births. These counties, therefore, if we are to judge from these extracts, must have been *then* decreasing. The increase which appears at present is almost entirely the increase of the towns just mentioned; and if they are struck out, the remainder in this *first* account, as well as the *second,* will be little; and that little will shew a decrease in *Somersetshire,* no increase in *Nottinghamshire,* and only a small increase even in *Yorkshire.*

Mr. *Wales's third* list shews an increase at the beginning of this century so rapid in the diocese of St. *David's* as in 30 years to double the inhabitants of five deaneries; but, in the other parts of the diocese, so much flower, as in the same time not to add a *quarter* to the inhabitants.——It deserves notice farther, that they represent the increase which took place in the *first* period as changed into a decrease in the *second* and *third* periods. This will appear upon considering, that had the increase in the *first* period been continued to the end of the *second,* the annual averages at the end of this *second* period, (or which is nearly the same) the annual averages from 1760 to 1763, muft have been much greater than they are; for they muft have borne the fame proportion to the averages of the *second* period that the mean between thefe averages and the averages of the *firft* period bear to thefe laft averages. That is, in the five deaneries, the average of burials about 1760 fhould have been to 587 as the mean betwen 587 and 325 (or as 456) is to 325. It fhould have been, therefore, 823 (or fome number not very diftant from this) inftead of 580; which laft number is fo much too little as to be nearly equal to the annual burials about the middle of the fecond period; and, therefore, if not very wrong, proves a decreafe muft have taken place.

By the fame reafoning it will appear, that in the whole diocefe, if the increafe in the *firft* period had continued, the burials at the end of the *second*, or the beginning of the *third* period fhould have been nearly 1808, inftead of 1663. The fame conclufions may be deduced by computing from the births.

Thefe are circumftances which give a fufpicious appearance to this regifter evidence (*a*); but there is a third circumftance which deftroys its credit.

At

(*a*) One plain reafon of the inconfiftencies in thefe accounts has been intimated, namely, that the births and

At the fame time that, in the five deaneries, they fhew an extravagant increafe in the *firft* period, they give the births and burials nearly equal, and therefore make it impoffible there fhould have been any increafe (*b*).—The like will be obferved prefently of the whole diocefe.

That part of the kingdom where the parifh regifters give the ftrongeft proofs of an increafe is the diocefe of *Chefter*.——The following is a fummary of the extracts from them as I have received it from a friend in the diocefe.

		Births.	Burials.
In the archdeaconry of *Chefter*	in 1717	7703	6380
	in 1779	16791	12573
In the whole diocefe	in 1717	10604	8755
	in 1779	21463	16080

There appears here an increafe which has *doubled* the inhabitants in 62 years; and

and burials in former periods are given by the extracts much *more* below the truth than in the latter periods. And as far as this is the cafe, they prove nothing.

(*b*) The births in the firft period, in order to produce (in conformity to the extracts) a double number in 30 years, fhould have been more than double the burials; that is, fuppofing the burials not too high, the births fhould have been about 700; and both the births and burials in the *fecond* period, inftead of being 715 and 587, fhould have been double thefe numbers.

there is no reason to doubt but that this part of the kingdom (including in it some of the chief manufacturing towns in *Lancashire*, *Cheshire*, and *Yorkshire*) has considerably increased. I cannot, however, trust my belief of this merely to these extracts (*a*); for they destroy their own authority by giving a proportion of the births to the burials, which is inconsistent with any such increase, as will appear from the following observations.

If the annual average of burials about 1717 is multiplied by 35 (a multiplier which, in the case of a large *country* district cannot be much too high), it will appear that the whole number of inhabitants in the diocese was then 306,000 The excess of the births above the burials was 1849, or the 166th part of the inhabitants; and this is an excess which, supposing the increase produced by it uniformly accelerated, without being once checked by sickly seasons

---

(*a*) The author of the pamphlet entitled, *The Uncertainty of the Population of the Kingdom*, mentions a very material circumstance relating to the registers of births kept in *Lancashire*, and some other northern counties.—
" I am assured," says he, " by the most authentic in-
" formation, that, in consequence of the late multipli-
" cation of chapels, it is no uncommon thing for bap-
" tisms (and sometimes burials) to be entered, in some
" parishes in these counties, twice over; first in the cha-
" pel register, and afterwards, for greater security, in
" that of the mother church, p. 28."

and emigrations (that is, suppofing it a much greater increafe from a given furplus of births than there is reafon to expect), could not have doubled the inhabitants in lefs time than 115 years, as may be found by computing in the manner directed in the Note, Vol. I. p. 279. If, therefore agreeably to the parifh extracts, they were doubled in 62 years, it muft have been the effect, not of the excefs of the births above the burials (the only general caufe of the increafe of countries), but of an influx of people from other parts of the kingdom; and, therefore, proves no more than that one part of the kingdom has gained by taking away from other parts. And this may probably have happened in this diocefe. The truth, however, more probably is, that the parifh regifters do not give us true information in confequence either of having been more deficient formerly, or not having been duly preferved. See the Notes in p. 321, &c.

This obfervation is applicable to all the other accounts which I have met with taken from parifh regifters.——In the diocefe of St. *David*'s there appears, by the extracts, to have been an addition (between 1715 and 1760) of *three fifths* to the inhabitants. But the excefs of the births above the deaths will not account for more than a *third* of this increafe; and as very probably more people leave WALES than flock into it, either (in conformity to the excefs of the births) there may have been no increase, or the regifter in the firft period muft have been fo deficient as to give the births near a third lefs than the truth *(a)*.

This argument holds equally with refpect to the fecond of the accounts taken from Mr. *Wales*. And his firft account carries, as before obferved, impoffibility on the face of it.

The following is a fummary of Mr. *Howlett*'s accounts, taken from p. 128 of his *Examination*, &c.

Annual average of births and burials for 20 years about the Revolution, compared with the annual average for the laft 20 years, in 68 parifhes in *Kent*, 43 in *Effex*, and 17 in *Surry*.

	Births.	Burials.
About the *Revolution* —	2993	3054
For the laft 20 years —	3947	3983

In the fame parifhes, with the addition of 18 in *Suffex*, 15 in five fouthern counties, 29 in *Suffolk*, the city of *Norwich*, and five parifhes in *Wales*.

	Births.	Burials.
About the *Revolution* —	7553	7740
For the laft 20 years —	10023 *(b)*	10175

To

(a) If the burials are fuppofed deficient, as certainly they ought, the births muft have been proportionably more deficient than the third here reckoned.

(b) There are many errors in Mr. *Howlett*'s numbers, but I have not difcovered any that will materially affect the proportion of the totals here given

POSTSCRIPT. 329

To thefe accounts Mr. *Howlett* has added (in p. 13) a comparifon of the births and burials for two periods of *five* years in 62 parifhes in 26 counties ; the firft period beginning with 1758, 1760, or 1761 ; and the fecond with 1773, 1775, or 1776.

	Annual average of births.	Annual average of burials.
In the firft period	9527	9710
In the fecond period	1191	1060

This is all the regifter evidence which Mr. *Howlett* has produced, exclufive of Mr. *Wales*'s, and that taken from the parifh regifters in the diocefe of *Chefter* already noticed. This evidence he has difplayed with great pomp, and infifted upon as a full proof of an *aftonifhing* increafe in our population. But never before was an evidence offered fo abfurd and felf-deftructive. For it fhould be obferved, that, according to thefe accounts, the deaths in the kingdom from the Revolution to the prefent time have exceeded

In a poftfcript he has added to the parifhes abovementioned the births and burials in 17 others; and all together make the annual averages.

	Births.	Burials.
At the Revolution	8375	8493
At prefent	11195	11382

the

POSTSCRIPT.

the births *(a)*. Mr. *Howlett*, therefore, will, I hope, some time or other, inform us how the increase in which he triumphs has been produced.——But to be serious. An excess of deaths cannot exist long in any kingdom. The appearance of it, therefore, in

(a) It may be said, that the excess of burials in this and the other accounts before noticed, is occasioned by a great over-proportion of omissions in the registration of births. But what confidence can be placed in registers which admit of such defects? or how is it to be known that they were not much greater formerly, agreeably to the observations in the Note p. 321?

The omission of still-born and unbaptized infants scarcely deserves notice, because they contribute nothing to population, and are probably, in most places, omitted in the burials as well as the births. And with respect to other omissions, were we to reckon them a *tenth* of the births, and only *half* as much of the burials, still an excess of births would be left, which would be almost equally inadequate to the increase.

In short; let the registers of births be ever so deficient, the increase they shew must have taken place if they were not more deficient formerly than they have been lately: And yet, this increase could not take place unless they were deficient to a degree which is incredible, and which, were it credible, would render them unworthy of much notice.——The increase, for instance, which on this supposition must have taken place in the diocese of *Chester*, cannot be accounted for from the excess of births without reckoning the omissions in the registers of births equal in both periods to at least a *third* of the registered births, even though the registers of burials are reckoned correct and complete. This will appear to any one who will calculate in the manner explained in p. 326, &c. The supposition, therefore, must be wrong that the registers of births were not more deficient formerly than they have been lately.

The

in thefe extracts muft be owing either to their being miferably erroneous; or to their being taken moftly from *towns*; for in thefe it feldom happens that an excefs of deaths does not take place; nor is there any worfe caufe or fymptom of depopulation than their increafe.

All the evidence taken from the parifh regifters has been now laid before the reader, as far as I am acquainted with it. I am informed that Mr. *Wales* and Mr. *Howlett* are proceeding with their enquiries *(a)*; and I hope they will be able hereafter to offer to the public fome more confiftent and probable accounts. When, however, I confider the reafon there is for believing that

the

The effect which the omiffion only of baptifms among Diffenters may have, will appear from the following fact.——The number of baptifms at *Sandwich* in *Kent*, among Proteftant Diffenters (exclufive of *Baptifts*) was

From 1690 to 1699	—	120
From 1730 to 1739	—	58
From 1770 to 1779	—	13

The number of baptifms in the fame town for the fame periods refpectively was, exclufive of Diffenters, 755, 744, and 758

(a) I have not fought for any accounts of this kind, not chufing to give trouble to obtain fo indecifive and percarious an evidence. The following are all I can add from my own information to thofe already given.

Lincoln.

the parish registers were in former periods particularly defective, I cannot help doubting

	Annual births	Annual burials	Annual marriages
Lincolnshire—*Swinderby* parish 10 years to 1690	7.3	7.5	2.5
to 1720	5.8	5.0	2.0
to 1770	7.1	5.0	1.4
Durham—*Staindrop* parish 10 years to 1745	37.6	28.5	7.0
to 1771	49.3	44.8	12.9
Kent——*Tenterden* parish 20 years to 1729	29.8	33.6	9.1
to 1769	34.5	34.0	11.9
Sandwich parish 10 years to 1629	148.3	159.6	41.3
to 1689	103.2	95.8	11.7
to 1739	74.4	70.4	16.3
to 1779	75.8	68.8	21.3
Eastry parish 10 years to 1629	20.1	12.1	6.4
to 1689	13.7	12.2	2.6
to 1739	17.3	13.0	4.2
to 1779	20.7	13.4	5.2
Word parish 10 years to 1739	7.6	4.9	1.2
to 1779	6.7	4.8	2.0
Woodnesborough parish 10 years to 1719	15.5	10.9	7.3
to 1779	14.8	12.4	4.1
Ash parish 20 years to 1578	27.7	25.7	6.6
to 1777	50.0	39.7	11.9
Cornwall——*Liskeard* parish 20 years to 1719	51.7	45.3	13.0
to 1769	48.3	45.3	12.8
Devonshire—*Okeford* parish 20 years to 1719	12.2	8.0	
to 1769	12.2	7.5	
Staffordshire—*Biddulph* 20 years to 1719	20.3	15.6	4.3
to 1739	27.8	21.1	4.4
to 1769	38.9	21.1	6.1

whether

whether any examination of them is capable of furnishing with sufficient evidence to prove that our population has not decreased since the *Revolution*, I question even whether it can inform us properly of the proportion of births to deaths in the kingdom. This alone, could it be ascertained, would enable us to form some judgment of the present state of our population, and to determine, with some probability, whether it is increasing or decreasing. If we unite all the extracts before given, rejecting Mr. *Howlett*'s, this proportion will come out $\frac{128}{100}$. Were these extracts to be depended on, they would probably give this proportion too high for the kingdom at large, because taken chiefly from the register of the diocese of *Chester*, the most populous and flourishing part of the kingdom (*a*). We may, however, argue upon it, and reckon it the just proportion for

---

(*a*) Dr. *Short* has employed much time and pains in collecting extracts from the registers of a great variety of market-towns and country parishes and villages in different parts of the kingdom for two periods, the first extending from the reign of Queen *Elizabeth* to the middle of the last century; and the second from different years at the end of the last century to the middle of the present century: and from a comparison of these extracts it appears, that in the former period the births exceeded the burials in the proportion of 124 to 100: but that in the latter they exceeded them only in the proportion of 111 to 100

334 POSTSCRIPT.

for *England* and *Wales*, exclusive of *London* and its environs; on which suppofition, if we reckon the annual burials such as, in consequence of multiplying by 35, will make the inhabitants of *England*, exclusive of *London*, four millions and a half, the annual burials will be nearly 128,000, and the births 164,000, leaving an annual excefs of 36,000; and this is an excefs which would produce an increafe in moft other countries, notwithftanding the wafte in their capitals, and all the other caufes which ufually check the increafe of countries (*a*) But

This, were there fufficient evidence for it, would manifeft too plainly an encumbered and declining population. It appears (as Dr. *Short* fpeaks) with no lefs evidence from the regifters *than that the fun fhines in a cloudlefs day at noon*; and he concludes from it, that in confequence of the irregularities and debauchery occafioned fince the Revolution, by increafing opulence and luxury, the kingdom has been for many years growing lefs healthy. But the truth is, that the regifters (having certainly been more defective formerly than they are at prefent) cannot be trufted as a juft foundation for any conclufions.—— See Dr. *Short's New Obfervations*, Tables 1ft, 2d, and 3d, and p. 80.—See likewife the Preface to his *Hiftory of the Comparative Increafe and Decreafe of Mankind*; and the Tables at the end.

(*a*) The proportion of births to deaths in all SWEDEN for 9 years to 1763 was } 130 to 100

In the kingdom of NAPLES for 5 years to 1777 — — — } 144 to 100

In all FRANCE for 5 years to 1774 as 928,918 to 793,931, or — — } 117 to 100

Annual

But perhaps there are few kingdoms now exifting in which moft of thefe caufes operate
fo

Annual average of births, deaths, and marriages in *Breflaw*, *Glogaw*, and the other *towns* of SILESIA for four years to 1778.

Births.	Deaths.	Marriages.	Proportion of births to marriages.	Proportion of births to deaths.
10900	10935	2409	45 to 10	996 to 1000

Annual average of births, deaths, and marriages in the *country parifhes and villages* of SILESIA for the fame period.

Births.	Deaths.	Marriages.	Proportion of births to marriages.	Proportion of births to deaths.
53694	42894	11848	45 to 10	125 to 100

SILESIA appears from hence to confift of near two millions of inhabitants; of whom the inhabitants of towns are about a *fixth* part.

The following accounts (copied from the Tables at the end of the Firft Volume of Mr. *Sufmilch's Gottliche Ordnung*, 3d Edition) will fhew, in fome meafure, the ufual progrefs of population in a country. They will alfo ferve for a contraft to the inconfiftent extracts which I have given from our parifh regifters; for it will appear that inftead of fhewing an increafe too great for the furplus of births, they always (in confequence of fickly years and other caufes) fhew a much fmaller increafe than it was capable of producing.

In the old PRUSSIAN dominions and the provinces of *Brandenburg*.

Annual average.	Births.	Burials.	Marriages.	Proportion of births to marriages.	Proportion of births to burials.
4 years to 1701	66247	44680	18145	30 to 10	148 to 100
7 years to 1728	82934	60821	20726	40 to 10	136 to 100
6 years to 1756	102935	78865	24487	40 to 10	136 to 100

In

POSTSCRIPT.

fo much as in this. Few kingdoms have been engaged within fo fhort a period in fo many defolating wars. Few kingdoms have had fuch armies and garrifons and fettlements to maintain in fo many diftant regions, and

In the kingdom of *Pruſſia* and dukedom of *Lithuania*.

Annual average.	Births.	Burials.	Marriages.	Proportion of births to marriages.	Proportion of births to burials.
10 years to 1702	21963	14718	5908	37 to 10	150 to 100
5 years to 1716	21602	11984	49 8	39 to 10	180 to 100
5 years to 1756	28392	19154	5599	50 to 10	148 to 100

N. B. In 1709 and 1710 a peftilence carried off 247,733 of the inhabitants of this country; and in 1736 and 1737 epidemics prevailed, which again checked its increafe.

In the *Churmark* of BRANDENBURGH.

Annual average.	Births.	Burials.	Marriages.	Proportion of births to marriages.	Proportion of births to burials.
5 years to 1702	13433	7605	3597	37 to 10	176 to 100
4 years to 1756	23486	18840	6646	38 to 10	124 to 100

Duchy of POMERANIA.

Annual average.	Births.	Burials.	Marriages.	Proportion of births to marriages.	Proportion of births to burials.
6 years to 1702	6540	4647	1810	36 to 10	140 to 100
6 years to 1708	6455	4208	1875	39 to 10	177 to 100
6 years to 1726	8432	5627	2131	39 to 10	150 to 100
4 years to 1756	12767	9281	2957	43 to 10	137 to 100

In this inftance the inhabitants appear to have been almoft doubled in 56 years, no very bad epidemic having once interrupted the increafe; but the three years immediately following the laft period (to 1759) were years fo fickly that the births were funk to 10,229, and the burials raifed to 15,068

Neumark

and in such unhealthful climates. No kingdom ever supported such a navy, or carried on so extensive a foreign commerce, or wanted, on these accounts, such a supply of *men* for the sea-service : Nor was there ever a king-

Neumark of BRANDENBURG.

Annual average.	Births.	Burials.	Marriages.	Proportion of births to marriages.	Proportion of births to burials.
5 years to 1701	5433	3483	1436	37 to 10	155 to 100
5 years to 1726	7012	4254	1713	40 to 10	164 to 100
5 years to 1756	7978	5567	1891	42 to 10	143 to 100

Epidemics prevailed for 6 years from 1736 to 1741, which checked the increase.

Dukedom of MAGDEBURG.

Annual average.	Births.	Burials.	Marriages.	Proportion of births to marriages.	Proportion of births to burials.
5 years to 1702	6431	4103	1681	38 to 10	156 to 100
5 years to 1717	7590	5335	2076	36 to 10	142 to 100
5 years to 1756	8850	8069	2193	40 to 10	109 to 100

The years 1738, 1739, 1740, 1741, 1750, and 1751 were particularly sickly.

Duchy of HALBERSTADT.

Annual average.	Births.	Burials.	Marriages.	Births to marriages.	Births to burials.
4 years to 1692	2366	1478	604	39 to 10	160 to 100
5 years to 1746	2803	2052	712	39 to 10	136 to 100
6 years to 1756	2917	2621	778	37 to 10	111 to 100

Duchy of RAVENSBERG.

Annual average.	Births	Burials.	Marriages.	Births to marriages.	Births to burials.
5 years to 1692	3899	2552	964	40 to 10	152 to 100
4 years to 1756	5041	3814	1371	36 to 10	132 to 100

a kingdom which confifted fo much of people employed in trades and manufactures, which

Dukedom of CLEVE and County of *Mark.*

Annual average	Births.	Burials.	Marriages.	Births to marriages.	Births to deaths.
4 years to 1701	6249	4132	1729	36 to 10	151 to 100
5 years to 1739	7358	5535	1741	42 to 10	134 to 100
4 years to 1756	7612	5567	1966	38 to 10	136 to 100

AUSTRIAN MILANESE;

Confifting in 1774, of 211,479 families, and 1,116,859 inabitants; and in 1769, of 1,101,723 inhabitants, of whom 9638 were priefts, 5616 friars, and 7140 monks and nuns.

Annual average of	Births.	Burials	Marriages.	Births to marriages.	Births to deaths.
1769, 1773 and 1774	44030	40030	9619	45 to 10	110 to 100

N. B. The laft of thefe years appears to have been particularly fickly; for the burials exceeded the births, and were 9156 higher than the average of the years 1769 and 1773.

DENMARK.

Annual average of	Births.	Burials.	Births to burials.
5 years to 1747	22996	18864	121 to 100
5 years to 1756	24298	21706	112 to 100

Epidemics prevailed in 1755, and 1756, which made the burials in thofe years nearly equal to the births.

The medium of thefe ten years is nearly 20,000; and, multiplying it by 35, will make the number of inhabitants then in *Denmark* 700,000.

NORWAY.

Annual average of	Births.	Burials.	Births to burials.
5 years to 1747	17522	10955	160 to 100
14 years to 1756	19947	14661	136 to 100

Multiplying 16000 (the average of burials in *Norway* for four years to 1756) by 35, will make the number of inhabitants 560,000 in 1756. In

POSTSCRIPT.

which shorten life, or whose metropolis was so large, or *half* so large, in comparison with the number of its inhabitants.——If we include in LONDON all the parishes and little towns near LONDON, where, almost universally, the burials exceed the births, it is moderate to reckon that the former exceeds the latter in this part of the kingdom about 10,000 annually; and that, consequently, LONDON demands a recruit of people every year equal to this number. Forty years ago there was this excess of burials within the bills only. This will make the annual surplus for the whole kingdom 26,000 which may probably be sufficient, or perhaps more than sufficient, to supply all the waste occasioned by sickly seasons, emigrations to the colonies, and the other causes I have mentioned.——But the truth is, that it cannot be reckoned with any degree of

In 1056 country parishes and villages in the *Churmark* of *Brandenburgh*, consisting (in 1748) of 106,204 males and 107,540 females.

Annual average of	Births.	Burials.	Marriages.	Births to marriages.	Births to burials
10 years to 1748	7099	5561	1966	36 to 10	127 to 100

In seven market-towns and 54 country-parishes in *England*, consisting (in 1740) of 10434 families and 46,650 inhabitants, according to Dr. Short's *New Observations*, p. 133.

Annual average.	Births.	Burials.	Marriages.	Births to marriages.	Births to burials.
In 1748	1575	1360	399	40 to 10	115 to 100

confidence, that there exifts any fuch furplus.

Mr. *King*, in 1693, ftated the births of the kingdom, exclufive of thofe in *London*, at 170,000, and the burials at 148,000, which makes the proportion of the former to the latter as 115 to 100. See Dr. *Davenant*'s Works, Vol. II. p. 180. Mr. *King* deduced this from the affeffments then impofed on births, marriages and burials; and he has fhewn fuch fagacity in his other eftimates, that I cannot help paying fome regard to him in this. If he was right, the kingdom has probably been decreafing, fuch a furplus being incapable of fupporting a population fo encumbered as ours, and which ever fince Mr. *King*'s time has had fuch increafing demands upon it.

I cannot help taking this opportunity to obferve, that there is reafon to believe that poor countries (provided the ground fupplies them with plenty of food, and the poverty of the inhabitants confifts only in their wanting *conveniencies* and *elegancies*, in other countries deemed *neceffaries*) increafe fafter than *rich* countries. The reafon is obvious. The greateft enemies of population are the artificial wants, the accumulation of property, and the luxury and vices which are the conftant attendants of opulence, and which prevent a regular and early union between the fexes. The inhabitants of poor countries are more fimple,

more

more healthy, and more virtuous; and, wanting little befides food, families are no burdens, and the prolific powers of nature have free fcope to difplay themfelves.— Perhaps IRELAND is one inftance of this. If we may depend on an account in the Philofophical Tranfactions (Abridgement, Vol. III. p. 666.) the number of people in *Ireland*, in 1695, did not much exceed a million. At prefent they are, I fuppofe, about two millions.——According to an account publifhed annually at *Dublin*, in *Watfon*'s Almanack, the houfes in *Ireland*, in 1754, were 395,439. In 1767 they were increafed to 424,046; and in 1777 to 448,426. But I have been informed that this account is of no authority, and deferves little credit. Nor can I learn that there are in *Ireland* any *documents* from which a judgment tolerably correct can be formed of the progrefs and prefent ftate of its population. It might have been expected, that the hearthtax would have furnifhed fuch *documents*: But this is not the cafe; and all that is known with certainty is the yearly produce of the tax; the average of which for the laft five years to 1781, having been 60,648*l*. makes the number of hearths that pay the tax (at 2*s*. per hearth) to be 606,480. It is fuppofed that a houfe may be allowed for every *two* hearths, and that a *third* of the houfes are excufed on account of inability and, on these suppositions, the number of houses will exceed 400,000 (*a*); and, consequently, the inhabitants will be (as just reckoned) about two millions (*b*).

(*a*) In the year 1787 the following account was returned to the House of Commons of Ireland, of the number of houses in that kingdom paying hearth-money.

No. of Houses containing Hearths.		No. of Houses containing Hearths.		No. of Houses containing Hearths.		No. of Houses containing Hearths.	
1	397,644	15	99	29	4	45	4
2	24,031	16	127	30	16	46	1
3	7,562	17	46	31	4	50	3
4	5,542	18	42	32	4	55	1
5	4,062	19	23	33	6	56	1
6	3,556	20	61	34	3	67	1
7	3,330	21	13	35	3	92	1
8	2,209	22	10	36	6	112	1
9	985	23	9	37	1	Houses exempted by law 23,075	
10	772	24	20	39	1		
11	316	25	20	40	7		
12	295	26	10	41	3		
13	147	27	5	42	3		
14	139	28	8	44	2		

From this table it appears that the number of hearths (exclusive of those exempted by law) is 612,577; and therefore, on the supposition adopted in this postscript, the whole number of houses in Ireland will be 408,384.—But if the preceding accounts be accurate, their real number amounts to 474,234, and consequently the inhabitants will rather exceed two millions and a quarter. E<small>D</small>.

(*b*) A survey of B<small>ELFAST</small> was made in *Jan.* 1782, from which it appeared, that it consisted of 2026 houses, containing 13,105 inhabitants, 6133 of whom were males, and 6972 females.——Looms 388; and houses for selling beer and spirits 119, or a 17 part of all the houses.
——On *Jan.* 1, 1757, the number of looms was 399, and the houses 1779, containing 8549 inhabitants, of whom 7993 were *Protestants,* and 556 *Papists.*

Sweden,

POSTSCRIPT.

Sweden, Norway (*a*), and the kingdom of *Naples*, are increafing faft; and alfo RUSSIA, if we may judge from the following facts.

In the viceroyalty of *Tweer* (in 1780) there died 4315 males; 3646 females; but there were born 11948 males, and 9013 females. The marriages were 6074.

In the eparchy of *Vologda* the deaths in the fame year were 2688 males, and 2377 females, The births were 6517 males, and 5366 females. The marriages 3232.

In both thefe provinces, therefore, the births were confiderably more than *double* the deaths; and the increafe muft be rapid.

At the beginning of the fame year (1780) there were found in the diftrict of Moscow 137,698 males, and 134,918 females; of whom died in the courfe of the year 2101 males and 1601 females, or the 65th part of the males, and 84th part of the females. But there were born in the courfe of the year 4546 males, and 4075 females, which added 5919 (or a 46th part) to the inhabitants; and the number of inhabitants actually counted at the end of the year was 140,143 males, and 137,392 females (*b*)

(a) See the Preliminary Obfervations to Table XLII, p. 146; and the Effay on the *Population of England*, p. 14.

(b) Thefe accounts have been given by authority in RUSSIA; and were communicated to me by Mr. *Howard*; who with views of unparalleled humanity, travelled through that country in 1781——To Mr. *Howard*'s enquiries I likewife owe the account in the note p. 335 of SILESIA.

POSTSCRIPT.

But there exifts probably among mankind no fuch increafe as that among the United States of NORTH-AMERICA, according to the account of it in Vol I. p. 276, &c.

The reflection on thefe facts muft be mortifying to this country (the richeft upon earth) if it be indeed true that our population is declining. But we muft comfort ourfelves by confidering that in this cafe, *value* is of more confequence than *number*. Commerce, arts, and liberty, once placed the little ftate of *Athens* at the head of the world; and the fame caufes once raifed this ifland to the fame eminence.

To the direct evidence already ftated of a decreafe in our population, it is proper to add the following facts.

1ft. The decreafe of LONDON. This I muft reckon certain, till fome other fatisfactory reafon (a) can be given for a diminution fince 1727, of more than 7000 *per ann.* in the regiftered burials, and near 2000 in the regiftered births.

(a) The new burying grounds (taken notice of in the Notes p. 255 and p. 260, Vol. I.) have been opened but lately; and therefore, cannot account for this diminution; nor do the burials in them amount to a number equal to it.

Annual medium of regiftered burials in LONDON.
For five years to 1722 inclufive 26,443
     to 1727   26,747
     to 1732   26,582

Secondly. The decreafe in the produce of the hereditary and temporary excife upon beer. This was almoft the only excife that exifted before the Revolution; and though the country was then poorer, it produced a *quarter* more than it has lately. This fact, together with the objections to the inference I have drawn from it, may be found diftinctly ftated in the Effay on the *Population of England*, &c. p. 18, &c. and p. 45, &c.

Thirdly. The growing diftrefs among the lower orders of people, who are the majority of the nation, deferves to be parti-

For five years to 1737	26,848
to 1742	28,344
to 1748	23,884
to 1753	22,006
to 1758	20,875
to 1763	22,593
to 1768	23,319
to 1773	22,754
For four years to 1777	20,945
For three years to 1780	20,438
For two years to 1782	19,313

Annual medium of regiftered births in LONDON.

For five years to 1727	18,898
to 1768	16,291
to 1782	16,966

The decreafe which this Table fhews to have taken place lately in the excefs of burials above the births, has been afcribed to an improved ftate of LONDON with refpect to its influence on the health of its inhabitants; but the true reafon is the fact referred to at the beginning of this note.

cularly

cularly attended to on this subject. The increase of the poor rates proves this fact; and it seems to be universally acknowledged. A people at their ease will increase; but increasing difficulties in procuring the means of subsistence, producing a forced industry, and an aversion to marriage, must depopulate.

The increased produce of the taxes on candles, leather, &c. the inclosures of waste lands, and the improvements in agriculture which have taken place lately, have been urged in opposition to these facts. But I am afraid they only prove that luxury has increased consumption more than it has lessened the number of our people.

Upon the whole. I beg it may be remembered, that my opinion, in this instance, is by no means a clear and decided conviction. I may probably be influenced too much by a desire to maintain an assertion once delivered.——Some time or other, perhaps, the Legislature will think this a point worth its attention. Much light may be thrown upon it, and the state of our population kept constantly in view, by only ordering exact registers to be kept of the births, burials, and marriages in the kingdom. This is done in other kingdoms. It has lately been done in *France*; and the result has been a discovery that the population of FRANCE exceeds all that had been conjectured

POSTSCRIPT.

jectured concerning it *. Should a like discovery be the consequence of carrying such an order into execution here, it will give the kingdom an encouragement which at present it greatly wants; and I shall rejoice in my own confutation.

* See the Appendix to a Discourse on the Love of our Country, delivered by the Author on November 4th, 1789, to the Society for commemorating the Revolution in Great Britain.—In this Appendix it is observed, that the medium of annual deaths, births, and marriages, in the kingdom of France, was

Of births for four years, to 1774   914,710
Of deaths — — —   793,931
Of marriages — — —   192,180
Of births, for six years, to 1780   958,419
Of deaths — — —   834,865
Of marriages — — —   228,170

If 834,865, the number of deaths to 1780, be multiplied by 35, agreeable to the rule in p. 326, it will appear that the whole number of inhabitants in this kingdom exceeds *twenty-nine millions*. ED.

VIEW

OF THE

AGRICULTURE

OF

MIDDLESEX;

WITH

OBSERVATIONS ON THE MEANS OF ITS IMPROVEMENT,

AND

SEVERAL ESSAYS ON AGRICULTURE IN GENERAL.

DRAWN UP FOR THE CONSIDERATION OF

THE BOARD OF AGRICULTURE,

BY

JOHN MIDDLETON, ESQ.

OF WEST-BARNS FARM, MERTON, AND OF LAMBETH, SURREY,

LAND SURVEYOR;

Member of the London Society for the Encouragement of Arts, Manufactures, and Commerce, and Corresponding Member of the Board of Agriculture.

ACCOMPANIED BY THE

REMARKS OF SEVERAL RESPECTABLE
GENTLEMEN AND FARMERS.

LONDON:

PRINTED BY B. MACMILLAN,
PRINTER TO HIS ROYAL HIGHNESS THE PRINCE OF WALES;
FOR G. NICOL, PALL-MALL, BOOKSELLER TO HIS MAJESTY,
AND THE BOARD OF AGRICULTURE; AND SOLD BY
G. G. AND J. ROBINSON, PATERNOSTER-ROW;
J. SEWELL, CORNHILL; CADELL AND DAVIES,
STRAND; W. CREECH, EDINBURGH; AND
JOHN ARCHER, DUBLIN.

1798.

Republished in 1973 by Gregg International Publishers Limited
Westmead, Farnborough, Hants., England

LETTER FROM THE REV. JOHN HOWLETT
TO THE AUTHOR, ON POPULATION.

———

SIR,

I WAS not at home when your very obliging letter of the 15th arrived here, or I should have endeavoured to have answered it sooner. And now I am set down for that purpose, I will begin by correcting my own errors, with respect to the population of the kingdom, and that of the metropolis in particular.

The former, in my examination of Dr. Price's essay, &c. I made to be between eight and nine millions. This estimate was formed upon principles so extremely unfounded, which I did not then know, but very soon discovered,

covered, as rendered the final result utterly erroneous. From a more minute, and accurate investigation of the subject, about fourteen or fifteen years ago (which I intended to publish, but did not, and I believe never shall), I am nearly confident our population did not then amount to seven millions and a half, and that at present it does not exceed eight millions. It is somewhat extraordinary, that the fallacy which misled me, neither the public nor the keen penetrating eyes of Dr. Price ever saw. The Doctor indeed pointed out a misapprehension which he supposed me to be under; but that was entirely groundless.

With regard to the number of inhabitants within the London bills of mortality, I confess I felt no small degree of confusion, upon finding I had asserted they were between 8 and 900,000; having long been inclined to think that they have never yet amounted to 700,000. I have turned to the passage in which I have given my estimate of 8 or 900,000, and find the reasoning upon which it is founded, too vague and precarious to be safely depended upon.

In my examination of Dr. Price's essay on the population of England and Wales, I have stated the annual deficiency of burials in the metropolis, as given in the bills of mortality, at 11,273; which, added to those then in the bills, 20,668, makes the total of annual burials 31,941*. Dr. Price very justly observes, I have made

---

* That the deficiency of burials registered in the bills has been considerably increased since the year 1780, is, I believe, notorious; and that this increase is now at least 1000, is, I presume, by no means an extravagant estimate. The burials in the bills for 1795, were 21,179; that is, 511 more than those of 1780; adding these to the thousand, the increased deficiency of burials, together with the allowed deficiency in 1780, and we have 31,511 for the present total deficiency of the bills, which multiply by 20, (the acknowledged proportion of the inhabitants of the capital to its burials being nearly as that number to 1), and there comes out 630,220 as the actual proportion *within* the bills; and by making the proper deductions and additions, that for Middlesex 634,200.

no allowance for the numbers annually brought from the neighbouring country villages to be interred in London, as I ought to have done, and as I actually did with regard to those carried out of the city, and buried in the country, to the amount of 2000. Now, making proper deductions for this, and some other particulars that might be noticed, I think it requisite to reduce the 31,941 stated above as the total actual number of burials annually within the bills of mortality, to about 30,000. Dr. Price has shewn, with great plausibility, that the annual mortality of the city of London is about 1 in 20 of its entire population; multiplying its 30,000 burials then by 20, we have 600,000 for the entire number of inhabitants *within* the bills.

The population of Middlesex may be computed, by ascertaining the proportion between the number of taxed houses and the number of people in an adequate number of places. This method of calculation Dr. Price himself pointed out, which is unexceptionable; and had Mr. Lysons given us the number of taxed houses only in those parishes of which the infinitely greater, but necessary trouble was taken, actually to enumerate the inhabitants, we should have been able to make it for the county of Middlesex with tolerable precision. And even now, we are not totally destitute of data for this purpose. But before I proceed to calculate upon them, it may not be amiss to say a few words upon the nature of the Tax-office returns.

Now these returns are of two leading descriptions: the first contains the number of taxed and taxable houses; the second, the number of cottages excused on account of poverty.

These returns, for the year 1781, for the whole kingdom stand thus:

Number

Number of houses taxed and taxable - 728,699
Ditto of cottages excused on account of poverty 277,111

Total - - 1,005,810

Were both these kinds of returns perfectly correct, the population might be easily settled; but this is far from being the case. The taxed and taxable houses are returned by the district surveyors upon *oath*, and are therefore tolerably accurate; but as to the number of cottages, no *oath* is required, and seldom, if ever, are any returns made by them for particular parishes, and those for whole districts are mere lumping random conjectures, most astonishingly defective. For illustration of this, take the county of Essex:

The return of taxed and taxable houses for 1781, is 18,422
Ditto of cottages excused on account of poverty 9,664

Total - - 28,086

This proportion of cottages, one would at first sight be inclined to think, would be amply sufficient; for it is more than a third part of the whole return. But upon full inquiry, how different turns out the fact. My parish of Dunmow contains above 300 houses, out of which not 120 are returned as taxed and taxable; and in the parishes of Bocking, Braintree, Halstead, Coggeshall, &c. the deficiency is greater still; and throughout the whole county, I have a sufficient number of actual enumerations of the inhabitants of parishes of every description, fully to authorize my concluding, that our population, compared with our taxed and taxable houses, is above the ratio of $13\frac{1}{2}$ to 1. Were the same proportion to take place in Middlesex, multiplying the taxed and taxable houses,

75,171,

75,171, as returned for that county for 1781, by 13½, we make its number of inhabitants about 1,004,808 ; if we adopt 76,527, the number sent to you for the year 1796, and use the same multiplier, we raise it to about 1,033,114. But this cannot be admitted, because the proportion of houses excused on account of poverty, is not nearly so great in Middlesex as in Essex, that being a manufacturing county, and its manufacture greatly declining.

I have the number of inhabitants and taxed houses in Uxbridge, and three country parishes in Middlesex; the former amount to 4,487, the latter to 522 *; this gives a proportion of persons to taxed houses of scarcely 8 to 1 †; which is certainly as much too low for the whole county as the other is too high, and would give us only 612,216 as the total population of Middlesex.

The number of people in the parishes of Mortlake, Putney, and Wandsworth, in Surrey, by Mr. Lysons' enumeration, is 8,614; of the taxed houses which I procured from the parochial duplicates, 755.

In twelve country parishes in the same county, the inhabitants are 3860; taxed houses 416. To these add the four parishes in Middlesex, as just above given—Persons 4,487, taxed houses 522, and the total amount of the nineteen parishes in the two counties, is 16.961 inhabitants and 1,693 taxed houses; which yields a proportion of the former to the latter, of something more than 10 to 1 ‖. Multiply therefore the Tax-office return sent you, 76,527

---

* The accounts of these parishes were sent me in the year 1781 ; and likewise twelve country parishes in Surrey.

† This should be 8 6-10 to 1, which, being applied to Middlesex, would be 76,526 × 8 6-10 = 6,8,133. —*J. M.*

‖ These observations of Mr. Howlett's can only be applied to the country part of the county.—*J. M.*

by

by 10, and there comes out 765,270*, for the total population of Middlesex. This, I am inclined to think, is not very short of the truth. Perhaps you may approach somewhat nearer, if you obtain, as I suppose you easily might, from the parochial surveyors or collectors of the six parishes of Hayes, Heston, Isleworth, Teddington, Twickenham and Twyford, the number of taxed and taxable houses in their several parochial duplicates, each respectively.

Of the several calculations I have hazarded, I think the last by much the best, and nearest the fact. I presume not, however, to place entire confidence in it. Of this, however, I think myself nearly certain, that the population of Middlesex has never yet amounted to 800,000; I keep my mind, however, entirely open to conviction, upon the appearance of adequate evidence.

I am Sir, &c.

JOHN HOWLETT.

Dunmow, April 23, 1797.

---

* If we combine the three computations, and take the average, we have about 681,316 for the total population of Middlesex; which, for any thing I certainly know to the contrary, may be nearer the truth than any one of them separately. I should be happy to see the matter more clearly investigated.

AN

ESTIMATE

OF THE

NUMBER OF INHABITANTS

IN

GREAT BRITAIN

AND

IRELAND.

BY

SIR FREDERICK MORTON EDEN, Bart.

" THESE CONSTITUTE A STATE."

SIR W. JONES.

PRINTED FOR J. WRIGHT, PICCADILLY.

1800.

Republished in 1973 by Gregg International Publishers Limited
Westmead, Farnborough, Hants., England

AN

ESTIMATE, &c.

A Bill, for afcertaining the population of Great Britain, being now under the confideration of the Legiflature, I am induced to avail myfelf of the opportunity, which the difcuffion of this fubject prefents, to lay before the public a comparative eftimate of our numbers at the clofe of the feventeenth and eighteenth centuries. Part of this eftimate is felected from a work which I publifhed three years ago; the remainder is the refult of communications, recently obtained from diftricts, principally, if not entirely, agricultural.

Of the various fubjects to which political arithmetic has been applied, none, perhaps, have furnifhed fo much matter for ingenious difputation

difputation as our population. Twenty years ago, Dr. Price maintained, upon the authority of the returns of the Tax-Office Surveyors, that the number of houfes in England and Wales, in the year 1777, amounted to 952,734; and, averaging the various accounts he had received, that five perfons *per* houfe were more than a fair allowance: he, therefore, inferred, that the number of inhabitants in the fouthern part of the empire did not exceed 5,000,000.* His opponents contended that, with refpect to cottages, (or houfes exempted from affeffment,) the returns of the Surveyors were extremely inaccurate; that five perfons *per* houfe, including public buildings, were probably lefs than the average of the kingdom; and that inftead of 5,000,000, 8,000,000, or even 10,000,000 might be affumed as the population of England and Wales. There are many who now think, that a ftill higher number is nearer the truth. The information, however, which individuals can obtain, forms fo fmall a part of the mafs of knowledge that is wanted upon fo intricate a fubject, that general conclufions ought not to be admitted, without many qualifications. He who

* Price's Effay on the Population of England, firft publifhed in 1779.

looks

looks for more than probabilities, will be disappointed. Moral certainty cannot, in inquiries of this nature, be expected to refult from inveftigations into the number of baptifms, burials, taxed houfes, cottages, and inhabitants, in particular diftricts. With this impreffion on my mind, I offer to the confideration of others thofe documents which have afforded conviction to myfelf; and I offer them with the lefs hefitation, as any errors in this eftimate (errors which will be readily excufed, by all who are accuftomed to fuch difquifitions) muft foon be detected. I fhall probably clofe the lift of thofe who, in refearches concerning the progrefs of one of the moft important (perhaps the moft important) of our national refources, are obliged to collect information from returns of taxed houfes; or from excifes on confumable commodities; or (ftill more perplexing tafk) to

> Search it there, where, to be born and die,
> Of rich and poor makes all the hiftory.

The propofed enumeration of the people will fuperfede the ufe of ingenious gueffes and plaufible fpeculations, drawn from fuch *data;* and (I truft) prove, beyond the poffibility of doubt, that, among the diftreffes of the times, we have not to deplore a declining population.

(4)

In the following ten Tables, which were formed from materials contained in " The State of the Poor," (the work above alluded to), the baptifms, burials, and marriages, are the number annually, on the average of the laft feven years, that could be procured, ending with 1793, 1794, or 1795; except in the following inftances:

> Stapleton is for the year 1795.
> Overingham is the average of fix years, ending with 1794.
> Monkwearmouth, of four years, ending with 1794.
> North Shields, of two years, ending with 1795.

The larger numbers, in Table VII. are not the refult of actual enumeration; yet, as great pains were ufed to obtain both the affeffed houfes, and number of inhabitants in the manufacturing towns, I offer them as approximations to the truth.

TABLE

TABLE I.

AGRICULTURAL PARISHES.

COUNTY.	PARISH.	Baptisms.	Burials.	Affected Houses.
Bedford	Houghton-Regis ...	$14\frac{3}{7}$	$13\frac{1}{7}$	47
Bucks	Maids-Morton	$8\frac{1}{7}$	8	19
	Winflow	$38\frac{1}{7}$	$24\frac{5}{7}$	101
Cumberland ..	Caftle-Carrock	$8\frac{2}{7}$	3	31
	Gilcrux	$5\frac{2}{7}$	$3\frac{3}{7}$	24
	Cumrew	$5\frac{5}{7}$	$3\frac{1}{7}$	27
	Cumwhitton	$11\frac{6}{7}$	$6\frac{6}{7}$	50
	Harrington	$34\frac{2}{7}$	$24\frac{6}{7}$	101
	Sebergham	$23\frac{4}{7}$	$14\frac{3}{7}$	80
	Kirkofwald	$17\frac{5}{7}$	$14\frac{6}{7}$	97
Devon	Clyft, St. George ..	$8\frac{4}{7}$	$5\frac{3}{7}$	18
Gloucefter ...	Stapleton	53	38	84
	Rodmarton	$11\frac{5}{7}$	$6\frac{3}{7}$	9
Herts	Chipping-Barnet ...	53	$32\frac{6}{7}$	120
Kent	Chalk	$7\frac{2}{7}$	$8\frac{5}{7}$	15
	Cobham	$15\frac{4}{7}$	$15\frac{1}{7}$	40
	Hothfield	$11\frac{2}{7}$	$5\frac{6}{7}$	40
	Meopham	$22\frac{2}{7}$	$13\frac{5}{7}$	48
Leicefter ...	Kibworth-Beauchamp	$28\frac{5}{7}$	$25\frac{1}{7}$	124
	Alford	$36\frac{1}{7}$	$18\frac{4}{7}$	48
	Spilfby	$26\frac{1}{7}$	$16\frac{2}{7}$	121
	Swinefhead	$63\frac{1}{7}$	$46\frac{5}{7}$	166
	Willoughby	$9\frac{3}{7}$	8	41
Northampton .	Brixworth	$21\frac{5}{7}$	20	36
Nottingham ..	Overingham	$9\frac{4}{7}$	$5\frac{5}{7}$	24
Oxford ...:	Deddington	48	31	102
Rutland	North-Luffenham ..	10	$7\frac{6}{7}$	23
Surry	Efher	$24\frac{3}{7}$	$23\frac{2}{7}$	96
	Reigate	59	$46\frac{4}{7}$	206
	Walton-on-Thames .	$45\frac{3}{7}$	$37\frac{4}{7}$	158

AGRICULTURAL PARISHES, CONTINUED.

COUNTY.	PARISH.	Baptisms.	Burials.	Affected Houses.
Suffex	Chailey	$20\frac{5}{7}$	$17\frac{1}{7}$	57
Warwick	Southam	28	$19\frac{5}{7}$	86
Weftmorland	Orton	$34\frac{2}{7}$	$22\frac{5}{7}$	205
Worcefter	Inkborough	$43\frac{1}{7}$	$25\frac{3}{7}$	72
York	Great Driffield	$37\frac{5}{7}$	$26\frac{3}{7}$	160
	Pocklington	$41\frac{2}{7}$	$38\frac{2}{7}$	150
	Stokefley	$53\frac{1}{7}$	$42\frac{4}{7}$	158
Denbigh	Llanferras	$17\frac{4}{7}$	$9\frac{5}{7}$	46
		$1007\frac{6}{7}$	$731\frac{1}{7}$	3030

TABLE

TABLE II.

TOWNS and MANUFACTURING PARISHES.

COUNTY.	PARISH.	Baptisms.	Burials.	Affected Houses.
Bedford	Dunstable	$29\frac{6}{7}$	$23\frac{4}{7}$	115
Bucks	Buckingham	$73\frac{3}{7}$	$40\frac{2}{7}$	230
Berks	St. Mary, Reading . .	78	$89\frac{4}{7}$	240
Derby	Chesterfield	$153\frac{3}{7}$	$112\frac{6}{7}$	370
	All-Saints, Derby . .	$91\frac{3}{7}$	$79\frac{5}{7}$	300
	St. Michael. Derby .	$20\frac{5}{7}$	$23\frac{5}{7}$	65
	St. Werburgh, Derby .	$71\frac{1}{7}$	$64\frac{3}{7}$	228
Devon	South Tawton	$53\frac{3}{7}$	$28\frac{3}{7}$	73
Durham	Monkwearmouth . . .	$127\frac{3}{7}$	163	274
	Tanfield	$75\frac{4}{7}$	$6+\frac{4}{7}$	130
Essex......	All-Saints, Colchester	$47\frac{2}{7}$	$9\frac{4}{7}$	58
Hereford	All-Saints, Hereford .	$55\frac{4}{7}$	45	160
	St. Nicholas, Hereford	16	$11\frac{3}{7}$	102
Herts	Abbey-Ch. St. Albans	$49\frac{1}{7}$	$32\frac{6}{7}$	97
Lancaster ...	Bury	$478\frac{4}{7}$	$288\frac{3}{7}$	325
Leicester....	Ashby-de-la-Zouch . .	$65\frac{3}{7}$	$60\frac{2}{7}$	195
	St. Martin, Leicester .	76	$73\frac{6}{7}$	520
Lincoln	Louth	$119\frac{1}{7}$	$92\frac{3}{7}$	392
Middlesex ...	Ealing	$168\frac{5}{7}$	$167\frac{6}{7}$	355
Monmouth...	Monmouth	$68\frac{2}{7}$	$66\frac{5}{7}$	351
Norfolk	Norwich	$1082\frac{1}{7}$	$1122\frac{5}{7}$	2200
Northampton .	All-Saints, Northampton	$99\frac{5}{7}$	$91\frac{5}{7}$	408
Northumberland	North Shields	366	362	740
Nottingham ..	Newark	$219\frac{6}{7}$	$151\frac{6}{7}$	605
	St. Mary, Nottingham	764	482	1200
Somerset....	Minehead	30	$19\frac{6}{7}$	110
Warwick ...	Sutton-Colefield ...	$91\frac{1}{7}$	$57\frac{6}{7}$	203
Wilts	Scend	$39\frac{3}{7}$	$23\frac{3}{7}$	63

York,

TOWNS AND MANUFACTURING PARISHES, CONTINUED.

COUNTY.	PARISH.	Baptisms.	Burials.	Assessed Houses.
York	Burton	34 1/7	22 3/7	51
	Ecclesfield	168 5/7	110 1/7	328
	Leeds	935 2/7	838 3/7	1836
	Sheffield	1608 3/7	1213 3/7	2365
	Skipton	60 2/7	55 2/7	121
		7318 4/7	6089 4/7	14810
	Brought over from Table I.	1007 6/7	731 3/7	3030
	Total	8326 3/7	6821	17840

Baptisms to Burials as 10 to $8\frac{1}{5}$.
Assessed Houses to Baptisms as 10 to $4\frac{2}{3}$.

TABLE

(9)

TABLE III.

AGRICULTURAL PARISHES.

COUNTY.	PARISH.	Baptisms.	Marriages.
Bucks	Maids-Morton ...	$8\frac{1}{7}$	4
	Winflow	$38\frac{1}{7}$	$7\frac{4}{7}$
Cumberland ..	Cumrew	$5\frac{5}{7}$	2
	Sebergham	$23\frac{4}{7}$	$4\frac{5}{7}$
	Kirkofwald	$17\frac{5}{7}$	$4\frac{5}{7}$
Devon	Clyft, St. George .	$8\frac{4}{7}$	$2\frac{1}{7}$
Gloucester ...	Stapleton	53	17
	Rodmarton	$11\frac{5}{7}$	2
Kent	Chalk	$7\frac{2}{7}$	$5\frac{6}{7}$
	Cobham	$15\frac{4}{7}$	6
	Hothfield	$11\frac{2}{7}$	$2\frac{3}{7}$
	Meopham	$22\frac{2}{7}$	$5\frac{3}{7}$
Leicester ...	Kilworth-Beauchamp	$28\frac{5}{7}$	$9\frac{6}{7}$
Northampton .	Brixworth	$21\frac{5}{7}$	$5\frac{1}{7}$
Oxford	Deddington	48	$8\frac{2}{7}$
Rutland	North Luffenham..	10	$2\frac{2}{7}$
Surry	Esher	$24\frac{3}{7}$	$4\frac{6}{7}$
	Reigate	59	$15\frac{2}{7}$
Warwick ...	Southam	28	$7\frac{5}{7}$
Westmorland .	Orton	$34\frac{2}{7}$	$7\frac{5}{7}$
York	Great Driffield ...	$37\frac{6}{7}$	10
	Pocklington	$41\frac{2}{7}$	$13\frac{5}{7}$
	Stokesley	$53\frac{1}{7}$	$12\frac{2}{7}$
Denbigh	Llanterras	$17\frac{4}{7}$	$2\frac{3}{7}$
		627	$163\frac{3}{7}$

TABLE IV.

TOWNS and MANUFACTURING PARISHES.

COUNTY.	PARISH.	Baptisms.	Marriages.
Bedford	Dunstable	$29\frac{6}{7}$	$8\frac{2}{7}$
Bucks	Buckingham	$73\frac{3}{7}$	$20\frac{6}{7}$
Berks	St. Mary, Reading	78	$26\frac{2}{7}$
Devon	South Tawton	$53\frac{3}{7}$	$13\frac{1}{7}$
Durham	Monkwearmouth	$127\frac{3}{7}$	52
	Tanfield	$75\frac{4}{7}$	$16\frac{6}{7}$
Essex	All-Saints, Colchester	$47\frac{2}{7}$	$21\frac{6}{7}$
Herts	Abbey-Church, St Albans	$49\frac{1}{7}$	$12\frac{5}{7}$
Hereford	All-Saints, Hereford	$55\frac{4}{7}$	$14\frac{1}{7}$
	St. Nicholas, Hereford	16	$7\frac{3}{7}$
Lancaster	Bury	$478\frac{4}{7}$	$167\frac{6}{7}$
Leicester	Ashby-de-la-Zouch	$65\frac{4}{7}$	$21\frac{3}{7}$
Middlesex	Ealing	$168\frac{5}{7}$	$60\frac{5}{7}$
Monmouth	Monmouth	$68\frac{2}{7}$	19
Northampton	All-Saints, Northamptn	$99\frac{5}{7}$	40
Northumberland	North Shields	366	127
Somerset	Minehead	30	6
Warwick	Sutton-Colefield	$91\frac{1}{7}$	$15\frac{1}{7}$
Wilts	Seend	$39\frac{3}{7}$	$7\frac{2}{7}$
York	Ecclesfield	$168\frac{5}{7}$	$43\frac{6}{7}$
	Sheffield	$1608\frac{5}{7}$	429
	Brought over from Table III.	$3790\frac{4}{7}$ 627	$1130\frac{6}{7}$ $163\frac{3}{7}$
	Total	$4417\frac{4}{7}$	$1294\frac{2}{7}$

Baptisms to Marriages, as 1 to 3 nearly.

TABLE

TABLE V.

AGRICULTURAL PARISHES.

COUNTY.	PARISH.	Baptisms.	Population.
Bucks	Winflow	$38\frac{1}{7}$	1,100
Cumberland . .	Caftle-Carrock . . .	$8\frac{2}{7}$	232
	Cumrew	$5\frac{5}{7}$	146
	Gilcrux	$5\frac{2}{7}$	207
	Harrington	$34\frac{2}{7}$	1,412
	Kirkofwald	$17\frac{5}{7}$	937
Gloucefter . . .	Stapleton	53	1,377
Kent	Meopham	$22\frac{2}{7}$	612
Northampton .	Brixworth	$21\frac{5}{7}$	800
Nottingham . .	Overingham	$9\frac{4}{7}$	240
Rutland	North Luffenham . .	10	310
Worcefter . . .	Inkborough	$43\frac{1}{7}$	889
		$239\frac{1}{7}$	8262

TABLE

TABLE VI.

TOWNS and MANUFACTURING PARISHES.

COUNTY.	PARISH.	Baptisms.	Population.
Derby	Chesterfield	$153\frac{3}{7}$	3,987
	All-Saints, Derby .	$91\frac{3}{7}$	2,675
	St. Michael, Derby .	$20\frac{5}{7}$	640
	St. Werburgh, Derby	$71\frac{1}{7}$	1,935
Devon	South Tawton ...	$53\frac{3}{7}$	2,500
Durham ...	Monkwearmouth ..	$127\frac{3}{7}$	5,000
Lancaster ...	Bury	$478\frac{4}{7}$	4,500
Leicester ...	St. Martin, Leicester	76	2,825
York	Leeds	$935\frac{2}{7}$	31,500
	Sheffield	$1,608\frac{5}{7}$	35,000
Norfolk	Norwich	$1,082\frac{1}{7}$	36,000
Nottingham .	Newark	$219\frac{6}{7}$	7,000
		$4,918\frac{1}{7}$	133,562
	Brought over from Table V.	$239\frac{1}{7}$	8,262
	Total	$5,157\frac{2}{7}$	141,824

Baptisms to Population as 1 to $27\frac{3}{4}$.

TABLE

TABLE VII.

AGRICULTURAL PARISHES.

COUNTY:	PARISH.	Affeſſed Houſes.	Population.
Bedford	Humberſhoe	15	170
Bucks	Winſlow	101	1100
Cheſter	High-Walton	15	110
Cumberland ..	Ainſtable	50	434
	Caſtle-Carrock	31	232
	Croglin	26	163
	Cumrew	27	146
	Gilcrux	24	207
	Harrington	101	1412
	Heſket	160	1150
	Kirkoſwald	97	937
	Warwick	28	347
	Wetheral	172	1413
Derby	Wirkſworth	152	2800
Dorſet	Durweſton	10	300
Durham	Holy-Iſland	62	691
	Stanhope	520	3600
Glouceſter ...	Stapleton	84	1377
Kent	Meopham	48	612
Northampton .	Brixworth	36	800
Nottingham ..	Overingham	24	240
Rutland	North Luffenham ..	23	310
Salop	Biſhop's Caſtle, Borough	128	1100
	————————, Hamlet	28	250
Surry	Epſom	238	1671
Weſtmorland .	Kirkby-Lonſdale ...	135	1081
Worceſter ...	Inkborough	72	889
		2407	23,542

TABLE

TABLE VIII.

TOWNS and MANUFACTURING PARISHES.

COUNTY	PARISH.	Affeſſed Houſes.	Population.
Derby	Cheſterfield	370	3,987
	All-Saints, Derby	300	2,675
	St. Michael, Derby	65	640
	St. Werburgh, Derby	228	1,935
Devon	South Tawton	73	2,500
Durham	Monkwearmouth	274	5,000
	South Shields	550	12,000
Eſſex	St. Mary, Colcheſter	15	250
Hants.	Southampton	700	9,000
Lancaſter	Bury	325	4,500
	Lancaſter	612	8,000
	Mancheſter	4,572	66,980
Leiceſter	St. Martin, Leiceſter	520	2,825
Lincoln	Louth	392	4,000
Middleſex	Ealing	355	4,500
Norfolk	Norwich	2,200	36,000
	Yarmouth	750	13,000
Northumberland	North Shields	740	10,000
Nottingham	Newark	605	7,000
Warwick	Birmingham	4,000	65,000
Weſtmorland	Kendal	430	7,154
York	Leeds	1,836	31,500
	Sheffield	2,365	35,000
		22,277	333,446
	Brought over, from Table VII.	2,407	23,542
	Total	24,684	356,988

Aſſeſſed Houſes to Population, as 1 to 14½.

TABLE

(15)

TABLE IX.

TOWN and COUNTRY PARISHES.

COUNTY.	PARISH.	Marriages.	Assessed Houses.
Berks	New Windsor	$22\frac{6}{7}$	470
Bucks	Buckingham	$20\frac{5}{7}$	230
	Maids-Morton	4	19
	Winflow	$7\frac{4}{7}$	101
Cumberland	Cumrew	2	27
	Kirkofwald	$4\frac{5}{7}$	97
	Sebergham	$4\frac{5}{7}$	80
Devon	Clyft, St. George	$2\frac{1}{7}$	18
	South Tawton	$13\frac{1}{7}$	73
Durham	St. Margaret, Durham	$20\frac{1}{7}$	200
	South Shields	$50\frac{5}{7}$	550
	Tanfield	$16\frac{6}{7}$	130
Effex	All-Saints, Colchefter	$21\frac{6}{7}$	58
Gloucefter	Rodmarton	2	9
	Stapleton	17	84
Hereford	All-Saints, Hereford	$14\frac{1}{7}$	160
	St. Nicholas, Hereford	$7\frac{3}{7}$	102
Herts	Abbey-Ch. St. Alban's	$12\frac{5}{7}$	97
Kent	Chalk	$5\frac{6}{7}$	15
	Cobham	6	40
	Meopham	$5\frac{3}{7}$	48
Lancafter	Bury	$167\frac{6}{7}$	325
Leicefter	Afhby-de-la-Zouch	$21\frac{3}{7}$	195
	Kibworth-Beauchamp	$9\frac{6}{7}$	124
Middlefex	Ealing	$60\frac{3}{7}$	355
Monmouth	Abergavenny	$20\frac{4}{7}$	302
	Monmouth	19	351
Northampton	Brixworth	$5\frac{1}{7}$	36
	Northampton	40	408
Northumberland	North Shields	127	740

TOWN AND COUNTRY PARISHES, CONTINUED.

COUNTY.	PARISH.	Marriages.	Affessed Houses.
Oxford	Deddington	$8\frac{2}{7}$	102
Rutland	North Luffenham ..	$2\frac{2}{7}$	23
Somerset ...	Minehead	6	110
Surry	Epsom	11	238
	Esher	$4\frac{6}{7}$	96
	Farnham	$37\frac{2}{7}$	340
Warwick ...	Southam	$7\frac{5}{7}$	86
	Sutton-Colefield...	$15\frac{1}{7}$	203
Westmorland .	Orton	$7\frac{5}{7}$	205
Wilts.	Seend	$7\frac{2}{7}$	63
York	Ecclesfield	$43\frac{6}{7}$	328
	Great Driffield ...	10	160
	Sheffield	429	2,365
	Pocklington	$13\frac{5}{7}$	150
	Stokesley	$12\frac{2}{7}$	158
Denbigh ...	Llanferras	$2\frac{3}{7}$	46
Pembroke ...	Narbeth	$10\frac{3}{7}$	96
		1363	10,213

Affessed Houses to Marriages, as 78 to 10.

TABLE

TABLE X.

AGRICULTURAL PARISHES.

COUNTY.	PARISH.	Marriages.	Population.
Bucks	Winflow	$7\frac{4}{7}$	1,100
Cumberland	Cumrew	2	146
	Kirkofwald	$4\frac{5}{7}$	937
Devon	South Tawton	$13\frac{1}{7}$	2,500
Gloucefter	Stapleton	17	1,377
Kent	Meopham	$5\frac{3}{7}$	612
Northampton	Brixworth	$5\frac{1}{7}$	800
Rutland	North Luffenham	$2\frac{2}{7}$	310
Surry	Epfom	11	1,671
		$68\frac{2}{7}$	9,453

Marriages to Population as 139 to 1.

The following TABLE, of the number of charged and chargeable houfes, and of cottages, returned by the furveyors of the houfe and window duties, was obtained from the Tax-Office laft winter.

D TABLE

TABLE XI.

Number of Houses in England and Wales charged or chargeable with the Duties on Houses and Windows or Lights, as also the Number of Houses exempted from the Payment of the Duty, distinguishing the Number in each County.

COUNTIES.	Houses inhabited.	Houses uninhabited.	Houses exempted from Duty.	Total.
Bedford	4,714	55	579	5,348
Berks	7,249	181	6,174	13,604
Bucks	7,924	105	6,398	14,427
Cambridge . . .	8,538	56	5,563	14,157
Chester	16,175	324	10,885	27,384
Cornwall . . .	13,262	1,260	6,305	20,827
Cumberland . .	12,408	374	2,294	15,076
Derby	12,665	347	5,944	18,556
Devon	26,708	1,640	15,263	43,611
Dorset	10,320	104	4,210	14,634
Durham	11,533	150	2,069	13,752
Essex	17,245	751	9,640	27,636
Gloucester . . .	13,887	233	346	14,466
Hereford	7,124	154	754	8,032
Hertford	7,917	195	4,024	12,136
Huntingdon . .	3,167	79	1,402	4,648
Kent	29,862	1,900	5,189	36,951
Lancaster . . .	40,081	969	12,399	53,499
Leicester	12,461	215	7,224	19,900
Lincoln	22,720	199	3,094	26,013
London	12,937	556	1,582	15,075
Middlesex . . .	42,468	2,380	9,420	54,268
Monmouth . . .	3,961	69	89	4,119
Norfolk	18,007	713	10,409	29,129
Northampton .	9,286	151	11,810	21,247

TABLE XI. CONTINUED.

COUNTIES.	Houses inhabited.	Houses uninhabited.	Houses exempted from Duty.	Total.
Northumberland	12,024	235	6,572	18,831
Nottingham . .	10,806	130	1,621	12,557
Oxford	8,634	237	7,050	15,921
Rutland	1,451	18	115	1,584
Salop	10,958	358	3,313	14,629
Somerset	23,685	719	13,609	38,013
Southampton . .	15,741	455	7,004	23,200
Stafford	16,246	559	6,665	23,470
Suffolk	16,944	587	8,804	26,335
Surry	10,853	710	3,990	15,553
Southwark . . .	10,703	394	5,448	16,545
Sussex	11,296	247	6,986	18,556
Warwick . . .	13,888	767	18,307	32,962
Westmorland .	4,745	990	1,733	7,468
Wilts	11,499	246	5,862	17,607
Worcester . . .	7,736	388	13,328	21,452
Westminster . .	16,249	670	612	17,531
York	72,377	1,827	30,870	105,074
Anglesea	2,455	56	2,000	4,511
Brecon	2,814	374	620	3,808
Cardigan	2,492	19	738	3,249
Carmarthen . .	5,547	35	1,088	6,670
Carnarvon . . .	2,494	96	1,483	4,071
Denbigh	4,994	57	835	5,886
Flint	2,722	80	601	3,403
Glamorgan . . .	5,246	35	85	5,366
Merioneth . . .	2,891	11	471	3,373
Montgomery . .	4,803	237	879	5,919
Pembroke . . .	3,120	49	287	3,456
Radnor	1,813	32	532	2,377
Total . .	689,845	23,803	294,574	1,008,222

Respecting the houfe and window duties, it feems material to remark, that, of the returns, made up at the Tax-Office, of charged and chargeable houfes, at different periods during the prefent century, fome include certain defcriptions of houfes, which are not included in others.

By the 7th and 8th W. III. c. 18, paffed in 1696, all inhabited houfes in England and Wales, excepting thofe not paying to church or poor, were fubjected to an annual duty of 2s.—Every houfe having 10, and fewer than 20 windows, 6s.—Every houfe having 20 windows, and upwards, 10s.

It appears from a paper, ftill remaining in the Tax-Office,* that the produce of this tax, for the year 1700, was 115,226l.

The oldeft lift of houfes, which fpecifically paid the tax of 1696, is the following account, made up for the year 1708; we owe its difcovery to the active refearches of Mr. Chalmers.

* Chalmers's Eftimate, edit. 1794, page 175.

		£
248,784 houses, at	2s. produced	24,878
165,856	6s.	49,757
93,876	10s.	46,938
508,516		£ 121,573

The 8th Anne, c. 4, imposes an additional duty of 10s. on 20 windows, and 20s. on 30 windows.

In 1710, the old duty produced only 115,675*l*.

The 20th Geo. II. c. 3, passed in 1747, repealed the former acts; but re-imposed the 2s. duty on inhabited houses; and raised the duty on houses, containing

From 10 to 14 windows, to 6d. *per* window.
From 14 to 20 . . . . 9d.
Above 20 . . . . 1s.

Houses, having less than 10 windows, and not paying to church, or poor, were exempted.

The old and new duties, for the year ending at Lady-day, 1748, produced . . . . £ 208,093

And

And (probably in confequence of an explanatory law paffed in 1748) in 1749 . . . . £ 220,890

In 1750, the number of charged and and chargeable houfes, returned to the Tax-Office, was . . . . , £ 729,048

The 31ft Geo. II. c. 22, paffed in 1757, raifed the houfe-duty to 3s.; and impofed an additional duty of 6d. *per* window, on houfes containing above 15 windows.

Houfes having lefs than 10 windows, and not paying to church or poor, were exempted from the houfe and window duties impofed by either of thefe acts. The account, therefore, of charged and chargeable houfes, in 1759, when no farther alteration had taken place, muft contain the fame defcription of houfes, as the account of 1708.

The charged houfes, in 1708, were 508,516.

What the number of chargeable houfes was, is difficult to determine; but allowing 25,000, the number, in 1761, or even twice that number, the charged and chargeable, in 1708, may be ftated at 550,000

The charged and chargeable houses, in 1759,* were 704,053

The higher number of charged and chargeable houses, in 1750, it is justly observed, by Mr. Chalmers, was probably owing to the act, 20th Geo. II. c. 3, which had just passed. New modes of circumvention had not then taken place; but means of evading the law having been found, the duties decreased year after year; and the window-duty having, in 1766, been extended, by 6th Geo. III. c. 38, to houses containing only seven windows, we are informed, that, of 400,273 houses, having exactly seven windows, nearly two-thirds were reduced to houses having only six windows.†

The 6th Geo. III. c. 38, repealed the former acts, and imposed a duty of 3*s.* on every inhabited house, (repealed in 1792,‡ as far as it affected houses having less than seven windows,) and a progressive duty from 2*d. per* window, on houses having seven windows, to 2*s. per* window on houses having 25, and upwards.

---

* Price's Observations on Reversionary Payments, 5th edit. ii. 299.

† Price's Essay, p. 10. ‡ By 32d Geo. III. c. 2.

In 1781, the charged and chargeable
houses were .... 724,351.

The commutation-act, 24th Geo. III. c. 38, passed in 1784, added 3s. to the 3s. inhabited house-duty, imposed by former acts, and more than doubled the window-duty: and additional duties on inhabited houses, according to the number of windows, were imposed by 37th Geo. III. c. 105, and other acts.

The 38th Geo. III. c. 40, by which the window and commutation taxes were consolidated, has extended the window-duty to houses having only six windows.

           £. s. d.
Houses having 6 windows, and of less rent than 5l. now pay 0 4 6 ann. duty.
  6 windows, if the rent is 5l. 0 6 0
  7 ——— 0 14 6
  8 ——— 1 1 0
  9 ——— 1 7 0

Houses, containing six, or fewer windows, and exempted, on account of poverty, from church and poor rates, pay no duty.

Considering the temptation which these taxes hold out, to the lower classes, to stop up their windows,

windows, it is not aftonifhing, that the prefent number of charged and chargeable houfes, though it includes houfes having fix windows, fhould be lefs than the returns in 1781, 1759, or 1750.

The preceding Tables furnifh the following refults:

1. That the baptifms are to the burials, as . 10 to $8\frac{1}{5}$
2. That the affeffed houfes are to the baptifms, as 10 to $4\frac{2}{3}$
3. That the baptifms are to the marriages, as . 1 to 3 nearly
4. That the baptifms are to the population, as 1 to $27\frac{3}{4}$
5. That the affeffed houfes are to the population, as 1 to $14\frac{1}{2}$
6. That the affeffed houfes are to the marriages, as 78 to 10
7. That the marriages are to the population, as 139 to 1

As the charged, or affeffed, houfes may be ftated (from Table X.) in round numbers, at 690,000, the baptifms (according to refult 2) will be 322,000; which, multiplied by $27\frac{3}{4}$, (according to refult 4), will yield a population of 8,935,500.

The baptifms being 322,000, the burials (by refult 2) will be 264,000:
And the marriages (by refult 3) 107,000 nearly;
or (by refult 6) 88,460

The average of thefe 2 numbers, 97,730 marriages.

The proportion of affeffed houfes to population, or $14\frac{1}{2}$ to 1 (found by refult 5), gives a population of 10,005,000.

88,460 marriages (found by refult 6), multiplied by 139 (according to refult 7), make the population 12,295,940: but the population in Table X. on which refult 7 is founded, not having been afcertained by actual enumeration, and being only the population of a few places, I do not offer it as equally correct with the information contained in the other tables. 139 to 1, is, without doubt, too high for the proportion of population to marriages. From accurate obfervations, made on 7 market towns and 54 country parifhes, about 50 years ago, Dr. Short found the marriages were to the population as 1 to 117.*

It is obfervable, that of country-parifhes, thofe inhabited principally by agricultural labourers furnifh the greateft proportion of baptifms, and the leaft of affeffed houfes: but, as in the above tables, very few are parifhes of this defcription, the proportion of affeffed houfes to baptifms (10 to $4\frac{1}{2}$) muft be higher than the fair average of England. In the Cumberland parifhes, for

* Price's Obf. on Rev. Paym, ii. 339.

inftance

inftance, the great number of *ftatefmen*, as they are called, who cultivate their own land, renders the proportion of affeffed houfes very high. Making, therefore, a fair allowance for agricultural labourers, (the moft numerous clafs in the kingdom), I cannot but think that the annual baptifms, in England and Wales, muft, at leaft, amount to 340,000.

According to refult 4, the baptifms are to the population as 1 to $27\frac{3}{4}$. From Dr. Short's obfervations, above-mentioned, they are as 1 to 29: and from various inquiries, recently made, in Suffolk,* as 1 to 30: the following correct account, formed from actual enumerations, give 1 to 33, as the proportion of baptifms to population.

* See Young's Agricultural Report, page 286.

TABLE XII.

COUNTY.	PARISH.	Years.	Annual Average of Baptiſms.	Population.
Eſſex . . .	Barking . .	1790-4	$128\frac{4}{5}$	4,12
	Weſt Ham .	1790-4	169	5,806
Kent * . .	Beckenham .	1790-4	$28\frac{4}{5}$	1,877
	Foots-Cray .	1790-4	$11\frac{2}{5}$	100
	Bromley . .	1790-4	$82\frac{1}{5}$	2,000
Middleſex	Hayes . . .	1790-3	$23\frac{3}{4}$	707
	Heſton . . .	1790-3	$59\frac{1}{4}$	1,632
	Iſleworth . .	1790-3	$137\frac{1}{4}$	4,190
	Teddington	1780-94	$19\frac{1}{5}$	580
	Twickenham	1790-4	$98\frac{2}{5}$	3,355
Surry	Mortlake . .	1784-91	$49\frac{3}{4}$	1,766
	Putney . . .	1780-91	$59\frac{1}{6}$	2,294
	Wandſworth	1780-91	$135\frac{1}{4}$	4,554
			1,002	32,984

Baptiſms to Population, nearly as 1 to 33.

Upon the whole, I believe the *medium* of this table and the Suffolk Report, or 1 to $31\frac{1}{2}$, to be nearly the general proportion of baptiſms to population. If my conjectures be well-founded, 340,000 baptiſms, multiplied by $31\frac{1}{2}$, will give 10,710,000, as the number of inhabitants in

* The whole of this Table (excepting the population of the three Kent pariſhes, which will be noticed in a ſubſequent Table) conſiſts of actual enumerations extracted from various parts of Mr. Lyſon's "Environs of London."

England

England and Wales; and, if feamen and foldiers (who are not included in the accounts of particular parifhes) be added, the aggregate amount of the population of South Britain will be nearly 11,000,000.

The number of inhabitants in England and Wales being thus afcertained, the number of houfes, containing them, may be determined with fufficient accuracy, from the average number of perfons *per* houfe, in different parts of the kingdom.

It appears, from the following accurate enumerations in Mr. Lyfon's work, that, in country parifhes, round London, the number of inhabitants *per* houfe is $5\frac{3}{4}$.

TABLE

TABLE XIII.

COUNTY.	PARISH.	No. of Houses.	Population.		
Surry ..	Mortlake	301	1,766		
	Putney	440	2,294		
	Wandsworth ..	690	4,554		
		1431	8,614	or $6\frac{1}{50}$ to a house	
Middlesex	Hayes	141	707		
	Heston	281	1,632		
	Isleworth	712	4,190		
	Teddington ..	118	580		
	Twickenham .	610	3,355		
	Twyford	1	10		
	Part of Hackney	475	2,521		
		2338	12,995	or $5\frac{1}{2}$ to a house	
Essex ..	Barking	752	4,123		
	West Ham ...	1057	5,806		
		1809	9,929	or $5\frac{1}{2}$ to a house	
Totals	{ Surry ..	1431	8,614		
	Middlesex	2338	12,995		
	{ Essex ..	1809	9,929		
		5578	31,538		

General average $5\frac{3}{4}$ persons to a house.

Dr.

Dr. Price, in his laſt treatiſe on the ſubject of population, from accounts of 45,217 houſes and families, containing 231,842 inhabitants, ſeems inclined to allow $5\frac{1}{8}$ to a houſe;* but, as theſe accouuts conſiſt of *families* as well as *houſes*, no ſatisfactory deduction can be made from them, reſpecting the number *per* houſe. Mr. Howlett, from a no leſs extenſive ſurvey, reckons the number *per* houſe at $5\frac{2}{5}$.† That this eſtimate is very moderate, is evinced by the Agricultural Report of the County of Suffolk, in which 7,767 houſes are ſtated to contain 44,416 ſouls, or $5\frac{3}{4}$ *per* houſe.‡ By returns, lately made to the Biſhop of Rocheſter, from the clergy in his lordſhip's dioceſe, it appears, that in 17,864 *families*, there are 95,335 ſouls, or nearly $5\frac{1}{3}$ in a family.

Of theſe returns the following, I believe, may be depended on:

---

* Price's Obſ. on Rev. Paym. ii. 310.

† Examination of Dr. Price's Eſſay.

‡ Suffolk Report, page 286.

TABLE

TABLE XIV.

PARISH.	Families.	Souls.
Barming	160	313
Trotfcliffe	40	160
Tunbridge	782	3,500
Beckenham	176	1,877
North Cray	24	130
Foots-Cray	20	100
Shipborne	56	325
Southfleet	100	497
Milton	330	1,500
St. Nicholas, Rochefter	450	3,000
Bromley	358	2,000
	2,496	13,402

Number of inhabitants, *per* family, nearly $5\frac{1}{2}$.

It is deferving of obfervation, that in St. Nicholas's parifh, Rochefter, the number of perfons *per* family is $6\frac{1}{2}$. The proportion in London is, probably, not lefs than $6\frac{1}{2}$ *per* houfe; and nearly the fame in our great manufacturing towns. From an accurate enumeration of the inhabitants of Manchefter and Salford, made in 1773, it appeared, that there were $6\frac{1}{2}$ perfons to a houfe. It feems, therefore, not unreafonable to infer, that the average number *per* houfe

In our cities, including towns containing above 1,500 souls, must be about $6\frac{1}{4}$; and in country parishes, about 5; and that the average of England and Wales, is nearly $5\frac{1}{2}$.

Dr. Beeke has recently shewn, from the actual state of the hundred of Desborough, in Buckinghamshire, and from other circumstances, that the population, connected with husbandry, in England and Wales, (excluding towns containing 1,500 souls and upwards), cannot be less than 7,000,000.* This agricultural population, at 5 persons to a house, will require 1,400,000 houses. The population of the towns, taken at 3,710,000,† at $6\frac{1}{4}$ to a house, will require 593,600 houses. It may therefore be concluded, that, as the number of charged and chargeable houses is 713,803, the number of cottages, instead of the number stated in Table X. must be, at least, 1,200,000; and, that the aggregate number of houses in England and Wales, including its appendages, Jersey, Guernsey, and Alderney, must exceed 2,000,000.

That the proportion, between assessed houses and population, found by result 5, is the same,

* Letter to a County Member, p. 72.
† See p. 28.

or nearly the fame in many parts of the kingdom, is evident, from the following table, which contains the population of feveral counties, according to fuch proportion, and likewife as ftated by the Reports drawn up by order of the Board of Agriculture.

TABLE XV.

COUNTIES.	Population mentioned in the Agricultural Report.	Affeffed Houfes in each County.		Suppofed Population, proportioned to Affeffed Houfes, as fourteen one-half to one.
Berks .	115,000	7,249	multiplied by 14½, give	105,110
Durham	150,000	11,533		167,228
Hants. .	200,000	15,741		228,244
Norfolk	220,000	18,007		261,101
Rutland	20,000	1,451		21,039
Stafford	250,000	16,246		235,567

In other counties, no doubt, the proportion varies greatly, according to the fub-divifion of property, the nature of tenures, the wealth, occupations of the inhabitants, and many other circumftances. In the counties of Dorfet, Lancafter, and Lincoln, I fhould apprehend the affeffed houfes were lefs, but in Kent and Cumberland (in both which counties there is a numerous yeomanry) more, than two-29ths of the population.

The

The ftatiftical accounts of Scotland have, in the moft authentic manner, determined the exact amount of its population. From them it appears, that the

Number of inhabitants, in 1798, was 1,526,492
Between 1743 and 1755 1,265,380

Increafe within 50 years 261,112*

The enumeration, between 1743 and 1755, was made by Dr. Webfter, for the purpofe of obtaining *data*, for forming a fociety for the benefit of the widows of the clergy. He afterwards drew up a general report, particularizing, 1.The population;—2. The incomes of the clergy;—3. The patrons of livings;—4. The number of fencible men, which he computed at 253,076.

If it were poffible to add to the above account every native of Scotland ferving in the navy, army, and other profeffions, in England, Ireland, or the colonies, I am perfuaded, the exifting race of North Britons might be ftated, without ex-

* Statiftical Account of Scotland, xx. 621, and App. lxxxviii.

aggeration,

aggeration, at 1,600,000 or 1,700,000. The biographer of Robert Burns, the celebrated Ayrſhire Poet, eſtimates the number of abſentees from Scotland at 150,000.*

Ireland furniſhes a more extraordinary inſtance of the progreſs of population.

Sir William Petty, in 1672, ſtated the number of houſe, at 200,020
And the number of inhabitants, at 1,100,000†

From an account in the Philoſophical Tranſactions, which has been mentioned by Dr. Price in the poſtſcript to his Obſervations on Reverſionary Payments, ‡ it appears, that, in 1695, when the country had ſcarcely emerged from the horrors of rebellion, the population did not much exceed 1,000,000

---

* Dr. Currie's Life of Burns, prefixed to the laſt edition of the works of the Poet.

† Political Anatomy, 2d edit. page 8. Sir W. Petty uſes *families,* as ſynonymous with *houſes.*

‡ Obſervations on Reverſionary Payments, ii. 341.

Dean

Dean Swift, by a rough calculation,
in 1724, made it 1,500,000*

Dr. Duigenan informs us, that a *cenſus*, taken by order of government, in 1732, aſcertained the number of inhabitants to be leſs than ..... 2,000,000†

Another writer eſtimated it, from the ſame document, at more than . 2,200,000‡

According to an account, publiſhed annually, at Dublin, in Watſon's Almanack, the houſes in Ireland, in 1754, were 395,439; and, in 1767, they had increaſed to .... 424,046 §

I inſert the following Table of the produce of the hearth-tax, at different periods, as it, in a great meaſure, confirms the Table which immediately follows, and is an unequivocal proof of the regular progreſs of population in Ireland.

---

* Refutation of Dr. Duigenan's Appendix, 1800, p. 4.
† Political State of Ireland, p. 235.
‡ Refutation of Dr. Duigenan's Appendix, p. 5.
§ Obſervations on Reverſionary Payments, ii. 341.

TABLE XVII.

Produce of the Tax of 2s. *per Hearth, impofed by* 14*th and* 15*th C.* II. *c.* 17, *on all Hearths in Ireland, excepting thofe of Perfons living on Alms, and unable to live by Work.*

	£
Average of 5 years, ending with 1687 .	32,416
Average of 3 years, ending with 1732 .	42,457
Average of 3 years, ending with 1762 .	55,189
Average of 7 years, ending with 1777 .	59,868
Produce in the year . . . . 1778 .	61,646
Produce in the year . . . . 1779 .	60,617
Average of 5 years, ending with 1781 .	60,648
Produce in the year . . . . 1781 .	63,820

The following Table exhibits the number of houfes in Ireland, in 1772, 1781, 1787, and 1791.

TABLE

TABLE XVII.

HOUSES.	Statement transmitted by Mr. Beresford to Mr. Howlett. 1772.*	1781.†	From Returns to the House of Commons in 1787.‡	From Returns to the House of Commons in 1791.§
Under 2 Hearths	375,444	......	......	483,990
With 2 and 3 Hearths	31,785	} with 2, 3,	} 397,644	67,663
With 4, 5, and 6 Hearths	13,273	} 4, and 5, Hearths 400,783	} 41,197	With 2 or more Hearths
With 7, 8, and 9 Hearths	6,738	43,980		
With 10, 11, & 12 Hearths	1,672	with more than } 15,098	12,318	15,025 No. of Hearths unascertained.
With 13 to 20 Hearths	685	5 Hearths }		21,868 New Houses
Above 20 Hearths	162			
	429,759	459,861	451,159	588,546
Houses exempted		17,741	23,075	112,556
		477,602	474,234	701,102

* See Howlett's Essay on the Population of Ireland, p. 20.   † Ibid. p. 13.   ‡ Obs. on Rev. Paym. ii. 342.
§ Account presented to the Irish House of Commons, by Mr. Bushe, 22d of March, 1792.

It seems evident, from a comparison of the 2d and 3d columns, that paupers' houses were omitted in the account sent to Mr Howlett; and, I am persuaded, that, even in the return of 1787, their number is as inaccurate as that of English cottages in the returns of the Tax-Office; for, in the return of 1791, the number of houses exempted, or paupers' houses, is five times as great as the corresponding article in the return of 1787.

I have very great doubts of the accuracy of that part of the return of 1791, which relates to houses having only one hearth. The progress from 1772 to 1787, is such, as might naturally be expected; but it is not easy to conceive how 86,346 houses with one hearth, and 51,041 other dwellings, making altogether 137,387, (a number sufficient to contain above 750,000 persons, at $5\frac{1}{2}$ *per* house), could have been added to the number of houses existing in Ireland, in 1787, exclusive of those inhabited by paupers. Had not the return of 1791 been published, with every mark of accuracy and authenticity, I should have concluded, from previous accounts, that the number of houses in Ireland, at the present time, allowing for a fair increase since 1787,

1787, muſt be leſs than 600,000, and the number of inhabitants leſs than 3,500,000.

If the return of 1791 be correct, (and, till it is proved to be otherwiſe, we muſt conſider it as ſuch), the population of Ireland, at $5\frac{1}{2}$ perſons to a houſe, according to Dr. Beaufort's reaſonable allowance, will be 3,856,061 ;* and, after a fair deduction for the loſs, which the ſiſter country has lately ſuſtained, from civil war and emigration, her people may be reckoned, in round numbers, at 3,800,000.

I cannot conclude this account of the population of Ireland, without expreſſing an opinion, with Mr. Douglas,† that the common eſtimates of the progreſſive increaſe of population, in Ireland and Scotland, during the preſent century, are erroneous ; that the numbers in Ireland have, of late, been greatly exaggerated ; and thoſe in Scotland much under-rated. I believe that an actual enumeration would prove the population of the former to be leſs than 4,000,000, and of the latter to be nearly, if not quite, 2,000,000. That the actual reſident population,

---

* Memoir of a Map of Ireland, page 142
† Now Lord Glenbervie. Speech on the Union with Ireland, page 112.

in Scotland, has not increased in an equal ratio with that of Ireland, during the present century, I readily admit: but, this circumstance is easily explained, without derogating from the benefits arising to Scotland from her Union with England; benefits, which are now distinctly felt, and generally acknowledged. " By the articles
" of the Union, the barrier was broken down
" which divided the two British nations, and
" knowledge and poverty poured the adventu-
" rous natives of the North over the fertile
" plains of England, and, more especially over
" the colonies which she had settled in the East
" and in the West. The stream of population
" continues to flow from the North to the South;
" for the causes that originally impelled it con-
" tinue to operate; and the richer country is
" constantly invigorated by the accession of an
" informed, and hardy, race of men, educated
" in poverty, and prepared for hardship and
" danger, patient of labour, and prodigal of
" life." *

In forming estimates of our aggregate population from partial enumerations, taken within

* Dr. Currie's Life of Burns, p. 7.

the laſt ſeven years, we ſhould add to the account a conſiderable portion of thoſe claſſes, which may properly be ſaid to belong to the whole, and not to any particular part, of the Britiſh empire; the army, navy, and militia, the crews of regiſtered veſſels, ſeamen employed in the Iriſh coaſting trade and fiſheries, and in the Bri tiſh fiſheries, in veſſels not decked, or in decked veſſels of leſs than 15 tons.

Of the numbers in theſe different claſſes, a tolerable idea may be formed from the following ſtatement, which I am perſuaded is not exaggerated.

TABLE XVIII.

Forces in Great Britain, Jerſey, Guernſey and Alderney.

Regular cavalry and waggon-corps	20,766
Regular infantry	31,663
Invalids	5,797
Garriſons	302
Militia of South Britain	39,404
Ditto of North Britain	6,026
Corps of miners	633
Fencible infantry	8,775
Military force in Gt. Britain	113,366

Forces in Ireland.

Regular cavalry . . .	3,900
Regular infantry . . .	9,500
Fencible infantry . .	19,700
Militia of Ireland . .	22,000

───Military force in Ireland 55,100

Forces in the Plantations, Mediterranean, Cape of Good Hope, and New South Wales.

Regular cavalry . . .	2,815
Regular infantry . . .	62,712

───Military force in Mediterranean, &c . 65,527

Forces in the Eaſt Indies.

King's infantry . . .	14,239
King's cavalry . . .	1,885
Company's European infantry and artillery .	5,063
Native cavalry . . .	4,843
Native infantry . . .	81,079
(Excluſive of about 3,000 volunteers and militia)	

───Military force in Eaſt Indies 107,109

The corps of artillery (of which detachments are ſerving in all parts of the world) about 6,000
Foreign corps in the ſervice of Great Britain . . 17,976
Black corps in the Weſt Indies, about 5,000
The returns of volunteer corps, in Great Britain, were 140,000; their effective ſtrength may be ſtated at 80,000 infantry, and 20,000 cavalry 100,000
The Iriſh yeomanry and volunteers, effective ſtrength, not leſs than 20,000

Total 490,078

To this liſt may be added ſea-fencibles, Eaſt and Weſt India militia, and other corps of various deſcriptions, making the aggregate of military force, now embodied for the defence of the Britiſh Empire (excluſive of the navy) more than 500,000

	Seamen.
The number of seamen and marines, voted for the navy, this year, is	125,000
Men and boys employed in vessels belonging to different ports of the British Empire, of whom, however, a considerable number are foreigners *	130,000
It is not easy to ascertain how many persons, besides seamen belonging to registered vessels, are employed in the British and Irish fisheries, but their number is certainly very considerable: the herring fishery, in the Forth, last year, I am credibly informed, employed above 300 vessels, and probably more than	3,000
From a report of a committee of the House of Commons, on the British fisheries, made in June, 1800, it appears that, of the fisheries in Scotland, the Buss fishery employed 300 busses of 50 tons each (equal to 15,000 tons) and	3,366
The boat fishery	2,400
Liverpool, 61 smacks	437
Isle of Man { herring fishery, 80 boats, 880 men / mackarel ... 45 ... 450 .. }	1,330

* That our merchant-ships, notwithstanding the number of seamen required for the navy, are still well supplied with crews, the following account (laid before the House of Commons six months ago) affords very satisfactory proof.

On the 30th of September in	Vessels belonging to British Ports.	Tonnage.	Men & Boys usually employed.
1789	14,310	1,395,172	108,962
1790	15,015	1,460,823	112,556
1791	15,647	1,511,401	117,113
1792	16,079	1,540,145	118,286
1793	16,329	1,564,520	118,952
1794	16,806	1,589,758	119,629
1795	16,728	1,574,451	116,467
1796	17,069	1,519,278	120,979
1797	16,903	1,614,906	124,394
1798	17,295	1,666,481	126,546
1799*	16,902	1,693,253	128,083

* The returns from many ports not being received, this year is not complete.

A re-

A regifter, ftating the tonnage of boats of burden, on rivers and canals, and of the men actually employed in navigating them, would enable us to add to the above lift. Without fuch documents, any attempt to afcertain our population on rivers and canals muft be mere conjecture: that it is not inconfiderable, may be prefumed from this circumftance, that, near the metropolis alone, 3,436 craft, and 3,000 wherries, employ about 10,000 boatmen and boys; and that, exclufive of the bufinefs which they tranfact, there are 800,000 tons, of different commodities, carried up and down the river every year.*

The aggregate population of Great Britain and Ireland will, therefore, be

England and Wales, about ... 10,710,000
Scotland, at leaft 1,500,000
Ireland 3,800,000
Maritime and military population,
exclufive of Indian and foreign corps, 500,000

Total population of the Britifh Ifles, 16,510,000

* Colquhoun's Police of the River Thames, p. 16 and 498.

Without

Without meaning to confider the fubject " too curioufly," I fhall proceed to inquire, whether England and Wales have experienced an equal increafe in the number of their inhabitants with that which, it appears, has taken place in the courfe of the prefent century, both in Scotland and Ireland; but, as no actual enumerations of the people have been made, during this period, and as an actual enumeration, if it were now made, would itfelf, alone, furnifh no proof whether our population was progreffive, retrograde, or ftationary, we muft be fatisfied with rational inferences, drawn from the parifh regifters of different periods. An appeal to them will (as Lord Hale expreffes it) "give a greater demonftration of the increafe of mankind than a hundred national arguments." Such arguments, indeed, as may very properly be called *national*, might be drawn from the profperous circumftances of England, fince the Revolution; and would fatisfy us in believing, that an increafe of induftry, wealth, produce, and confumption, muft neceffarily be attended with an increafe in the number of confumers. But, as this is not the beft evidence which the cafe admits, our attention fhould be directed to comparifons of baptifms, burials, and marriages, at different periods; fources of information, which are allowed to be of peculiar importance * for the elucidation of this queftion.

That our numbers have increafed, fince his majefty afcended the throne, there can, now, be little doubt. Our towns are confeffedly larger, and more populous, than they were forty years ago; but, even in this enlightened age, there are political economifts, who gravely lament, that great cities are inimical to the multiplication of the fpecies; that a devouring metropolis drains the country of its inhabitants; that the confolidation of fmall farms leffens the number of cultivators; and that, though trade and manufactures may flourifh, the hardy ftock of independant yeomen, and induftrious peafants, decays. Such complaints, to fay the leaft of them, are unwarrantable, if not mifchievous.

" Deferted villages" in Great Britain are now only to be found in the fictions of poetry. The refult of thefe inquiries, I am perfuaded, will prove (as far as indirect evidence can prove) that our agricultural parifhes are better ftocked than they were 100 years ago, when induftry had

* Obfervations on Reverfionary Payments; ii. 319.

not purged the country of its fuperfluous mouths, and the vifionary evils afcribed to the exiftence of commercial and agricultural capitalift did not exift.

From an account, which Sir John Call laid before the Board of Agriculture, in 1798,* drawn up from returns from 28 agricultural parifhes, in the counties of Devon and Cornwall, it appeared, that the baptifms in the eftablifhed church
During the preceding 10 years, amounted to 6,956
And the burials, including all defcriptions of fectaries, to 4,645

Leaving an excefs of baptifms equal to one-third of their number 2,311

In order to afcertain whether an increafe in the fame ratio had taken place throughout England, Sir John Call determined to procure extracts from the regifters of four difperfed and diftant parifhes in every county; and with this

* Communications to the Board of Agriculture, ii. 479.

view he prepared a general form, for ftating the annual baptifms and burials, which he fent with circular letters, explaining his motives to fome of the country members, and to other gentlemen, refiding in the feveral counties. Middlefex was omitted, its increafed and increafing population being indifputable. In 50 of the remaining 51 counties, 200 returns were obtained from parifhes, whofe inhabitants were, in general, permanently refident, and not drawn together from other places, to carry on any manufacture, or other particular object.

The following fummary, fhews the general refult of this inquiry: and it may not be unimportant to remark that it coincides with the returns from the 28 parifhes, in Cornwall and Devon:

	Males.	Females.	Total.
Total of baptifms, in 200 parifhes, for 10 years, ending 31ft Dec. 1797	37,661	35,974	73,635
Total of burials in ditto, for ditto	24,852	25,290	50,142
Excefs of baptifms . .	12,809	10,684	23,493

From

From this abstract it appears that there are about 19 males born for 18 females.

One objection to this mode of attempting to prove an increase in the population, Sir John Call thus endeavours to obviate: it might be urged (he says) " that great numbers of males have died, been killed, or lost, by land or sea, in the service of their country." To ascertain what that contingent might be, he had recourse to the totals of baptisms, from which it appeared, that the number of males baptized exceeded that of females, by 1687, and that the number of females buried was more than the males, by 438: these two sums, added together, amount to 2125, or about 1 in 11 of the apparent increase; an allowance probably sufficient to cover the loss of males, by war, commerce, emigration, and colonization.

It appears from the following returns, which I have lately received, in answer to a circular letter sent to the ministers of above 200 parishes, that our agricultural population has increased, and is increasing. Four parishes were originally applied to in each county in England, and two in each county in Wales; but several unsatisfactory returns

returns having been made, from places where the regifters were imperfect, or wholly deftroyed, frefh parifhes were applied to. Satisfactory returns have been obtained from 114 parifhes; and, with regard to their circumftances, it may be proper to obferve, that they are principally, if not altogether, agricultural; that the increafe of their inhabitants is not owing to their being favoured by commerce or manufactures; and that they are, moftly, at a diftance from high roads, rivers, canals, and great towns. The ready and obliging manner in which information on this fubject has been communicated by the clergy to an individual, perfonally unknown to them, and from whom no application was made before the 21ft of laft October, would furnifh proofs (if proofs were wanting) of their difpofition to facilitate the progrefs of ftatiftical inquiries.

TABLE

TABLE XIX.

An Abstract of Baptisms, Burials, and Marriages, in Agricultural Parishes, in England and Wales, at different Periods, containing (in Four Lines of Figures, placed opposite to their respective Parishes) the Baptisms, Burials, and Marriages of such Parish, in the following Order, except in a few Instances, noted in the Margin.

1st line, 10 years, from 1688 to 1697, both inclusive.
2d ---- 10 ———— 1788 — 1797,
3d ---- 6 ———— 1788 — 1793,
4th ---- 6 ———— 1793 — 1799,

COUNTY.	PARISH.	BAPTISMS.			BURIALS.			Marriages	REMARKS.
		Males	Females	Total	Males	Females	Total		
Bedford....	1 Colmsworth....	30	34	64	17	15	32	6	6 years, 1692 to 1697
		18	21	39	16	11	27	18	6 years, 1792 to 1797
		20	19	39	15	15	30	18	
		26	25	51	21	11	32	20	

COUNTY.	PARISH.	BAPTISMS.			BURIALS.			Marriages	REMARKS.
		Males	Females	Total	Males	Females	Total		
Bedford....	2 Clifton......	38	53	91	28	34	62	18	
		51	53	104	38	35	73	31	
		27	30	57	20	19	39	18	
		33	31	64	22	19	41	17	
	3 Toddington....	122	108	230	75	81	156	25	At the clofe of the laſt century, Toddington had a well-frequented market: it has been difcontinued about 80 years.
		211	178	389	120	114	234	64	
		118	121	239	60	57	117	41	
		136	95	231	94	86	180	44	
Berks......	4 Lamborn......	219	191	410	131	137	268	28	
		292	318	610	205	223	428	137	
		181	192	373	130	124	254	80	
		196	186	382	112	133	245	92	
	5 White Waltham	63	60	123	44	43	87	31	
		112	112	224	85	98	183	51	
		66	79	145	39	56	95	30	
		56	51	107	57	58	115	31	

(55)

Bucks	6 Bradwell	22	26	48	18	22	40	6	
		27	24	51	30	22	52	26	
		12	16	28	16	13	29	18	
		19	14	33	18	14	32	15	
	7 Hampden	25	16	41	18	23	41	11	
		58	44	102	33	33	66	12	
		38	24	62	15	21	36	9	
		30	38	68	21	19	40	7	
	8 Fullmer	26	17	43	22	19	41	34	
		41	49	90	28	17	45	19	
		22	33	55	12	11	23	12	
		34	30	64	21	15	36	12	
Cambridge	9 Chatteris	123	102	225	147	102	249	51	
		319	328	647	266	242	518	206	
		198	171	369	171	131	302	136	
		201	221	422	146	166	312	119	
	10 Foulmire	34	49	83	37	34	71	16	This parish is full of Dissenters, many of them Anabaptists; whose names are omitted in the baptisms, and, if they die before the age of maturity, they are omitted in the burials.
		49	38	87	40	38	78	46	
		31	18	49	22	28	50	24	
		29	36	65	22	16	38	32	

(56)

COUNTY.	PARISH.	BAPTISMS.			BURIALS.			Marriages	REMARKS.
		Males	Females	Total	Males	Females	Total		
Cambridge..	11 Stretchworth.	37	31	68	25	28	53	7	
		54	49	103	40	38	78	15	
		33	39	72	22	20	42	8	
		37	33	70	23	23	46	11	
	12 Whittlefea ...	208	152	360	157	134	291	98	
		267	217	484	200	195	395	138	
		418	447	865	346	396	742	231	
		558	460	1018	399	391	790	239	
Chefter	13 Aftbury......	300	291	591	202	305	507	88	3 years, 1695 to 1697
		483	473	956	338	485	823	293	3 years, 1795 to 1797
	14 Woodchurch..	89	83	172	81	96	177	28	5 years, 1693 to 1697
		106	114	220	72	79	151	40	5 years, 1793 to 1797
		67	73	140	39	51	90	22	
		57	61	118	44	41	85	30	

(57)

Cornwall	15 Kilkhampton	69	74	143	71	71	142	27	
		111	113	224	65	54	119	45	
		64	68	132	38	32	70	27	
		81	70	151	36	33	69	33	
	16 Padstow	126	119	245	115	113	228	45	
		196	183	379	101	121	222	104	
		108	121	229	67	68	135	60	
		125	90	215	80	77	157	58	
	17 St. Stephen's	113	96	209	109	151	260	71	
		152	142	294	224	197	421	137	
		98	89	187	119	116	235	78	
		84	82	166	166	134	300	91	
Cumberland	18 Beaumont	11	11	22	3	6	9	7	3 years, 1695 to 1697
		12	11	23	9	4	13	4	
		16	29	45	11	12	23	11	
		23	24	47	14	7	21	5	
	19 Millom	99	94	193	70	70	140	31	3 years, 1795 to 1797
		102	80	191	53	40	93	65	The baptisms of 1689 being wanting, the average of the remaining 9 years is added.
		61	56	117	30	22	52	45	
		63	45	103	41	25	66	29	

COUNTY.	PARISH.	BAPTISMS.			BURIALS.			Marriages	REMARKS.
		Males	Females	Total	Males	Females	Total		
Cumberland .	20 Kirklington ..	89	95	184	13	8	21	4	
		231	200	431	78	96	174	83	
		139	138	277	52	54	106	54	
		128	107	235	48	56	104	47	
	21 Wigton	180	204	384	138	143	281	119	
		396	330	726	238	308	546	208	
		226	184	410	136	174	310	116	
		266	229	495	167	206	373	122	
Derby......	22 Glossop......	59	58	117	87	86	173	49	6 years, 1692 to 1697
		160	168	328	127	164	291	372	6 years, 1792 to 1797
		165	163	328	142	159	301	370	The sexes not being distinguished in
		188	187	375	134	154	288	382	the last century, arranged as in Cheshunt.
	23 Chapel in Frith	116	117	233	196	214	410	41	
		390	345	735	269	284	553	198	
		228	190	418	158	177	335	118	
		247	221	468	163	159	322	102	

County	Parish								Years
Devon	24 Bampton	157	171	328	194	197	391	64	
		173	177	350	105	106	201	95	
		112	105	217	55	56	111	62	
		93	101	194	65	71	136	48	
	25 Comb-Martin	123	127	250	123	112	235	58	
		108	101	209	67	69	136	53	
		63	61	124	38	40	78	36	
		76	67	143	44	39	83	31	
Dorset	26 Bradford-Abbas	28	31	59	40	48	88	17	
		80	75	155	48	60	108	30	
		49	51	100	25	40	65	20	
		39	35	74	32	27	59	14	
	27 Burton Bradstock	56	58	114	39	23	62	18	The disproportion between males and females in the burials is owing to the situation of this parish, which encourages a seafaring life.
		85	81	166	31	50	81	36	
		53	56	109	14	22	36	21	
		45	50	95	24	37	61	30	
	28 Swanage	60	56	116	36	45	81	24	7 years, 1691 to 1697
		152	151	303	64	85	149	65	7 years, 1791 to 1797
		124	111	235	46	75	121	46	5 years, 1789 to 1793
		90	105	195	55	49	104	46	5 years, 1794 to 1798

(60)

COUNTY.	PARISH.	BAPTISMS.			BURIALS.			Marriages	REMARKS.
		Males	Females	Total	Males	Females	Total		
Durham....	29 Dalton......	54	45	99	34	28	62	23	
		29	31	60	18	16	34	19	
		20	20	40	10	13	23	13	
		14	17	31	8	6	14	12	
	30 Norham......	248	239	487	169	157	326	142	
		83	82	165	187	203	390	27	
		49	51	100	99	112	211	18	
		57	49	106	111	127	238	14	
	31 Norton.....	90	64	154	92	76	168	74	
		121	130	251	108	140	248	68	
		69	84	153	63	80	143	47	
		73	74	147	70	94	164	35	
	32 Whitburn ...	74	65	139	47	62	109	39	
		99	85	184	94	86	180	54	
		60	57	117	47	62	109	35	
		68	45	113	60	39	99	32	

Essex	33 Writtle......	112	129	241		143	303	80
		288	265	553	160	92	188	108
		172	157	329	96	76	188	68
		165	166	331	105		181	68
Gloucester..	34 Marshfield ...	155	135	290	147	149	296	54
		176	187	363	129	125	254	96
		104	112	216	76	76	152	65
		111	115	226	74	72	146	41
Hants......	35 Bishops Waltham	179	193	372	147	128	275	57
		304	252	556	173	156	329	100
		181	145	326	99	91	190	66
		180	163	343	116	97	213	54
	36 Fordingbridge .	240	220	460	182	174	356	59
		372	335	707	162	199	361	168
		219	198	417	71	84	155	114
		221	201	422	146	161	307	95
	37 Kingsclere...	269	214	483	156	134	290	141
		383	360	743	221	246	466	80
		230	206	436	128	155	283	89
		232	227	459	133	89	222	

(62)

COUNTY.	PARISH.	BAPTISMS.			BURIALS.			Marriages	REMARKS.
		Males	Females	Total.	Males	Females	Total		
Hereford...	38 Bramyard....	257	223	480	205	190	395	150	
		429	373	802	233	211	444	149	
		279	218	497	132	135	267	105	
		228	240	468	149	124	273	63	
	39 Hope-Manfell.	35	38	73	21	14	35	8	
		17	26	43	14	14	28	15	
		11	16	27	7	7	14	12	
		9	15	24	11	10	21	6	
Herts.....	40 Berkhamftead.	89	91	180	136	125	261	52	The regifter of burials, in 1688 and 1689, being wanting, 26, the average burials, for the next 8 years, have been added to the males, and the fame number to the females, to make up the burials for 10 years.
		241	237	478	184	200	384	127	
		150	147	297	107	114	221	79	
		135	122	257	114	110	224	74	
	41 Cheshunt.....	276	290	566	343	325	668	75	The fexes not being always noticed in the regifter of the laft century, in fuch omiffions, the entries have been made, male and female, alternately.
		440	442	882	373	362	735	193	
		275	265	540	237	224	461	135	
		244	266	510	199	209	408	86	

Herts	42 Bishops Stortford	262	259	521	186	180	366	115
		323	293	616	281	250	531	151
		186	174	360	181	151	332	92
		194	185	379	158	156	314	88
	43 Hemel-Hemsted	206	190	396	195	194	389	88
		373	373	746	301	250	551	182
		219	205	424	187	161	348	113
		251	239	490	169	137	306	120
Huntingdon	44 Fenstanton	54	59	113	77	81	158	101
		105	111	216	65	79	144	61
		70	68	138	41	42	83	35
		56	59	115	35	55	90	34
	45 Great Paxton and Tofeland	35	31	66	37	33	70	31
		60	71	131	30	24	54	33
		37	48	85	22	20	42	11
		29	35	64	19	13	32	30
	46 Little Paxton	21	19	40	20	19	39	10
		20	38	58	21	18	39	17
		13	20	33	9	9	18	10
		14	27	41	16	10	26	13

(64)

COUNTY.	PARISH.	BAPTISMS.			BURIALS.			Marriages	REMARKS.
		Males	Females	Total	Males	Females	Total		
Kent......	47 Minfter......	73	80	153	76	59	135	48	
		121	118	239	79	74	153	63	
		82	80	162	48	41	89	41	
		70	66	136	43	42	85	32	
Lancafter ..	48 Halfall	111	92	203	113	91	204	26	
		134	159	293	142	145	287	72	
		79	98	177	78	83	161	41	
		84	88	172	87	81	168	47	
	49 Kirkham	399	421	820	595	570	1165	134	There are above 200 Roman Catholic families in this parifh: their burials are inferted in the regifter; but not their baptifms.
		736	683	1419	608	658	1266	420	
		432	420	852	384	403	787	238	
		485	396	881	358	391	749	281	
	50 Ulverfton.....	163	155	318	201	238	439	114	A Diffenters chapel having been open-ed, within the laft 30 years, about 10 of their baptifms, and a few Quakers, may have been omitted.
		475	448	923	248	299	547	210	
		288	257	545	141	181	322	129	
		288	278	566	154	170	324	124	

Leicester...	51 Kegworth...	82	73	155	66	74	140	24
		237	203	440	120	120	240	104
		125	120	245	88	74	162	66
		148	129	277	60	70	130	64
	52 MarketBosworth	156	165	321	100	94	194	45
		158	222	380	167	153	320	170
		167	125	292	112	99	211	90
		137	153	290	84	83	167	109
Lincoln....	53 Skidbrook-cum-Saltfleet.....	41	26	67	23	24		21
		26	25	51	19	14	47	30
		27	14	41	6	12	33	20
		18	21	39			18	18
	54 Wainfleet...	51	71	122	36	44	80	46
		83	91	174	43	46	89	39
		49	49	98	31	28	59	24
		51	58	109	18	30	48	29
	55 Wintringham.	63	67	130	50	46	96	27
		118	90	208	60	64	124	66
		62	57	119	37	39	76	30
		85	58	143	36	34	70	52

The year 1690 being wanting, the average of the remaining 9 years is added.

(66)

COUNTY.	PARISH.	BAPTISMS.			BURIALS.			Marriages	REMARKS.
		Males	Females	Total	Males	Females	Total		
Middlesex	56 Hadley	63	53	116	118	75	193	11	
		141	127	268	56	62	118	34	
		73	86	159	22	28	50	17	
		98	68	166	56	52	108	26	
	57 Hillingdon	140	146	285	157	178	335	72	The marriage register imperfect, in 1694, and 95.
		240	236	476	269	234	503	231	
		137	132	269	146	149	295	129	
		151	150	301	165	131	294	148	
	58 Uxbridge	172	156	328	200	172	372		The burials, in 1690, 91, and 92, being wanting, 110 (37 being the average of the remaining 7 years) have been added; half to males, and half to females.
		325	326	651	228	204	432		
		206	200	406	121	123	244		
		190	196	386	151	120	271		
	59 South'Mimms	169	141	310	148	142	290	167	The incumbent is said to have performed the marriage ceremony, in 1694, 95, and 96, for a very small fee. This accounts for the number of marriages (101) solemnized in those years.
		171	172	343	203	161	364	92	
		98	99	197	114	104	218	63	
		109	110	219	125	90	215	45	

County	Parish								Notes
Middlesex	60 Sunbury	83	69	152	75	57	132	21	
		200	206	406	144	139	283	59	
		117	123	240	85	73	168	35	
		132	123	255	93	104	197	38	
Monmouth	61 Abergavenny	379	305	624	220	220	440	38	The deficiency of the years 1689, 90, and 91, supplied as in Uxbridge.
		310	300	610	277	338	615	202	
		182	180	362	162	169	331	121	
		189	185	374	165	165	330	116	
Norfolk	62 Aylsham	95	100	195	60	64	124	—	6 years, 1692 to 1697
		138	121	259	99	80	179	83	6 years, 1792 to 1797
		135	132	267	88	101	189	86	
		149	122	271	99	84	183	78	
	63 Snettisham	67	67	134	56	64	120	33	
		118	130	248	61	77	138	53	
		67	65	132	39	40	79	31	
		84	93	177	50	49	99	30	
	64 Watton	84	94	178	81	81	162	56	
		77	92	169	52	75	127	42	
		42	55	97	27	43	70	30	
		55	53	108	43	45	88	20	

(68)

COUNTY.	PARISH.	BAPTISMS.			BURIALS.			Marriages	REMARKS.
		Males	Females	Total	Males	Females	Total		
Northampton	65 Cliffe-Regis ..	133	134	267	103	99	202	24	
		172	163	335	111	141	252	86	
		109	104	213	58	84	142	56	
		93	104	197	79	81	160	44	
Oxford	66 Bampton	216	176	411	140	134	274		The year 1694 being wanting, the average of the remaining 9 years is added.
		251	202	453	156	103	259	95	
		154	133	287	102	95	197	52	
		152	125	277	82	94	186	60	
	67 Bicefter......	221	218	439	166	206	372	48	
		311	313	624	190	221	411	155	
		192	176	368	127	126	253	92	
		182	215	397	117	149	266	91	
	68 Watlington ..	192	156	348	130	148	278	48	
		164	164	328	108	97	205	66	
		95	95	190	56	59	115	39	
		112	114	226	59	61	120	44	

(69)

									6 years, 1692 to 1697 6 years, 1792 to 1797
Salop	69 Cleobury Mortimer	159	159	318	115	122	237	22
		207	189	396	136	150	286	97
		123	107	230	84	95	179	61
		117	121	238	78	76	154	55
	70 Hodnet	130	119	249	115	108	223	34
		205	174	379	130	135	265	106
		117	109	226	80	83	163	65
		122	108	230	66	66	132	66
	71 Winftanton	74	65	139	62	52	114	21
		102	102	204	51	43	94	—
		63	65	128	32	32	64	—
		62	57	119	23	24	47	3
Stafford	72 Abbots-Bromley	171	188	359	122	139	261	58
		201	183	384	134	134	268	90
		119	104	223	71	87	158	53
		122	126	248	88	71	159	52
	73 Swinerton	41	39	80	25	32	57	6
		56	62	118	28	28	56	23
		53	63	116	28	29	57	22
		58	63	121	33	36	69	20

(70)

COUNTY.	PARISH.	BAPTISMS.			BURIALS.			Marriages	REMARKS.
		Males	Females	Total	Males	Females	Total		
Stafford	74 Walfall	730	608	1338	1597	1551	3148	220	
		1983	1865	3849	955	962	1917	758	
		1288	1141	2429	955	805	1653	481	
		1068	1052	2120	848			404	
	75 Wednefbury	218	217	435	184	135	319	75	
		894	848	1742	519	459	1078	207	
		520	502	1022	317	292	609	160	
		572	501	1073	331	293	624	73	
Suffolk	76 Bildefton	121	103	224	94	83	177	33	
		86	78	164	63	71	134	42	
		51	44	95	37	44	81	23	
		49	53	102	35	40	75	29	
	77 Mildenhall	363	308	671	263	269	532	126	
		309	330	639	161	233	394	178	
		181	211	392	90	129	219	100	
		201	179	380	109	139	248	121	

Suffolk	78 Orford	58	82	140	78	57	135	17
		118	106	224	82	89	171	72
		64	52	116	47	58	105	47
		81	74	155	60	53	113	39
Surry	79 Godalming	227	200	427	229	235	464	115
		448	454	902	295	301	596	167
		261	271	532	166	176	342	122
		278	262	540	190	175	365	75
	80 Malden	23	21	44	12	14	26	7
		61	51	112	29	13	42	4
		36	26	62	16	6	22	17
		32	36	68	17	9	26	14
	81 Cheffington, chapel of eafe to Malden	32	13	45	24	10	34	2
		45	50	95	26	25	51	22
		31	28	59	12	13	25	11
		25	29	54	17	15	32	16
	82 Reigate	241	254	495	274	259	533	86
		323	332	655	226	246	472	127
		208	195	403	132	134	266	74
		174	190	364	153	153	306	82

(72)

COUNTY.	PARISH.	BAPTISMS.			BURIALS.			Marriages	REMARKS.
		Males	Females	Total	Males	Females	Total		
Surry...	83 Weybridge....	53	73	126	74	67	141	20	
		102	128	236	76	92	168	23	
		69	76	145	50	52	102	15	
		67	76	143	44	56	100	16	
Suffex....	84 Angmering...	68	62	130	70	53	123	23	
		126	118	244	53	57	110	40	
		73	72	145	39	34	73	24	
		81	81	162	33	36	69	26	
	85 Rottingdean..	20	17	37	11	11	22	14	
		92	99	191	57	55	112	34	
		58	52	110	30	30	60	24	
		51	69	120	35	26	61	16	
	86 Selfey......	60	39	99	52	43	95	35	
		79	65	144	41	31	72	40	
		43	38	81	24	21	45	18	
		47	48	95	27	15	42	31	

(73)

Warwick	87 Bitford	129	132	261	72	80	152	27	
		171	144	315	83	70	153	43	
		110	84	194	53	37	90	29	
		93	88	181	44	146	90	26	
	88 Colefhill	172	164	336			259	28	The decreafe, fince the laft century, is probably owing to a confiderable manufactory having been removed to Banbury, about 40 years ago.
		218	238	456	186	181	367	98	
		132	141	273	110	99	209	63	
		145	143	288	104	119	23		
	89 Shipfton	174	163	337	117	126	243	30	
		161	141	302	123	126	249	78	
		97	86	183	72	72	144	51	
		100	85	185	69	70	139	50	
	90 Southam	63	75	138	58	60	118	41	
		127	137	264	98	96	194	63	
		85	90	175	54	53	107	42	
		59	69	128	58	61	119	42	
Weftmorland	91 Amblefide	58	73	128	38	58	96	19	
		79	77	156	51	60	111	23	
		41	45	86	28	35	63	18	
		62	52	114	34	31	65	9	

L

(74)

COUNTY.	PARISH.	BURIALS			BAPTISMS			Marriages	REMARKS.
		Males	Females	Total	Males	Females	Total		
Westmorland	92 Crosby-Garrett	33	30	63	31	19	50	19	
		33	22	55	25	28	53	22	
		15	14	29	19	12	31	11	
		27	14	41	13	21	34	13	
	93 Haversham....	162	170	332	176	185	361	63	The years 1688, 89, 90, and 91, being wanted, 1698, 99, 1700, and 1701, are substituted.
		241	315	556	196	216	412	148	
		155	179	334	104	128	232	91	
		140	204	344	126	132	258	78	
Wilts......	94 Albourn......	147	143	290	113	91	204	35	
		211	210	421	134	114	248	111	
		122	112	234	73	56	129	55	
		145	146	291	83	83	166	74	
	95 Mere	314	271	585	219	266	485	33	
		314	323	637	203	221	424	132	
		198	193	391	125	120	245	84	
		171	193	364	120	144	264	69	

(75)

Worcester..	96 Bayton......	35	38	73	25	28	53	17
		67	61	138	49	29	69	15
		43	39	82	30	11	41	9
		32	32	64	24	14	38	10
	97 Broadway....	90	114	204	66	85	151	23
		187	173	360	125	126	251	89
		110	108	218	74	76	150	54
		112	108	220	72	82	154	47
	98 Kings-Norton.	181	213	394	151	145	296	74
		272	232	504	239	205	444	144
		155	124	279	140	115	255	98
		157	158	315	139	137	276	67
York...... North Riding	99 Masham......	239	226	465	213	203	416	93
		291	273	565	162	178	340	141
		161	156	317	93	96	189	78
		185	199	384	101	118	219	100
East Riding..	100 Howden.....	342	363	705	367	439	806	266
		395	353	748	338	332	670	232
		223	211	434	190	215	405	175
		284	235	519	210	185	395	173

L 2

COUNTY.	PARISH.	BAPTISMS.			BURIALS.			Marriages
		Males	Females	Total	Males	Females	Total	
East Riding	101 NorthGrimston	21	12	33	17	12	29	5
		12	17	29	19	11	21	6
		7	13	20	6	6	12	5
		12	9	21	7	8	15	6
	102 Patrington	100	92	192	81	86	167	31
		160	158	318	122	119	241	56
		98	97	195	78	75	153	38
		98	103	201	66	66	132	30
West Riding.	103 Armthorp	21	27	48	24	27	51	89
		46	33	79	23	16	39	15
		29	15	44	16	10	26	12
		27	27	54	11	11	22	6
	104 Dent	211	208	419	199	197	396	106
		223	210	433	195	219	444	96
		143	129	272	115	116	231	57
		135	131	266	99	137	236	66

West Riding.	105 Heptonftall	1681 1003 997	1544 913 912	1169 3225 1916 1909	1049 619 621	1152 635 743	917 2201 1254 1364	392 899 565 502	In the first period the sexes are not distinguished.
North Wales. Anglesea	106 Beaumaris	128 234 151 126	111 267 172 128	239 50 323 254	132 156 91 92	126 171 111 91	258 327 202 183	37 102 67 59	
Carnarvon.	107 Caerhun	64 84 57 37	62 71 38 51	126 155 95 88	65 64 35 41	47 57 33 38	112 121 68 79	24 55 29 35	
	108 Llanbedr	46 114 67 67	52 96 65 54	98 210 132 121	53 64 43 37	55 53 33 26	108 117 76 63	17 37 23 21	The burials of 4 years are wanting.
Flint.......	109 Hawarden	366 762 436 485	317 644 390 401	693 1406 826 886	283 401 228 243	272 387 233 229	555 788 461 472	108 256 163 141	The sexes not being diftinguished in a few entries of baptifms and burials laft century, they have been fupplied, as in Cheshunt.

COUNTY.	PARISH.	BAPTISMS.			BURIALS.			Marriages	REMARKS.
		Males	Females	Total	Males	Females	Total		
Flint......	110 Whitford	192	208	400	153	127	380	57	
		474	431	905	284	258	542	162	
		312	270	382	166	161	327	101	
		249	235	484	170	152	322	91	
Montgomery.	111 Llanidloes	91	105	196	96	84	180	94	6 years, 1692 to 1697
		167	156	323	110	104	214	78	6 years, 1792 to 1797
		191	302	393	107	120	227	112	
		162	155	317	81	78	159		
South Wales. Caermarthen.	112 Langharne ..	95	98	183	112	113	225	60	
		207	216	423	107	122	229	88	
		123	129	252	62	73	135	55	
		134	130	264	61	70	131	47	
Radnor.....	113 Kiwelly.....	118	100	218	76	75	151	41	
		196	199	395	165	162	327	100	
		132	131	263	112	101	213	55	
		101	93	194	83	87	170	63	

Glamorgan	114 Neath	72	71	143	78	79	157	6 years, 1692 to 1697
		247	209	450	126	126	252	117
		201	211	412	122	110	23?	132
		256	210	466	127	136	263	101

The following is a general Abstract of the preceding Table.

	Number of Parishes returned.	Baptisms.	Number of Parishes returned.	Burials.	Number of Parishes returned.	Marriages.
1st period	114	30,207	111	25,365	—	—
2d period	114	50,384	114	36,067	—	—
3d period	113	30,942	113	21,712	111	7,794
4th period	113	31,442	113	21,815	111	7,327

At the period of the revolution, the number of houfes in England and Wales, according to Dr. Davenant,* was 1,319,215
And the population, with his allowance of 6 perfons to a houfe . . . 7,900,000
His contemporary, Gregory King, at $4\frac{1}{2}$ perfons to a houfe, reckoned the people at 5,500,000
The firft allowance feems too high; the latter too low : the *medium* will be 6,700,000

If my eftimate of our annual baptifms, 340,000, and of our prefent population, be correct, and if the proportion between baptifms and population were the fame at the clofe of the 17th and 18th centuries, as the baptifms of 114 parifhes, for 10 years, ending with 1797, namely, 50,384, accompany a population of 11,000,000, the baptifms of the fame number of parifhes, for 10 years, ending with 1697, being 30,207, will determine our population, at the revolution, to have been 6,600,000, or nearly the medium of Davenant and King's eftimates. In the fame manner, fuppofing the population, at the revolution, to have been 6,700,000, our prefent population may be fhewn to exceed 11,000,000.

Whitworth's Davenant, i. 62.

The following is the general Refult of the Returns from different Parifhes.

RETURNS.	Baptifms.	Burials.	Marriages.
Sir J. Call. { From 28 parifhes, for 10 years, ending with 1797	6,956	4,645	—
From 200 parifhes, for 10 years, ending with 1797	73,635	50,142	—
From 113 parifhes, for 6 years, ending with 1793	30,942	21,712	7,794
From 113 parifhes, for 6 years, ending with 1799	31,442	21,815	7,327

The baptifms, therefore, are to the burials, as 3 to 2 nearly; and if our baptifms, as I here fuppofe, amount to 340,000, the burials will not exceed 240,000, leaving an annual excefs of 100,000 baptifms; an excefs fully fufficient to account for our increafed, and increafing, population.

Such an excefs of baptifms, however great it may feem, is not uncommon. The baptifms, in the county of Suffolk, are ftated, in the Agricultural Report of the county, to be as 3 to 2; and the fame proportion between births and burials has been afcertained to have taken place, in various

various parts of the continent, during the prefent century.*

This rapid increafe in our population is the natural refult of the great demand for labour, arifing from an extended commerce, from multiplied manufactures, and from a fpirited fyftem of agriculture, that primeval employment, which is, perhaps, the moft efficient caufe of the multiplication of the fpecies.

The internal improvement of the country, by roads and canals, which have facilitated the tranfportation of furplus produce, and furplus population, from one part of the kingdom to another, mufthave effentially promoted the progrefs of population. It muft have been promoted by the introduction of machinery, which is, in effect, an addition to the national capital.

To thefe caufes may be added the fuperior fobriety, and cleanlinefs, of the people in modern times. Inoculation for the fmall-pox has, probably, had its fhare in producing the extraordinary excefs of baptifms, mentioned in thefe pages. The fubftitution of the vaccine, for the

* Obf. on Rev. Paym. ii. 335.

variolous,

variolous, inoculation, promifes to exempt mankind from a difeafe that is dreadful, even in its mildeft form; and we may hope that the fmallpox, like the plague, will, in future ages, be known only by defcription.

Improvements, very conducive to the prolongation of life, have taken place in the metropolis. The inhabitants are lefs crowded together, than they were a hundred years ago;* wide ftreets have been opened; immenfe warehoufes have been erected on the fcite of private dwelling houfes; the cuftom of keeping country houfes is very general; and many thoufand lives are annually faved by the act, (paffed in confequence of Mr. Hanway's humane fuggeftions,) by which the parifhes, within the bills of mortality, are obliged to fend the children of their poor to be nurfed in the country.

* This is proved by the creafe of annual births in the 97 parifhes within the walls: according to Dr. Price, the medium of annual births was,

```
From 1655 to 1664 . . . . . . . . . 3264
     1680    1690 . . . . . . . . . 2139
     1730    1740 . . . . . . . . . 2316
     1758    1768 . . . . . . . . . 1620
     1781    1784 . . . . . . . . . 1354  Obf. on Rev. Paym. i. 255.
     1793    1799 (both inclufive) 1172  From the bills of mortality.
```

No part of the empire has made a greater progrefs in all thofe arts of civilized life, which moft efficiently promote population by encouraging induftry, than the northern half of Great Britain. In Scotland, the happy effects of the Union are now manifefted in the increafe of her people, her trade, and her manufactures.

                                            Inhabitants.
Glafgow, which in 1663 contained 12,298
    and in . 1701 only 14,000
    contained in 1798 (according to Mr. Dundas) 77,042

The population of Edinburgh, in 1678, was 35,500
. . . . 1722 40,420
. . . . 1791 84,886

Paifley, at the Union, did not contain above 2,500
    but in 1792 19,903

Dundee, in 1651 8,057
    1792 24,000

Aberdeen, at the Union, about 12,000
    now about 25,000

And the other principal towns of Scotland, Perth, Ayr, Montrofe, Invernefs, have experienced a fimilar increafe of population.*

* See Mr. Dundas's Speech on the Union with Ireland, p. 20; and a pamphlet, publifhed in Dublin in 1799, intituled, " Ireland profiting by Example," p. 11.

Scotland,

Scotland, in the laſt century, probably did not poſſeſs more than a million of inhabitants; (De Foe, indeed, aſſigns her two millions); yet, till lately, this country, perhaps, was over-peopled; for, from no parts of this iſland was emigration more prevalent. At length, however, full employment has been found for her people, even in diſtricts the moſt inauſpicious to induſtry; on her weſtern coaſt, eternally buffetted by the Atlantic, thriving villages, and nurſeries for ſeamen, have been eſtabliſhed in places, which, before the preſent reign, were, " antres vaſte and deſarts idle." There the tillage of the ſea offers crops more abundant, (and in the preſent period no leſs important) than the produce of the earth. Britons have at length diſcovered that colonies may be planted on the ſhores and waſtes of their own country. They are now generally convinced that there is no " happier iſland in the watry waſte" than their own; and that in no part of the world have they a fairer chance of bettering their fortunes than in the cultivated plains, and buſy cities, of Great Britain: they know that they might ſeek,

" in vain,
" For feats, like theſe, beyond the weſtern main."

How

How far this computation is correct, will, I trust, be determined, by the operation of the bill, now before the House of Lords, for ascertaining the population of Great Britain.

That such a measure should have been so long delayed is truly astonishing. One attempt, indeed, to number the people, appears on the Journals of the House of Commons. In 1753, a bill was brought into that house, by Mr. Potter, son of the Archbishop of Canterbury, for taking and registering an annual account of the total number of people; and of the total number of marriages, births, and deaths; and also of the total number of persons receiving alms in every parish, and extra-parochial place in Great Britain. Some of the clauses of the bill, I understand, were very objectionable. It was violently opposed by Mr. Thornton, the member for York, as subversive of the last remains of English liberty; and was thrown out, on the second reading, in the House of Lords.

Notwithstanding the very popular arguments which were urged against this measure, and, which it is probable, caused its rejection, I think it is much to be regretted, that a part, at least, of Mr. Potter's bill did not pass into a law. Of political

political arithmetic, or " the art of reasoning by figures, on matters relating to government," a correct knowledge of the numbers and conditions of the people seems to be the principal foundation. To ascertain, by enumerations, taken from time to time, that the population of a country is gradually increased, is, perhaps, in other words, to determine, that the great business of government has been wisely and prosperously administered. Davenant assures us, that, " as the wealth of all nations arises from the " labour and industry of the people, a right " knowledge of their numbers is necessary to " those who will judge of a country's power " and strength. And this is so far from being " a matter of mere speculation, as some think, " that many conclusions may be drawn from " thence, useful and reducible to practice."*

A modern writer well observes, that " if the " various states of Europe kept and published " annually, an exact account of their popula-
" tion, nothing carefully, in a second column, " the exact age at which the children die, this " second column would shew the relative merit " of the governments, and the comparative hap-

* Whitworth's Davenant, i. 138.

" piness

" pinefs of their fubjects. A fimple arithmetical
" ftatement would, then, perhaps be more con-
" clufive than all the arguments that could be
" adduced."*

It is fingular that the countries, now at war with Great Britain, have all preceded us in enumerations of the people.

From the inquiries directed to be made by the National Affembly, in 1790, (which A. Young fuppofes, were executed with great accuracy), the population of France, including Corfica, appeared to be above 26,000,000.

Necker, a few years before, by multiplying 963,207, the annual births, (on an average of 5 years, ending with 1780), by $25\frac{1}{2}$, (his fuppofed proportion of population to births), allowed 24,800,000 inhabitants to France.

There can be little doubt that, fince the year 1790, fhe has loft not lefs than 3,000,000 of her inhabitants, by premature deaths, and emigrations; and that of the remaining popula-

* Sir Francis d'Ivernois's Survey of the Loffes of the French Nation, 1799, p. 15.

tion of France, (I do not speak of the conquered countries) not one-fourth is capable of bearing arms.

" It would, however, (as Sir Francis D'Ivernois properly remarks), " be a great error to con-
" sider their numerical amount as a complete
" abstract of all their losses. Those have yet to
" learn the first principles of political arithmetic
" who imagine it is in the field of battle, and
" in the hospitals,* that an account can be taken
" of the lives a revolution or a war has cost.
" Much less important is it to inscribe that aw-
" ful register with the number of men who are
" killed than with that of the children it has pre-
" vented, and will still prevent, from coming into
" the world. This is the deepest wound the
" population of France has received." †

From an accurate enumeration made in Spain, in 1787, the number of inhabitants was found to be 10,409,879.‡

Mr. Chalmers, from a document in the British Museum, has estimated the population of

* Of 19,800 deaths at Paris, last year, 8,200 were " aux hospices."—*Moniteur.* † Survey, p. 15.
‡ See the printed account, intituled, " Censo Espanol."

Spain, at the epoch of the armada, at about 5,000,000.* The author of the Memoirs of the Duke de Ripperda fays, that the duke, in 1727, reckoned it at no more; but this authority is not to be depended on: thefe memoirs have more the appearance of romance than of hiftory. La Induftria Popular, a work publifhed in 1777, ftates the population of Spain, and the adjacent iflands, at 11,000,000.

The remark which A. Young has made, refpecting other parts of the continent, feems peculiarly applicable to Spain. He fays, "There " is, probably, no corner of Europe, barbarous " Turkey alone excepted, in which the people " do not increafe confiderably: we ought not, " therefore, in England, to take too much cre- " dit for that rapid augmentation which we ex- " perience. It is found under the worft govern- " ments, as well as under the beft, but not " equally."†

From a cenfus, made with great precifion throughout the feven provinces of Holland, in 1796, in order

---

* Eftimate, Dedication, p. 5.
† Young's Travels in France, ii. 284.

to afcertain the number of reprefentatives which each diftrict fhould fend to the Dutch National Affembly, the refident population, exclufive of foreigners, was afcertained to be lefs than *1,800,000

Including foreigners, it probably, now, does not exceed 2,000,000

The ordinary eftimate of the refident inhabitants and foreigners in Holland, ten years ago, was 2,500,000

The population of France and her dependants, the Batavian Republic, and Spanifh Monarchy, fhould not appal us, whilft our enemies are befieged at home by our fleets, which blockade their ports from the Texel to Gibraltar, and the Britifh Empire is protected by a military force of half a million of men.

* Holland, according to Boetticher's Statiftical Tables, contains 10,000 fquare miles, or 6,400,000 acres. The extent of England and Wales being about 38,500,000 acres, and their population, according to this eftimate, 11,000,000, our number of inhabitants, *per* acre, is greater than in Holland, in the following proportion; in England and Wales, the number of inhabitants, *per* fquare mile, is 183; in Holland, 180. England has about $3\frac{1}{2}$ acres *per* head; Holland, $3\frac{5}{9}$.

"Thefe

" Thefe are the fubftance, finews, arms, and ftrength " of this " Heaven-protected Ifle : "— whilft fhe poffeffes fuch means of defence, her arts and induftry, her colonies and her commerce, will continue to flourifh, and her inhabitants live profperous and free.

At the clofe of the laft century, Davenant made the following remark on our population ; taking it at 5,500,000, according to Gregory King's eftimate,(which is confeffedly too low),and eftimating the quantity of land, in England and Wales, at 39,000,000 of acres, (which is probably near the truth), he fays, " we feem now " to have about 7¼ acres *per* head ; but there " are many reafons to think, that England is " capable of nourifhing double its prefent num- " ber of people, which, fuppofing them now to " be 5,500,000, would be 11,000,000, and even " then there will be as many acres *per* head, as " they have in Holland. And, when we have " this complement of men, either in the natural " courfe of time, or fooner, by the help of good " conduct, we fhall be in a ftate of power to " deal with any ftrength in Europe."* That

* Whitworth's Davenant, ii. 221.

we

we have attained " this complement of men" cannot admit of much doubt: that we are " in a ſtate of power to deal with any ſtrength in Europe," has been proved by our exertions in the preſent awful conteſt: and I truſt we ſhall long continue, what we now are,

" A land, that diſtant tyrants hate in vain."

THE END.